STUDIES IN PLAY AND GAMES

THE GAMES OF THE AMERICAS
A Book of Readings
Part I: Central and South America
Part II: North America

Brian Sutton-Smith, Editor

ARNO PRESS

A New York Times Company

New York — 1976

Editorial Supervision: SHEILA MEHLMAN

———◆———

Reprint Edition 1976 by Arno Press Inc.

Copyright © 1976 by Arno Press Inc.

STUDIES IN PLAY AND GAMES
ISBN for complete set: 0-405-07912-5
See last pages of this volume for titles.

Manufactured in the United States of America

Publisher's Note: This book has be reproduced
from the best available copies.

———◆———

Library of Congress Cataloging in Publication Data

Main entry under title:

The Games of the Americas.

    (Studies in play and games)
    CONTENTS: pt. 1. Central and South America.--
pt. 2. North America.
    1. Indians--Games--Addresses, essays, lectures.
I. Sutton-Smith, Brian. II. Series.
E59.G3G25   398'.355   75-35081
ISBN 0-405-07929-X

ACKNOWLEDGEMENTS

HOME DIVERSIONS OF THE AZTEC CHIEF by Arthur J. O. Anderson;
LEGENDS OF THREE NAVAHO GAMES by Lisbeth Eubank; and
SIX GAME PIECES FROM OTOWI by Marjorie Ferguson Tichy have been
reprinted by permission of *El Palacio,* published by the Museum of New Mexico,
Santa Fe, New Mexico.

THE MAYA BALL GAME POK-TA-POK by Frans Blom is reprinted by
permission of the Middle American Research Institute, Tulane University,
New Orleans, Louisiana.

THE COURT BALL GAME OF THE ABORIGINAL MAYAS by William A.
Goellner is reprinted by permission of the American Alliance for Health,
Physical Education, and Recreation.

TYPES OF BALL COURTS IN THE HIGHLANDS OF GUATEMALA
by A. Ledyard Smith is reprinted by permission of the publishers from *Essays in
Pre-Columbian Art and Archaeology,* by Samuel K. Lothrop, et al., Cambridge,
Massachusetts: Harvard University Press, © 1961 by the President and Fellows of
Harvard College.

A CHOCKTAW BALL GAME by George Catlin has been reprinted from
Primitive Heritage: An Anthropological Anthology edited by Margaret Mead and
Nicolas Calas, originally published by Random House, Inc.

CANUTE by Reginaldo Espinosa; INDIAN "OLYMPICS" by Joe Simon Sando;
and INDIAN TRACK MEET by Clee Woods have been reprinted by permission
of *New Mexico Magazine.*

SOCIAL MECHANISMS IN GROS VENTRE GAMBLING by Regina Flannery
and John M. Cooper has been reprinted by permission of Regina Flannery and
the *Journal of Anthropological Research.*

THE CHIPPEWA OR OJIBWAY MOCCASIN GAME by George A. Flaskerd
has been reprinted by permission of the Minnesota Archaeological Society.

THE GAME OF DOUBLE-BALL by Melvin R. Gilmore has been reprinted by
permission of the Museum of the American Indian.

INDIAN GAMES by L. F. Hallett has been reprinted by permission of the
Massachusetts Archaeological Society, Inc.

NOTES ON A WEST COAST SURVIVAL OF THE ANCIENT MEXICAN
BALL GAME by Isabel Kelly in Carnegie Institution of Washington, *Notes on
Middle American Archaeology and Ethnology,* Vol. I, No. 26, November 10, 1943,
has been reprinted by permission of the Carnegie Institution of Washington.

AMERICAN LOVE OF BALL GAME DATES BACK TO INDIANS by John
Rinaldo is reprinted by permission of the Field Museum of Natural History.

CONTENTS

Part II: *North America*

Beauchamp, W. M.
IROQUOIS GAMES (Reprinted from *Journal of American Folk-Lore,* Vol. IX,
No. XXXV, October-December, 1896, pp. 269-277). Boston, 1896

Blasiz, R.
THE PRACTICE OF SPORTS AMONG THE INDIANS OF AMERICA,
Translated by Fred E. Foertsch (Reprinted from *Mind and Body,* Vol. 40,
Nos. 416-417, December-January, 1933-1934, pp. 216-219). New Ulm,
Minnesota, 1933-1934

Catlin, George
A CHOKTAW BALL GAME (Reprinted from *Primitive Heritage:
An Anthropological Anthology,* edited by Margaret Mead and Nicolas Calas,
pp. 289-295). New York, 1953

Daniel, Z. T.
KANSU: A Sioux Game (Reprinted from *American Anthropologist,* Vol. V,
No. 3, July, 1892, pp. 215-216). Washington, D.C., 1892

Espinosa, Reginaldo
CANUTE: A Game Handed Down from the Indians to Spanish Settlers in New
Mexico Still Lives in Native Homes (Reprinted from *New Mexico,* Vol. XI,
No. 5, May, 1933, pp. 16-17, 46-48). Santa Fe, New Mexico, 1933

Eubank, Lisbeth
LEGENDS OF THREE NAVAHO GAMES (Reprinted from *El Palacio,*
Vol. LII, No. 7, July, 1945, pp. 138-140). Santa Fe, New Mexico, 1945

Flannery, Regina and John M. Cooper
SOCIAL MECHANISMS IN GROS VENTRE GAMBLING (Reprinted from
Southwestern Journal of Anthropology, Vol. 2, No. 4, 1946, pp. 391-419).
Albuquerque, New Mexico, 1946

Flaskerd, George A.
THE CHIPPEWA OR OJIBWAY MOCCASIN GAME (Reprinted from
The Minnesota Archaeologist, Vol. XXIII, No. 4, October, 1961, pp 86-94).
Minneapolis, Minnesota, 1961

Gilmore, Melvin R.
THE GAME OF DOUBLE-BALL, OR TWIN-BALL (Reprinted from *Indian
Notes,* Vol. III, No. 4, October, 1926, pp. 293-295). New York, 1926

Haddon, Alfred C.
A FEW AMERICAN STRING FIGURES AND TRICKS (Reprinted from
American Anthropologist, New Series, Vol. 5, No. 2, April-June, 1903,
pp. 213-223). Washington, D.C., 1903

Hallett, L. F.
INDIAN GAMES (Reprinted from *Massachusetts Archaeological Society Bulletin,* Vol. XVI, No. 2, January, 1955, pp. 25-28). Attleboro, Massachusetts, 1955

Kelly, Isabel
NOTES ON A WEST COAST SURVIVAL OF THE ANCIENT MEXICAN BALL GAME (Reprinted from Carnegie Institution of Washington, *Notes on Middle American Archaeology and Ethnology,* Vol. I, No. 26, November 10, 1943). Cambridge, Massachusetts, 1943

McCaskill, J. C.
INDIAN SPORTS (Reprinted from *Indians at Work,* Vol. III, No. 22, July 1, 1936, pp. 29-30). Washington, D.C., 1936

McKenzie, B.
THE SEMINOLES WERE RECOGNIZED AS THE LEADING BALL PLAYERS YEARS AGO (Reprinted from *American Indian,* Vol. 1, No. 5, 1927, p. 10). Tulsa, Oklahoma, 1927

Matthews, Washington
NAVAJO GAMBLING SONGS (Reprinted from *American Anthropologist,* Vol. II, No. 1, January, 1889, pp. 1-19). Washington, D.C., 1889

Moses, Alma Louise
CHOCTAW SPORTS (Reprinted from *Indians at Work,* Vol. III, No. 14, March 1, 1936, pp. 15-16). Washington, D.C., 1936

Myounge, Orpha
CREEKS, CHOCTAWS AND CHEROKEES LOVE GAMES (Reprinted from *Indians at Work,* Vol. II, No. 24, August 1, 1935, p. 24). Washington, D.C., 1935

Rinaldo, John
AMERICAN LOVE OF BALL GAME DATES BACK TO INDIANS (Reprinted from *Chicago Natural History Museum Bulletin,* Vol. 26, No. 1, January, 1955, pp. 3-4) Chicago, 1955

Sando, Joe Simon
INDIAN "OLYMPICS" (Reprinted from *New Mexico,* Vol. XXX, No. 4, April, 1952, pp. 22-43, 45, 47). Albuquerque, New Mexico, 1952

Tichy, Marjorie Ferguson
SIX GAME PIECES FROM OTOWI (Reprinted from *El Palacio,* Vol. XLVIII, No. 1, January 1941, pp. 1-6). Santa Fe, New Mexico, 1941

Walker, J. R.
SIOUX GAMES [PARTS] I-II (Reprinted from *Journal of American Folk-Lore,* Vol. XVIII, No. LXXI, October-December, 1905, pp. 277-290 and Vol. XIX, No. LXXII, January-March, 1906, pp. 28-36). Boston, 1905-1906

Wolfe, K. E.
A CHEROKEE INDIAN BALL GAME (Reprinted from *Red Man,* Vol. 3, 1910, pp. 76-77). Carlisle, Pennsylvania, 1910

Woods, Clee
INDIAN TRACK MEET (Reprinted from *New Mexico,* Vol. XXIV, No. 3, March, 1946, pp. 16-17, 41, 43, 45, 47). Albuquerque, New Mexico, 1946

Part I

CENTRAL AND SOUTH AMERICA

HOME DIVERSIONS OF THE AZTEC CHIEF

Arthur J. O. Anderson

HOME DIVERSIONS OF THE AZTEC CHIEF

ARTHUR J. O. ANDERSON*

IN THE important Aztec household, well-organized amusements were devised so that for the men, at least, time would not hang heavy. Some of these Fr. Bernardino de Sahagún describes in Lib. VIII, cap. x, of his *Historia general de las cosas de Nueva España*—the *tlatoani* or chief out for a walk, singing, playing *tlachtli*, playing *patolli* (a kind of dice), shooting and snaring birds, enjoying flower-gardens, watching buffoons, and even collecting people and animals. Sahagún must have seen it all, even though his descriptions are really those of informants. Fr. Juan de Torquemada also probably knew some of the games and pastimes at first hand; his description of the game of *palo,* in which an acrobat, lying on his back, kept a log dancing in the air with the soles of his feet, says he had watched it, and it may be inferred that he likewise had witnessed *patolli* and *tlachtli*.[1]

An English version of Lib. VIII, cap. x (Of the Pastimes and Recreations of the Lords), of the Nahuatl of the *Florentine Codex* follows.[2]

* * *

When the chief goes forth from his house, he carries in his hand [a small stick] tapered to a point, with which he points out, as if with his finger, what he speaks of. His young men[3] guide him through the lines of people, advancing on either side of him, [shielding him from] those who stare at him, [and so] none pass in front of him, none come before him, nor look up at him, nor join him.

*Dr. Arthur J. O. Anderson is Associate in Charge, Department of History, Museum of New Mexico.

1. *Segunda parte de los veinte i un libros rituales i monarchia indiana* (Madrid: Nicolas Rodriguez y Franco Anade, 1723), P. 551

2. With the exception of the description of the *tlachtli* game, which is to appear elsewhere. In footnotes, Fr. Alonso de Molina's *Vocabvlario en lengua mexicana y castellana* (Leipzig: B. G. Teubner, 1880; ed. facsim.) and Rémi Siméon's *Dictionnaire de la langue nahuatl* (Paris: Imprimerie Nationale, 1885) will be referred to as "Molina" and "Rémi Siméon" respectively.

This passage has been translated and is here printed by permission of Dr. Sylvanus G. Morley, Director, Museum of New Mexico and School of American Research.

3. *In icaoan*—his younger brothers (Molina). Sahagún, in the Spanish of the *Florentine Codex,* says *los principales.*

He sings and learns songs, he sings songs of praise.[4] They tell
stories and proverbs to pass the time. . . .

They play *patolli* with four large, round beans whose surfaces
are drilled with holes. In the following way they are disposed by
the hand of him who spreads them over the ground: The four
beans form a figure on the mat; its design, in black, goes back
and forth; for the mat on which *patolli* is played, is marked.[5]
There, then, are counted the counters—twelve [of them], six on
each side for each player, counters for each of the contenders.[6]
The winner in *patolli* takes everything of value—gold ornaments,
green stones, turquoises, bracelets set with round [cut] jewels of
green stone or turquoise, rich plumes, valuable houses, corn-fields,
costly mantles, mattresses [*i. e.*, beds], large capes, green stone
labrets, gold earrings, capes of duck-feathers. And if that player
of *patolli*, when he rolled the beans, [threw] one bean so that it
stood up on one end, that was held as an omen; it was regarded
at a great wonder. Then the winner loses all of value, whatever
it is; he does not take what he was to receive. Thus it is agreed;
thus [the game] is ended.

[Also] they shoot with the bow, bending it, at tree-trunks,[7] and
with darts for birds, and with arrows.

With his pages, the lord goes wearing bracelets set with great
round green stones or turquoises on his wrists. With a blow-gun
he shoots stones, his servant [carrying] a net for the stone pellets
to be shot, through a hollow rod, at small birds. They hunt with

4. *Cuica ehecoa*. Spanish text reads: "*deprendia los cantares, que
suelen dezir en los areytos*"—he learned the songs which they custom-
arily say in the ceremonies.

5. With two diagonal and two transverse lines, according to Francesco
Saverio Clavigero, in his *Storia Antica del Messico* (Cesena: Gregorio
Biasani, 1780), Vol. I, p. 185. Torquemada (*loc. cit.*) says the design
was in the form of a St. Andrew's cross (*hechas ciertas raias, à manera de
aspa*) with other lines crossing (*y atravesando otras*).

6. Depending upon the place, with reference to the lines traced on
the mat, where the beans landed, certain variously-colored pebbles, or
counters, were taken up or put down. The player who took up three
pebbles consecutively was winner. *Cf.* Rémi Siméon (*Patolli*); Clavigero, *loc. cit.;* Torquemada, *loc. cit.*

7. *Tipontica:* prob. *tepuntica*. Torquemada, *op. cit.*, Lib. XIV, cap.
iii, says archers of Tehuacan could shoot two or three at once as if
they were a single arrow.

a net which can be closed, with a bird-net, so that various birds can be taken with the hand.

There were fields and walls of flowers, and they looked at all the various flowers.

Also they had buffoons who amused and solaced them, who took a pole with their feet. gladdening them with their well-done accomplishment, making them laugh. And it was marvelous how with the soles of his feet, thrusting it up from below, a man makes a thick column of wood dance;[8] lying on his back, with the soles of his feet he throws the column of wood up, pushing it up with only the soles of his feet—a well-done trick which he performs to provide recreation.

Also there were his younger relatives, his servants, who accompanied and amused him, dwarfs, cripples crawling on all fours, hunchbacks, pages.

And they kept eagles, ocelots, wolves,[9] mountain cats, and a variety of birds.

The Maya Ball-game *Pok-ta-pok*

(Called *Tlachtli* by the Aztec)

By FRANS BLOM

BALL-COURTS IN THE MAYA AREA

THE MAYA BALL-GAME *POK-TA-POK*

(Called *Tlachtli* by the Aztec)

By Frans Blom

PRACTICALLY all students of the Maya civilization have stated that the presence of Atlantean figures, serpent columns, and ball-courts in northern Yucatán are proof of an influence of Toltec culture on the so-called "New Empire" period of Maya history.[1] The great ball-court at Chichén Itzá has always been held up as an example, probably due to its size and good state of preservation. It is possible that the Atlantean figures and the serpent columns are genuinely Toltec, as are also the multitude of figures carved on walls and square pillars at the same place. Furthermore the historical data brought to us through the books of Chilam Balam and through Landa confirms the fact that Toltec mercenaries took part in the wars of the last period of Maya history. The large ball-court at Chichén is certainly strongly stamped by the Toltec culture, but this does not imply that the ball game was of Toltec origin. It is the aim of this paper to show that the game which played so great a role in the life of the Middle American peoples was of Maya origin.

Even a rapid survey of the Aztec and Zapotec codices, even a superficial acquaintance with the writing of the early Spanish historians show us that the ball game called TLACHTLI in the Nahua language, and POKOLPOK in Maya, was of much importance in the daily life of the people.[2]

Innumerable are the drawings of ball-courts in the codices, and Sahagún, Duran, Torquemada, Herrera and other historians[3] give us descriptions of the game and also of the ceremonies and gambling connected with it. It is therefore strange to realize that not a single ball-court has yet been discovered in the Toltec-Aztec area—at least to my knowledge.

In the National Museum at Mexico City, and on the principal squares of many of the towns in the valley of Mexico—as, for ex-

---

1 The designations "Old" and "New Empire" as the major periods of Maya history are decidedly misnomers. "Empire" infers a centralized rule and our knowledge of Maya history is at present too scant for such a definite classification. Recent investigations of the early history of the Maya and historical data extracted from the Books of Chilam Balam and post-Conquest reports show us that the Maya were divided into a multitude of capital-city-states, frequently at war with each other.

2 Maya from the Motul dictionary and Pio Perez 1866-77, Quiché from the Popol Vuh, Brasseur Edition, and Basseta's vocabulary. Nahua from Molina, 1571.

3 Sahagun, Bustamante Edition, 1829; Duran, 1880; Torquemada, 1723; Herrera, 1726-28.

ample, coyoacan and Texcoco—stand **stone** rings (Nahua—*tlachte-malacatl*) which once were used in the **ball** game, but excavators have not as yet found ruins of the courts **from** where they came.

As a matter of fact the court at **Chichén Itzá** has been for a long time practically the only example. **The** walls of the ball-court at Uxmal have been given scarce recognition and the many courts lo-

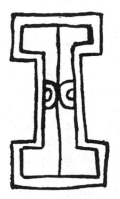

cated by Sapper and **Seler**[4] have been ignored; or, as they occur on the **southern** fringe of the Maya area, they have been considered a late Toltec-Aztec intrusion.

The ball-court at **Chichén Itzá** is of super-size, but otherwise it fits **the** description which we have of ball-courts among **the** Aztec. Based on this, the records of the early Spanish historians, and the pictures in the codices, it is not difficult to reconstruct such a court.

Fig. 1—Ball-court.
Codex Mendoza
8, 31, 36.

Torquemada calls the ball-court TLACHO in the Nahua language **and** in the Codex Mendoza on pages 8, 31 and 36 this word is shown as a glyph for the name of the town **Tlacho**, as shown in Fig. 1.

The descriptions by the Spanish **writers** are much alike and we will quote Duran.[5]

". . . they built ball-courts enclosed **with** fine walls, and well ornamented, with the whole floor inside **very** smooth and covered with mortar, with many paintings of effigies of idols and devils to whom

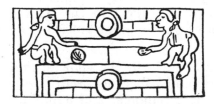

Fig. 2—Ball-court and players.
Codex Florentino
Lam. LI, Libr. VIII, No. 86-92.

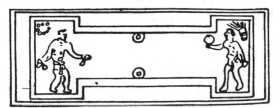

Fig. 3—Players in ball-court.
Duran, Cap. 23°, La. II.

that game was dedicated and whom **the** players had for protectors in that sport. These ball-courts were better **in** some places than others and built after the design shown in **the** picture, narrow in the center, and at the ends, broad with corners **made** purposely so that if the ball entered there the players would be **at** disadvantage and lose a point (Figs. 2 and 3).

4 Sapper, 1895, 1897; Seler, 1896, 1901.
5 Duran, 1880, vol. II, cap. CI, p. 242.

"The walls measured 1½ to 2 estados in height (10 to 12 feet) all around, and outside of which they planted for superstitious reasons, some wild palms or some trees with red beans, the wood of which is very soft and light in weight and from which crucifixes and images are now made. On all the walls were either towers or effigies of stone placed at intervals and filled with people when there was a general game among the rulers, which was when the occupation of waging war, because of truce or for other reason, had ceased and left them time to play.

"The ball-courts were one hundred, one hundred and fifty and also two hundred feet long between where they ended in said cor-

Fig. 4—The lords of the day and the night in the ball-court with their followers.
Codex Colombino P.XI.

ners . . . In the center of this enclosure were placed two stones in the wall one opposite the other; these two (stones) had a hole in the center, which hole was encircled by an idol representing the god of the game . . . These rings also served them as cord, because straight in front of them (*derecho*) on the ground was a black or green line made with a certain herb, which for reason of superstition had to be made with a particular herb and with no other"[6] (Fig. 4).

6   Sahagun, Lib. VIII, Cap. X, auh yn oncan vel inepantla tlachtli onoca tlecotl tlaxotlalli yn tlalli; "y en medio del juego estaba una raya questa al proposito del juego"; and in the middle of the court was a line which was pertaining to the game. Sahagun, Lib. III, Cap. XVI; auh yn tlanepantla yn ocan icac tlecotl; "y en medio del juego se puso una señal o raya que se dice tlecotl"; and in the middle of the court was placed a sign or line called tlecotl.

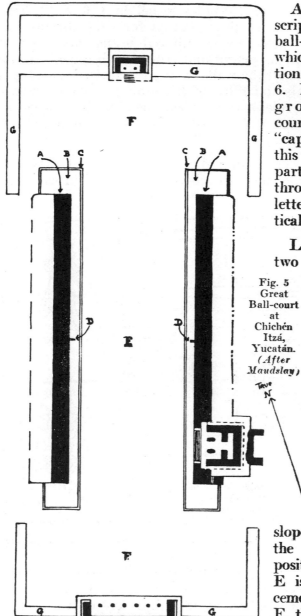

Fig. 5
Great
Ball-court
at
Chichén
Itzá,
Yucatán.
(*After
Maudslay*)

As stated above this description agrees with the large ball-court at Chichén Itzá, of which a ground plan and section is shown in Figs. 5 and 6. Fig. 5 gives us the typical ground plan of the ball-courts, i. e., the shape of the "capital I." The letters on this plan refer to distinct parts of the structure and throughout this paper these letters will be used for identical features in other courts.

Letter A indicates the two parallel walls of the court. In the type of ball-court which we are discussing at present, i. e., the large court at Chichén, the one at Uxmal, and those described by the Spaniards, these walls of what might be called a standard court were 15 to 20 feet high.

At the inner side of these walls is a low terrace, marked B, which ends in a stone-clad slope, C, towards the floor of the court. D indicates the position of the stone rings. E is the level, smoothly-cemented floor of the court. F, the wide ends, and G, the low wall enclosing these ends.

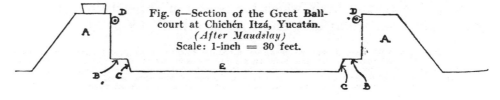

Fig. 6—Section of the Great Ball-court at Chichén Itzá, Yucatán.
(*After Maudslay*)
Scale: 1-inch = 30 feet.

On Fig. 7 we see the east wall of the Chichén Itzá court, and can easily distinguish its separate features.

Next we come to the game itself.

The players were both amateurs and professionals, the latter being called *Ollamani*, in Nahua (Fig. 8). They were dressed only in loin-clouts (Maya—*Ex;* Nahua—*Maxtli*) over which they carried a protective cover of leather (Maya—*Keuel;* Quiché—*Tzuum;* Nahua —*cuatl*) and gloves (Maya—*Hup Kab Keuel;* Quiché—*Pach Kap;* Nahua—*Maycuatl*).

For description we quote Duran:

". . . to speak of the ball game of which a description is offered according to that promised in the chapter head, and the drawing

Fig. 7   East side of the Great Ball-court at Chichén Itzá, Yucatán.
A—Vertical wall.   B—Ramp.   C—Slope.
D—Ring.   G—End-wall.

shows. It was a game of much recreation to them and enjoyment specially for those who took it as pastime and entertainment, among which were some who played it with such dexterity and skill that they during one hour succeeded in not stopping the flight of the ball from one end to the other without missing a single hit with their buttocks, not being allowed to reach it with hands, nor feet, nor with the calf of their legs, nor with their arms. They were so clever both those of one side and those of the other in not allowing the ball to stop that it was marvelous—for if to see those of our country (Spain) play ball with their hands gives us such pleasure and surprise, then seeing skill and speed with which some of them play, how much more must we praise those who with such skill and dexterity and elegance play it with buttocks and with knees, counting it a foul to touch the ball with hands or any other part of the body except the two said parts, the buttocks or the knees. And with the practice there were such skillful and excellent players, that they not only were held in high esteem, but the rulers made them gifts and lodged them in their houses and courts, and they were honoured with special insignia.

"Many times have I seen this being played and in order to satisfy myself of how much it enchanted the old ones to copy the ancient, but as the best (most important?) was lacking, which was the enclosure inside of which they played and the holes (rings) through which they drove and passed the ball, and over which the combat and dispute was held, it was soft now as compared to how it was in the time of their infidelity and differed as much as the live from the painted. And so that we may understand the way it was done and enjoy the art and dexterity which this game was played it should be understood that in all the cities and towns which had some renown and standing and serious authority, as well among the citizens as among

Fig. 8—Ball-court and player.
Codex Fejervary Mayer.

the rulers (of which they made much) and in order not to be inferior, one to the other, they built ball-courts enclosed with fine walls, and well ornamented, with the whole floor inside very smooth and covered with mortar, with many paintings of effigies of idols and devils to whom the game was dedicated and whom the players had for protectors in that sport.

". . . and at the ends of the court they had a quantity of players on guard and to defend against the ball entering there, with the principal players in the middle to face the ball and the opponents. The game was played just as they fought, i. e., they battled in distinct units. In the center of this enclosure were placed two stones in the wall one opposite the other; these two (stones) had a hole in the center, which was encircled by an idol representing the god of the game. He had a face like that of a monkey, whose feast, as we see in the calendar, was celebrated once every year. That we may understand the purpose which these stones served it should be known

that the stone on one side served that those of one party could drive
the ball through the hole which was in the stone; and the one on the
other side served the other party and either of these who first drove
his ball through (the hole in the stone) won the prize. Those rings
also served them as cord, because straight in front of them (*derecho*)
on the ground was a black or green line made with a certain herb,
which for reason of superstition had to be made with a particular
herb and with no other. All the time the ball had to pass this line
in which case they did not lose, because even when the ball came
rolling on the ground, as they had hit it with the seat or knee as
soon as it passed the line, though only two fingers distance, then it
was not a default, but counted as such if it did not pass. He who hit
the ball through said hole in the stone was surrounded by all, and
they honored him and sang songs of praise and danced a while with
him and they gave him a certain special prize of feathers or loin-
clouts, a thing they valued highly, though the honor was what he
appreciated most and most highly esteemed, because they practically
honored him as a man who in special battle of even sides had con-
quered, and ended the dispute.

"All those who entered this game, played with leathers placed
over their loin-clouts and they always wore some trousers of deerskin to protect the thighs which they all the time were scraping
against the ground. They wore gloves in order not to hurt their
hands, as they continuously were steadying and supporting themselves on the ground . . . A great multitude of nobles and gentlemen
took part, and they played with such content and joy, changing now
some and later others, from time to time, in order all to enjoy the
pleasure and so content that the sun would go down before they
knew of it. Some of them were carried dead out of the place and
the reason was that as they ran, tired and out of breath, after the
ball from one end to the other, they would see the ball come in the
air and in order to reach it first before others it would rebound on
the pit of the stomach or in the hollow, so that they fell to the
ground out of breath, and some of them died instantly, because of
their ambition to reach the ball before anybody else. Some were so
outstanding in playing this game and made so many elegant moves
in it that it was worth seeing and I will specially relate one which I
saw done by Indians who had practiced it, and it was that they used
a curious thrust or hit, when seeing the ball in the air, at the time it
was coming to ground. They were so quick in that moment to hit
with their knees or seats that they returned the ball with an extraordinary velocity. With these thrusts they suffered great damage
on the knees or on the thighs, with the result that those who for

smartness often used them, got their haunches so mangled that they had those places cut with a small knife and extracted blood which the blows of the ball had gathered."[7]

The ball was of solid rubber, up to one foot in diameter. It must have been quite heavy, and it is no wonder that when driven with force it would leave blue spots on the bodies of players. Most of our sources describe the ball, and tell us that it was made out of the milk or blood of a tree. Oviedo,[8] when speaking of the game called *batey,* describes the ball as follows:

"The balls are made out of roots of trees and herbs and juices and mixture of wax and pitch. Bringing together these and other materials they boil it all and make a paste, then they give it a round shape and make the ball of the same size as those filled with air made in Spain, and some they make larger and some smaller; the mixture

Fig. 9—"Ollamani," ball-player statuette in Museo Nacional, Mexico.
Cat. No. 283. 57 cm. high.

Fig. 10—Ball-player.
Codex Mendocino.

has a black shining surface and does not stick to the hand. After it is dry it becomes somewhat spongy, not because it has any holes or vacuum as sponges have, but it becomes light and is soft and quite heavy. Without comparison these balls jump much more than those filled with air because by simply dropping it from your hands on the ground it jumps much higher in the air and gives a jump and another, one more and another and as many more, the jumps becoming smaller every time."

This, to my knowledge, is the first European description of the rubber ball.

"This ball is—as some people may have seen—as large as a small ball used in playing nine-pins. The material of which the ball is

7 Duran. Op. cit.
8 Oviedo. 1851, Vol. I, p. 165.

made is called Olin, which I have heard to be called 'batel'[9] in our Spanish which is a rosin of a special tree which when boiled becomes like sinews. It is plentiful and used by the natives both as medicine and as offering. It has one property which is that it jumps and rebounds upwards, and continues jumping from here to there so that those who run after it become tired before they catch it."[10]

In Maya the word KIK means blood and also rubber; KIKCHE means rubber-tree. In the Popol Vuh we find the ball used in the ball game called QUIC, which also means blood.

UOL, UOLOL in Maya mean ball, pellets and all round things. UOLOL CIB means a ball of wax. UOLLIC is translated "round," the round shape of something, and UOUOLOC is a round spherical thing.

Looking upon the Nahua names for rubber and the ball and the ball-game we find the following in Molina's dictionary:[11]

OLLAMA:	Jugar a la pelota con las nalgas; to play ball with the buttocks.
OLLAMALIZTLI:	Juego de pelota de esta manera, el acto de jugar; to play ball in this way, the act of playing.
OLLAMANI:	Jugador de tal; player of this game (Figs. 9 and 10).
OLLAMIA:	Jugar a la pelota con las nalgas; to play ball with the buttocks.
OLLAMIA:	Jugar con otros este juego; to play this game with other persons.
OLLANQUI:	Jugador desta manera; one who plays in this way.
OLLI:	Cierta goma de arboles medicinales, deque hazen pelotas para jugar con las nalgas; certain gum of medicinal trees, of which they make balls with which they play with their buttocks
OLLO:	Cosa que tiene desta goma; a thing which contains this gum.
OLOLIUHCAYOTL:	Redondez de bola, o de otra cosa spherica; the roundness of a ball or other spherical things.
OLOLIUHTIMANI:	Corillo de gente ayuntada; a congregation of many people brought together.
OLOLTIC:	Cosa redonda como bola o pelota; a round thing like a ball or a ball to play with.

We note that the Maya called a round thing UOLLIC and it is most likely that the Aztec used the similar word, OLOLTIC, from which they derived OLLI to indicate rubber. Maya traders brought their

9 *Batel* may be derived from *batey*, the name of the ball-game in the islands of the West Indies.
10 Duran. Op. et loc. cit.
11 Molina, 1571.

round balls of rubber to the Toltec-Aztec. The Maya word UOLLIC represents the form, whereas the Aztec use this word not only for the form but also for the material; and went still further by using the word OLLI, *rubber,* as part of the words which refer to the game played with the rubber ball. From OLLI the conquerors got their name for rubber, which is HULE.

Rubber grows chiefly along the Gulf coast of Mexico and in Yucatán, as well as on the tropical part of the Pacific coast. *It does not grow* in the country of the Toltec-Aztec. Rubber was brought to them by trade, and it would be just as natural for them to name it after the Maya word as it was for the conquerors to name rubber after the Nahua word.

Just as we find in Molina a list of designations pertaining to the ball game in the Nahua language so do we find a similar list in the large Pio Perez dictionary[12] in connection with the Maya word POK. which means a ball.

POK:	Jugar pelota, saltar y el salto; play ball, to jump and the jump. (POK—the stroke that throws the ball. Juan Martínez H.)
POKCHINTAH:	Arrojarlo o abarrajarlo contra la pared; to thrust or hurl it (the ball) against the wall.
POKLEMCAB:	Pelear, luchar; to fight, to struggle.
POKCHAHAL and POKTAL:	To fill with pus, as a sore or from a blister.
POKOLPOKTAH:	Pelotear la pelota; to play ball.
POKYAH:	El juego de la pelota; the game of the ball[13] (the Ball-court).
POKOL:	Herirse o desollarse recio en pie, pierna, rodilla, cobdo, o rostro con alguna caida; to wound or bruise oneself badly on foot, leg, knee, elbow or face by a fall.
POKOLPOC:	Juego de la pelota y jugarla; the ball game and to play it.
KAMALPOK:	Pelotear, jugar a la pelota; to play ball (kamal—received; kamal kam—from hand to hand; kamal kamtah—to carry from hand to hand, alternatively).
POKOLPOK:	Jugar a la pelota; to play ball.

Regarding the roots *pok* and *uol,* Mr. Ralph L. Roys writes me the following: "There is every reason for deciding that both of

---

12 Perez. Pio 1866-77.
13 Pio Perez, 1866-1877, has also EKEL EK—juego de pelota. ball-court; the Motul Dictionary translates *Ekelek u nok* as: andar enlutado por tristeza. go wrapped in sorrow, literally. go in mourning of sadness. I am inclined to believe that Pio Perez's translation is erroneous

the words are good old Maya roots, *pok* and *uol,* and that they are neither of them borrowed from Nahoa or any other foreign source.

1. These monosyllabic roots are usually old Maya and not borrowed.

2. Both roots are fertile compounds, which does not indicate borrowing, but quite the contrary.

3. Both roots are employed as numerical suffixes, a feature which goes deep into the heart of the old language.

4. We find the duplicative form of *uol* in *uouol* and *uouol- uol,* indicating in my opinion that the root is an old one; also *pokolpoktah:* "to play ball."

The Spanish authors used the words "juego de la pelota" both to indicate the game of ball and the place where the game is played, i. e., the ball-court, for which reason I think it is permissible to call both the game and the court POKOL-POK or POK-TA-POK.

After discussing the question with Juan Martínez Hernández, the outstanding Maya linguist of today, I have adopted the word *pok-ta-pok* to signify the game.[14]

Even when taking all the sources into consideration we have only a vague picture of how the game was conducted. It could be played by one, two or more on either side. When many persons played, the principal players stood in the narrow space, E (Fig. 6), between the two high walls, A, and by hitting the ball with their knees, thighs, or buttocks they sought to drive it through one of the stone rings. The line drawn on the floor of the court from ring to ring probably divided the field of the two parties, and is the one referred to by Duran when he states that: "the ball at all times had to pass this line, etc."

This seems to indicate that one party, X, must keep the ball on the move while it was on their side of the line, and strive to drive it into the field of the opposing party Y. While X was doing this Y would interfere (Fig. 11).

The line running lengthwise through the center of the court, as we frequently see it depicted in the codices, may have been a division referring to the stone ring, i. e., that the party X defended the ring on one side as theirs, while they at the same time attacked the ring on the opposite side belonging to the party Y (Fig. 11).

---

14 TZELTAL, pocibon—jugar a la pelota con los pies; pocibil—jugador asi.
  ZAPOTEC, lachi—pelota de los indios; gotiialachi—jugar pelota (tlachtlilachi).
  OTOMI, Ndamxey—lugar en el que se juega la pelota, o el mayor juego de pelota.
  TARASCA, querétaro—juego de pelota.

It is not clear whether the game was played across the court from ring to ring, or lengthwise from one end to the other. In any case we learned that guards stood at the broad ends, F, of the court to stop the ball from entering there.

The bouncing of the ball against the wall was probably of much importance, and many of the finer tricks of the game were undoubtedly based on this. It is easy to understand the excitement of the spectators when the ball was driven through the stone ring. Especially so when one considers, first, that the ball could not be hit with hands or feet; secondly, that it was large and heavy; and thirdly, that it was without doubt made of uneven material and most likely was not even perfectly round in shape.[15]

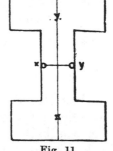

Fig. 11.
Ball-court.

The game was immensely popular, and Torquemada tells us that ball-games often were played in the market-place during fairs. Duran declares that every town had its ball-court, more or less elaborate according to its wealth; and in the Codex Mendoza we see that twenty-two towns located on the Gulf Coast between northern Oaxaca and the Gulf paid 16,000 rubber balls as tribute every year (Fig. 12) to the court of Mexico. The towns mentioned in the

Fig. 12—Symbol for
"16,000 rubber
balls."
Codex Mendocino.

Mendoza codex all lie on the slopes of the Oaxaca mountains, and in the alluvial plain watered by a multitude of rivers that all fall into the Gulf approximately by Alvarado. It is a very rich country, and was once the home of the Olmeca nation—Olmeca means the rubber people. The territory borders the western fringe of the Maya area, and is probably the country of the "ball playing and fisher people" referred to in the Popol Vuh.

The court, the ball and the stone ring had their protecting gods to whom offerings were made, and no game was started until religious ceremonies had first been conducted. "Each ball-court was a temple because they placed two images in it, the one was the god of the game and the other of

15 Size of stone rings in Mus. Nac. de Mexico.

Catalog No.	Diameter of Ring	Diameter of Hole	Catalog No.	Diameter of Ring	Diameter of Hole
160	87 cm	19 cm	551	32 cm	8 cm
161	80 cm	16 cm	695	94 cm	23 cm
162	72 cm	17 cm	756	94 cm	23 cm
163	88 cm	17 cm	963	57 cm	17 cm
164	95 cm	31 cm	693	92 cm	20 cm
			Texcoco	102 cm	21 cm

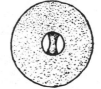

In ring No. 693 in the Museo Nacional the hole is not fully perforated.

the ball, on the top of the two lower walls, at midnight, on a day of good omen, with certain ceremony and witch-craft and in the middle of the floor they made similar ceremonies, while singing songs: thereafter one of the priests of the main temple with some of his ministers came to bless it with certain words (if the detestable superstition can be called blessing) ;[16] he threw the ball four times in the ball-court and with this they said that the court was consecrated, and they could play in it and not before then: this was made with much display of grandeur and attention because they said that in it lay rest and comfort for the hearts. The owner of the ball-court (who always was a ruler) did not play ball without first making certain ceremonies and offerings to the idol of the game, from which can be seen how superstitious they were, because even when they were concerned with their amusement they would take account of their idols."[16a]

In the codices we continually see the gods on the ball-court. The Codex Colombino, p. XI, shows us the Lord of the Day and the Lord of the Night, each with two followers, approaching each other on the court (See Fig. 4). Codex Borgia, p. 21, shows the black and the red Texcatlipoca, and in the Borbonicus, p. 21, we see Xochipilli and Ixtilton facing Quetzalcoatl and Coatlicue for a game. We hear of Quetzalcoatl—the green feathered Serpent—that he was an expert player, skilfully hitting the ball with his buttocks, and as the ring on the wall of the court pictured on page 21 of the Codex Borgia is a Serpent's Head, this court may have been dedicated to him (Fig. 13).

Fig. 13—Ball-ring.
Codex Borgia, 21.

The same may be the case with the big Chichén Itzá court. Duran tells us that "These two (stones) had a hole in the centre, which hole was encircled by an idol representing the god of the game. He had a face like that of a monkey . . ."[17] At Chichén Itzá we see two plumed serpents encircling the hole in the stone ring, and as Quetzalcoatl, alias Kukulcan, was the hero god of the Toltec, it is most likely that both the court and the temple on the east wall were dedicated to him (Fig. 14).

The Nahua sources mention Xochiquetzal, the Aztec Venus, goddess of love, lust and gambling, as the protector of the game. She is pictured in the Tonalamatls of the Borbonicus and the Aubin manuscripts.

---

16 This parenthesis is a quotation.
16a Torquemada, 1723, pp. 552-554.
17 A stone ring with a monkey, tail and all, is in the Museum of Toluca.

Xoltol is pictured in the Codex Magliabecchiano (XIII 3.f.33) with the statement: "Otro que se llamava Xubotl el qual poenen en los juegos de pelota pintado o de Bulto."

Seler, in several of his papers, believes that every god who played ball was a protector of the game. I think that there is not enough definite evidence in the texts to support this. On the other hand, from a purely human point of view, it is very likely that they were. Baseball fans of today idolize Babe Ruth and would undoubtedly like to worship him in a niche if it could be done.

Fig. 14—Ball-ring from Chichén Itzá.
(Photo Carnegie Institution of Washington)

None of the Maya source-books, such as the codices, the inscriptions, or the Spanish records disclose as yet who was the Maya god of the game.

From Duran's description we have already heard that the rulers and nobles played games between themselves, betting jewelry, slaves, rich stones, handsome cloaks, adornments of war and also young women. Some of the games of the nobles were played for stakes and others were played in order to decide disputes. Several authors tell us of the game between Axayacatl of Mexico and Xihuiltemoc of Xochimilco. The stakes were several towns against the revenues of the market and the lake of Mexico. The lord of Xochimilco won the game and apparently was assassinated by the loser.

Famous is the game between Nezaualpilli, lord of Texcoco, and Moctezuma of Mexico to decide whose version of different prognostications was the correct one.

Professional players took part in the games of the common people. Great crowds attended these games and Duran gives us a very vivid description of the ceremonies and gambling which was connected with them.

"Having recounted the ways of the nobles when playing this game of ball for their recreation and enjoyment, we will now deal with those who played it for gain and as a vice, setting all their happiness and effort not to lose but to win, as gamblers who had no other business, who did not live from other sources nor had any other occupation than this, whose children and wives always lived on borrowed bread and begging from their neighbors, molesting everybody, as even among our people happens, that they send here for bread today, and tomorrow there for vinegar and another day for oil, etc. In this way these usually poor and adventurous people lived without sowing nor harvesting nor knowing anything other than gambling, and of these gamblers some would find themselves prosperous without any enlightenment and thus moved and persuaded by desire and greed to win, they made a thousand ceremonies and super-stitious deeds and invent-ed prognostications and idolatries of which I will now tell.

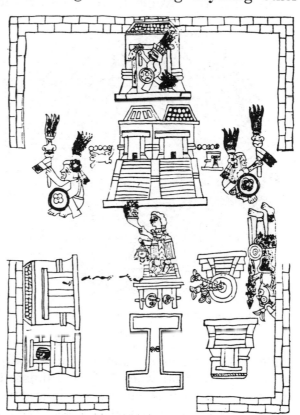

Fig. 15—Temple square with ball-court at Tenochtitlan.

"First it should be known that these gam-blers by nightfall took the ball and placed it on a clean plate with the leather loincloth and the gloves, hanging it all on a pole and, crouching be-fore these instruments of the game, they wor-shipped them and spoke to them with certain words of superstition and incantations with much devotion, praying to the ball that it should be favorable that day. For this purpose they—in the incantation which they made to the ball—invoked the aid of the water and springs, the ravines, the trees, the wild animals and serpents, the sun, the moon and the stars, the clouds, the rains and at last all created things and to the gods which they had invented for each thing.

"Having terminated the wicked and godless prayer they took a handful of incense and placed it in a small incense vessel which they had for this purpose and offered sacrifice to the ball and leather and while the copal (gum used as incense) burned they went away and brought back a meal of bread and a poor stew and wine and made offering of it before those instruments and left it there until morning, and when it was day they consumed the food which they had offered and then they left to search for some one with whom to play, and after this they were so certain and confident that they would win, that they would fight to death anyone who would say they were to lose and they would place seven lives in defense of this infidelity, which I doubt if they would do now in defense of our own true religion.

Fig. 16—Tlachtemalacatl from Tepoztlan.
(After Seler)

"What the low class people gambled was jewelry of small value and worth and as he who has little wealth on hand usually loses it, they were in necessity of gambling their houses, fields, maize-stores, maguey plants and of selling their children in order to gamble and even of gambling themselves away and of becoming slaves, to be sacrificed if they did not redeem themselves in time, as has already been told. Their way of gambling was that when they had finished losing the valuables which they carried such as cloaks, beads and feathers, they would gamble on their word, saying that they had certain valuables in their houses. When they retrieved their loss by this it was good, if not, he who won would go to the house of the loser and was given the jewelry or the valuables which had been gambled on his word, and if he did not have them, nor anything with which to make payment, he was thrown in jail, and if his wife and children did not redeem him he would come out as a slave of his creditor, it being the law of the country that he could be sold for the amount he owed and not for more, because in case he wished to free himself or found himself with means, nothing more should be said for the reason why he was condemned, and he who paid more for him lost it, and this is the way it was with all the games."

Before describing the numerous ball-courts in the Maya area, I will mention that courts were found at the time of the Conquest in the Temple enclosure at Tenochtitlan, as depicted by Sahagun.[18]

Seler found a *tlachtemalecatl* (Fig. 16), or stone ring for the game at Tepoztlan,[19] and also speaks of courts found in the ruins at Tamplax and Cerro del Cangrejo in the Huaxteca.[20]

Batres speaks of a ball-court at La Quemada[21] but neither his ground plan nor his photographs support his statement.

Recently Alfonso Caso has described a ball-court which he located at Xochicalco.[22]

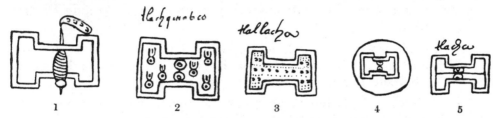

Fig. 17—Place-name glyphs containing the ball-court plan:
1—Tlachmalacac—Libro de tributos, 15.
2—Tlachquiabco—Codex Mendocino, 45.
3—Tlalacho—Codex Mendocino, 45.
4—Tlachyahualco—Codex Mendocino, 45.
5—Tlachco—Codex Mendocino, 31.

Hernando Vargas in his "Relacion" of 1582[23] tells us that where now lies the town of Querétaro, there used to be a ball-court.

We also hear of courts in Michoacan, and a series of place names as Tlachmalacac, Tlachquiabco, Tlalachco, Tlachyahualco and Tlachco[24] indicate that important ball-courts were found in these towns.

In Clavijero's time, about 1765[25], the game was apparently being played by people in the north, the Nayarit, Opatas and Tarahumares, and Dr. Hermann Beyer heard a few years ago from Mr. Kurt Hähnel that the Indians near Mazatlan still play a game which they call *ollimani*.

18 Sahagun. Paso y Troncoso facsimile.
19 Seler. Vol. II, pp. 213-214. Fig. 21.
20 Seler, Vol. II, p. 172-173.
21 Batres, 1903.
22 Caso, 1929.
23 Velazquez, 1898, Vol. I, pp. 1-48.
24 Tribute list in Codex Mendoza.
25 Clavijero, 1917, p. 405.

As will be seen from the above, our material on the ball-game is very scant, and in order to give a picture of the game and to get an impression of its importance we have been forced to use Nahua and other Mexican sources. The written records are rich in such information, but the architectural remains of ball-courts in the supposed home of the game are practically nil.

The reverse is the case in the Maya field, where we have sparse written records and innumerable ruins of ball-courts.

Karl Sapper and the late Eduard Seler are both pioneers to whom we owe a great debt because of their thorough investigations. It was these two who first located ball-courts in the southern part of the Maya area.

Sapper mapped a number of sites in the State of Chiapas, Mexico, and among these the ruins at Sacramento, Bolonchac, and El Rosarito in Chiapas, and also at Utatlan[26] or Cumarkah, in the Quiché, Saculeo, in Huehuetenango, Guatemala, and Leon de Piedra, El Salvador.

In the Zapotec country Seler reported a ball-court at Guiengola by Tehuantepec[27] (Fig. 19) and in his book on Chaculá he shows courts at Uaxac Canal.[28]

Unfortunately neither Sapper nor Seler give cross-sections of the ball-courts they found, but Seler's descriptions give us some important information.

As Dr. Seler's German style is quite heavy, I prefer to give the texts as they stand rather than run the risk of a too free translation alone.[29]

Uaxac Canal (Seler, 1901, p. 27):

"Die Seitenwände des schmalen Teils des Ballspielplatzes . . . von zwei parallelen, wallartigen Hügeln oder länglichen Pyramiden

26   Sapper, 1897.
27   Seler, 1896. Ges. Abh., Vol. II.
28   Seler, 1901, p. 27, fig. 12.
29   Uaxac Canal (Seler, 1901, p. 27):
      "The lateral walls of the narrow part of the ball-court . . . formed by two parallel mounds or elongated pyramids, from each one of which descends a moderately-inclined talus to the bottom of the court. The enlarged T-like ends are either represented simply by the ends of the ball-court, which is sunken into the ground, or they are formed by very low terraces; often mere rows of stone indicate them. A peculiarity of the ball-court, Fig. 12—which also occurs in other ball-courts of the Chacula region surveyed by Dr. Sapper, but which by no means is found everywhere—is that the downward-sloping tlachmatl wall, which projects two meters, has before it still another low, plain terrace of three meters' width—'similar to a sidewalk,' says Dr. Sapper—which slopes down in one or two layers of stone to the bottom of the ball-court."
   Uaxac Canal, Ventana Group (Seler, 1901, p. 57):
      "The two side-walls are pyramids of 11 meters in length and three meters in width, having before their inner side an inclined, smoothed wall of one meter in width, and a broad, plain terrace of two meters' width, marked with two rows of stones against the soil."
   Chacula, Ball-Court by East Temple (Seler, 1901, p. 64):
      "The side-walls are represented by two pyramids, 16 meters long, 1.75 meters high, four meters broad at the base, and two meters at the top, which slope apparently uniformly towards the interior. At about half a meter above the sunken level of the court there is joined to the inner side of these walls a wall which projects one meter and descends one-fourth of a meter, and to this again is joined a terrace two meters in width and one-fourth meters high, separated from the bottom by two inclined layers of stones."

gebildet, von denen je eine mässig geneigte, schräge Fläche sich bis auf den Boden des Ballspielplatzes herabsenkt. Die T-artig erweiterten Enden dagegen sind entweder nur durch die Wände der Vertiefung die der Ballspielplatz darstellt, oder durch ganz flache Terrassen, häufig auch nur durch blosse Steinreihen markiert, Eine Eigenetümlichkeit des Ballspields Ab. 12—die ebenso auch bei andern Ballspielen der Chaculä-Gegend und auch bei verschiedenen der von Dr. Sapper aufgenommenen Spielplätze, aber durchaus nicht überall vorkommt — ist, das *der um zwei Meter vorspringenden, schräg absteigenden tlachmatl-Wand noch eine drei Meter breite niedrige, ebene Terrasse vorgelagert ist—'ähnlich einem Trottoir,' sagt Dr. Sapper—die mit ein bis zwei schrägen Steinlagen zum Boden des Ballspielplatzes absteigt . . .''*

Uaxac Canal, Ventana Group (Seler, 1901, p. 57):

"Die beiden Seitenwälle sind Pyramiden von 11 m Länge und 3 m Breite, denen auf der Innenseite aine schräge zum Boden absteigende geglättete Wand von 1 m Breite und *eine 2 m, breite ebene Terrasse, die mit zwei schrägen Steinlagen gegen den Boden abgesetzt ist, vorgelagert sind.''*

Chaculá, Ball-Court by East Temple (Seler, 1901, p. 64):

"Die Seitenwälle werden von zwei 16 m langen, 1.75 m hohen und an der Basis 4 m, oben 2 m breiten Pyramiden gebildet, die anscheinend mit gleichmässiger Schräung nach innen abfallen. In einer Höhe von 1/2 m über dem vertieften Boden des Platzes schliesst sich an die Innenseite dieser Seitenwälle eine 1 m vorspringende und bis 1/4 m herabgehende schräge Wand, und dieser wiederum ist *eine 2 m breite, 1/4 m hohe ebene Terrasse vorgelagert, die durch zwei schräge Steinlagen gegen den Boden abgegrenzt ist . . .''*

From the above it is clearly seen that the courts found by Seler did not have vertical walls, as did the courts at Chichén and Uxmal and those described by the Spaniards. Furthermore, both Seler and Sapper speak of a low terrace at the foot of the main wall, and parallel with it towards the court.

When we first described the large court at Chichén Itzá we noted that a similar terrace, B and C, was found at the foot of the great wall, A, in Fig. 5.

The "capital I" shape is found in every case reported by Sapper and Seler, and they both state that the sloping side of the main wall and the low terrace are covered with cut stones.

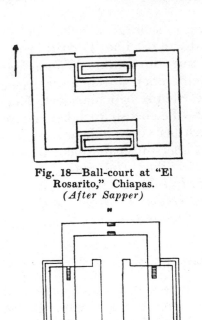

Fig. 18—Ball-court at "El
Rosarito," Chiapas.
(After Sapper)

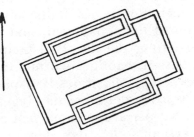

Fig. 19—El Resguardo, ruins
of Utatlan, Guatemala.
(After Sapper)

Fig. 20—Guiengola, Oaxaca.
(After Seler)

Fig. 21—Uaxac Canal,
Guatemala.
(After Seler)

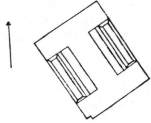

Fig. 22—Uaxac Canal, Ven-
tana Group, Guatemala.
(After Seler)

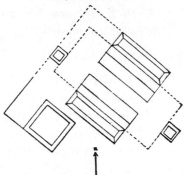

Fig. 23—Ball-court at foot of
East Temple, Chaculá.
(After Seler)

Fig. 24—Ball-court (?) at Rabinal, Guatemala.
(After Maudslay)

Also it will be noted that none of these courts has a stone ring.

In "Glimpses at Guatemala" by A. C. and A. P. Maudslay[30] is a drawing of a structure having the form of a ball-court (Fig. 24).

Let us now turn to the ball-courts located by the John Geddings Gray Memorial Expedition, conducted by the Department of Middle American Research of the Tulane University of Louisiana, in 1928.

On the northeast side of the broad valley where many smaller rivers join to form the Rio Grande de Chiapas, are a great many ruined cities of the Maya. As a rule these ruins lie on the top of hills, or on spurs on the main range which protrude into the valley.

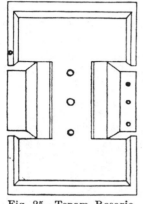

Fig. 25—Tenam Rosario, Chiapas.

The common name for a group of ruins in that region is *tenam,* and in order to distinguish the multitude of tenams, one from the other, we added the name of the ranch on whose property they were located.

The first major group of ruins to be visited was Tenam Rosario (Fig. 25), one day's ride to the southeast of Zapaluta, Chiapas. The top of a very extensive hill has been levelled, and dense low bush covers a great many ruined stone buildings and pyramids. On the eastern edge of the plateau lies a ball-court of shape and construction like those reported by Sapper and Seler, but with the difference that three circular altars are set into the floor of the court, and three similar altars lie on the top of one of the walls. The wide ends of the court are enclosed by walls, and the entire enclosure looks like a "sunken court." The two main parallel walls, A, are clad with cut stones, set close together, which form a smooth surface sloping toward the court. We also find the low terrace, B, and its stone-set slope C.

These altars set into the floor of the central part, E, of the court, on a level with its surface, remind me of three small circular altars with figures carved on their surfaces which Merwin found at the Rio Grande ruins in British Honduras, now called Lubaantun. These three small altars were found set into the floor of a passage between two parallel mounds. Mr. J. Eric Thompson kindly inspected these mounds, A and B, on the map of the site made by him[31] and

30   A. C. and A. P. Maudslay, 1889, p. 104.
31   Report on the British Museum Expedition to British Honduras, 1927. Royal Anthrop. Inst., Vol. LVII, July-Dec., 1927.

5 and 6 on the map made by Merwin in 1914-1915.[32]   In a letter he states as follows: "I looked carefully at the possible ball-court there, but without excavating it seemed to me that there wasn't any evidence that they were so employed.   There is no sign of a narrow terrace at the base of the insides of the mounds, but the south end has a kind of TAU shape, missing, however, at the north end."

As the low terraces are rarely over two feet high they can well be hidden under debris and humus.   The fact that only one broad end of the court has an enclosing wall, we shall see duplicated at Yaxchilan.   It should be interesting to make a cross-section trench at mounds A and B at Lubaantun.

The three altars found by Merwin, and now in the Peabody Museum of Harvard University, have two human figures carved on their surface, and between them is a circular object which could well be a ball.   These figures are similar to those on Altar 2 at Cankuen (Fig. 26) on the Rio de la Pasion in Guatemala.   Unfortunately Maler's small plan of the Cankuen[33] ruins only gives the location of the two stelae, and Morley,[34] who located the altar in question, has not published any plan.

Fig. 26 – Altar 2.   Cankuen, Guatemala. (Photo by Morley)

About three hours' ride from Tenam Rosario one reaches the small ranches by Cieneguilla and Soledad. Several groups of ruins are located in the vicinity of these, but we will only speak of Tenam Soledad here. On the top of a mountain spur, at a short distance from the Soledad ranch, lies a sizeable group of mounds and pyramids around plazas. Towards the point of the spur we find a ball-court consisting of two parallel mounds.   The sides facing each other are covered with cut stones and slope towards low terraces.   All the typical features of the ball-court mounds of the region are present, the only departure being that the east mound terminates in a vertical wall on the side away from the court (Fig. 27).

A few hours' ride further on we reached the narrow fertile valley of Sacchaná, enclosed by steep mountains.   High over the valley, on a prominent mountain from which one has a magnificent view over the surrounding country, lies another group of temples

32 Map compiled by Blom from Merwin's unpublished field notes.
33 Maler, 1908, pp. 36-49.
34 Morley, 1915 a., p. 344.   Morley, 1922, p. 123.

named Desconsuelo. Here we found an excellently-preserved ball-court. We measured it with great care and took photographs. Unfortunately, our pictures were destroyed by heat and moisture, but our plan is shown in Fig. 28.

After a trip through the untracked parts of the Tzendales jungle we reached the abandoned lumber-station, now called Montería

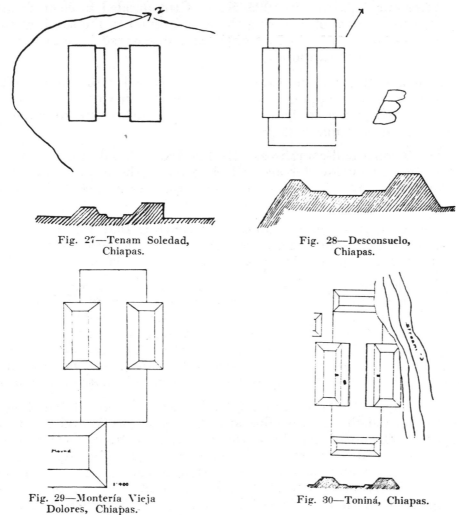

Fig. 27—Tenam Soledad, Chiapas.

Fig. 28—Desconsuelo, Chiapas.

Fig. 29—Montería Vieja Dolores, Chiapas.

Fig. 30—Toniná, Chiapas.

Vieja de Dolores, located at the junction of the Tzaconehá and the Chacpuyil rivers. An old trail leads through a group of ruins, and cuts across one end of a ball-court of the type already described (Fig. 29).

In 1925 the First Tulane University Expedition spent some days at the Tonina ruins making a map of the most prominent part.

To the south of the main ruins lay a level stretch of land entirely covered by dense undergrowth. Señor Auro Cruz, owner of the land where the ruins are located, is one of those rare persons who is really interested in taking care of the ancient buildings and monuments, and he promised us to be on the look-out for objects of interest.

After our departure in 1925, Señor Cruz decided to clear a part of the dense vegetation covering the level ground to the south of the main ruins in order to plant coffee, and discovered several carved figures lying on the ground.

Reaching the ruins in 1928, we were received with this cheerful news, and while mapping the mounds on the newly cleared land found a well-preserved ball-court. These courts were apparently becoming an epidemic with us.

The Toniná ball-court is exactly like those already described. It is surrounded by low terraces which gives it the appearance of a sunken court. On the low terrace along the foot of the west mound lies a stone tablet with a short inscription.

The prominent feature about this court is that we found two stone tenons, opposite each other in the center of the main walls, as shown on our Fig. 30. We shall return to these later.

Crossing the Tzendales forests from west to east, we arrived at Yaxchilan on the Usumatsintla river in the heart of the area inhabited by the old Maya. On his map of these ruins Maler[35] writes between the structures 13 and 14, on the river terrace: Plaza de Juego, and in the text he states: "Did these two incomprehensible structures once enclose a playground like those of the Yucatan cities?" We can now answer his question in the affirmative (Fig. 31).

The sides of the two mounds 13 and 14 are covered with cut stones forming a smooth slope; we find also the low terrace B and the small slope C. The broad end F towards the river, i. e., towards the northeast, is enclosed by terraces, but the end towards the city is open, and a circular altar lies at some distance along the axis of the court. As the broad ends, F, were not of primary importance in the game the outline of the end in question may have been indicated by a low wall or stones which now are buried under a thick layer of humus.

Due to scarcity of water, I was able to spend only a few hours in Tikal, one of the most extensive of the Maya ruins, and time did not permit a search for ball-courts. But on the trail from Peten,

---

35 Maler. 1903 pl. XXXIX, text p. 134. See Appendix for more information on Yaxchilan ball-courts.

Guatemala, we encountered a large group of mounds and ruined buildings. Among these ruins was also a ball-court, as in Fig. 32.

Lothrop[36] describes a couple of ball-courts in El Salvador, Cihuatan and Tehuacan and one in Honduras, at Tenampua. He also suggests that the structures XXXVII and XXXVIII on Ricketson's map[37] of Piedras Negras might be a ball-court. This completes our information on courts in the southern Maya area, and the regions immediately adjacent to it.

In the northern area we have, first, the giant court at Chichén Itzá, and two small courts; next the well-known court at Uxmal.

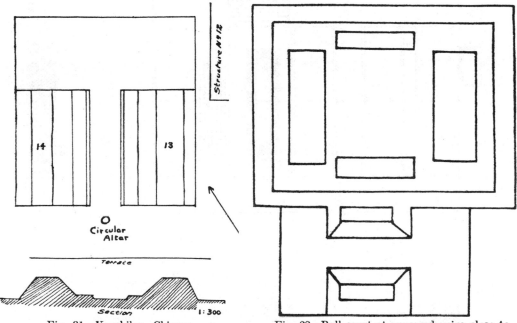

Fig. 31—Yaxchilan, Chiapas.   Fig. 32—Ball-court at unnamed ruins close to Kash-uinik, British Honduras.

To these should be added a court figured by Charnay[38] at Aké and two courts recently reported by Eric Thompson and Harry Pollock at Cobá. Quoting a letter from Pollock[39] I also give his plan of one of the courts at Cobá (Fig. 33).

"The sills at either side of the floor are about 10 cm. high, and 35 cm. broad. Above these the wall slopes up to a little vertical moulding projecting 20 cm. and 25 cm. high. The rings, the western fragment was found in place, were set just under the moulding.

36 Lothrop, 1927.
37 O. G. Ricketson's unpublished map for Carnegie Institution of Washington.
38 Charnay, 1887.
39 Pollock—letter.

The eastern ring, about half of it was found, has an outside diameter of 90 cm., an inside diameter of 50 cm. and is 18 cm. thick." We recognize here the sill B, familiar from other courts and note that the wall of the court was *sloping* and that *stone rings were in these walls.*

Thompson and Pollock also report a court at Nohoch Mul about 1½ km. from Cobá.

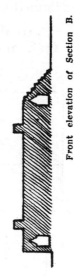

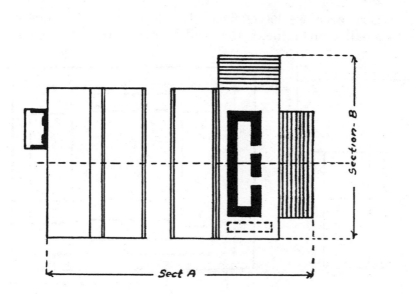

Side elevation of Section A.

Fig. 33—Ball-court at Cobá, Quintana Roo.
(Courtesy of J. Eric Thompson. Harry Pollock and Carnegie Institution of Washington)

In 1930, during the Chicago World's Fair Expedition to Uxmal, conducted by Tulane University, the writer located a ball-court at Sayil, a court of the typical "capital I" shape and with slanting walls (Fig. 34).

[40]Having now reviewed all the ball-courts known for the present in the area we can establish the following facts:

---

40 See post-script to this paper.

First of all, it will be noted that there is no rule as to how the ball-courts are placed in relation to the cardinal points. In a few cases the longitudinal axis of a court runs north-south, but it is far from a rule. This does away with the theory that the courts were oriented to the cardinal points, and that the movement of the ball represented the sun or the moon. Some of the drawings of courts found in the codices show the floor of the courts painted in sections in four different colors, which in some, but far from all cases, coincide with the cardinal points. As a whole, though, evidence to support this theory is scant.

All ball-courts, both northern and southern, have the "capital I" shape.

The walls, A, always have a smooth surface, and are usually sloping towards the court and are vertical only in some cases in the north.

The low terrace, B, is present in all cases, both north and south.

The stone-clad slope, C, from terrace to floor of court is always present.

Stone rings in the walls are found only in the north.

The absence of the stone ring, a most important feature in the game as it was played by the Toltec-Nahua, is astonishing until we study the documentary evidences from the southern area. Most outstanding of these is the Popol Vuh, and in it the ball-game is constantly mentioned.

There are several statements, but as they are practically identical I will only mention a few of them.

Hunhun-Ahpu and Vucub-Hunapu spent every day in playing ball, and were heard by Hun Came and Vukub Camé, lords of Xibalba, the under-world. The noise annoyed those sinister gentlemen, and they sent a message to summon the offenders to a game.

Reaching the ball-court of Hunhun Ahpú and Vucub Hunahpu the messengers ordered them to: ". . . bring their instruments, their rings, their gloves and also their ball . . ."

". . . qui bate, qui pachgab, chi pe naipuch ri qui quiq . . ."

Bate is translated both by Brasseur and Raynaud[41] as ring. Ximenez[42] translates it as "pala," which is a wooden shovel in Eng-

---

41 Brasseur. 1861. pp. 77, 83, 127, 129, 139, etc. Raynaud. 1925. p. 30, etc.
42 Ximenez in Scherzer.

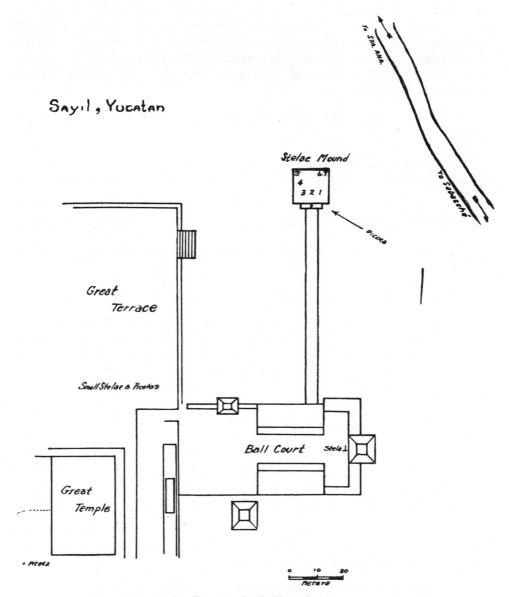

Fig. 34—Sayil, Yucatán.

lish, and the Villacorta-Rodas[43] edition shows its weakness in this as in so many other cases by translating it as arrows (p. 215), masks (p. 219), and lances (pp. 249, 253, 277, etc.)

The word BATE leads to speculations. From many sources we know that the Spaniards encountered a ball-game named *batey* on the Isla Española, the present Haiti. We have already quoted Oviedo's description[44] of the rubber ball used in their game.

Duran states that "the material of which this ball is made is called *olin*, which I have heard to be called 'batel' in our Spanish." Here he may well have heard the name given to the substance, rubber, on the Island of Española.

The puzzle arises when we encounter the word BATE, in the Quiché language meaning the ring used in a game with a rubber ball.

PACHKAP is gloves, from PACH, to cover and KAP, a hand.

QUIQ, or QUIC, is blood; QUIQCHE is bleeding tree, hence QUIQ is also rubber. In the case of the two latter words Villacorta-Rodas again translates erratically.

The above-mentioned instruments, i. e., the ring, the gloves and the ball, are frequently mentioned in the Popol Vuh, always in the same order and always as *portable* objects, which first Hunhun-Ahpu and Vucub-Hunahpu, and later Hunahpu and Xbalanque are told to bring with them to Xibalba.

It is therefore evident that the ring in early times was not a fixture on the wall of the court, and this explains its absence from the courts in the southern, i. e., the oldest area, as already pointed out by Raynaud,[45]

In the Popol Vuh we mostly hear of the court, the game and its instruments, and only in one case do we get a short, and quite unsatisfactory description of a game in progress:[46]

"Then the rulers of Xibalba threw the ball. Xbalanque went out to meet it, it flew straight for the ring, hit it, and went out again, passing over the ball-court, and entering directly into the mouldings of the cornice."[47]

43   Villacorta. 1927.
44   Oviedo, 1851, vol. 1, p. 165.
45   Raynaud, 1925, p. 30, note 2.
46   Brasseur, 1861, pp. 168-169; Pohorilles, 1913, pp. 55-56; Raynaud, 1925, pp. 65-66.
47   A close comparison of all translations has been made, and the Quiché text has been checked with the help of Brasseur, 1862, and Basseta's manuscript vocabulary. As a curiosity the Villacorta-Rodas translation of this passage is presented (p. 277): "deteniéndose frente a su lanza, e inmediatamente la arrojó de un puntapié sobre la casa del juego"; "(the ball) stopping in front of his lance, and immediately he hurled it with a kick of his foot over the house of the game." Remember that lances do not belong to the implements of the game, and that the players were not allowed to touch the ball with their hands and feet.

It appears that the game in its early stages was played in courts with slanting side walls, and with portable wooden (?) rings. The stone tenons which we found in the center of the side walls at Toniná may belong to a second stage in the evolution of the game, and the last development was a court with vertical walls, and fixed stone rings.

Therefore, it may be correct to state that the ball-game played in courts with vertical walls and with fixed stone rings was a Toltec feature. The fact remains that the game of POK-TA-POK, or *tlachtli* was played with much enthusiasm by the mythological ancestors of the highland Maya of the Old Area, as well as by their descendants, the Mayance Indians of the South.

Exploration in the Maya area is still in its infancy, and many more ball-courts will be found; therefore, the map (frontispiece to this paper) shows what we know today, and the list of ball-courts in the Maya area, both north and south, with which I conclude this paper, is overwhelmingly in favor of my contention.

Fig. 35—Ball-court at Uxmal, Yucatán (foreground). Ruins of
nunnery quadrangle to rear.

POST-SCRIPT

A short summary of the finding of ball-courts in the southern area was given in a paper delivered before the Twenty-third Congress of Americanists held in New York in 1928. It was entitled: "Preliminary Notes on Two Important Maya Finds," and the ball-courts were described on pages 167 to 171 of the volume published by the Congress.

As a result of this paper the search for ball-courts was intensified, and I herewith take the opportunity to express my thanks to my colleagues who most generously supplied me with information upon their findings. I want especially to mention Dr. S. G. Morley of the Carnegie Institution of Washington; Messrs. Alfonso Caso, J. Eric Thompson, Harry E. D. Pollock, Karl Ruppert and J. S. Boles.

In the magnificent discovery made by Mr. Alfonso Caso in tomb seven at Monte Alban, there was among many other incredibly beautiful objects a pectoral of gold, which represents the sky, the sun, the moon and the earth. The sky is represented by the outline of a ball-court, and in *aplique* of gold thread are two players holding their rubber game-ball. The sun is depicted with the usual sun-disk, the moon by the Aztec glyph *tecpatl,* and the earth by the Aztec glyph *cipactli.*

The fact that the sky is represented by a ball-court and two ball-players proves plainly why this game was not only a favorite sport but also was of a high religious and ceremonial importance among the natives of Middle America, and further stresses my contention that probably every city of importance had at least one ball-court.

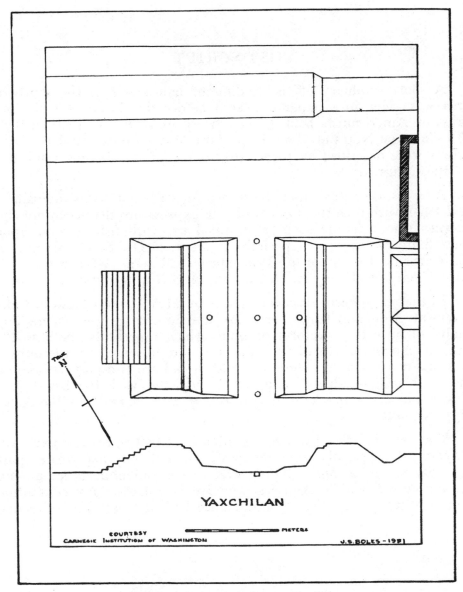

Fig. 36—Ball-court No. 1 at Yaxchilan.

APPENDIX

Ball-Courts of the Maya Area

Located By	At	Area
Sapper	Sacramento, Chis., Mexico	South
"	Bolonchac, Chis., Mexico	"
"	Saculeo, Guatemala	"
"	Kalamté, Guatemala	"
"	Sajcabaja, Guatemala	"
"	Resguardo (Utatlan), Guatemala	"
"	Rosarito, Chis., Mexico	"
"	Leon de Piedra, El Salvador	"
Seler	Guiengola, Oaxaca, Mexico	"
"	Uaxac Canal, Guatemala	"
"	Uaxac Canal, Ventana Group, Guatemala	"
"	Chaculá, Guatemala	"
J. G. Gray Memorial Expedition and Maler	Tenam Rosario, Chis., Mexico	"
"	Tenam Soledad, Chis., Mexico	"
"	Desconsuelo, Chis., Mexico	"
"	Chacpuyil, Chis., Mexico	"
"	Toniná, Chis., Mexico	"
"	Yaxchilan, Chis., Mexico	"
"	Kash-uinik, British Honduras	"
Maudslay	Rabinal, British Honduras	"
Lothrop	Chiuatan, El Salvador	"
"	Tehuacan, El Salvador	"

519

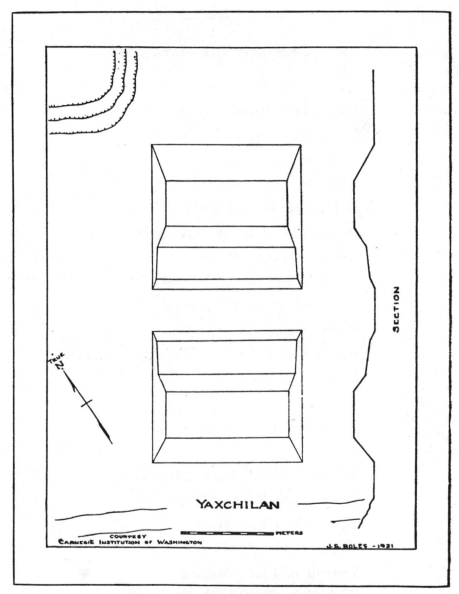

Fig. 37—Ball-court No. 2 at Yaxchilan.

Located By	At	Area
Lothrop	Tenampua, El Salvador	South
"	Piedras Negras, Guatemala	"
Burkitt	Chipal, Guatemala	"
"	San Francisco, Guatemala	"
"	Chichel, Guatemala	"
"	Xolchun, Guatemala	"
	Cankuen, Guatemala	"
	Lubaantun, British Honduras	"
	Chichén Itzá No. 1, Yucatán	North
	Chichén Itzá No. 2, Yucatán	"
	Chichén Itzá No. 3, Yucatán	"
	Uxmal, Yucatán	"
Charnay	Aké, Yucatán	"
Carnegie Expedition }	Cobá No. 1, Quintana Roo	"
"	Cobá No. 2, Quintana Roo	"
"	Nohoch Mul, Quintana Roo	"
Chicago-Tulane Expedition }	Sayil, Yucatán	"

With Guiengola and Leon de Piedra as the geographical extremes of the Maya country, we have 32 ball-courts in the southern area, against eight in the north. I am inclined to believe, though, that we must expect to find at least one ball-court in every city of any importance, both in the north and in the south.

BIBLIOGRAPHY

ALVARADO TEZOZOMOC, FERNANDO:
    1878   Cronica Mexicana, Mexico.

ARA, DOMINGO DE:
    1571   MS—Bocabulario en lengua tzeltal. Photostat.

BANCROFT, HUBERT HOWE:
    1874-76 The Native Races of the Pacific States of North America. D. Appleton & Co., New York.

BASSETA, DOMINGO:
    Vocabulario de Lengua Quiche. Photostat in D. M. A. R., Tulane University, New Orleans.

BATRES, LEOPOLDO:
    1903   Visita a los Monumentos Arquelogicos de "La Quemada," Zacatecas. F. Diaz de Leon, Mexico.

BLOM, FRANS:
    1928   Preliminary Notes on Two Important Maya Finds—paper before 23rd Congress of Americanists, New York.

BRASSEUR ("DE BOURBOURG") CHAS. ETIENNE:
    1857-59 Histoire des Nations Civilisées Mexique et de l'Amérique-Centrale. A. Bertrand, Paris.
    1861   Popul Vuh. A. Durand, Paris.
    1862   Gramatica de la Lengua Quiche. Grammairē de la Langue Quichée. A. Bertrand, Paris.

CASO, ALFONSO:
    1929   Informe de las Labores Realizadas en la Direccion de Arquelogia Durante el Mes de Julio de 1929. Boletin de la Secretaria de Educacion, Mexico.

CHARLOT, JEAN:
    1932   (See THOMPSON, J. ERIC).

CHARNAY, DESIRE:
    1887   The Ancient Cities of the New World. Harper & Bros., New York.

CHAVERO, ALFREDO:
    1901   Colección Chavero. Pinturas Jeroglificos. Imp. del J. E. Barbero, Mexico.

CLARK, J. COOPER:
    1912   The Story of "Eight Deer" in Codex Colombino. Taylor & Francis, London.

CLAVIJERO, FRANCISCO JAVIER:
 1917   Historia Antigua de México. Vol. I. Mexico.

CODEX BORBONICUS:
 1889   Manuscrit Mexicain de la Bibliotheque du Palais Bourbon. (Livre
         Divinatoire et Ritual Figuré). E. Leroux, Paris.

CODEX BORGIA:
 1904-09 Eine Altmexikanische Bilderschrift der Bibliothek der Congregatio
         de Propaganda Fide. Druck von Gebr. Unger, Berlin.

CODEX LAUD:
 1928   Manuscrito Pictorio Mexicana Donado a la Universidad de Oxford
         por el Arzbispo Laud y que se Conserva en la Biblioteca Bodlei-
         ana. Mexico.

CODEX MAGLIABECCHIANO:
 1904   Manuscrit Mexicain Post-Colombien de la Bibliotheque Nationale de
         Florence; Reproduit en Photochromographie aux Frais du Duc de
         Loubat. Danesi, Rome.

CODEX MENDOZA:
 1829   Sahagún, Bernardino de: Historia General de las Cosas de Nueva
         España. Madrid.

CODEX NUTTALL:
 1902   Facsimile of an Ancient Mexican Codez Belonging to Lord Zouche
         of Harynworth, England, with an introduction by Zelia Nuttall.
         Cambridge, Mass.

DURAN, DIEGO:
 1867-80 Historia de las Indias de Nueva-España y Islas de "Tierra Firme,
         J. M. Andrade y F. Escalante. Mexico.

FEWKES, J. WALTER:
 1913   Porto Rican Elbow-Stones in the Heye Museum, with Discussion of
         Similar Objects Elsewhere. New Era Printing Co., Lancaster,
         Pennsylvania.

FRIAS, VANETIN F.:
 1910   Las Calles de Querétaro.

GOMARA, FRANCISCO LOPEZ DE:
 1554   Historia de Mexico, Con el Descvbrimirnto dela Nueva España, Con-
         quistada por el Muy Illustre y Valeroso Principe Don Fernando
         Cortes, Marques del Valle. En Envers, en Casa de Iuan Steelsio.

HERNÁNDEZ, JUAN MARTÍNEZ:
 1930   Diccionario de Motul. Talleres de la Compañia Tipografica, Merida,
         Yuc., Mexico.

HERRERA Y TORDESILLAS, ANTONIO DE:
 1726-28 Historia General de los Hechos de los Castellanos en las Islas i Tierra
         Firme del Mar Oceano. Imprenta Real de Nicolas Rodriguez
         Franco, Madrid.

HOLMES, WILLIAM HENRY:
    1895-97 Archaeological Studies Among the Ancient Cities of Mexico. Chicago.

KINGSBOROUGH, EDWARD KING, VISCOUNT:
    1831-48 Antiquities of Mexico. R. Havall, London.

LOTHROP, SAMUEL KIRKLAND:
    1927   Pottery Types and their Sequence in El Salvador. Heye Founda-
             tion, New York.

LOVEN, SVEN:
    1924   Uber die Wurzeln der Tainischen Kultur. Elanders Boktryckeri
             Akitiebolag, Goteborg, Sweden.

MALER, TEOBERT:
    1901-03 Researches in the Central Portions of the Usumasintla Valley. Cam-
             bridge, Mass.
    1908   Explorations in the Upper Usumasintla Valley and Adjacent Region.
             Cambridge, Mass.

MAUDSLAY, ALFRED PERCIVAL:
    1889-1902 Biologia Centrali Americana.

MAUDSLAY, A. C. AND A.P.:
    1899   A Glimpse at Guatemala, and Some Notes on the Ancient Monu-
             ments of Central America. J. Murray, London.

MEDINA, BALTHASAS DE:
    1682   Chronica de la Santa Provincia de San Diego de Mexico, de Re-
             ligiosos Descalços de N. S. P. S. Francisco en la Nueva España.
             J. de Ribera, Mexico.

MERWIN, B.:
    MS.   Unpublished Field Notes, Peabody Museum, Harvard University.
             Cambridge, Mass.

MOLINA, ALONSO DE:
    1571   Vocabvlario en Lengva Castellana y Mexicana. Antonia de Spinosa,
             Mexico.

MORLEY, SYLVANUS GRISWOLD:
    1915   An Introduction to the Study of Maya Hieroglyphs. Washington.
    1922   History and Chronology in Ancient Middle America.

MOTUL DICTIONARY:
    MS.   Diccionario de Motul, Maya-Spanish, Spanish-Maya. Photostat.

MUNOZ CAMARGO, DIEGO:
    1892   Historia de Tlaxcala. Oficina Tip. de la Secretaria de Fomento.
             Mexico.

NEVE Y MOLINA, LUIS DE:
    1767   Reglas de Orthographia, Diccionario, y Arte del Idiona Othomi.
             Impr. de la Bibliotheca Mexicana, Mexico.

OVIEDO Y VALDES, GONZALO FERNANDEZ DE:
  1851-55 Historia General y Natural de las Indias, Islas y Tierra-firme del
          Mar Oceano. Imp. de la Real Acedamia de la Historia. Madrid.

PEREZ, JUAN PIO:
  1866-77 Diccionario de la Lengua Maya. J. F. Mólina Solis. Merida.
  1898   Coordinacion Alfabetica de las Voces del Idioma Maya que se Hallan
          en el Arte y Obras del Padre Fr. Pedro Beltran de Santa Rosa.
          Imp. de la Ermita, Merida.

POHORILLES, NOAH ELIESER:
  1913   Das Popol Vuh, Die Mutische Geshichte der Kice-Volkes von Guate-
          mala. Leipzig.

POLLOCK, HARRY:
  MS.   Letter to Blom in D. M. A. R., Tulane University, New Orleans.
  1932   See also THOMPSON, J. ERIC.

POPUL VUH:
  1861   Popul Vuh. Le Livre Sacré et les Mythes de l'Antiquité Américaine,
          Avec les Livres Héroïques et Historiques des Quichés. Brasseur
          edition. Durand, Paris.
  1923   El Popol-vuh, ó Libro Sagrado de los Antiguos Votánides. Docu-
          mento de Capital Importancia para el Estudio de la Historia Pre-
          colombina. Precididó de un Estudio Preliminar por el Doctor
          Santiago I. Barberena. "Pluma y Lapiz," Merida.
  1927   Manuscrit de Chich i Castenango (Popul buj). Estudios Sobre las
          Antiguas Tradiciones del Pueblo Quiché. Por J. Antonio Villa-
          corta C y Flavio Rodas N. Guatemala.

QUADERNO DE YDIONA ZAPOTECO DEL VALLE:
  1793   Que Contiene Alguna Reglas las mas Comunes del Arte, un Vocabu-
          lario Algo Copioso, un Confessonario y Otras Cosas que Veera el
          Christiano Lector. Sn. Martin Tilcaxete. MS. in D. M. A. R.,
          Tulane University, New Orleans.

RAYNAUD, GEORGES:
  1925   Popul Vuh. Les Dieux, les Héros et les Hommes de l'Ancien Guaté-
          mala d'Apres le Livre du Conseil. E. Leroux, Paris.
  1927   Popul Vuh. Los Dioses, los Héros y los Hombres de Guatemala
          Antiqua. Tr. de la Versión Francesca del Prof. Georges Raynaud
          . . . por . . . Miguel Angel Asturias y J. M. Gonzalez de Mendoza.
          Ed. Paris-America, Paris.

REINOSO, DIEGO DE:
  1916   Vocabulario de la Lengua Mame. Impr. de la Secretaria de Fomento.
          Mexico.

RICKETSON, O. G., JR.:
          Unpublished Map for Carnegie Institution of Washington.

ROYAL ANTHROPOLOGICAL INSTITUTE:
  1927   Report on British Museum Expedition to British Honduras in 1927.

SAHAGÚN, BERNARDINO DE:

1829   Historia de la Conquista de Mexico . . . Pub. por Separado de sus Demás Obras Carlos Maria de Bustamante . . . Impr. de Galvan á Cargo de M. Arévalo. Mexico.

1829-30 Historia General de las Cosas de Nueva España. Impr. del Cuidadano A. Valdés. Mexico.

1905-06 Historia General de las Casas de Nueva España. Edición Parcial en Facsimile de los Códices Matritenses en Lengua Mexicana que se Custodian in las Bibliotecas del Palacio Real y de la Real Academia de las Historia. Fototipia de Hauser y Menet. Madrid.

SAPPER, KARL:

1895   Altindianische Ansiedlungen in Guatemala und Chiapas.

1897   Das Nördliche Mittel-Amerika Nebst Einem Ausflug Nach dem Hochland von Anahuac. F. Vieweg und Sohn, Braunschweig.

SCHULTZ, WOLFGANG:

1913   Einleitung in das Popol Vuh. J. C. Hinrichs'sche Buchhandlung, Leipzig.

SELER, CECILIE:

1925   Auf Alten Wegen in Mexiko und Guatemala. Strecker und Schröder, Stuttgart.

SELER, EDUARD:

1901   Die Alten Ansiedelungen von Chaculá im Distrikte Nenton des Departements Huehuetenango der Republic Guatemala. D. Reimer, Berlin.

1902-19 Gesammelte Abhandlungen Zur Amerikanischen Sprachund Alterthumskunde. A. Asher & Co., Berlin.

SPINDEN, HERBERT J.:

1913   A Study of Maya Art; its Subject Matter and Historical Development. The Museum, Cambridge, Mass.

1922   Ancient Civilizations of Mexico and Central America. 1-3 Ed., American Museum Press, New York.

1927   Study of Dead City of "Rubber People," New York Times.

THOMPSON, J. ERIC:

1927   The Civilization of the Mayas. Field Museum, Chicago.

THOMPSON, J. ERIC; AND POLLOCK, HARRY E. D.; AND CHARLOT, JEAN:

1932   Cobá Report, Carnegie Institution.

TORQUEMADA, JUAN DE:

1723   Primera (Segunda, Tercera) Parte de los Viente i vn Libros Rituales i Monarchia Indiana. N. Rodriguez Franco, Madrid.

VARGAS, HERNANDO:

1582   Relacion de Queretaro. Published in Velazquez, P. F., 1898. Documentos para la Historia de St. Luis Potosi.

VELAZQUEZ, P. F.:

1898   Documentos para la Historia de St. Luis Potosi.

VEYTIA, MARIANO:
    1836   Historia Antigua de Méjico. J. Ojeda, Mexico.

VILLACORTA C., J. ANTONIO:
    1927   Popul Vuh. Manuscrito de Chichicastenango (Popul buj). Por J
            Antonio Villacorta C y Flavio Rodas N. Guatemala.

VOCABULARIO CASTELLANO-ZAPOTECO:
    1893   Vocabulario Castellano-Zapoteco. Pub . . . con Motivo de la Cele-
            bración del Cuarto Centenario del Descubrimiento de America.
            Oficina tip. de la Secretario de Fomento. Mexico.

XIMENEZ, FRANCISCO:
    1857   Popul Vuh. Las Historias del Origen de los Indios de esta Provincia
            de Guatemala. C. Gerold é Hijo, Vienna.

INDEX

GAMES AND GAMBLING

John M. Cooper

GAMES AND GAMBLING

By John M. Cooper

Dancing, singing, feasting, and, in the distribution area of alcoholic beverages, drinking sprees are probably, all things considered, the favorite recreational activities of the Indians of southern Middle America, the West Indies, and South America. The present article is concerned with recreational activities other than these—with games, sports, and kindred amusements.

For convenience of reference we are using the following areal terms: Middle American (Honduras to Panamá, including the *Cuna*), Antillean (West Indies), Andean (Highlands and adjacent west coast from northern Colombia to Middle Chile), *Araucanian* (including Chiloé and *Araucanian* territory east of Andes), Orinocoan (especially territory watered by left affluents of the Orinoco), Amazonian (watershed of Amazon west of mouth of the Río Negro to the north and of the Xingú River to the south, and including the Montaña), Guiana (Guianas to Amazon), Eastern Brazilian (area south of the Amazon and east of the Xingú and the Paraguay Rivers, down to about latitude 30° S.), Eastern Bolivian (Bolivia and immediately adjacent area, east of the *Aymara-Quechua* region), Chacoan (including also the *Chiriguano* and *Chané*), Pampean (Uruguayan and Argentine plains, south to Río Negro), Patagonian (Río Negro to Strait of Magellan), Fuegian (*Ona, Yahgan, Alacaluf*).

Field data on games are very imperfect and spotty. We have what appears to be full or fairly full information for the following areas: The Guianan (esp. Roth, W. E., 1924); parts of the Amazonian (esp. Karsten, 1930, 1935; and Koch-Grünberg, 1909–10); Chacoan and parts of Eastern Bolivian (esp. Nordenskiöld, 1910, 1919 a, 1920, and Karsten, 1930, 1932); *Araucanian* (esp. Manquilef, 1914); Fuegian (Gusinde, 1931, 1937). As regards the Middle American, Antillean and Andean areas, our data are relatively scant. The bulk of our information on games comes from the great forest and savanna region to the north—especially the Amazonian, Guianan, Eastern Brazilian, Eastern Bolivian, and Chacoan—and from the *Araucanian* and Fuegian areas to the south.

Our chief distributional studies are those of Nordenskiöld (esp. 1919 a, 1920).

We shall deal first with nongambling games and amusements, and afterward with gambling ones.

NONGAMBLING GAMES AND AMUSEMENTS

We shall take up in order games and amusements distributed (1) very generally over most or all of the continent and adjacent islands, (2) widely within two or more areas therein, and (3) locally within quite limited ranges. In view of the many lacunae in our earlier and later sources, lines between these three divisions have to be drawn somewhat loosely. Moreover, the writer can at best hope to block out the broad outline of the continental picture as a working basis for later completion and emendation as further data are salvaged from the field or gleaned from our endless scattered literature.

Continental and near-continental distributions.—Games of ball are the only games that are specifically recorded as played within each of the 13 areas listed above. The balls are more commonly of maize leaves or rubber, sometimes of stuffed hide or other material. The games vary from the simple throwing or volleying of the ball from player to player, as among the Fuegians, or the kicking of a football, as among the Pampean women, to the elaborate organized hockey and pillma games and the rubber-ball games with or without a court proper. The more important and distinctive of these will be dealt with presently.

Specifically recorded as distributed over many or a majority of the 13 areas, including the Andean and the Fuegian, are wrestling and racing, and the use of dolls. In wrestling, various holds are customary, such as: hair (*Araucanian*), upper arm (*Island Carib*), neck (*Tapirapé*). In some areas, as the Andean (*Aymara*) and Guianan, team wrestling occurs, the *Aymara* teams representing moieties. Racing may be on foot, on horseback, or on water. Dolls are made of wood, clay, wax, gum, bone, straw, or other material. Probably general, widely recorded types of recreation, such as imitative or prevocational play with bows and arrows, slings, bolas, and so forth, and perhaps some specific types recorded from marginal as well as central areas, such as hide-and-seek (*Ona*, *Araucanian*, *Guaraní*, Guiana, *Mosquito-Sumo*) and "jaguar" (fig. 166) (*Mosquito-Sumo*, *Macushí*, *Taulipáng*, Chacoan—also not uncommon in North America), will be found near-continentally distributed when all the field data are in. The "jaguar" game, known under other names also, and nearly identical with our playground fox-and-geese, is a children's game, in which a group line up in a row, headed by a leader; another player, the

FIGURE 166.—Jaguar game, *Taulipáng, Macushi.* The boy hopping on his hands and one foot is the "jaguar." His raised right leg represents the jaguar's tail. (After Koch-Grünberg, 1917–28, vol. 3, fig. 10.)

"jaguar," endeavors to seize or tag the last child of the line, while the group and its leader try to ward him off.

Games of more limited distribution.—A good many games have wide distribution in two or more of our 13 areas, but are conspicuously absent from a number of them, particularly from the Andean, Pampean, Patagonian, and Fuegian.

The Andean area, apart from dice games to be dealt with later, and the Pampean, Patagonian, and Fuegian areas appear from our sources to have relatively meager game complexes and to lack a number of games, amusements, and toys that are of widespread distribution on the rest of the continent. The well-studied Fuegian area evidently has a very simple recreative culture; and seemingly so too have or had the Pampean and Patagonian, especially if we strip off the games and amusements derived after the beginning of the 18th century from *Araucanian* and Spanish sources—pillma ball game and hockey, playing cards, and horse racing. Whether the meagerness in the recorded game complex of the Andean area is due to lacunae in our earlier and more recent studies or to actual meagerness is not so clear; the latter explanation seems to be the slightly more probable one.

Of wide or fairly wide distribution east of the Andes and north of the Pampean area are ball games with the use of rubber or maize-leaf balls, hockey, hoop-and-pole, stilts, log race, snow-snake, ring-and-pin, cat's cradles, tops, bullroarers, buzzers, corncob darts, and bean shooters. Lacking in or at least unreported for the Pampean, Patagonian, and Fuegian areas are all of these; unreported for the Andean, all except cat's cradles, tops, and bull-roarers (bull-roarers reported for *Chocó* and *Aymara*); unreported for the *Araucanian*, all except tops, stilts, and hockey.

Ball games with the use of solid or hollow rubber balls are, or were earlier, found in the Middle American, Antillean (rubberlike ball of tree gum), Orinocoan, Amazonian, Guianan, Eastern Brazilian, Eastern Bolivian, and Chacoan (*Chané*) areas.   The games with rubber balls are more commonly team games played by youths or adult men between tribes, villages, or other units.   In the majority of tribes the ball is propelled toward the goals at either end of the playing field by the player's head, shoulder, knee, or part of the body other than the hands and feet; in a minority, as among the *Witoto, Macushí, Pata-mona, Sherente,* and *Mojo,* by the feet and/or hands.   Among the *Apinayé,* the rubber ball is batted with flat and cylindrical battledores; among the earlier *Otomac* the women struck at it with straight thick-ended clubs.   Sunken ball courts with walls of stone slabs were used in Porto Rico and Santo Domingo, but stone courts are not reported anywhere on the continent south of Middle America.   Betting accompanied the game among the *Taino* of Hispaniola and the *Otomac* of the Orinoco.

Ball play with balls or "shuttlecocks" made of maize leaves (fig. 167) is very widespread in the Amazonian, Orinocoan, Guianan, Eastern Bolivian, Eastern Brazilian, and Chacoan areas.   These balls are usually volleyed with the palm of the hand or else thrown.

Hockey, played with sticks curved at the distal end (fig. 168), and with balls usually of wood, sometimes of plaited rope, or of stone, may

FIGURE 167.—Maize-leaf ball, *Taulipáng, Macushí.*   (Redrawn from Koch-Grün-berg, 1917–28, vol. 3, pl. 36.)

be called the national game of the Chacoan and *Araucanian* peoples.
From the latter it spread to the *Tehuelche*. It is more commonly
played by teams; in the Chaco these represent bands. Men, women,
and children play the game among the *Araucanians*. Various magico-
religious rites were carried out by the *Araucanians* in connection with
the game, such as fumigation and anointing of the sticks and abstention from sexual intercourse.

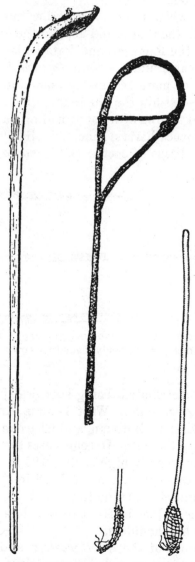

FIGURE 168.—Hockey stick and rackets. *Left:* Palm-leaf stalk hockey stick,
Choroti. (⅑ actual size). *Right:* Spoon-shaped racket, *Chiriguano.* (¹⁄₁₆
actual size.) *Center:* Side-meshed racket, *Chamacoco.* (After Rosen, 1924,
fig. 174; Nordenskiöld, 1910, fig. 8; and Baldus, 1931, p. 109.)

Among the *Chiriguano* and *Chamacoco*, the stick used in the game of hockey is a racket—of the spoon-shaped type (fig. 168, *right*) among the former, of the side-meshed type (fig. 168, *center*) among the latter. Wegner (1934, p. 70, pl. 34, fig. 5) reports that he found in a child's grave of pre-Columbian date at Nazca, South Perú, a miniature side-ringed racket. What interpretation should be given this reported find is doubtful. No other indications of earlier hockey are found in Peruvian archeological sites.

Pillma, a game in which the players gather in a circle and a ball is thrown from beneath the thighs and kept in the air, is peculiar to the *Araucanians* and to the Pampean and Patagonian peoples who in the early 18th century came under strong *Araucanian* influence.

A hoop-and-pole, or more accurately hoop-and-arrow, game is recorded sporadically—within the Guianan, Amazonian, Chacoan, and Fuegian areas. In it arrows are shot at rolling papaw fruit (*Arawak* of Pomeroon and Moruca Rivers), hoop of solid wood (*Tupí-Cawahíb* of Madeira River), discus of cactus (*Chiriguano*, fig. 169), or grass hoop (*Ona*).

FIGURE 169.—Arrows used in *Chiriguano* hoop-and-arrow game. The arrows are decorated so that each player can easily identify his own. (After Nordenskiöld, 1924 b, fig. 6.)

Stilts are widely distributed, being specifically reported from the Middle American, *Araucanian*, West Indian, Amazonian, Guianan, Eastern Brazilian, Eastern Bolivian, and Chacoan areas, but not from the Pampean or south thereof. In some cases these may well be post-Columbian. Extraordinarily high stilts—3.20 m. (10.7 feet) or more long, with the foot rests 1.70–2.00 m. (5.7–6.8 feet) above ground—are used by *Apinayé* hunters returning to the village, the ends of the pole being grasped by the walker in front of his chest, not held under his armpits and behind his shoulders.

The "national game" of the *Northwestern* and *Central Ge* of the Eastern Brazilian area, recorded from since the 17th century in the region, is the relay race by male adolescents and adults carrying sections of tree trunks. These logs may weigh up to about 200 pounds (90 kg.). The race is commonly by teams, the team themselves being drawn among some tribes from moieties or societies. A race with lighter logs is run by *Canella* girls and women. Logs are used in dancing and were carried by the *Southern* and *Northern Cayapó*, but the log race proper is lacking as it is among the *Caingang*. The log race is reported clearly only from *Ge*-speaking peoples.

Games resembling North American dart or snow-snake are reported from the Chacoan and Eastern Brazilian areas. The *Abipón*, *Mocoví*, and *Chané* (fig. 170) throw rods, clubs, or sticks along the ground, making them rebound; the *Canella* shoot arrows along smooth ground making them rebound, while the *Apinayé* slide them.

Games similar to North American ring-and-pin are found in the Chacoan and Amazonian (*Panoans*, *Ticuna*) areas. Among the *Mbayá*, 56 to 60 rings on a string were tossed up to be caught on a stick—a game still played by the *Chamacoco*. In a ring-and-pin game, reported only among the *Sherente*, a player tries to catch on a

FIGURE 170.—"Snow snake," *Chané*. (After Nordenskiöld, 1920, fig. 32.)

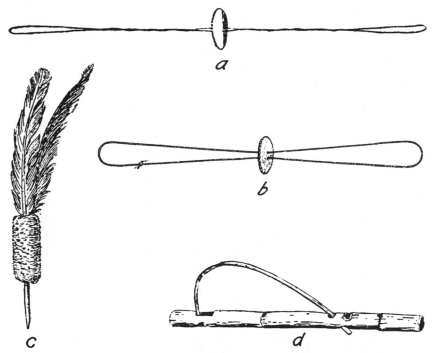

FIGURE 171.—Miscellaneous gaming implements. *a, Taulipáng* buzzer. (⅙ actual size.) *b. Chané* buzzer. (⅙ actual size.) *c, Chané* corncob dart. (⅓ actual size.) *d, Chané* bean shooter. (⅙ actual size.) (After Koch-Grünberg, 1917–28, vol. 3, pl. 36; Nordenskiöld, 1910, fig. 9; and Nordenskiöld, 1920, figs. 33, 34.)

12-inch (0.3 m.) stick a hoop about 12 inches in diameter thrown by his opponent.

Cat's cradles are reported from all the areas north of the *Araucanian* and Pampean, except the West Indian and Orinocoan. They appear to be particularly developed in the Guianan.

Tops, of various shapes and materials, and either humming or silent, are reported for the Middle American, Andean, *Araucanian*, West Indian, Amazonian, Guianan, Eastern Brazilian, Eastern Bolivian, and Chacoan areas.

Among children's toys bull-roarers, buzzers, corncob darts, and bean-shooters are widely distributed east of the Andes and down to the Chaco, but are lacking apparently in the Andean (apart from records of bull-roarers among the *Chocó* and *Aymara*), *Araucanian*, Pampean, Patagonian, and Fuegian areas. Bull-roarers as toys are common in the Amazonian, Eastern Brazilian, Eastern Bolivian, and Chacoan areas; buzzers (fig. 171, *a, b*), in the same areas and also in the Guianan. Darts made of a bit of corncob with a feather stuck in or through it (fig. 171, *c*) are reported for the Guianan and Chacoan areas and from the *Chimila* of Colombia; the beanshooter, made with a flexible strip of bamboo or other material to provide power (fig. 171, *d*), in the

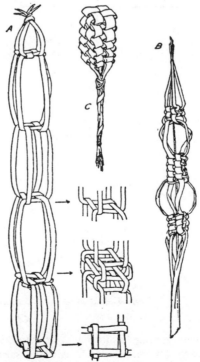

FIGURE 172.—Leaf-strand figures. *A*, Clouds; *B*, a lamp; *C*, a rattle. British Guiana. (After Roth, 1924, fig. 243.)

viously, which would give a date around the middle of the 18th century, and that before this the Pampeans had no gambling. It was about this same time that the *Mocoví* of the Chacoan area took over gambling at cards and dice from the Spanish colonists (Fúrlong, 1938, p. 139). Gambling with playing cards and dice can be traced among the *Tehuelche* of the Patagonian area back to the time of the Malaspina expedition of 1789.

The taba game is played with the astragalus of a cow or llama (fig. 174). The bone is thrown by hand, the count depending on which side lands up. The game is in use among some of the Peruvian, Bolivian, and Argentine *Quechua*, some of the Chaco Indians and the *Chiriguano* and *Chané*, and the *Araucanians*, as it is among the Gauchos of Argentina and the upper classes of the Argentine provinces.

FIGURE 174.—Taba die, *Quechua* of Cuzco region, Perú. (After Karsten, 1935, fig. 17.)

By far the greater weight of evidence points to the conclusion that the taba game, i. e., with use of the astragalus, is an importation from Spain. It has only recently spread into *Araucanian* territory from Argentina. The *Chiriguano* and *Chané* learned it in the sugar mills (Nordenskiöld, 1912 b, p. 165), while only those Chacoan Indians play it who have worked in these mills (Nordenskiöld, 1910, p. 430). The name "taba," although resembling *Quechua* tauva or tahua ("four"), means "astragalus" in Spanish. The game itself, also called taba, is played in Spain with one astragalus (of sheep or lamb) by children or with four as a game of hazard by adults, and in southern Europe goes well back into classic Greco-Roman times. Moreover, not only the game but also divination with astragali occurs among the Peruvian *Quechua*, as it does in Spain and did in classic times. The same game with astragali is found under the same name, "la taba" or "tábatci," among the modern *Tarahumara* of México. (For presentation of theory of native origin, cf. Rivet, 1925.)

The date of the game's introduction into South American Indian life is very uncertain; our specific records go back only several decades. Very interestingly, since its introduction it has become assimilated in function, as a funeral game, among the *Quechua* of Cuzco and of Bolivia at least, to the huayru game (see infra) of the *Quechua*-speaking Indians of the Sierra. Played during the wake, it helps the departed father of a family on his way to heaven, is a mark of friendship toward the deceased, and gives the winner some of the property of the dead man. Among the *Quechua* of the Puna de Jujuy in Northwest Argentina, at the feast of the departed, taba is played to find who should pronounce the prayer for the deceased. Among the Gauchos and Argentinians, however, taba is purely a gambling game, without relation to mortuary customs. (Karsten, 1935, pp. 487–489; Rosen, 1924, pp. 247–248.)

NATIVE GAMBLING SPORTS AND GAMES

(1) **Sports.**—Of the many native South American Indian sports, there are chiefly three, all of them ball games—the rubber-ball game, pillma, and hockey—that are recorded as being or having been attended with gambling.

In earlier times gambling was associated with the rubber-ball game among the *Taino* of Hispaniola and the *Otomac* of the Orinoco. Among the former such gambling as occurred appears to have been lightly regarded, and the stakes wagered by members of the two teams (and by others?) were objects of little intrinsic value (Casas, 1875–76, 5:507). Acquisition, however, bulked large in the consciousness of the *Otomac;* they played not merely for the fun of the game but to win the substantial stakes. These consisted of baskets of maize, strings of glass beads, and, when necessary, of everything the players had in their houses. The onlookers also bet on their favorites. Association of wagering with the ball game among the 18th-century *Otomac* of Gumilla's and Gilij's day, the period of first close White contact, points to pre-Contact origin and suggests a probable earlier prehistoric connection of some kind with the Mexican or Antillean ball game.

Quite recently, the *Kepkiriwat* of the Guaporé River have been reported as playing the head-ball game to win arrows.

Apart from the above three cases, gambling is not recorded, to the writer's knowledge, as associated anywhere else on the South American continent with the rubber-ball game, and is nowhere so associated with the maize-ball game.

Gambling with pillma and hockey has a more southern distribution, namely, in the *Araucanian* and Chacoan areas. Gambling by the *Mapuche-Huilliche* of Chile is consistently attested by our sources, and for as far back as the first half of the 17th century by Rosales, Ovalle, and Bascuñan, who were the first to give us any appreciable details on *Araucanian* games and sports. At that early date gambling was associated with at least four distinct native pastimes— two ball games and two dice games. It is almost certainly of pre-Hispanic origin among the *Mapuche-Huilliche*, although their later passionate addiction to gambling may be partly attributable to Spanish influence.

The *Mapuche-Huilliche* of the 17th century gambled at a ball game very like, and seemingly the ancestor of, modern *Araucanian* pillma. They likewise wagered, and heavily it seems, on hockey, with stakes of shirts, bridles, horses, and so forth (fig. 175).

Moduo ludendi indorum ... *Vocatur ala chueca*

FIGURE 175.—Hockey game. *Mapuche-Huilliche* of early seventeenth century. Stakes are seen hung on tree. (After Ovalle, 1646, opp. p. 92.)

Much of the betting on hockey, still in vogue, takes the form of paired betting, each member of one team betting with a given member of the other team. The spectators also lay wagers. Sometimes serious affairs of public concern were decided by the outcome of a hockey game. We have no evidence, however, that gambling in either ball or dice games is or was resorted to by the *Mapuche-Huilliche* as a magico-religious rite in connection with deaths, harvests, and so forth.

In the Chacoan area, hockey is commonly played for stakes: among the *Mataco*, between villages for large stakes; among the *Toba-Pilagá*, for valuable stakes put up by the team captains or some one else and distributed at the end of the game among the members of the winning team. Our records for gambling with hockey—and for that matter, gambling of any kind except at cards, dice, and horse racing introduced around the middle eighteenth century—among the Chacoan tribes are all very recent, dating only from the last several decades. For all we know, gambling at hockey, taba, and stick-dice (cf. infra) may be of very recent introduction into the Chacoan area.

While both hockey and pillma occur in the general Pampean-Patagonian region, there is no record of gambling in connection with them among non-*Araucanian* Indians. In the middle 18th century, the "Pampa Indians" of Sánchez Labrador were playing a game of "pelota" (hockey? or pillma?), but apparently without stakes. Both games are recorded from the Patagonian area among *Tehuelche*, but again without mention of wagers.

To complete the record for the continent we may add two final instances of gambling at sports: among the early *Chibcha*, betting among the young men at the races held in connection with the solemn sacrifices at Guatavita (Acosta, 1901, p. 136); among the modern *Apinayé*, winning of the arrows of the other players by the boy who slides his dart farthest on the ground.

(2) **Dice games.**—Native games of hazard played with one or more "dice" have a distinctly western distribution in South America, being found only in the Andean and *Araucanian* areas, and in limited regions adjacent thereto, namely, the Chacoan area and one small section of the extreme northwestern fringe of the Amazonian.

Single-die games.—A number of games differing somewhat one from the other but all having much in common were played with a single die, and some are today played, in the Highland Ecuadorean and Peruvian sections of the Andean area and in the *Araucanian* area. Among the early Peruvians these went under various names (cf. Romero, E., 1941). The more common earlier and modern names are: wayru, huayru (meaning uncertain), pisca, pichka (*Quechua*, "five"), chunkara (*Quechua:* chunka, "ten"), among *Quechua*-speaking peoples; pasa (*Quechua*, "100"), among *Aymara* and *Quechua* of Perú; quechucáhue (*Mapuche:* quechu, "five"; quechucáhue, "instrument to play quechu"), among the *Mapuche-Huilliche* of Chile. The numbers from which the names are derived refer to marks on the die, to points scored on the throw, or to points required to win the game.

The die itself, of bone or wood, is or was of various forms: a right quadrangular prism, among the modern *Canelo;* a seven-faced one or hexangular pyramid, among the *Aymara* of Perú and some of the modern *Quechua*-speaking peoples of Ecuador and Perú (figs. 176, 177); a five-faced one or pyramid with oblong or squarish base, among the early and modern *Mapuche-Huilliche* and some of the modern Ecuadorean Indians.

In the game, the die is thrown or let fall from a slight height. Among

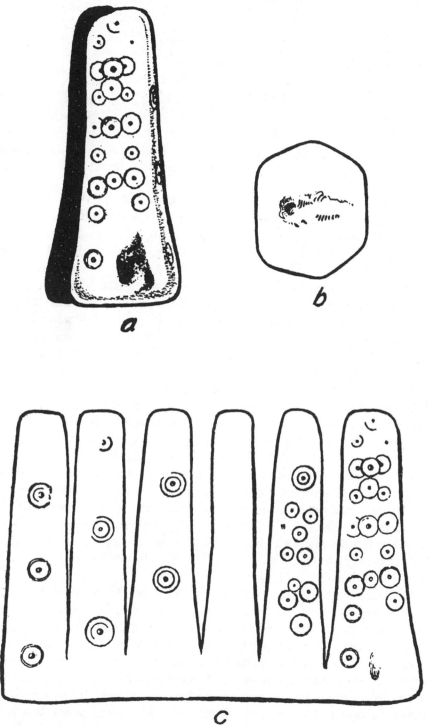

FIGURE 176.—Huayru die, *Quechua* of Ecuador. *a*, Face; *b*, base; *c*, schematic drawing of the six sides with circles indicating count. (After Nordenskiöld, 1930 c, figs. 29–31.)

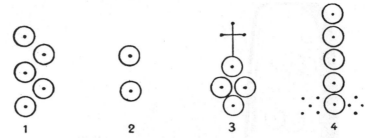

FIGURE 177.—Huayru die, *Quechua* of Ecuador.   Counts cut on the four faces of
the pyramidal die.   (After Rivet, 1925, fig. 1.)

the modern *Mapuche-Huilliche*, count is kept with small sticks which
are advanced along in certain holes made in the ground.   Among the
early Peruvians, it was kept in some of the single-die games with beans
or pebbles which were moved around holes excavated in a board or
flat stone.

Among the *Mapuche-Huilliche*, the game was and is played seriously
for the winnings.   Among the early Peruvians it was also played,
sometimes at least, for gain—with stakes of guinea pigs, according to
Morúa, writing about 1577, or of mantles and live stock, according to
Cobo, writing in 1653; but they played "more for fun than from greed
of gain" (Cobo, 1890–93, 4:228) and evidently took their gambling
much more lightly than do the *Mapuche-Huilliche*.

Among the Andean and some adjacent peoples, but not, so far as
our evidence goes, among the *Mapuche-Huilliche*, the game had and
has death-rite functions in addition to or in place of those of recreation and gain.   Arriaga (1920, p. 60; 1st ed., 1621) recorded that in his
day the Peruvians at their 5-day wakes played pisca "to keep away
sleep" and that afterward the clothes of the deceased were washed in
the river.   His terse statement is confirmed and illuminated by
Karsten's studies (1920 c, 1935) of the modern *Quechua*-speaking
people of the Ecuadorean Sierra who at wakes must keep from sleeping
and must play huayru, while on the fifth day the clothes of the deceased
must be washed.

At the modern Ecuadorean Sierra wake for the head of a family
or for a housewife the huayru game is played with a hexangular pyramidal die by the invited male adolescent and adult guests, but not by
near relatives of the deceased.   The winners receive stakes generally
consisting of domestic animals owned by the deceased.   The animals
are either slaughtered and eaten in common by the guests and hosts
or are taken home by the winners to be eaten there.   The game is to
honor the dead.   The luckiest winner is regarded as the one to whom
the deceased feels most friendly, for it is the deceased's invisible hand
that causes the players to throw winning or losing casts of the die.

Among the *Quechua*-speaking *Canelo* of the Montaña adjacent to the Ecuadorean Sierra, a similar game, called by them huairitu, is played, at the wake of a father or mother of a family, with a right rectangular prism die of manioc (fig. 178, *left*), against a similar conceptual background and for similar ends; and among the nearby *Semigae* (*Shimigay*) Indians of the middle Pastaza, related to the *Záparo*, practically the same game for the same ends, with a conical die made of manioc and called singu. (See also supra on role of taba game in the mortuary complex of the *Quechua* of Cuzco and Bolivia.) The *Colorado* Indians of Santo Domingo in western Ecuador play games at wakes, but not for the property of the deceased nor for winnings.

Figure 178.—*Canelo* gaming die and disk. *Left:* Prism die. *Right:* disk-board for maize-grain game. (After Karsten, 1935, figs. 12, 13.)

Multiple-dice games.—The two most important gambling games played with more than one die are lligues in the *Araucanian* area and tsúka in the Chacoan.

The lligues game, which can be traced back in our sources to the beginning of the 17th century and as a gambling game to the middle thereof, and which is almost certainly aboriginal, is played by 2 people, with 8 to 12 beans, blacked on one side and white or natural color on the other. The player shakes the beans in his hand and throws them down, counting his points according to whether the blacked or noncolored sides turn up, and using small and large sticks

as tallies. In Colchagua the game is said to be played with shells of
nuts; in another region, probably the province of Maule, with four
buttons. This bean game is not recorded from any part of the Andean
area; whether there be any historical connection between the *Araucanian* use of beans as "dice" and the Andean use of them as tallies is
problematical.

The tsúka game (tsukoc, houka, chunquanti, chukanta, chucaray, and
other variants, from *Quechua*, chunka, "ten": Nordenskiöld, 1910,
1919 a; Rosen, 1924; Karsten, 1932) is confined to the Chacoan
area, where it is played by a number of the Chacoan tribes proper as
well as by the *Chiriguano* and *Chané*. Four stick dice of wood are
used, convex on one side and flat or concave on the other, and about 10

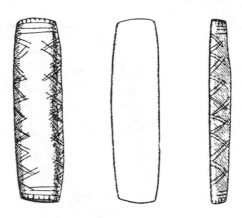

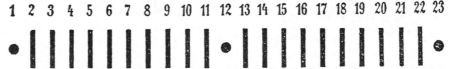

FIGURE 179.—Tsúka game of the Chaco. *Top: Ashluslay* stick-die. *Bottom:*
Chané counting holes. (After Nordenskiöld, 1910, figs. 1, 2.)

cm. (4 in.) long (fig. 179, *top*). The player takes two of the dice in
each hand and throws them against one another so that they touch as
they fall to the ground. Points are won according to fall with convex side up. In counting (fig. 179, *bottom*) the two opponents start
from their respective "homes", holes 1 and 23 (or 21) on opposite
ends of a straight or crescent row of 23 (or 21) holes in the ground,
each player with an arrow in his "home" and with pegs called "sheep"
in holes 2 to 11 and 13 to 22, respectively. Hole 12, the "river," serves
as a trap. According to count on the throw, the player moves his ar-

row back and forth across the whole row, "killing" his opponent's "sheep" as he does so.

The tsúka game is nearly always played for stakes, and often for very substantial ones. It has no role whatever in the mortuary complex. Among the *Choroti*, Karsten was told that it is played to increase the edible wild fruits and to prevent starvation.

The origin of this game is a puzzling mystery. Our first records of it go back only to the beginning of the present century. Many words of *Quechua* origin are used in it, which would suggest an Andean origin. But no dice game like this is reported in early or recent sources from the Andean area. The tsúka game is strikingly similar in many respects to the stick-dice game of North America (Culin, 1907; Spier, 1928, pp. 341–342, 347–351).

A game somewhat similar to tsúka, and called chukareta, is played by the *Chiriguano* and *Chané*, with a heap of sticks—apparently, from the context, as a gambling game (Nordenskiöld, 1920, pp. 99–100).

The *Canelo* of the Ecuadorean Montaña had a multiple-dice game, now largely given up, which they played at wakes, for purposes similar to those described previously for the *Canelo* huairitu game. On a disk-shaped board with a figure representing the deceased and with seven holes, the players in turn threw four grains of maize at a time, with the object of having them fall into the holes on either side of the figure (fig. 178, *right*).

Guessing games of chance, such as the widespread stick games, hand game, and moccasin game of North America, are reported from nowhere on the South American continent.

DISTRIBUTIONAL AND HISTORICAL SUMMARY

Gambling in earlier post-Contact days had and today still has a quite limited and distinctly western distribution in South America. Apart from the sporadic *Otomac*, *Kepkiriwat*, *Canelo-Semigae*, and *Apinayé* occurrences cited above, it is not recorded in either early or recent sources, to the writer's knowledge, for the Middle American (Nicaragua to Panamá), Orinocoan, Amazonian, Guianan, Eastern Bolivian, Eastern Brazilian, or Fuegian areas. Prior to about the middle of the 18th century, when gambling at European cards, dice, and horse racing was introduced from the Spanish colonists, gambling was lacking in the Patagonian and Pampean areas. In view of the silence of our earlier sources regarding gambling in the Chacoan area, more probably gambling there is of post-Contact introduction, from European, Andean, and perhaps Pampean-*Araucanian* influences; gambling at Spanish cards and dice came in around the middle 18th century, betting at horse racing perhaps a little earlier; gambling at hockey, taba, and stick dice—with clear indications of some Andean influence in the latter two—is recorded only within very recent decades. The *Canelo* and *Semigae* gambling at wakes is pretty obviously due to borrowing, probably fairly recent, from the adjacent Ecuadorean Sierral culture. On the possible age of the *Kepkiriwat* and *Apinayé* gambling, such as it is, we have no evidence.

In early Colonial times gambling, dating from pre-Contact days, was in vogue in: the Andean area, at dice games for gain and as a mortuary custom among the Peruvians, from whom it apparently spread, perhaps quite early, to the Ecuadorean Sierral Indians, and in one recorded instance at races among the *Chibcha* of Guatavita; the *Araucanian* area, at dice and ball games; the Antillean area among the *Taino* of Hispaniola and Orinocoan area among the *Otomac* only, at rubber-ball games.

So far as our evidence goes, all these peoples, except perhaps the *Mapuche-Huilliche* and *Otomac*, took their gambling gains very lightly. In the main, passionate addiction to gambling, such as is later recorded in the *Araucanian*, Chacoan, Pampean, and Patagonian areas, appears to be, in large part at least, a reflection of the gambling frenzy that pervaded Old World Spanish society in the 16th and 17th centuries (cf. Pfandl, 1929; Ballesteros y Beretta, 1918–41, 4: pt. 2), and that was carried by the early settlers and adventurers to the New World, where it found a congenial climate on the Colonial frontier.

Gambling in the Andean area and among the *Canelo* and *Semigae* has been and is mainly a mortuary custom, although light gambling for gain was earlier in vogue in Perú. Elsewhere it was and is practiced mostly or exclusively for recreation and gain.

We have no intensive field studies on the dynamic aspects of gambling among any of the peoples of South America—on the factors responsible for its presence or absence in given tribes and areas or for the acceptance of or resistance to the spread of European or native gambling complexes, or on its integrating or disintegrating effects upon native culture, society, or personality. Hence any attempt to treat in the present article the dynamics of gambling in South America would be little more than speculation and guesswork. Such intensive field studies for aboriginal South America—and incidentally for literate as well as nonliterate peoples of the rest of the world— are urgent desiderata. Anthropologists and sociologists alike have given the subject stepmotherly treatment.

GENERALIZATIONS AND COMPARISONS

Some of the more striking general features of the game and amusement complex of South American Indian culture are: The relative poverty of the game pattern in the Fuegian and early Patagonian and Pampean areas, and strangely enough in the Andean, as compared with that of the areas north and east of these; the particularly rich pattern of the Chacoan area, at least in the modern period; a seeming predominance of quiet games, mostly dice games, in the Andean area, contrasting with the prominence of active, often strenuous or violent, sports in the *Araucanian* area to the south and in most of the remaining areas of the continent east of the Andean Cordillera; the absence of team games toward the southern end of the continent, in the Fuegian area and earlier it seems in the Patagonian; the marked western distribution of gambling, in earlier times confined almost entirely to the *Araucanian* and middle Andean areas, and even in more recent days found almost exclusively in areas (Patagonian, Pampean, Chacoan, Northern Andean) adjacent to and influenced by these. The *Araucanian* area links typologically and probably historically with both the Andean through its characteristic dice games and gambling and with the Chacoan through its equally characteristic hockey game.

A comparison of the South American games and amusements in which implements are employed with those of North America reveals some interesting resemblances and contrasts. It is not our purpose to offer any interpretation of these, but merely to call attention to the facts.

Culin (1907) lists such North American games and amusements as follows: (*a*) Games of chance: dice games, guessing games (stick, hand, four-stick, moccasin); (*b*) games of dexterity: archery, snow-snake, hoop and pole, ring and pin, ball (racket, hockey, double ball, ball race, football, ball juggling, and four additional highly localized and specialized ball games); (*c*) minor amusements: shuttlecock (with and without battledore), tipcat, quoits, stone throwing, shuffleboard (resembling ninepins), jackstraws, swing, tilts, tops (hand-, cord- and whip-spun, simple and humming), bull-roarer, buzzer, popgun, beanshooter, and cat's cradles.

Of these all are found in South America except guessing games of chance, double ball, ball race, the four specialized and localized ball games, tipcat (European?) and jackstraws (European?). The chief North American games lacking in South America are the first three of the foregoing: guessing games of chance, double ball, and ball race.

Of the implement games found in South America but lacking in North America the most striking are the log race of the *Ge* of the Eastern Brazilian area and the pillma ball game of the *Mapuche-Huilliche* of the *Araucanian*.

The data are not available for an adequate corresponding comparison of South American with North American games and amusements in which implements are not used, but so far as our data go, they seem to show an equally high proportion of resemblances and low proportion of contrasts.

BIBLIOGRAPHY

Acosta, 1901; Arriaga, 1920; Baldus, 1931; Ballesteros y Beretta, 1918–41; Casas, 1875–76; Cobo, 1890–93; Culin, 1907; Fúrlong, 1938; Gusinde, 1931, 1937; Karsten, 1920 c, 1930, 1932, 1935; Koch-Grünberg, 1909–10; Manquilef, 1914; Nordenskiöld, 1910, 1912 b, 1919 a, 1920, 1930 c; Pfandl, 1929; Rivet, 1925; Romero, E., 1941; Rosen, 1924; Roth, W. E., 1924; Sánchez Labrador, 1936; Spier, 1928; Wegner, 1934.

THE COURT BALL GAME
OF THE
ABORIGINAL MAYAS

William A. Goellner

The Court Ball Game of the Aboriginal Mayas[1]

WILLIAM A. GOELLNER

1000 Richmond Road
Cleveland 24, Ohio

THE SPORTS AND recreational pursuits of aboriginal and modern primitive peoples have always been of deep interest to those concerned with physical education or its related fields. Unfortunately, physical educators have done relatively little research in this area and the studies that have been made are usually by men trained in one of the branches of anthropology. While this has resulted in some excellent studies, the results have not always been adapted to the physical education viewpoint. As a consequence the full benefits of many of these investigations have escaped us. The possibilities for research in the fields of archaeology, ethnology, and cultural anthropology stressing the physical education viewpoint were pointed out in an article by Stumpf and Cozens (33).

To have a complete understanding of the culture of any peoples, aboriginal or modern, it is necessary to have an adequate appreciation of the role played by their games, sports, and recreational amusements. Of the three great native civilizations of the New World, the Aztec, Inca, and Maya, the most enduring was that of the Mayas. An integral part of this brilliant civilization which lasted for 1100 years was the court ball game originated by them. Its mythological origin and religious significance is inextricably bound with the rise and fall of their nation. Many existing codices, manuscripts, and written accounts of both the pre-and post-Conquest era attested its importance as part of the Maya culture.

Purpose of the Study

The expressed purposes of this study are: (1) A determination of the origin, development and diffusion of the court ball game in ancient Middle America; (2) The specific rules, techniques and equipment used plus the construction of the ball courts; (3) The cultural importance of the ball game to the Mayas and the tribes who subsequently played it.

Review of the Literature

Studies relating to the role of games, sports, and recreational amusements of modern primitive peoples have been made by Stumpf and Cozens on the New Zealand Maoris and the Fiijians (34). A similar study was completed by Dunlap (12) with respect to the Samoans. Many archaeologists and travelers

[1] This study was made while the author was a graduate student in the School of Health, Physical Education, and Recreation at Indiana University.

have written on some phase of the ball court sites but the work of Maudsley (1) is particularly valuable. A thorough investigation was submitted by Blom (3) in the Middle America Research Series. Both of these reports are the work of renowned archaeologists and have stressed that aspect in their writings. With the exception of these studies, all others may be classified as more or less descriptive references of the actual ruins of ball court sites or brief mention of such a game having formerly been played by the Mayas and Aztecs.

Procedure

The basis of the study rests upon two visits made by the author to Mexico, Yucatan, and Guatemala. During the course of these trips several visits were made to the ball courts at Chichen Itza and Uxmal in the northern section of the Peninsula of Yucatan, and the court site of Monte Alban in the State of Oaxaca. Black and white and kodachrome still pictures were taken by means of an Argus C-3 camera. A Ciné Kodak 8 mm. camera was used for motion pictures. Tape measurements and compass directions of the court layout supplemented the above.

In addition to this work in the field, extensive use was made of the archaeological collections of the museums in Mexico City, Oaxaca, Merida, and Guatemala City. Miniature scale models of the main ball court at Chichen Itza were available for study in the Chicago Field Museum of Natural History as well as the museum in Merida.

A critical review was undertaken of the works of 16th century writers who dealt with the period of the Spanish Conquest and the history and culture of the Indians of Middle America. The John G. White Collection of Folklore and Orientalia of the Cleveland Public Library was particularly helpful in making available authentic facsimiles of codices and manuscripts which were impossible to secure otherwise.

Geographic Locale and History

The geographic region of the aboriginal Mayas consisted of the present day states of Yucatan, Campeche, Tabasco, Quintana Roo and the eastern half of Chiapas in the Republic of Mexico. These with the southern highlands and Department of Peten in Guatemala, all of British Honduras, and the adjacent western part of the Republic of Honduras combined to form an area of approximately 150,000 square miles.

The term "Mayan civilization" is defined by Morley (22) as applying exclusively to that ancient American culture which had as its two principal material manifestations unique hieroglyphic writing and chronology and, so far as North America is concerned, a unique stone architecture involving the use of corbel-stone roof vaults. Wherever these two cultural traits existed in Middle America—that is southern Mexico and Northern Central America—the Mayan civilization may be considered as having existed.

The birthplace of the Mayan civilization is believed to have originated in the climatically favorable north central section of the Department of Peten, Guatemala in the 4th century A.D. Two great periods of development followed. The first and greatest was the Old Empire era, which began in 317 A.D. and reached its zenith in the 8th century. From this time on, the old Empire deteriorated rapidly until by the year 987 the large cities were deserted and the era was completed.

The New Empire era began in the 10th century with a spectacular period of renaissance which was confined to northern Yucatan and was fostered by the arrival of Toltec tribes from central Mexico who modified the existing Maya culture. A period of initial growth reached its culmination in the 13th century to be followed by cultural corruption and decay so that the New Empire was dying when the Spaniards first arrived in Yucatan in 1527. The last independent Mayan political entity existed on an island in Lake Peten Itza, Guatemala, and was brought under Spanish domination in the year 1697.

This brilliant native civilization developed independently of outside influence as the result of favorable climatic and geographical conditions coupled with the native genius of the Mayas. The eventual cause of its decay is still a matter of debate. One theory is that, since it was a maize-culture civilization, the peculiar milpa method of agriculture depleted the soil to such an extent that the civilization could no longer exist (10, 11). The Mayas made great progress in the arts and sciences. Independently they developed a system of hieroglyphic writing and a positional arithmetic with the concept of zero. The calendar employed by them at the time of their first meeting with the Spaniards was more exact than that in use at the time in Europe.

The People

Today almost two million people live in the area once occupied by the ancient Mayas.

The present-day Maya is physically of small stature, the average height for men is 5 feet 1 inch and 4 feet 8 inches for women. The physique is very broad-shouldered and deep-chested, with comparatively long hands and feet. The cephalic indexes of 85.8 for the men and 86.4 for women make them one of the broadest-headed people in the world (31). Black, straight, and rather coarse hair is combined with a skin color of a coppery brown which may vary slightly with the individual. Body hair is relatively scarce. An Asiatic origin is strongly suggested by the epicanthic eye fold, the so-called "Mongolian spot" at the base of the spine, and the line patterns of the palms of the hands (22).

The modern-day Maya may be described as an active, energetic, and hardworking individual. There is little desire for supremacy and a marked spirit of conservatism which makes them cling to their ancient customs and beliefs.

THE BALL GAME

Origin, Name, Diffusion

The origin of the court ball game has been a question of debate among Middle American archaeologists ever since the discovery of ball court sites. These may be divided into three main groups depending upon their belief. The first group hold that the ball game was originated by the ancient Mayas; the second group holds a similar viewpoint for the Toltecs of central Mexico; the third group holds out for an origin different from the two above. Broadly speaking, the Toltec may be considered as the forerunners of the Aztecs who subsequently occupied the same region.

The earliest reference to the ball game is to be found in the Popol Vuh (5, 16, 30). This book was held sacred by the Quiche Mayas of the Guatemalan highlands. In Part II of this book, reference is made to two divine heroes, the brothers Hunhun-Ahpu and Vukub-Hunahpu, who were fond of playing the ball game. One of these games was played near Xibalba, the underworld and place of the dead. The monarchs of this region became annoyed at the ball game in progress and challenged the intruders to a game with the intent of defeating and disgracing them. The brothers accepted the challenge but were betrayed by the Lords of the Underworld and put to death. Other references to the ball game are to be found in the Popol Vuh following this initial mention. From this earliest of references it is seen that the ball game is considered to have been of divine origin.

The Popol Vuh is estimated to have been written around the year 700 A.D. The above account far precedes that from any other known source and dates the ball game as having been played by the Mayas at least 200 years prior to any other reference to it by a source outside of the Maya area.

Gann (14) was of the opinion that the ball game was introduced to the Mayas by the Toltecs about 1200 A. D. However, this statement was made when very few ball court sites had been discovered in the Maya area. Subsequently, many more courts were uncovered by various archaeological expeditions. The Toltec theory of origin is also supported by Vaillant (37) who states that game was introduced by Topiltzin, the 9th king of the Classical Toltecs. Since accurate accounts of the dynasties of the Toltec rulers are available, this would have been around the year 900 A.D. which still falls 200 years after the first Mayan reference, cited in the Popol Vuh.

Thompson (35) has postulated a possible South American origin for the game but has given no details as to how he arrived at this opinion. Most bizarre of all the theories of origin is that advanced by Mitchell (21). A study of various related parallels in the Popol Vuh as compared with ancient Egyptians has convinced him that the ball game is of Egyptian origin. He supports this opinion by pointing out that in Part II of the Popol Vuh there is a description of recovering the head of Hun-Ahpu, one of the sons who was treacherously slain by the Lords of the Underworld during a game of ball. This incidence is taken by him to be a symbolic representation of the fight for, and the recovery of, the body of Osiris in Egyptian mythology. In later years the recovery of the actual body was dispensed with and the symbol of the head used instead. However, since this theory is based solely on the religious significance of certain parallel rites and is unsupported by any other evidence as to just how the Egyptian game arrived in Middle America it is scarcely held tenable and is cited for its curiosity value.

Archaeological expeditions of the Carnegie Institute of Washington, the Peabody Museum of Harvard University, and those of other foundations and universities, have discovered more than 40 ball court sites of which more than three-quarters have been located in the area formerly inhabited by the Mayas. Two of the foremost Middle American archaeologists of the present day, Blom and Morley, held that the weight of evidence is now distinctly in favor of attributing the origin of the ball game to the Mayas.

That the game was widely diffused is indicated by the presence of ball court sites from Guatemala and Honduras as far north as south-eastern Arizona (37). At the time of the first visit of the Spaniards to the Aztec capital of Tenochtitlan, the present Mexico City, a ball court was situated in the main plaza of the city (29).

In numerous Aztec codices there are representations of the gods playing in a ball court. The Codex Colombino (8) has an excellent illustration of the Lord of the Day and the Lord of the Night who are depicted as ready to play a game. A doubles game in progress is shown in the Codex Borbonicus. The gods Xochipilli and Ixtilton are playing as partners against the gods Quetzalcoatl and Caoutlicue (7).

Granting the Maya theory of origin as being the correct one, it seems probable that the ball game was taken up by the Toltecs who eventually passed it on to the Aztecs with whom it found great favor. The Aztecs in turn introduced the game to those tribes subjugated by them so that eventually the ball game had spread from Guatemala to the northern end of Mexico.

In an effort to trace the name used in describing the ball game it is necessary to go to the native language dictionaries compiled by the early Spanish friars. These vocabularies are of great aid in tracing words and word derivations referring to the game.

The ball game was called "Pok-ta-pok" by Mayas and "Tlachtli" by the Aztecs. In the Pio Perez dictionary of the Maya language, the following words refer to the game (28):

Pok: The stroke that throws the ball.
Pokolpoktah: To play ball.
Pokolpoc: The ball game and how to play it.

The Aztec name of "Tlachtli" is probably a derivation from the language of the Zapotecs who live in the southern part of Mexico. Hernandez (17) states that the Zapotec word 'lachi' meant, "pelota de los Indios" which translates as "ball game of the Indians." He also designates the word "tlachtlilachi" as meaning "jugar pelota" or, "to play ball" (17).

Torquemada (36) refers to the ball court as being called "tlacho" by the Aztecs and on several pages of the Codex Mendoza the word "tlacho" is shown as the name glyph for a town named Tlacho (9). The glyph of this town consists of the characteristic *I*-shaped character patterned on the actual ground shape of the ball courts.

A certain passage in the Popol Vuh refers to a country described as being that of, "the ball playing and fisher people." Probably this refers to the tribe later known as the Olmeca who inhabited a section of Mexico that bordered on the western part of the ancient Maya domain. The name meant "rubber people" and refers to the fact that rubber trees grew in their locale and they were familiar with its use. Approximately this same area is mentioned in the Codex Mendoza as being the site of 22 towns that paid an annual tribute of 16,000 rubber balls to the Aztec sovereign.

The Popol Vuh reference to the Olmeca as being the "ball playing and fisher people" is further substantiated by the following word derivations of the Nahua language in central Mexico (25).

Ollama: To play ball with the buttocks.
Ollamani: A player of the ball game.
Ollamia: To play the ball game with other people.

Popularity of the Game

Numerous writers who were eye witnesses of the Spanish conquest of Mexico, Yucatan, and Guatemala have left descriptions or references to the native game played by both the Mayas in Yucatan and the Aztecs in Mexico. Thus, Herrera (18) writes of Montezuma II, the Aztec emperor at the time of the conquest by Cortes:

"The King took much delight in seeing sport at ball, which the Spaniards have since prohibited, because of the mischief that often happened at, and was called by them Tlachtli, being like our tennis."

The banning of the ball game by the Spaniards was undoubtedly at the instigation of the clergy who wished to discourage the pagan beliefs and ceremonies which accompanied the ball games. These would have been continued by permitting the Indians to engage in their game. In fact, such was the appeal of this rugged sport that it was beginning to be played by the Spaniards themselves until the prohibition against playing it went into effect.

Each town of that time had its ball court, more or less elaborate according to the wealth and prestige of the town:

". . . It should be understood that in all the cities and towns which had some renown and standing and serious authority, as well among the citizens as among the rulers (of which they made much) and in order not to be inferior, one to the other, they built ball courts enclosed with fine walls, and well ornamented, with the whole inside smooth and covered with mortar, with many paintings of effigies and idols and devils to whom the game was dedicated and whom the players had for protectors in that sport." (13)

The popularity of the sport is shown by the fact that the kings and nobles played it. The Aztec emperor is described by Clavijero as being a participant (6).

"This game was in high esteem with the Mexicans, and in other nations of that kingdom, . . . The kings themselves played and challenged each other at this game; as Montezuma II did Nezahuapilli."

The game cited above was played to settle a difference of opinion in regard to the interpretation of certain omens. It was a common practice of that time for the people to play a game of ball in order to settle disputes.

The Ball Used

The ball used was one of solid rubber as may be judged from the accounts of Ovieda, Duran, and Herrera: The former describes the ball quite clearly (26).

"The balls are made out of the roots of trees and herbs and juices and mixture of wax and pitch. Bringing together these and other materials they boil it all and make a paste, then they gave it a round shape and make the ball the same size as those filled with air in Spain, and some they make larger and some smaller; the mixture has a black, shiny surface and does not stick to the hand. After it is dry it becomes somewhat spongy, and not because it has any holes or vacuum as sponges have, but it becomes light and soft and quite heavy. Without comparison these balls jump more than those filled with air because by simply dropping it from your hands on the ground it jumps much higher in the air and gives a jump, another, one more and another, and as many more, the jumps becoming smaller every time."

"The ball is—as some people may have seen—as large as a small ball used in playing nine-pins. The material of which the ball is made is called Olin, which I have heard to be called Batel in our Spanish which is the rosin of a special tree which when boiled becomes like sinews. It is plentiful and is used by the natives both as medicine and as offering. It has one property which is that it jumps and rebounds upwards, and continues jumping from here to there so that those who run after it become tired before they catch it." (13)

The reference to Batel is probably in connection with the native ball game encountered by the early Spaniards on the islands of Cuba and Haiti. This game was called Batey or Batel by the natives of those islands.

"The ball was made of the gum of a tree that grows in the hot country, which, having holes in it, distils great white drops, that soon harden, and being worked and molded together turn as black as pitch. The balls made thereof, tho' hard and heavy to the hand, did bound and fly as well as our footballs, there being no need to blow them . . ." (18)

The early Spaniards were among the first of the New World explorers to come into contact with rubber. They called this substance "caoutchouac" and were amazed by its peculiar physical properties. It has already been pointed out that the number of rubber balls paid in annual tribute to the crown of Mexico shows that large numbers were manufactured at that time. These balls varied in size and there is no evidence of any type of standardization in this respect. The size was partly determined by such factors as the diameter of the hole in the stone ring, size of the playing court, and it would be reasonable to assume that lighter and smaller balls would be made for the use of children and immature players.

The Ball Courts

Supplementing the written information derived from existing codices and the original accounts of the early Spaniards are the archaeological remains of several dozen ball courts. These edifices vary greatly in size and state of preservation. With the single exception of the court described by Vaillant as being in southeastern Arizona, the remainder are all situated in the Mayan-Mexican area of Middle America and Mexico. The largest and best preserved of these ball courts is the main court of Chichen Itza in Yucatan. It was rediscovered by Stephens after its existence had been forgotten to all but a few natives for almost three hundred years. His description of this court as he actually found it is important (32).

"It consisted of two immense parallel walls, each two hundred and seventy four feet long, thirty feet thick, and one hundred and twenty feet apart. One hundred feet from the northern extremity, facing the open space between the walls, stands on an elevation a building thirty five feet long, containing a single chamber, with the front fallen, and, rising among the rubbish, the remains of two columns, elaborately ornamented with sculpture; . . ."

"In the center of the great stone walls, exactly opposite each other, and at a height of twenty feet from the ground, are two massive stone rings, four feet in diameter, and one foot one inch thick; the diameter of the hole is one foot seven inches . . ."

"These walls . . . we considered identical in their uses and purposes with the parallel structures supporting the rings at Uxmal, of which I have already expressed the opinion that they were intended for the celebration of some public games. . . . At Chichen Itza all the principal buildings have names; . . . and there is historical authority which, in my opinion, shows clearly the object and uses of this extraordinary structure, I shall call it, as occasion requires, the Gymnasium of Tennis-Court."

Since the main ball court at Chichen Itza is the largest and most elaborate of all the courts rediscovered, it will be described in detail. As seen from the air the court has the general shape of the capital letter *I* or of two capital *T*'s placed base to base. The most accurate measurements available are those of Maudsley (1) which are cited here.

The two parallel walls that form the sides of the court are each 272 feet long and placed 119 feet apart. These walls are 39 feet thick at their bases and taper to a top width of 16 feet 3 inches. The angle of slope of this back-wall is 52 degrees. The inner side of the parallel walls are vertical and faced throughout with neatly-cut square blocks of stone. The height to the top of the walls from the playing surface of the court measures 27 feet. A terrace 5 feet 3 inches above the playing surface projects 10 feet outward from the inner side of each wall to end in a stone clad face which slopes toward the playing field. These sloping stone faces have 8 panels containing 84 figures carved in bas-relief. The terrace continues as a broad platform beyond the ends of each wall. The vertical face of the main walls rise 22 feet from the top of these terraces.

The two stone rings placed in the walls are 4 feet in diameter, 11 inches thick, with the diameter of the center hole being 19 inches. These rings are situated not in the exact center of the parallel walls as so many writers indicate, but are 134 feet from the south end of the walls and directly opposite each other. The center of the hole is 20 feet above the top of the terrace and 25 feet 3 inches above the ground level of the court.

Surmounting the southern end of the east wall is a restored temple named, "The Temple of the Jaguars" because numerous paintings of that animal are found on the walls of the temple room. A stairway with exceedingly steep risers leads up the back slope of the wall to side of the temple. The temple has a short flight of steps leading to the entrance which is flanked by two enormous feathered serpent columns.

On the top of the west wall are the remains of 3 small structures each of which consist of 2 parallel walls perpendicular on the inner side, but thicker at the top than the bottom, so that each wall has the appearance of leaning outward. The passage through these walls had apparently been roofed over and would have afforded sitting room for one person. Two of these similar corresponding structures are found directly opposite on the east wall. However, the site corresponding to the third such structure on the south end of the wall is occupied by the temple cited above. From their position at the boundaries of the court enabling the end spaces to be clearly observed and also directly above the rings Maudsley has concluded that they were used for umpire seats (1).

Approximately 100 feet beyond the ends of the parallel walls the playing field broadens out into the enlarged part of the *I* and this limitation is marked by end walls about 6 feet high with their extreme ends bent back at right angles to form a discontinuous part of the side walls of the ball court. A restored two-column temple is situated in the middle of the north wall and facing it from its position on the end wall of the south end of the court is another temple which is not, however, situated directly in the center of the end wall. Consequently there is a discrepancy in the symmetry of this end of the ball court.

The inside length of the playing field is 482 feet, by 119 feet in width between the parallel walls. The corresponding outside measurements are 545 feet and 225 feet respectively. The widths between the walls at the northern and southern end court areas are 222 feet and 208 feet respectively.

The massive stone rings are held in place by stone tenons which are firmly embedded in the stone blocks of the walls. The weight of these rings is considerable and reflects a high degree of engineering skill in placing them with such exactitude. Both rings were found in place by Stephens in his first visit to Chichen Itza although the court was several hundred years old at that time. Later on, the stone ring in the west wall was dug out by treasure seekers but was replaced when the court was restored by a archaeological party. Both rings are carved in bas-relief with a feathered serpent intertwining around the center hole.

The diagrams of the ground plan and cross sectional views of the court in Figure I will make the explanation clearer. The two parallel walls of the court are indicated by *A* with the stone terrace at the inner base designated as *B*. This stone terrace leads out to the sloping surface *C* which ends on the playing surface of the court *D*. The stone rings are shown by *E* and the sloping rear wall by *F*. The broadened ends of the playing field are marked *G* and both end walls indicated by *H*. The Temple of Jaguars surmounts the east wall as *I* with the two end wall temples marked as *J*. Remains of the possible umpires seats on both walls are labelled *K*.

There are no fewer than seven ball courts known at Chichen Itza. Of these six were in actual use when the city was last occupied by the Mayas and a seventh one, of earlier construction, lies buried under a later terrace located behind the Nunnery. In contrast to the large size of the main court detailed here is that of the smallest court in the same city. This court measures 65 feet in length and is 20 feet wide. It is situated behind the structure known as the Red House.

From the presence of certain characteristics archaeologists have concluded that the main court is neither pure Mayan or Toltec design but shows an intermingling of the characteristics of both cultures. While there are several indications of this Toltec influence the mere presence of feathered serpent columns

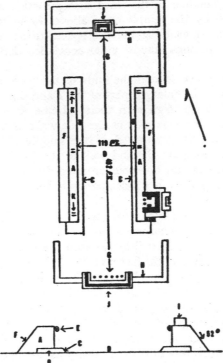

Fig. I. Main Ball Court at Chichen Itza, Yucatan. Cross Sectional View.

in the ball court temple serves as one of the easiest signs of such influence in the construction of the court.

The ruins of the ball court located at Uxmal show it to have been much smaller and less elaborate than the main court at Chichen Itza. The two parallel walls of the Uxmal court are situated 69 feet apart and are 155 feet long. The authors' measurements conflict with those of Gann who gave the same measurements as being 70 feet and 128 feet respectively. However, at the time that Gann took his measurements in the early 1920's, the ruins were incompletely excavated and the work done since that date in uncovering the court may account for the discrepancy in measurements. The two stone rings are still held *in situ* by means of the usual tenon. The outer portion of these rings has broken away but enough of each ring remains to determine the outside diameter of each as having been 4 feet. Sculptured on the north side of each ring is a band of hieroglyphics which date the erection of the ball court as having taken place in 1277 A.D. (14).

The walls of the court are in a poor state of preservation and so much debris has gathered under the stone rings that it is impossible to determine their exact height from the original playing surface of the court. This court did not have gallery space for the populace on top of the walls but was so constructed that it was possible to watch the game in progress by standing on two nearby edifices known as the Nuns' Quadrangle and the House of the Governor. Since the ball game was played over many centuries of time, some modification of the playing court gradually evolved. These points of resemblance and modifications have been noted by Blom as follows (3).

1. All ball courts have the characteristic *I* shape in their ground plan.

2. The inner surface of the side walls are always smoothly surfaced and usually slope toward the playing court. These side walls are vertical only in the case of some ball courts in the north. In this respect the author would point out that the restored court at Monte Alban, Oaxac which would certainly be considered in the northern area, has sloping side walls. However, this case may be considered an exception to the general rule.

3. The low terrace at the base of the playing walls is present in all courts.

4. The stone clad slope which leads from the terrace to the playing level of the court is found in the courts of all areas.

5. Stone rings are found only in the northern area courts or those courts which have been subjected to northern (Toltec) influence. Thus Joyce (19) feels that the Chichen Itza court displays the essential northern characteristics.

Descriptions of the ball courts have come down to us from many authentic sources. Sahagun records in his work (29):

"The ball courts were one hundred, one hundred and fifty, and also two hundred feet long between where they ended in said corners. . . . In the center of this enclosure were placed two stone rings in the walls one opposite the other; these two (stones) had a hole in the center, which hole was encircled by an idol representing the god of the game. . . ."

A somewhat more detailed account is rendered by Duran (13):

"They built ball courts enclosed with fine walls, and well ornamented, with the whole floor inside very smooth and carved with mortar. . . . These ball courts were better in some places than others and built after the plan shown in the picture, narrow at the center, and at the ends, broad with corners made purposely so that if the ball entered there the player would be at a disadvantage and lose the point. . . . The walls measured 1½ estados in height (10 to 12 feet) all around. . . . On the walls were either towers or effigies of stone placed at intervals. . . ."

It is a curious fact that archaeological excavations have discovered many stone rings in the northern area of the game but few actual court sites. In several of the towns of the Valley of Mexico, stone rings which were once used in the ball game have been erected in the town plaza. Such rings were formerly found in Coyocan and Texcoco.

The reverse is true of the southern area where many court sites have been uncovered but few, if any, stone rings. This was a puzzling fact to archaeologists for a long time until they reached the conclusion that the rings used in the game in the southern areas must have been made of wood or some other light material which would make them portable. This conclusion was justified when careful translations of the Popol Vuh indicated that in those passages referring to the ball game the rings are always written about in such manner that they must have been portable. Granting this explanation, coupled with the climatic assaults of many centuries, it is readily apparent that the portable rings would disappear whereas the stone ones would remain. Blom (3) believes that the use of stone rings represented an advanced stage in the evolution of the ball game.

In general the northern area of the ball game has been considered as that part of the Republic of Mexico north of the Peninsula of Yucatan. The northern section of Yucatan is considered an intermediate area in which the influence of both the Mayas and Mexicans was brought to bear. All areas of the ancient Maya domain south of this northern portion of Yucatan are considered to be in the southern area.

The actual size of the stone rings varied a good deal. The measurements of eight stone rings in the collection of the National Museum in Mexico City are shown in table 1 (3).

TABLE I

Comparison of Measurements Made of Stone Rings in the National Museum of Mexico City

	Diameter of Stone Rings	Diameter of Center Hole
Smallest...........................	32 cm.	8 cm.
Largest............................	102 cm.	21 cm.
Range.............................	32 to 102 cm.	8 to 31 cm.

There was no standardization of court size, as is apparent from the diverse measurements made of existing sites. Ball courts have been located in Chiapas, Oaxaca, the Valley of Mexico, Yucatan, Quintana Roo, Guatemala, British Honduras, and Honduras. Of a total number of 40 known sites, more than three-quarters have been located in the southern area and the measurements of these have shown as wide a variation as the courts in the northern area.

No doubt the larger courts were meant for team games with the smaller ones lending themselves to games of a singles or doubles nature. The possibility must not be overlooked that some of these smaller courts may have been constructed on a reduced scale to afford playing opportunity to the children of that time.

The placement height of the stone rings also varied from court to court. While the stone rings at Chichen Itza are placed a full 25 feet from the center of the ring to the playing surface, those at Uxmal, which are the same size, were estimated to have been placed only about 7 to 8 feet from the ground level of the court. Here again it is possible that the lower placement would lend itself well to the lesser skill and stamina of immature players. However, the reason for the variations in court size and ring height is not explained by any past writer so that we must fall back upon conjecture for an explanation

The direction of placement of the long axis of the court was not related to the cardinal points of the compass. Some of the early writers felt, owing to the religious significance of the game, that this matter of placement was important but the measurements of directions on the known court sites have varied as widely as in their respective sizes.

A study of the glyphs and depictions of the ball courts as found in codices shows that the floors of those courts with surfaced areas were frequently painted different colors in various sections of the court (7). Thus, the court might have each of its four sections painted a different color, or it may have been divided into two halves, either along the long axis of the court or from ring to ring, and each half painted a different color. No particular significance has been discovered in the sequence of colors or sections painted. Illustrations in the Codex Colombino (8) show one court painted in four quarters, with the upper left red, upper right green, lower left quarter yellow, and the lower right quarter brown. Another is shown in the same sequence as yellow, green, brown, red and still a third as brown, yellow, red, and blue.

Ground Plan of the Ball Court at Rabinal from Maudsley.

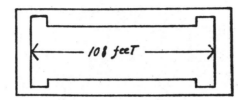

Ball Court Glyph Codex Mendoza.

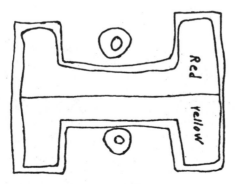

Ball Court Glyph Codex Borbonicus.

Fig. II.

Fig. III. Stone ring in Position in East Wall of the Main Ball Court at Chichen Itza, Yucatan.

Rules of Play

The ball game was played under a definite set of stringent rules, for all early Spanish writers mention that it was considered illegal to strike the ball with the hands or feet. All are agreed on this one point of play. Prominent mention is also made of the type of protective gear worn by the players during the course of the contest.

"All those who entered the game, played with leather placed over their loinclouts and they always wore some trousers of deerskin to protect the thighs which they all the time were scraping along the ground. They wore gloves in order not to hurt their hands, . . ."

"Some were so outstanding in the game and made so many elegant moves in it that it was worth seeing and I will specially relate one which I saw done by Indians who had practiced it, and it was that they used a curious thrust or hit, when seeing the ball in the air, at the same time it was coming to the ground. They were so quick in that moment to hit it with their knees or seats that they hit the ball with extraordinary velocity. With these thrusts they suffered great damage on the knees or on the thighs, with the result that those who for smartness often used them, got their haunches so mangled that they had those places cut with a small knife and extracted blood which the blows of the ball had gathered." (13)

Since the ball might be up to almost a foot in diameter and was made of pure rubber and was driven by the full force of a skilled player, it is easy to imagine that considerable damage would have resulted to any player who was unexpectedly struck by the ball. Along similar lines it is only necessary to recall some of the crippling and serious injuries which have resulted in modern playing of the Basque game of Jai-lai which in some respects is very similar to the ancient Mayan ball game.

Further evidence of the equipment worn by the players is given by the description taken from Sahagun's description (29):

> ". . . they did not play with their hands, but instead struck the ball with their buttocks; for playing they wore gloves on their hands and a belt of leather on their buttocks, with which to strike the ball."

A difference of opinion seems to have existed among certain writers as to what was considered legal and illegal in striking the ball. Some historians, like Sahagun, indicated that it was proper to use only the hips or the buttocks. A survey of the accounts of several early authors with respect to this point shows that the knees, thighs, hips, and buttocks were used for hitting the ball. There apparently was restriction in chesting and heading the ball, as in our modern-day soccer. Ovieda (26) is quite definite on this point:

> "They were so clever both those of the one side and those of the other in not allowing the ball to stop it was marvelous—for if to see those of our country (Spain) play ball with their hands gives us such pleasure and surprise, then seeing skill and speed with which some of them play, how much more must one praise those with such skill and dexterity and elegance play it with the buttocks and with the knees counting it a foul to touch the ball with any other part of the body except the two said parts, the buttocks and the knees."

There was general agreement on the wearing of leather hip and loin protectors by the players. In some of the drawings in the manuscripts and codices, the players appear to be wearing head protectors and gloves are mentioned as being worn in the accounts found in the Popol Vuh. No specific regulation on the uniform that could be worn seems to have existed. The players are sometimes depicted as wearing only a loin cloth and hip protectors and in other cases as fully clothed. A statuette of a ball player known as "Ollamani" in the National Museum of Mexico City shows the player to be wearing the loin cloth and hip protectors. Considering the activity involved in playing the game, it is probable that the players stripped down to a minimum in order to facilitate their play.

We are far less fortunate regarding more detailed rules of the actual playing than in the accounts dealing with equipment. It is certain that the object of the game was to score a goal by hitting the ball in a fair manner through the fixed ring. In the case of a goal being scored, the player scoring it had the right to the cloaks of all the spectators who immediately left the scene in an endeavor to save their apparel.

> ". . . and he that could strike it through won the game; and in token of it being an extraordinary success, which rarely happened, he had a right to the cloaks of all the lookers on, by ancient custom, and law amongst gamesters; and it was very pleasant to see, that as soon as the ball was in the hole, the standers-by took to their heels, running away with all their might to save their cloaks, laughing and rejoicing, others scurrying after them to secure their cloaks for the winner, who was obliged to offer some sacrifice to the idol of the tennis-court and stone through whose hole the ball had pass'd." (18).

The account set down above is further augmented by that of Brasseur de Bourbourg (4) in his record:

> "The decision was by a number of determined points and the skill consisted for the one of receiving and chasing the ball as their opponents sought to make a pass above the wall that they had chosen for their side. The one who touched it otherwise lost a point. So many points won a certain load of cloth or of chocolate."
>
> "If one of the players succeeded in making his ball pass through one of the rings in the wall this was regarded as a prodigious feat and of happiness without equal. He had the right of taking the cloaks of all the spectators;. . ."

Taking into account the large and heavy ball used, that in a large court such as at Chichen Itza the stone ring was placed 25 feet from the ground, and that the players were restricted from using their hands, it can be appreciated that a goal must have been a rather rare occurrence. The scoring of a goal appears to have ended the game as the players of the winning side immediately pursued the spectators to secure their cloaks for the player scoring the goal. In the case of a smaller court where the ring was set much lower and a goal scored more easily this may not have been the case. The reference to a certain set number of points determining a game would indicate that possibly several goals could be set to determine the winner of a game. No specific account exists which will tell us what was decided in the case of those games which ended without a goal being scored.

The number of players who could participate on a side was quite variable. The game is described as being played as singles, doubles, triples, and various combinations of these figures. The large court at Chichen Itza could have accommodated a great number of players but again no pertinent information on this point has been found.

Duran (13) describes a black and green-colored line which was drawn on the ground straight in front of the stone rings and says that this line was made with a special herb because of religious beliefs. This line divided the playing court into halves but it is not clear whether the line ran parallel to the length of the court or across the court from sidewall to sidewall. Two noted authorities in the field of Mayan archaeology hold opposing views on this question. Blom (3) believes that the dividing line was drawn lengthwise of the court, while Joyce (19) holds that it was drawn crosswise of the court. The importance of this dividing line is mentioned by Duran (13):

> "Those rings also served them as a cord, because straight in front of them (*derecho*) on the ground was a black or green line made with a certain herb, which for reason of superstition had to be made with a certain herb and no other. All the time the ball had to pass this line in which case they did not lose, because even when the ball came rolling on the ground, as they had hit it with the seat or knee as soon as it passed the line, though only two fingers distance, then it was not a default, but counted as such if it did not pass."

The game was similar to modern-day soccer and basketball in that it had players who definitely carried the attack to score while others were used to play guard or a defensive position.

"... and at the ends of the court they had a quantity of players on guard and to defend against the ball entering there, with the principal players in the middle to face the ball and the opponents. The game was played just as they fought, i.e., they battled in distinct units." (13).

A game was started by one of the priests throwing the ball into the air in such fashion that a player immediately received it on the hips or buttocks and put into play. With respect to the length of a game, time divisions, substitution, and other important elements, no definite knowledge is available. Although we know that the object of the game was to score a goal by hitting the ball through one of the rings, we are not even certain which ring was used. It is possible that a goal might have been scored using either ring although this runs contrary to modern-day games in which a specific goal is alloted to each team for scoring purposes. The answer to these questions awaits further research.

The careful construction of the inner playing walls of the courts, much care being expended in securing a smooth and uniform surface, would indicate that the rebounding and angling of the ball from the walls must have been an important skill for the players. While it is not known whether the teams played from one end of the court to the other or crosswise when many players were participating, the main effort must have been to keep the ball between the two side walls and in the vicinity of the stone rings.

The principal players stood between the walls (A), and attempted to strike the ball with their hips, buttocks, or knees in such fashion that they could drive it through one of the stone rings. The line mentioned by Duran had to be passed by that team having possession of the ball. One team had to keep the ball on the move while it was on their side of this line and attempt to drive it across into the field of play of the opposing team. In the meantime the other team would be free to interfere within the limits of the rules. The mention of a default counting against the team that failed to carry the ball in their possession across the dividing line probably meant loss of possession of the ball to the opposite team. This would be similar to the rules of modern basketball and similar games.

The courts were deliberately constructed with enlarged ends to pose a hazard for the ball and players were stationed there to stop the ball from entering. Since in all games involving the scoring of a goal the object is to keep the ball near the goal assigned to the team, it is reasonable to assume that such would have been the case in this ball game. In any case, a team which permitted the ball in its possession to be trapped in one of the wide end areas would have a poor chance of scoring a goal from that position. On the huge court at Chichen Itza this would be a physical impossibility.

Religious Significance

The impression of its deep religious significance is gained from the codices and the presence of numerous stone idols and bas-relief carvings at the actual court sites. Figure I indicates that no less than three temples are an integral part of the Chichen Itza court and religious ceremonies were held in connection with any game. This is very strongly emphasized by early historians who wrote of the importance of religion in the lives of the people:

> "Every tennis-court was a temple having two idols, the one of gaming, and the other of the ball. On a lucky day, at midnight, they performed certain ceremonies and enchantments on the two lower walls and on the midst of the floor, singing certain songs, or ballads; after which a priest of the great temple went with some of their religious men to bless it; he uttered some words, threw the ball about the tennis-court four times, and then it was consecrated, and might be play'd in, but not before. The owner of the tennis-court, who was always a lord, never play'd without making some offering and performing certain ceremonies to the idol of gaming, which shows how superstitious they were, since they had such regard to their idols, even in their diversions." (18)

Of the presence of stone idols on the walls of the ball courts Clavijero made the following remark (6):

> "The idols placed upon the wall were those of the god of the game, of whose name we are ignorant; but we suspect the name of one of them to have been Omacatl, the God of Rejoicings."

The stone rings at the main court of Chichen Itza have their center holes encircled by two carved serpents with their tails entwining. The Feathered Serpent called Kulkulcan by the Mayas, and Quetzalcoatl by the Aztecs, was a sacred symbol and used in carvings and decorations only in cases wherein it was desired to emphasize strongly something of a religious nature. The carving on the two rings, together with the three temples attached to the court, and the bas-relief carvings on the stone clad slope (C) all point to the religious significance of the ball game.

The deities associated with the game varied to a certain extent, as early accounts mention a fairly wide number of different gods and goddesses connected with the game. Duran (13) refers to a stone ring in one of the courts which had the center hole surrounded by a carving which appeared to have been the face of a monkey. Among the Aztecs Xochiquetzal, the goddess of love, lust, and gambling, was considered the protector of the game. At the time of the entrance of the Spaniards into Tenochtitlan, there was a ball court on the central plaza with statues dedicated to Oappatzan and Amapan to whom sacrifices were made at game time (19). The tenacles of ritual extended throughout the gamut of tribal activities, so that all sports and games were thought of in terms of their religious meanings.

A study of the religious connections of the game leads to the conclusion that there must have been two deities associated with it. One of these was connected with the game as a whole while the other was specifically associated with the ball and the stone ring. This conclusion seems to be supported by the studies of Bourbourg (4):

> "The ring had its god or special spirit as well as that of the local god himself and one offered on the occasion of sacrifices to these two divinities. The consecration of the new ball court took place at night, and one practiced there a large number of superstitious rites. For this effect they chose a good day and at midnight the priest of the temple descended to the court; one placed the image of the protecting spirit of the game on the wall, not less elevated than the gallery and on the side opposite one

protecting god of the ball and the stone ring. After the songs and hymns the priest pronounced some mystic formulas and having thrown the ball four times in the interior of the court the consecration of the place and of the equipment found itself ended."

Mention has already been made that a player fortunate enough to score a goal was expected to offer suitable thanksgiving to the ball game deity for his good fortune. In some cases the scoring of a goal was considered an ill omen and the sacrifice made by the scoring player was in the nature of a propitiation. It was undoubtedly the strong religious aspects of the ball game which led the Spanish friars eventually to prohibit its playing.

Gambling and Professionalism

At first the ball game was played by the nobles and general populace on a strictly recreational and amateur basis. However, as the sport became more firmly entrenched and began to evolve, professional players appeared on the scene and the character of the game began to change. Lords and nobles vied with one another in keeping the most skillful players for their teams. The purely amateur spirit of the original game is evident in the following excerpt:

> "He who hit the ball through said hole in the stone was surrounded by all, and they honoured him and sang songs of praise and danced a while with him and they gave him a certain special prize of feathers or loinclouts, a thing they valued highly, though honor was what he appreciated most and most highly esteemed,. . ." (13)

Before the advent of the professional player, the lords and nobles were accustomed to settle differences by playing a game of ball. This was the case shortly before the arrival of Cortes in 1519. At that period the emperor Montezuma II and Nezahuapilli, chief of the Texcocoans, had a dispute concerning the respective forecasts of their soothsayers. That of Nezahuapilli had prophesied the coming of white strangers to the land. So convinced was the latter of the correctness of this forecast that he wagered his kingdom against three turkey cocks, the result to be decided by a ritualistic game of ball to be played with Montezuma. The Aztec emperor won the first three games in a row but at that time the Texcoco chief made a strong comeback and succeeded in taking the last three games. This inconclusive tie further depressed Montezuma who was at that time exceedingly troubled by the ominous portents of the future (37).

Inevitably the decay and corruption of professionalism made itself felt in the life of the people. A curious parallel exists between our present-day problem of professionalism and gambling and that which confronted the aboriginal inhabitants of Middle America 500 years ago.

> "Having recounted the ways of the nobles when playing this game of ball for their recreation and enjoyment, then we will now deal with those who play it for game and as a vice, setting all their happiness and effort-not-to-lose, but to win, as gamblers who have no other business; men who did not live from other sources nor had any other occupation than gambling. Men whose children and wives always lived on borrowed bread and on begging from their neighbors, as even among our Spanish people may happen."

"What low class people gambled was jewelry and of small value and worth, and as he who has little weath on hand usually loses it, they went to gamble their houses, fields, maize storages, maguey plants, and they would even gamble themselves away to become slaves, to be sacrificed if they did not redeem themselves in time . . ." (13)

The heads of families would become such inveterate gamblers that they would stake their wives and children on the outcome of a game. This aspect of the game at the time of the first Spaniards was undoubtedly a sign of its degeneracy and the coming of the white man probably did little to destroy a sport which was at that time already showing signs of the decay that would have ultimately brought about its end or severe modification.

By the time the Spaniards arrived, the ball game had reached the peak of its development and no further modifications or expansion took place. Since it was banned very shortly by the friars, it came to be played less and less so that one of the last authentic records of its existence is that of Clavijero (6) who cites it as still being played by the Tarahuamare in northern Mexico during the year 1765. It may have continued to be played in isolated communities not closely observed by the clergy beyond this date, but the records are extremely vague.

From the earliest accounts mentioned in the Popol Vuh around the year 700 A.D., the ball game was played up to at least 1765 and probably beyond. This long span of over 1,000 years would make it the longest-played organized team game known to have existed among the aboriginal Americans.

Summary

The court ball game unique to Middle America was invented by the aboriginal Mayas about the year 700 A.D. It was called Pok-ta-pok by them and Tlachtli by the Aztecs. The ball game gradually diffused over a period of time so that it was played from Guatemala to southeastern Arizona, as proved by the existence of ball court sites. Its importance in the various cultures of those peoples who subsequently played it is attested to by the many references found in pre-Conquest manuscripts, codices, sacred books, and in the written accounts of the early Spaniards.

Although no definite set of rules has come down to us, the presence of numerous ball courts and other available data have made it possible to formulate a fairly accurate approximation of the way the ball game was conducted. On certain phases, such as the contruction of the courts, definite knowledge is available.

The court ball game became extremely popular with other aboriginal non-Mayan peoples and was being played by them at the time of the conquest. Under the instigation of the clergy, the ball game was prohibited but continued to be played until at least 1765 in a part of northern Mexico. Beyond that date authentic information is not available at this time. The total time during which the court ball game was played ranges from 700 A.D. to at least 1765. This span of almost 1100 years makes it the longest-played organized game known in the New World.

REFERENCES

1. *Biologia-Centrali-Americana; or Contributions to the Knowledge of Fauna and Flora of Mexico and Central America.* Archaeology by A. P. Maudsley, Vol. III and Plates, London: R. H. Porter, Edited by Duncan Godman, 1900.

2. BLOM, FRANZ. *The Conquest of Yucatan.* New York: The Houghton Mifflin Company, 1936, 238 pp.

3. ————. *The Maya Ball Game Pok-ta-pok* (called tlachtli by the Aztecs). Middle American Research Series, No. 4, Vol. 4: 431–56, Tulane University, New Orleans, 1932.

4. BRASSEUR DE BOURBOURG, CHARLES ETIENNE. *Histoire des Nations Civilisées du Mexique et de l'Amérque Centrale.* Paris: A. Bertrand, 4 volumes, 1857.

5. ————. *Popol Vuh. Le Livre Sacré et Les Mythes de l'Antiquité Américaine, Avec Les Livres Héroïque et Historique des Quichés.* Paris: A. Durand, Editeur, 1861, 386 pp.

6. CLAVIJERO, ABBÉ D. FRANCISCO SAVERIO. *The History of Mexico Collected from Spanish and Mexican Historians from Manuscripts and Ancient Paintings of the Indians* (Translated from the original Italian by Charles Cullen, Esq.). London: Joyce Gold, 1807, 476 pp.

7. CODEX BORBONICUS. *Manuscrit Mexicain de la Bibliothèque du Palais Bourbon* (Livre divinitaire et rituel figuré). Publié en facsimilé avec un commentaire explicatif par M. E. T. Hamy. Paris: Ernest Leroux, Editeur, 1899, 28 pp.

8. CODEX COLOMBINO. *Ho menaje a Cristobal Colon, Antiguedades Mexicanas, Publicades por la Junta Colombino de Mexico en el Cuarto Centenaria del Descubrimiento de América.* Mexico: Oficina Tipográfica de la Secretaría de Fomento, Calle de San Andres, Numero 15, 1892.

9. CODEX MENDOZA. *The Mexican Manuscript Known as the Collection of Mendoza and preserved in the Bodlein Library of Oxford.* (Edited and translated by James Cooper Clark). London: Waterlow and Sons, Ltd., 3 volumes (Vol. III), 1807, 71 codex pages.

10. COOK, O. F. *Milpa Agriculture, A Primitive Tropical System.* The Smithsonian Institute Annual Report, 1919, pp. 307–21.

11. ————. *Vegetation Affected by Agriculture in Central America.* U. S. Bureau of Plant Industry, Bulletin Number 145, Washington, D. C.

12. DUNLAP, HELEN. Games, Sports, Dancing, and Other Vigorous Recreational Activities and Their Function in Samoan Culture. *Research Quarterly* 22: 298–311 (Oct. 1951).

13. DURAN, DIEGO. *Historia de las Indias de Nueva-España y Islas de Tierra Firme.* Mexico: Imp. de J. M. Andrade y F. Escalante, 2 volumes and atlas, 1867–80.

14. GANN, T. W. F. *In an Unknown Land.* New York: Charles Scribner's and Sons, 1924, 263 pp.

15. ————. *Glories of the Maya.* Charles Scribner's and Sons, 1939, 279 pp.

16. GOETZ, DELIA, AND SYLVANUS G. MORLEY. *Popol Vuh, The Sacred Book of the Ancient Quiche Mayas.* English version from the Spanish translation by Adrian Recinos. Norman: University of Oklahoma Press, 1950, 267 pp.

17. HERNANDEZ, FRANCISCO. *De Antiquitatibus Novae Hispaniae.* Mexico: Edición facsimilar, Talleres gráficos del Museo Nacional de Arquiología, Historia, y Etnografía, 1926, 169 pp.

18. HERRERA, Y TORDESILLAS ANTONIO DE. *Historia General de los Hechos de los Castellanos en las Islas i Tierra-Firme del Mar Océano.* Madrid: Imprinte Real de Nicholas Rodriguez Franco, 5 volumes, 1726–30.

19. JOYCE, THOMAS A. *Mexican Archaeology, An Introduction to the Archaeology of the Mexican and Mayan Civilizations of Pre-Spanish America.* London: Phillip Lee Warner, 1920, 201 pp.

20. LANDA, DIEGO DE. *Relation des Choses de Yucatan (Relación de las cosas de Yucatán).* Texte espagnol et tr. française en regard. Paris: Jean Genet, Editeur, 2 volumes, 1928–29.

21. MITCHELL, J. LESLIE. *The Conquest of the Maya.* New York: E. P. Dutton and Company, Inc., 1935, 279 pp.

22. MORLEY, SYLVANUS G. *The Ancient Maya.* Stanford University Press, Stanford University, California, 1946, 520 pp.

23. ———. Chichen Itza, An Ancient American Mecca. *The National Geographic* (Jan. 1925):
    47: 63–93.
24. ———. The Maya. *Life* (June 30, 1947), 22: 51–67.
25. MOLINA, ALONSO DE. *Vocabulario en Lengua Castellana y Mexicana*. Madrid: Ediciones
    Cultura Hispánica, 1944.
26. OVIEDA, Y VALDES, GONZALO FERNANDEZ DE. *Historia General y Natural de las Indias,
    Islas y Tierra-firme del Mar Océano*. Madrid: Imprinte de la Real Academia de la His-
    toria, 4 volumes, 1851–55.
27. PENICHE, JOSÉ A. EROSA. *Guide Book to the Ruins of Uxmal* (English translation by Julio
    Granados). Merida, 1948, 50 pp.
28. PEREZ, JUAN PIO. *Diccionario de Lengua Maya*. Merida: Imprinte Litteraria, Juan F.
    Molina Solis, 1866–67, 437 pp.
29. SAHAGUN, FRAY BERNARDINO DE. *A History of Ancient Mexico* (Translation from the
    Spanish version of Carlos Maria de Bustamente by Fanny Bandelier). Fisk University
    Press, 1932, 315 pp.
30. SPENCE, LEWIS. *Popol Vuh. The Mythic and Heroic Saga of the Kiches of Central America*.
    In Popular Studies in Mythology, Romance, and Folklore, Number 16. London: David
    Nutt, 1908, 50 pp.
31. STEGGERDA, MORRIS. *Anthropometry of Adult Maya Indians: A Study of their Physical
    and Physiological Characteristics*. Carnegie Institution of Washington Publication Num-
    ber 434, 1932, 101 pp.
32. STEPHENS, JOHN L. *Incidents of Travel in Yucatan*. New York: Harper and Brothers, 2
    volumes, 1841.
33. STUMPF, FLORENCE, AND FREDERICK W. COZENS. Hidden possibilities for research in
    physical education and recreation. *Research Quarterly* 18: 104–08 (May 1947).
34. ———. Some aspects of the role of games, sports, and recreational activities in the cul-
    ture of modern primitive peoples. (In 2 Parts) Part I. The New Zealand Maoris. *Re-
    search Quarterly* 18: 198–218 (Oct. 1947); Part II. The Fijians. *Research Quarterly*,
    28: 2–20 (March 1949).
35. THOMPSON, J. ERIC. *The Civilization of the Mayas*. Field Museum of Natural History,
    Anthropology Leaflet Number 25, Chicago, 1936, 104 pp.
36. TORQUEMADA, JUAN DE. *Los veinte i un libros rituales y Monarquia Indiana*. Madrid:
    N. Rodriguez 3 volumes, 1723. 3rd edition, Mexico, 1943.
37. VAILLANT, C. G. *The Aztecs of Mexico*. New York: Doubleday, Doran and Co., Inc.,
    1944, 325 pp.

"shell game" and number of kernels or pebbles hidden in other's hand (*Aymara*), whole word from first syllable pronounced (*Araucanian*). Some of these, such as kites, are almost certainly of European introduction; others, such as jacks, hopscotch, blindman's buff, and riddles, probably so.

Vocalizing inarticulately and continuously and at the same time striking the mouth rhythmically with the palm of the hand—the familiar so-called "war whoop" of the North American Plains Indians—is recorded in connection with recreational and/or other gatherings and activities in the Chacoan, Pampean (*Araucanian* influence?) and *Araucanian* areas.

GAMBLING GAMES AND SPORTS

Gambling among South American Indians is confined to the risking of things of value on the issue of certain sports like hockey and horse racing or of games of hazard. Betting on present nesciences or on future contingencies of other kinds and the pledging of onerous acts are not recorded. Here and there prizes are or were offered to winners of sports: of ball games among the 16th-century *Itatin* of the Eastern Bolivian area; of club-throwing contests among the 18th-century *Abipón and Mocoví* of the Chacoan area; of archery contests among the *Pancararú* of the Eastern Brazilian area. But such awarding of prizes can hardly be called gambling.

Our factual data on South American gambling and gambling games and sports are scattered through a great number of sources, the more important of which are: Nordenskiöld (1910, 1919 a), Rosen (1924), Karsten (1920 c, 1930, 1932, 1935), Rivet (1925), Romero (1941).

In the present paper we shall deal first with gambling games and sports of European introduction, and afterward with those of native origin.

EUROPEAN GAMBLING GAMES AND SPORTS

The chief gambling games and sports of European introduction indulged in by the South American Indians are horse racing, playing cards, Spanish dice, and taba.

Gambling and betting in connection with one or more of the first three are or were passionately indulged in, often for very large stakes, in the Chacoan, Pampean (including the *Charrua*), Patagonian, and *Araucanian* areas; not however in the Fuegian. According to Sánchez Labrador (1936, pp. 48–49), the Pampean Indians were first taught how to play and gamble with Spanish dice and playing cards by Spaniards living among the natives as captives or as refugees from Colonial justice; he implies that this had taken place not so long pre-

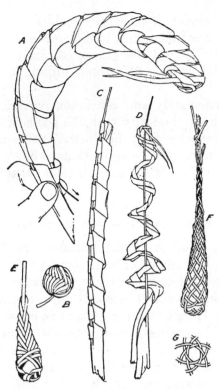

FIGURE 173.—Leaf-strand figures. *A*, Sweetheart's whereabouts; *B*, a ball; *C*, *D*, fancy forms; *E*, hassa fish; *F*, *G*, finger stalls. British Guiana. (After Roth, 1924, fig. 241.)

Eastern Bolivian and Chacoan. A particular game of patience, common in the Old World as well, and perhaps of European introduction, occurs in the Eastern Bolivian area; other forms, probably unrelated genetically, in the Guianan.

Characteristic leaf-strand toy figures (figs. 172, 173) are found in the Guianan, Eastern Bolivian, and Eastern Brazilian areas and among the modern *Carib* of Dominica; woven finger stalls (fig. 173, *F*, *G*) in the Guianan area and on the Tiquié River.

Localized distributions.—Among many games and amusements of local or very limited distribution may be mentioned: voladores (*Chorotega*, *Nicarao*); boxing (Chacoan area); mock battles of various kinds (Andean, Eastern Bolivian, and Eastern Brazilian areas); juggling (*Siusí*); shield game (*Warrau*); games like European jacks (*Araucanian*, Pampean), hop scotch (Pampean), and blind-man's buff (*Araucanian*, *Yahgan*); hoop rolling (Chacoan, Eastern Bolivian); games similar to quoits or duck-on-a-rock (*Quechua*, *Aymara*, *Chiriguano*) and to ninepins (*Chiriguano*, *Chané*); kites (*Mosquito-Sumo*); riddles (*Carib* of Dominica, *Aymara*, *Araucanian*); guessing games—

CEREMONIAL »BADMINTON« IN THE ANCIENT
CULTURE OF MOCHE (NORTH PERU)

Dr. Gerdt Kutscher, *Berlin*.

In the rich collection of ancient Peruvian pottery within the Berlin Museum für Völkerkunde is a vase of the culture of Moche, found in the Valle de Chicama[1]. Painted in the two-colour style so typical of this early, coastal culture of Northern Peru, the vase bears a lively scene swarming with figures. Max Schmidt has already published a photographic reproduction of this interesting specimen with the short comment »mythical scene«[2]. But only a complete projection of the scene can give one a clear notion of its exceeding richness, as is, indeed, true for all such works of art (vide fig. 1.)[3]. A stylized fish head adorns the spout which serves as a handle and rises in the shape of a stirrup to give the vase a total height of 29 cm. This fish head is a frequent motif in Moche art[4].

One of the two »faces« of the vase[5] is dominated by a »huaca«, one of the great step pyramids so characteristic of this culture. A big ramp leads from the right up into the second and topmost step of the pyramid. Upon the platform we see a box- or block-like seat which seems often to have crowned step pyramids[6]. Both this throne and the lower step of the pyramid display the same decorative design, namely, warriors marching toward the left, equipped with conical helmets and round shields and shouldering their heavy, ring-headed clubs. Such a motif is well known in vase painting.[7] These figures as well as the serpent coiling downward on the wall may be viewed as representations of murals. Unfortunately, very few examples of murals have survived in Moche art.[8]

Two magnificently dressed men stand upon the ramp. Their simple, cape-like mantles are rolled together and knotted upon their left shoulder with the two ends jutting out from the knot like coat-tails behind them. This method of wearing coats occurs elsewhere.[9] It would scarcely be some sort of »gesture of submission« before persons of high rank, as Jiménez Borja believes.[10] It may very well have arisen for purely practical reasons. The larger man's shirt is covered with crosses, while the sleeves are trimmed with a geometric motif very popular for decoration in those days.[11] The head-dress was obviously made from the skin of a beast of prey. It bears two paws which stretch their claws aloft and produces a dramatic effect[12]. The tail feathers of an osprey serve as a

CEREMONIAL BADMINTON IN THE
ANCIENT CULTURE OF MOCHE
(NORTH PERU)

Gerdt Kutscher

plume.[13] Both men carry a folded pouch of cloth or leather in their left hand. This little pouch belongs to the equipment of runners in the ritual races.[14]

Certainly not less imposing is the dress of the individual upon the throne. His short shirt reaches only to his hips. His collar in the shape of a wheel rests heavily upon the shirt. The disk adorning his nose is probably made of gold or a gold and copper alloy. Smaller disks surround the central one.[15] Whereas his left hand stretches diagonally downward, his right hand grasps a throwing stick with a missile laid upon it.

Behind the throne stands a person whose smaller stature and simpler garb identify him as a man of lesser importance. Surely, he is a sort of servant or noblemen's helper, as we see them in the deer hunting scenes. The long spear which this man is holding reaches far beneath the edge of the platform. Another individual, just as simply clothed, but somewhat larger, squats at the foot of the pyramid. Behind him stands upright a row of spears with their typical small rings and alternating light and dark bands.[16] On the upper edge of this scene is a wavy line which represents the hilly countryside. Seven small persons stand on either side of this line. One of them is wearing another head-dress plumed with the dark tail feathers of an osprey. The dots scattered about these persons indicate sand.

The section of transition to the other side of the vase is filled by three figures who face the vertical rear wall of the pyramid. One of them, his gaze slanting upward, stands at the foot of the structure. It seems as though he intended to pass a second spear to the man upon the platform. Behind this man at the foot of the pyramid appears a large figure much more richly clothed. His head-dress with its claws of a wild beast and its plume of osprey feathers and his ear ornament are already familiar to us from the first figure on the ramp. But these elements do not necessarily mean that the same person is here intended. The net-like painting of his face and the snake-like ornamental motif upon his short shirt sleeves are, in any event, new. While his left hand is grasping a spear, his right hand has poised the throwing stick behind him with its missile ready to be thrown.

The other »face« of the vase greets us with a scene every bit as brisk. Beneath six spear shafts ranged horizontally stand four individuals of various sizes. The central figure wears a head-dress made from the hide of an animal with pointed ears (fox or dog?). Another person behind him has draped a cloth decorated with crosses over his shoulders as though it were a sack. His left arm protrudes through the garment. Just like his companion to the lower left, he is wearing a head-dress of feathers which grow wider as they rise and then end bluntly. Feather ornaments of quite similar shape recur in other vase paintings[17] and in the frescoes of Moche.[18] Facing these three persons and standing in a landscape of sand dunes is a man whose body is bent backward, and with gaze turned

Fig. 1. Vase painting. Valle de Chicama. Museum für Völkerkunde, Berlin.

Fig. 2. Vase painting. Origin unknown. Museo de Antropología e Arqueología, Lima.

upward. He is poised to throw. Above his spear-thrower are three other persons. One, again, has painted his face like a net.

A wavy line indicates the landscape here just as on the other side of the vase. Two persons with five simple spears before them sit beneath the line. Above it are four pot-bellied clay jars. Each is closed and has a short rope around its neck. Similar jugs presumably filled with intoxicating beverages play a large part in festive dances and banquets of both the living and the dead.[19] Two jars appear to stand upon a support marked with parallel diagonal lines. The largest of the three small persons above the wavy line has another mantle slung across his shoulders like a bag. These three individuals raise the total population of the vase painting to 27 persons.

It is remarkable that almost all the larger figures, except the two men upon the ramp, are equipped with spears. Half a dozen spears constitute the central theme of one side of the vase. Not once, however, is a spear tipped with the needle-like point, otherwise so typical of the Moche spears.[20] These spears are not weapons, therefore, bus staffs which, like spears, are cast with a throwing stick. Another feature makes up for these missing spear heads. Near each end of the staff is fastened a cross-like part, particularly evident on the horizontal staffs. Moreover, objects shaped like flowers or rosettes are attached to the staffs.

The form and nature of these curious appendages become more apparent from various objects which are seen floating between the figures. A thin string connects a small peg to an object which looks like a bisected disk from the side. A frontal view, however, reveals it to be a disk bearing a cross. A series of leaf-like objecs cling to the disk. Whenever a frontal view of the disk occurs, as it does three times, one might at first be tempted to think of flower petals. Yet, shape and employment indicate feathers rather than petals, feathers which stem from the light-weight hemisphere. Thus, it seems to be a sort of shuttlecock (like the feathered ball in badminton) which is weighted down by a string with a wooden peg on the end.

Staffs equipped with small crosses and shuttlecocks were laid upon the throwing sticks and cast diagonally aloft, as one can see from the position of the marksman in the lower left-hand corner of the scene. In flight, the shuttlecock and string broke away from the spear shaft and floated through the air, while the wooden peg served as a sort of counterweight. To this exciting game, so full of movement, has flocked a large number of richly clad individuals, hence members of the upper class of the Moche culture. This is therefore no »mythical scene«, as Max Schmidt believed, but rather a ceremonial game which took place in the immediate vicinity of one of the great »huacas«, and, indeed, even on top of it.

Stylistically considered, the Berlin vase painting has been executed with a hasty, almost careless stroke of the brush. Yet, the very skill with which the artist worked, indicates that he knew his theme in all details. As the treatment here is so sketchy, one might object that any interpretation of this scene as a sort of ceremonial »badminton« game must be hypothetical. However, two other vase paintings treat the same subject with greater precision, one could even say, academically. When these two specimens are compared with the first, it is possible to arrive at a somewhat more accurate understanding of this interesting ceremony.

One of these two paintings occurs on a vase in the Museo Nacional de Antropología e Arqueología in Lima (Cat. No. 1/3494). It has not been published before (vide fig. 2)[21]. As in the Berlin painting, a pyramid with its two steps and large ramp attracts our attention first of all. The wall of the mighty building is decorated with a motif thrice repeated – a bird's head combined with a wavy line. This is a motif well known in the pottery of the Moche culture.[22]

The main figure on the platform far exceeds all his fellows in size and, hence,

significance. His dress and ornaments are more elaborate than in the Berlin painting. His cap-like head gear is surrounded by a thick, twisted band[23] and fastened
by a simple scarf knotted under the chin.[24] Another scarf is laid on the crown of
his head, while its ends dangle down over his back like two ribbons. The ribbons
are bordered with a saw-tooth motif.[25] His wheel collar is embellished with
two serpents placed side by side – a very popular decorative motif of those
times.[26] A skirt with slits along the bottom edge covers the lower part of the
body.[27] Besides a splendid ear ornament, the figure is wearing a nose decoration.
The two fangs indicate a being of superhuman rank.

The divinity grasps a throwing stick adorned with the head of a beast. His
other hand reaches out toward a man approaching him with deep reverence
and a fixed gaze upon the ramp. It seems as though the divine hand is about
to seize the goblet which the human being is offering him. The worshipper
presses a disk-like object against his breast with his left hand. This peculiar round
disk together with the large goblet is also present in other libation scenes.[27] It
must have fulfilled a special function which cannot be more precisely determined.

Between the large deity and the two worshippers are inserted two small individuals, each with two fingers pointing forward. They are equipped with the pouch
of a runner. Against the ramp appears a person seated before two great jars of
clay. One vessel has a thick rope handle. The other is capped by a calabash with
a sort of a spoon.[28] Nor is the servant on the rear of the platform missing. But
here he is holding several spear shafts.

All but three of the remaining figures, facing right, are armed with spears and
throwing sticks. In dress and ornaments they resemble the deity standing on the
platform. Several of them have already laid a missile on the throwing stick
and are poised for the throw. One of these marksmen has again fixed his gaze
heavenward. In contrast to the Berlin painting, the spears are here tipped with
long points. Yet, those two peculiar appendages, the crosses fastened to the shaft
and the shuttlecocks, are not missing. Lines running diagonally or perpendicularly
across the shaft demonstrate clearly how the string of the shuttlecock is wound
around the forward end of the shaft. The shuttlecocks themselves are viewed from
the side. Only once does a frontal view seem to have been intended, namely,
in the case of the figure to the upper right of the man with the goblet.

Two individuals in the top row of the painting have closed eyes, as is
characteristic of sleeping and also of dead men.[30] Equally as puzzling as these
two figures who may represent blind men is the small figure representing a
man with amputated arms on top of the vase. It is difficult to see any connection
between this figure and the ceremonial game.

While the awe-inspiring deity standing upon the »huaca« in this vase painting
is himself participating in the ceremony, the next painting which we are com-

Fig. 3. Vase painting. Origin unknown. After Jiménez Borja 1938.

paring with the Berlin work is a completely mythical scene (vide fig. 3). We are indebted to Jiménez Borja for its publication.[31]

As in the vase painting of the Museum in Lima, a great deity stands upon the pyramid consisting of three steps. Three serpents with saw-tooth backs hang down behind him. Two of them are, indeed, continuations of the saw-tooth band of the head-dress. The third may spring from the small of the god's back. Two smaller snakes whose heads are viewed from the front provide a sort of counterbalance on the other side, while four thin serpents rise like rays from the plume. The god has laid a long staff with an attached cross upon the throwing stick. Ready to throw, he gazes upward. Jiménez Borja has published another illustration of this deity with slight variations in several details.[32] If we may trust this enlargement, then the cross consists of two thin sticks tied together by a string wound diagonally around them.

Two animal demons – a beast of prey and a lizard demon – hasten toward the step pyramid. Each demon carries a staff, to which two crosses are fastened. Apparently, they wish to provide the deity standing upon the platform with fresh missiles. Above the lizard demon appears an owl demon characterized by the circle of feathers around his eyes. The demon clutches a mighty whip, as in a vase painting of the Berlin collection.[33] In both places he seems to be a sort of aide-de-camp for the great deity who is standing or enthroned behind him. At the foot of the pyramid stand the pot-bellied clay jars again. Two of them have a rope handle.

Behind the »huaca« are four other animal demons. The humming bird demon leading them may be plainly identified by his characteristic forked tail.[34] He is carrying a heavy bag on his shoulder – a motif already familiar to us from the Berlin painting. A humming bird demon with a bag also appears in a vase painting of a very intricate mythical battle scene.[35] Next follows a fox demon recognizable by his bushy, two-coloured tail.[36] His hands are propped on his thighs. Finally come two demon beasts of prey who are identified as a puma and a jaguar by their dark and spotted tails respectively. Both demons are in the same position. Gazing heavenward, they are about to launch the staff and shuttlecock lying upon their throwing stick. Here in all the clarity one could desire, the winding around the staff is evident. The small wooden peg is at the forward end of the staff, while the shuttlecock hangs down from the middle. Four identical shuttlecocks already accomplish their airy flight above the demons.

Jiménez Borja has confined himself to a short comment in his publication of this work. The vase painting is discussed in a section devoted to dance and music.

»Hay otras danzas en las que se despliegan bellos juegos de artificio. Parece como si los bailarines arrojasen al aire livianas pértigas en las que van apenas amarradas rosetas de plumas de colores. Las varillas saltan de las manos de los danzantes y caen luego al suelo mas dejan, méciendose en el cielo, la gracia de sus escarapelas.«[37]

Certainly, this is no dance as Jiménez Borja believes, since there is no trace of the chain formation so typical of the dances of both the living and the dead.[38] No, this is rather a festive game in which a shuttlecock attached to a staff is cast aloft with a throwing stick to float through the air like a balloon.[39]

While the significance of the shuttlecocks is clear, the function of the crosses fastened to the staffs and spears remains obscure. The scene published by Jiménez Borja seems to indicate that they are thin sticks tied together like a cross. In the Berlin vase-painting several staffs are equipped with shuttlecocks as well as crosses. Yet, in this as in the two other paintings the staffs are often enough provided with crosses alone. No doubt can remain that the spears furnished uniquely with crosses were also cast into the air. Indeed, the central figure of the painting published by Jiménez Borja proves it. Should one assume that the sticks of the cross were not firmly tied to the spear, but were mobily mounted, then the crosses may, possibly, have rotated in flight like propellers. This is, of course, purely hypothetical.[40]

Further paintings of the »badminton« game may, perhaps, be added from other collections. But already within the three vase paintings under discussion, a series of common elements stand out. The most important are compiled in the following table:

	Vase paintings		
	in Museum of Berlin	in Museum of Lima	published by Jiménez Borja
Step pyramid with ramp (»huaca«)....	×	×	×
Main figure (seated or standing) upon the pyramid.....................	×	×	×
Individual (or individuals) approaching upon the ramp..................	×	×	×

	Vase paintings		
	in Museum of Berlin	in Museum of Lima	published by Jiménez Borja
Small figure on the rear of the platform of pyramid	X	X	—
Spearmen gazing upward and poised to throw	X	X	X
Figures with mantle rolled together...	X	X	—
Figure carrying a bag	X	—	X
Figure with small pouch in his hand ..	X	X	—
Spear shafts (or staffs), needle-like point missing	X	—	X
Spear shafts (or staffs) with shuttlecocks	X	X	X
Shuttlecocks floating in the air	X	—	X
Spear shafts (or staffs) with stick crosses	X	X	X
Pot-bellied clay jars in a row.........	X	X	X

Several figures, on the other hand, are found only once: the man with goblet and disk (Lima), the men with closed eyes (Lima), and the owl demon equipped with a whip (Jiménez Borja).

But for all the great number of common elements, the differences among these three representations should not be forgotten. While the Berlin vase-painting offers us richly clothed and festively adorned human beings, the vase-painting of the Museum of Lima depicts a deity with his characteristic fangs as the central personnage upon the great »huaca« about to receive a drink offering from the man striding up the ramp. The throwing stick in the divine hand indicates that the god intends to participate in the game himself. This epiphany of the divinity among men is quite in keeping with the ancient tradition. Indeed, Antonio de la Calancha reports from the late period of the Chimu that the belief existed among the Indians of the North Coast that their demons in visible forms joined the dances, drinking bouts and festivals of the mortals.[41] Around the shrine of the divinity, whose name we do not know, the masses assembled to play »badminton«.

On the other hand, the vase painting published by Jiménez Borja is clearly a mythical scene, since all the participants in the game are gods or demons – representatives of the multiform pantheon of Moche. The deity standing upon the step pyramid, here again obviously the main personnage, is accompanied and served by numerous animal demons. Wild beast and lizard demons apparently bring him fresh missiles. A humming bird demon comes bearing a full bag.

An owl demon equipped with a whip is his aide-de-camp. Other animal demons amuse themselves at »badminton« like the main divinity himself.

Here is, consequently, an interesting parallel between human and divine-demonic action, just as in the sacred races which believers supposed to be performed by the demons themselves.[42] This concept of the correspondence between the-action of men and that of superhuman powers may surely be accounted for by the fact that the races as well as the »badminton« game were important ceremonies which were inaugurated by the gods and now in accordance with this commission were executed by men.

In conclusion, when one confronts the question of the deeper significance of this ceremonial game – if one be not satisfied to consider it pure recreation – then certain connections with the ritual races recur. One should note particularly the small pouches which, filled with beans essential to life, were the characteristic mark of the runner.[43] Not less significant is the appearance of the owl demon with a whip, as he awaits the approach of the row of running animal demons.[44] The divinity enthroned behind the owl demon in this vase painting is the actual goal of the race. He is quite similar to the great god in the vase painting published by Jiménez Borja. One is tempted to guess that they are representations of one and the same god, whose name we do not know.

Should this be true, then connections would exist with the fertility of the fields. Then we would have a picture into which not only the pouch full of beans and the whip, but also the humming bird demon carrying his bag, would fit as fertility symbols. Thus there are reasons to suspect that the strange »badminton« game of the ancient culture of Moche may have been connected with the ideas concerning the growth of the fruits of the field.

NOTES

[1] Moche culture, so named after its most important center, Moche, is the culture called »Proto Chimu« by Max Uhle, »Early Chimu« by A. L. Kroeber and Ph. A. Means and »Mochica« by R. Larco Hoyle. Since this ancient, advanced culture was first closely delineated by Max Uhle's excavations at Moche, it seems terminologically consistent to name it after its place of discovery, as is customary in Peruvian archaeology, particularly, since neither the ethnic nor the linguistic position of its people is known.

[2] Schmidt 1929 Fig. 197/2.

[3] Sincere thanks are offered here to Dr. H. D. Disselhoff, director of the Berlin Museum für Völkerkunde, for the permission to publish for the first time the projection made by Miss E. Armgardt.

[4] Kutscher 1954 Pl. 33 C–D.

[5] »Faces« here signifies the two vase sides which run parallel to the axis of the handle and which bear the principle decoration.

[6] Schmidt 1929 Figs. 156/3, 159/1.

[7] Jiménez Borja 1938 Fig. on p. (110).

[8] Kroeber 1930 P. XV. Schaedel 1951.

[9] Jiménez Borja 1955 Figs. on pp. 124–126.

[10] Jiménez Borja 1938 p. (101).

[11] Kutscher 1954 Pls. 7, 14 C.

[12] Baessler 1902 Pl. 24/112, 115.

[13] Kutscher 1954 Pls. 6 B – 8 A.

[14] Kutscher 1950 a, pp. 215 et seq.

[15] Kutscher 1954 Pl. 54 A.

[16] Jiménez Borja 1938 Fig. on p. (108).

[17] Kutscher 1950 Figs. 69, 72.

[18] Kroeber 1930 Pl. XV, second row.

[19] Larco Hoyle 1939 Pl. XXXI. Kutscher 1954 Pls. 30–31.

[20] Jiménez Borja 1938 Figs. on pp. (93), (111).

[21] To the director of the Museo Nacional de Antropología e Arqueología, my esteemed friend, Dr. Jorge C. Muelle, hearty thanks are due for kind permission to publish the projection which I made in August 1954 in Lima.

[22] Jiménez Borja 1938 Fig. on p. (9).

[23] Baessler 1902 Pl. 22/98. Baessler 1902. Pls. 4/16–17,5/21–23.

[24] Baessler 1902 Pl. 22/96.

[25] Baessler 1902 Pls. 23/103, 36/195.

[26] Jiménez Borja 1938 Fig. on p. (93). Kutscher 1954 Pl. 19 B, fourth figure.

[27] Yacovleff-Herrera 1934 Fig. 20. Jiménez Borja 1938 Fig. on p. (93).

[28] Kutscher 1950 Fig. 62. Larco Hoyle 1946 Fig. 20 c, second house.

[29] Montell 1929 Fig. 49.

[30] Kutscher 1950 Fig. 30.

[31] Jiménez Borja 1938 Fig. on p. (101).

[32] Jiménez Borja 1938 Fig. on p. (14).

[33] Kutscher 1954 Pl. 72.

[34] Kutscher 1950 Fig. 43.

[35] Kutscher 1954 Pl. 34 A–B.

[36] Kutscher 1954 Pl. 1 A–B.

[37] Jiménez Borja 1938 p. (101).

[38] Jiménez Borja 1955 Figs. on pp. 119–126. Kutscher 1954 Pls. 30–32.

[39] We have to admit that no such game has been reported from the Inca period, but the Inca goldsmiths are supposed to have known how to produce butterflies of sheet gold. Their wings were so delicate that they did not exceed a tenth of a millimeter. Flung into the air, these small images flew about for a while until they fell again to the ground (Wiener 1880 pp. 586–587).

[40] The principle of rotation was known to the ancient Peruvians, although they possessed neither the wheel nor the potter's wheel. Besides the spindle and the drill, we base this conclusion upon the reproduction of a child playing with a top in the Chronicle of Guaman Poma de Ayala (1936 fol. 208). The top, called *pisqoynyo* in Quechua (Rowe 1946 p. 288), is also found among several other tribes in South-America (Cooper 1949 p. 510).

[41] Calancha 1638 Lib. III Cap. II p. 556 rt. col. Kutscher 1950 p. 100.

[42] Kutscher 1550 a p. 224.

[43] Kutscher 1950 pp. 218 et seq.

[44] Kutscher 1954 Pl. 72.

BIBLIOGRAPHY

Baessler, Arthur: 1902. »Altperuanische Kunst. Beiträge zur Archäologie des Inca-Reichs.« Berlin-Leipzig. Band I–IV.

Calancha, Antonio de la: 1638. »Corónica moralizada del orden de San Agustín en el Perú, con sucesos egenplares en esta monarquiá.« Barcelona. Tomo I.

Cooper, John M.: 1949. »Games and Gambling.« Handbook of South American Indians. (Smithsonian Institution. Bureau of American Ethnology. Bulletin 143.) Washington. Vol. 5. pp. 503–524.

Guaman Poma de Ayala, Felipe: 1936. »Nueva Corónica y buen gobierno. Codex Péruvien Illustré.« Travaux et Mémoires de l'Institut d'Ethnologie. Paris. Tome XXIII.

Jiménez Borja, Arturo: 1938. »Moche«. Lima. (No pagination.)

Jiménez Borja, Arturo: 1955. »La Danza en el antiguo Perú. Epoca preinca.« Revista del Museo Nacional. Lima. Tomo XXIV. pp. 111–136.

Kroeber, Alfred Louis: 1930. »Archaeological Explorations in Peru. Part II: The Northern Coast.« Chicago Field Museum of Natural History. Anthropology, Memoirs. Chicago. Vol. II, No. 2.

Kutscher, Gerdt: 1950. »Chimu. Eine altindianische Hochkultur.« Berlin.

Kutscher, Gerdt: 1950a. »Sakrale Wettläufe bei den frühen Chimu (Nord–Peru).« Beiträge zur Gesellungs- und Völkerwissenschaft. Festschrift zum 80. Geburtstag von Professor Richard Thurnwald. Berlin. pp. 209–226.

Kutscher, Gerdt: 1954. »Nordperuanische Keramik. Figürlich verzierte Gefässe der Früh-Chimu – Cerámica del Perú septentrional. Figuras ornamentales en vasijas de los Chimúes antigous.« Monumenta Americana. Berlin. Band I.

Larco Hoyle, Rafael: 1939. »Los Mochicas.« Lima. Tomo II.—

Larco Hoyle, Rafael: 1946. »A Culture Sequence for the North Coast of Perú.« Handbook of South American Indians. (Smithsonian Institution. Bureau of American Ethnology. Bulletin 143). Washington. Vol. 2. pp. 149–175.

Montell, Gösta: 1929. »Dress and Ornaments in American Peru. Archaeological and Historical Studies.« Göteborg.

Rowe, John Howland: 1946. »Inca Culture at the Time of the Spanish Conquest.« Handbook of South American Indians. (Smithsonian Institution. Bureau of American Ethnology. Bulletin 143.) Washington. Vol. 2. pp. 183–330.

Schaedel, Richard P.: 1951. »Mochica Murals at Pañamarca.« Archaeology. Cambridge, Mass. Vol. IV. pp. 145–154.

Schmidt, Max: 1929. »Kunst und Kultur des alten Peru.« Berlin.

Wiener, Charles: 1880. »Pérou et Bolivie. Récit de Voyage suivi d'Études Archéologiques et Ethnographiques et de Notes sur l'Écriture et les Langues des Populations Indiennes.« Paris.

Yacovleff, Eugenio – Herrera, Fortunato: 1934. »El Mundo vegetal de los antiguos Peruanos.« Revista del Museo Nacional de Arqueología. Lima. Tomo III, No. 3. pp. 241–322. Tomo IV, No. 1. pp. 29–102.

TYPES OF BALL COURTS IN THE HIGHLANDS OF GUATEMALA

A. Ledyard Smith

Types of Ball Courts in the Highlands of Guatemala

The ball court was one of the first structures of ancient Middle American architecture that could be assigned a function. Carl Sapper and Edward Seler recognized their purpose; some thirty years later Robert Burkitt discussed the problem and in 1932 Frans Blom wrote his general survey of the Maya ball game in which he listed the courts in the Maya area.

Ball-court structures date from the Classic Period to the Spanish Conquest although the game itself is of great antiquity going well back into Pre-Classic times. Roman Piña Chan[1] shows a figurine from Tlatilco, in the Valley of Mexico, which depicts a ball player with a kneepad on right leg and what appears to be a ball in his right hand. The ball game, in various forms, also had a wide distribution in native America, extending into South America, the Antilles, and North America as well as Middle America. The present paper is limited to a discussion of the various types of ball courts found in the highlands of Guatemala.

When Blom published his paper on the Maya ball game, thirty-nine ball courts were known in the Maya area with only eleven in the Highlands of Guatemala. Since that time at least 132 ball courts, most of which fall into five categories or types, have been found in the Guatemala Highlands. In classifying them, Jorge Acosta, Linton Satterthwaite, and Acosta and Moedano have used as criteria the differences in structural profiles. I have used both profiles plus the over-all shape of the court in my classification.

The five types found in the Highlands of Guatemala have been called open-end, open-end *a*, enclosed, enclosed *a*, and "palangana." In an earlier publication[2] I distinguished four types: open-end, open-end *a*, enclosed, and intermediate. This classification has been changed for the present article. Two new types, see above, have been added and the "intermediate" classification has been replaced by the term "miscellaneous," a category that takes care of ball courts that are borderline cases and cannot be considered as belonging

a

b

FIG. 1. Chalchitan and Huil. *a:* Looking south at ball-court group at Chalchitan, Dept. of Huehuetenango. Open-end *a* type ball court. Restoration drawing by Tatiana Proskouriakoff. *b:* Looking southeast at Huil, Dept. of Quiché, showing open-end *a* type ball court. Restoration drawing by Tatiana Proskouriakoff.

to a definite type. These types will be defined below and discussed separately in detail.

The nomenclature of the various parts of a court is shown in figure 9; and for the different profiles of court types, see figure 8. The table at the end lists the 106 sites and the 133 ball courts upon which the types have been based. It gives, where possible, the ceramic periods of pottery recovered from sites, the type of ball court, and the main source of information. It should be understood that most of the pottery collections are from the surface; therefore, dating is open to revision. Time spans of the ceramic periods and a short definition of the several ball court types are also given in the table.

In discussing types of courts certain data are referred to. These data pertaining to courts are taken mostly from Acosta and Moedano. They are: *1*) geographical area; *2*) location; *3*) period; *4*) form of court; *5*) cross-section; *6*) longitudinal sections; *7*) orientation; *8*) degree of slope of playing wall; *9*) stone rings; *10*) tenoned heads set in playing walls or benches; *11*) alley markers; *12*) mortises to hold markers; *13*) hole in center of playing alley; *14*) niches; *15*) sculptured stones; *16*) stairs; *17*) buildings on ranges or at ends of courts; *18*) material used in construction; and *19*) relation of court to other structures. In the case of orientation there does not appear to be any definite pattern or custom so no further mention will be made concerning this datum. Benches at the face are from 20 to 80 cm. high. There seems to be no difference in this feature between the types except that in the open-end *a* ball courts benches never exceed a height of 50 cm. Another measurement that need not be mentioned later is bench width which may be anywhere from 1.20 to 3.60 m. The type that consistently has the narrowest bench is the enclosed type where the width never exceeds 1.80 m. All other types have benches from 1.80 to 3.60 m. wide. The only exception is the court at Tzicuay, one of the miscellaneous courts, where the bench width is only 1.55 m. wide.

OPEN-END TYPE BALL COURTS

The open-end ball court is the simplest of the types found in the Highlands of Guatemala (fig. 4, *a, b*). It consists of two parallel ranges of equal height and length bordering the playing alley. The ranges are from 24 to 32 m. long and, with the exception of the ball court at Nebaj, Group A, which has ranges about 9 m. high, average between 2.5 and 3 m. in height. The playing alley varies from 6 to 8 m. across from bench face to bench face. There are no walls defining end zones. It is possible that end zones were delimited by lines marked on the ground, but none were found. The profile

a

b

FIG. 2. Chutixtiox and Vicaveval. *a:* Looking north at Chutixtiox, Dept. of Quiché, showing enclosed type ball court. Restoration drawing by Tatiana Proskouriakoff. *b:* Looking southwest at Vicaveval, Dept. of Quiché, showing enclosed type ball court. Restoration drawing by Tatiana Proskouriakoff.

of this type ball court has a sloping bench face, a level bench top, and a sloping playing wall which sometimes had a vertical molding measuring .30 to .40 m. high, at the top (fig. 8, *a, b*). The slope of the playing wall varies from 45 to 59 degrees. This style profile is fairly similar to Acosta's Type A.[3] In some instances the benches extend around the ends of the playing walls. An example of this is shown in the ball court at Chichén which is situated on the west edge of that site (fig. 4, *b*). In those cases where it has been possible to note such details the backs of the ranges were terraced.

There are 19 open-end ball courts listed in the table at the end of this report of which two, Las Tinajas and Bucaral, are questioned, the former because it was badly cut away by farming activity, the latter because it was sketched from memory. Most of these courts are situated in valleys and were probably constructed in Late Classic times. An exception to this is La Lagunita where only Post-Classic pottery was found. Open-end ball courts are usually located at the edge of building groups but they occur, occasionally, near the center of building clusters (fig. 4). Because of their valley locations which are also the most desirable places for farming, many have been badly damaged and undoubtedly some completely razed. This type ball court has a wide distribution, being found in the Departments of Huehuetenango, Alta Verapaz, and Progreso as well as in the Sacapulas, Nebaj-Cotzal-Chajual, and San Andres Sajcabaja regions of the Department of Quiché.

Where masonry was visible it usually consisted of an outer facing of rough flat stones laid against a fill of earth or water-rolled stones. Although found in only a few cases, most ball courts probably had plaster surfaces. In some instances well-cut stones were used in the construction. The best-preserved open-end ball court is the one on the west edge of the ruins of Chichén. Here the masonry is a mixture of worked and unworked blocks. Large slabs were used in the playing walls, some extending from the bench to the vertical upper molding, 1.80 m. above. The central slab in the west playing wall has the profile of a bird carved on it. This carved stone has the same position as the ones in the playing walls of Strs. R-11a and R-11b at Piedras Negras[4] and may well have served as a marker also. The only other marker found in an open-end type ball court was a stone jaguar head with a large tenon found at the base of the center of the south side of the southernmost court at Chalchitan, Strs. 35 and 36.[5]

No traces of superstructures were seen on the ranges of this type of court.

OPEN-END "A" TYPE BALL COURTS

This type is an open-end ball court with one extremity leading into an adjoining plaza which normally has an altar platform in its center (fig. 1,

a

b

Fig. 3. Xolchun and Zaculeu. *a:* Looking south at Xolchun and Pacot on hill beyond, Dept. of Quiché. Ball court is in the miscellaneous group. Restoration drawing by Tatiana Proskouriakoff. *b:* Looking northeast at Zaculeu, Dept. of Huehuetenango from top of Structure 2. Ball court is in the miscellaneous group. Courtesy of United Fruit Company.

a and *b*). Often the plaza is completely surrounded by walls giving the impression of a sunken court as at Chalchitan (fig. 1, *a*). The ranges of all but Chalchitan vary from 17 to 26 m. in length and average between 2 and 3.50 m. in height. Chalchitan has ranges 5 m. high. The playing alley, where it was possible to get an accurate measurement between the bench faces, is a fairly consistent 6 to 7 m. across. With the exception of the two ball courts at San Francisco del Norte, and possibly at Acihtz, which have low enclosing walls forming end zones at that end of the court not leading into the adjoining plaza, there are no walls defining end zones connected with open-end *a* ball courts. These end walls at San Francisco del Norte are the only feature that differentiates these courts from others of the open-end *a* type. As suggested for the open-end ball courts, end zones may have been marked out with lines on the ground.

The profile of this type, which is quite similar to that of the open-end courts, has, with one exception, a vertical bench face. This face rises to a level or a slightly sloping bench top. The sloping playing wall has a vertical upper molding that projects 4 or 5 cm. from the playing wall and rises from 40 to 75 cm. above it (fig. 8, *d*). The exception is the court at Chalchitan, where the bench face is sloping (fig. 8, *c*). The playing wall of this court has a slope which varies from 45 to 65 degrees. This playing wall was built over an earlier wall of the Chalchitan court.[6]

In two instances, Huil and Oncap, benches extend around the ends of the playing walls.

Stairways occur on the ends and backs of ranges. One of the most elaborate stairways is on the back of the ball court at Huil. This is a stairway flanked by balustrades and divided in the center by a ramp with masonry block half way up the structure and another at the upper end of the ramp (fig. 1, *b*).

At six sites the court ranges had the remains of construction on top. At Acihtz and Chichel one of the ranges supported a low platform, and at Caquixay one carried a platform with the foundation walls of a superstructure on three sides. At Chipal there was evidence of a superstructure on both ranges. These had long narrow rooms opening on the side and overlooking the playing alley. The base of what had once been a stucco figure rested in the center of the top of the southwest range. At Chalchitan each range carries a long platform 40 cm. high that probably served as the foundation for buildings (see fig. 1, *a*). Both ranges at Huil had superstructures facing on the playing alley. The one on the southwest side is a long narrow room with

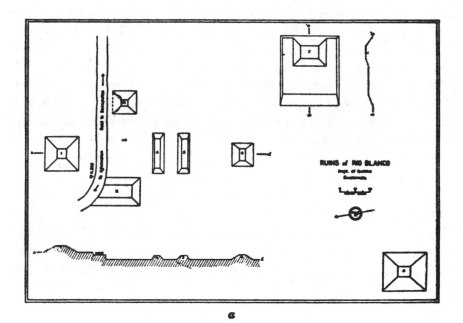

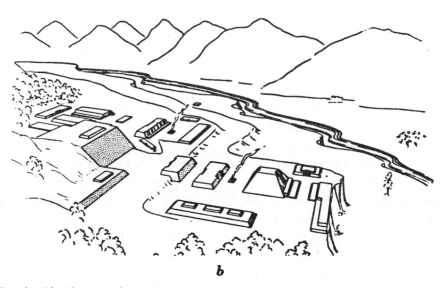

Fig. 4. Río Blanco and Chichén. *a:* Plan of Río Blanco, Dept. of Quiché. Structures 4 and 5 are the two ranges of an open-end ball court. *a,* small stone monument. *b:* Looking south at Chichén, Dept. of Alta Verapaz, showing two open-end ball courts, one on the west edge of the site and the other on the east. Rendering by Kisa Noguchi Sasaki of restoration by Stephen F. Borhegyi.

a doorway in the center of the back wall. Except for a small section of wall at either end, the front of this room was open. In the center of the room, in line with markers on the playing walls, is a round altar supporting a human figure lying on its back with legs hanging over the edge. Both altar and figure are of stucco. The superstructure on the northeast range at Huil consists of two long narrow rooms with a common medial wall but no front wall. One room looks on the playing alley and the other on a small court to the northeast of the ball court.

With the exception of two courts, Huitchun and Mutchil, which are on hills, the 18 open-end *a* type ball courts recorded are located in valleys or on side slopes of valleys. From the ceramic evidence they were constructed in either Post-Classic or Protohistoric times. Fourteen of these courts are in the Nebaj-Cotzal-Chajual region of the Department of Quiché. Of the remaining four, two are in the Department of Huehuetenango, one in the Department of Alta Verapaz, and one in the Department of Quiché in the San Andres Sajcabaja region.

In the courts of this type where masonry could be seen, it was of rough stone slabs laid up in mud mortar and covered with a smooth layer of plaster. At Pantzac, block masonry, nicely faced on the exposed surface, was used. The only paint on an open-end *a* ball court was found on the vertical molding above the playing wall of the southwest range at Oncap. Here are the remains of a red line, 2.5 cm. wide, with a row of dots, 5 cm. in diameter, above it.

There are several instances of markers located in the center of the two playing walls where they meet the upper molding. At Chalchitan, two stone jaguar heads, one still with its tenon intact, were found at the base of the playing walls near the center of the court. A hole in the middle of the playing wall of the east range, just below the vertical molding, probably held the head (figs. 1, *a* and 8, *c*, *1*). At Caquixay in the center of each playing wall, starting on the upper vertical molding and carrying onto the low sloping area, were the remains of what apparently were large stucco human heads with feathered headdresses and earplugs. At Huil, stucco markers adhered to the ranges of the court in the same position as those at Caquixay (figs. 1, *b* and 8, *d*, *2*). At Oncap, a rectangular hole in the center of the vertical upper molding of the playing wall may have held a marker.

An interesting feature in the open-end *a* ball court at Chalchitan is a circular depression 60 cm. in diameter and 25 cm. deep[7] in the plaster floor exactly in the middle of the playing alley. Both Theodore Stern[8] and Alfred Tozzer[9] mention a central opening in the playing field. Although such a

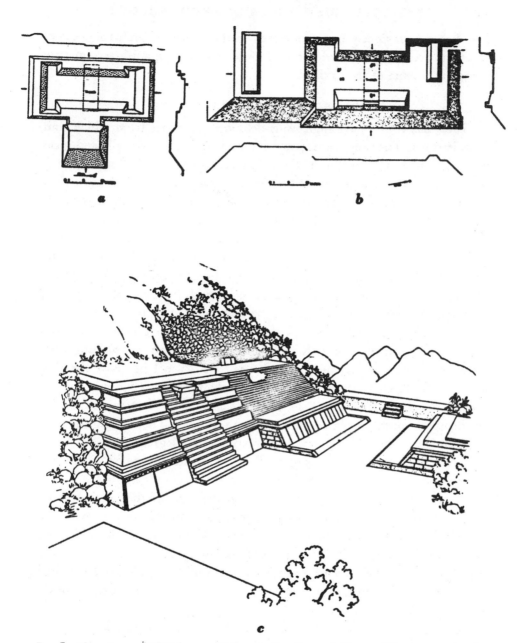

Fig. 5. Guaytan and Chijolom. *a:* Ball court 1 at Guaytan, Dept. of Progreso enclosed *a*
type. A, remains of playing alley floor (?). B, remains of bench floor of hard gray
adobe. C, gravel and dirt fill with a few large stones. *b:* Ball court at Guaytan, Dept.
of Progreso. Ball court is in miscellaneous group. A, natural rock. 1–5, tennoned serpent
heads. *c:* Looking south at Chijolom, Dept. of Alta Verapaz. Ball court is in the
miscellaneous group. Rendering by Kisa Noguchi Sasaki of restoration by Stephen F.
Borhegyi.

hole has not previously been uncovered in the course of archaeological excavations, according to Stern it is mentioned in certain Spanish accounts and is shown in some of the Codices.

ENCLOSED-TYPE BALL COURTS

These ball courts have high walls defining end zones from which stairways lead out. The ranges are always higher than these end walls and measure from 3 to 5 m. in height. The end walls are about 1 to 2.10 m. Although the two ranges of a court are of the same height, this is not always true of the end zone walls. For example, in the enclosed ball court at Chutixtiox, the walls of the end zones are 2.10 m. at one end and only .95 m. at the other. The width of the playing alley from bench face to bench face may be anywhere from 6 to 9.50 m. across, and the ranges vary from 20 to 30 m. long. End zones measure anywhere from about 9 to 19 m. across and 2.50 to 7.50 m. in depth. The plan of the enclosed ball court, with its long narrow playing alley and expanded end zones, takes the form of a "capital I" (figs. 2, *a, b;* 6, *a, b;* 7, *a, b*). The profile consists of a vertical bench face, a level bench top, and a sloping playing wall with a vertical upper molding that projects a few centimeters from the playing wall and rises from .45 to 1 m. above the playing wall (fig. 8, *e*). With the exception of the ball court at Chutixtiox, which has a sloping bench face (fig. 8, *f*), all the enclosed-type courts have the same profile which might be placed under Acosta's Type A. The slope in the playing wall varies from 64 degrees at Chutixtiox to 85 degrees at Mixco Viejo. The average angle of the playing wall is steeper in this type than in any other except the enclosed *a* which has a vertical playing wall.

Benches may or may not extend around the ends of the playing walls. Stairways were used to enter the end zones and to reach the top of the ranges. The former were placed in the center of the back wall of the end zones and the latter might be at the ends of the ranges, as at Comitancillo (fig. 7, *b*), or on the back of a range, as at Chuitinamit (fig. 6, *b*). Range backs were usually terraced and in most cases could have been used as means of access to the top.

Only four enclosed ball courts show evidence of superstructures on their ranges. At Chutixtiox and Comitancillo these were long narrow buildings indicated by low walls on three sides. The open side faced the playing alley (figs. 2, *a;* 7, *b*). At Chuitinamit the ball court in Group C has four small rectangular platforms, 40 cm. high, in line with, and equally spaced along, the top of the ranges (fig. 6, *b*). In the court in Group B at Mixco Viejo both ranges have a summit wall extending almost the whole length of the

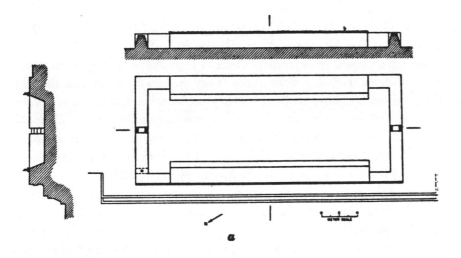

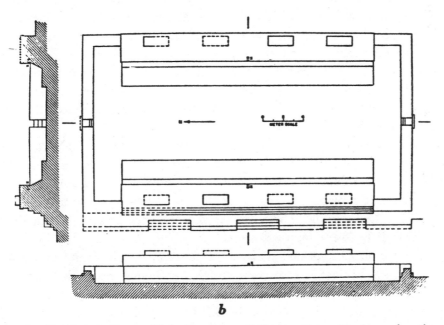

FIG. 6. Chuitinamit, Dept. of Baja Verapaz. *a:* Ball court, Group H, plan and sections. Enclosed type. *a,* drain. *b,* loose slabs placed along top of playing wall to make vertical upper zone or molding. *b:* Ball court, Group C, plan and sections. Enclosed type. X, mortise.

side farthest from the playing alley. Against this wall is a bench of the same length (fig. 7, *a*).

Of the 15 enclosed-type ball courts all but three, Comitancillo, Xolchun, and Patzac, are on hilltops and are defense sites. Even these three are on plateaus which could be defended. There is little doubt that all these courts were constructed in Protohistoric times. They are usually located on the edge of the group of buildings with which they are associated; but in a few cases, such as at Utatlan and Vicaveval, they are more centrally placed. Their distribution in the Highlands of Guatemala is fairly wide. They are found in the Departments of Guatemala, Chimaltenango, Huehuetenango, Baja Verapaz, and Quiché, especially in the Sacapulas region of the latter.

Many of the enclosed-type ball courts were in a very good state of preservation. Possibly, this is because they are located in fairly inaccessible places which are not well-suited to agriculture or grazing. Masonry of the courts varies a good deal in the type of rock used. Presumably, this depended upon what was available. For example, at Comitancillo, Xolpacol, Chutixtiox, Pacot and Vicaveval the masonry consists of rough slabs. At Mixco Viejo the slabs were well worked. At Xolchun well-cut stone blocks were used while at Chuitinamit schistose slabs were laid up horizontally. At Patzac, although the buildings were stripped, quantities of well-cut and faced tufa blocks were found. All stones were laid in mud mortar, and the walls were surfaced with one or two layers of thick plaster. At Comitancillo, traces of a design in red, yellow and blue were found on and directly below the vertical molding above the playing wall.

No markers occurred in or near the ball courts but they all had, when the wall was intact, mortises in the center of the playing walls, either in the upper vertical molding or just below it. The only possibility of a marker was the remains of a plaster-covered stone "adorno" below the hole in the playing wall at Comitancillo. These holes or mortises average about 40 cm. deep and from 20 to 40 cm. high and wide.

The fact that in not one instance was a tenoned stone found in a court is interesting because it adds some weight to Blom's theory that portable markers (he says rings) may have been used.[10] In the exact center of the early floor of the playing alley of the ball court at Xolchun, Department of Huehuetenango, there is a hole 20 cm. in diameter and 35 cm. deep.[11] This is the second case of a hole being found in this position; the other was in the open-end *a* court at Chalchitan. It is obvious that these enclosed courts must have had some method of disposing of water. Drains were found in the corners of the end zones, at Xolpacol, Xolchun, and Chuitinamit. Other

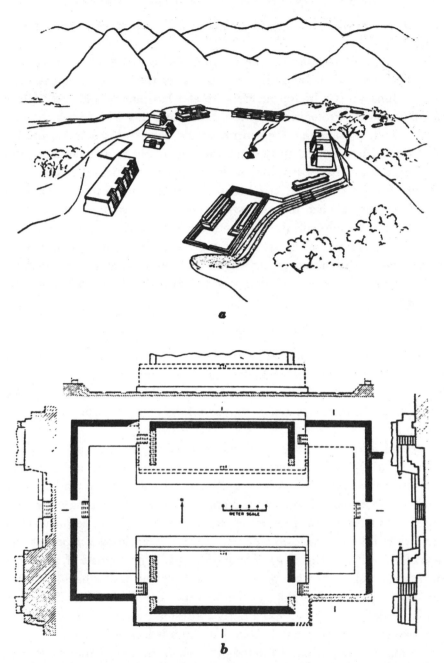

FIG. 7. Mixco Viejo and Comitancillo. *a*: Looking north at Group B, Mixco Viejo, Dept. of Chimaltenango. Enclosed type ball court in foreground. Rendering by Kisa Noguchi Sasaki of restoration by Stephen F. Borhegyi. *b*: Comitancillo, Dept. of Quiché, ball court, plan and sections. Enclosed type. 1, mortise. 2, reconstruction of possible type of carved stone and tenon set into mortise.

courts must have had drains, but were not seen as their corners were covered with debris.

The ball court at Chinautla, not far from Guatemala City, is questioned in the table because although Shook says it is of the late type, it has open ends.[12] Chinautla is a hilltop defense site and has pottery and architecture that belong in the Protohistoric Period. Discussing this with Shook, he told me that it was possible that the court once did have enclosed end zones because one end had broken away when the edge of the ravine caved in, and the other may well have been completely destroyed by agriculture. The court in figure 6, *a,* in Group H, at Chuitinamit, is shown because it was still under construction when the site was abandoned, indicating that this type of structure was being built right up until the Spanish Conquest. It is almost identical to the other ball court at the same site (fig. 6, *b*), but it has no benches, no plaster surfacing anywhere, and no vertical upper molding. There are slabs, however, laid along the top as if they were to be used for this purpose.

ENCLOSED "A" TYPE BALL COURTS

Very little excavation has been carried on in this type ball court. A trench was dug across the middle of Ball Court I at Asunción Mita[13] and Ball Court I at Guaytan,[14] but no court was thoroughly dug so, although we have data on the most essential parts, our information is not as complete as it might be.

The end zones are usually small but well defined by low walls about .50 to 2 m. in height. In a few instances one end may be as high as the ranges which are always the same, from 2 to 3 m. The width of the playing alley from bench face to bench face varies from 6 to 9 m., and the ranges measure from 18 to 36 m. in length. The end zones are from 3 to 8.50 m. deep and 11 to 19 m. wide. Like the enclosed-type ball court, the enclosed *a* type has the shape of a "capital I" (fig. 5, *a*). The profile (fig. 8, *g*) consists of a vertical bench face, a sloping bench top, and a vertical playing wall which is similar to Acosta's Type B.[15] The slope of the benches varies from 17 to 23 degrees and the vertical playing wall has a fairly consistent height of 1 m.

In two cases a small mound about 1 m. high is located in a central position on top of a range. On a mound set back from, but connected to, the south range of Ball Court I at Guaytan (fig. 5, *a*), slightly west of its center, is a low rectangular platform which may once have carried a structure overlooking the playing alley.

All of the eight enclosed *a* type ball courts are located in valleys, one near San Pedro Pinula in the Department of Jalapa, two near Asunción Mita, in

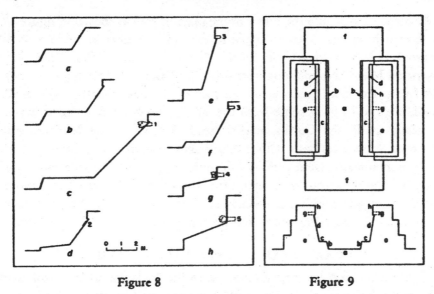

Figure 8   Figure 9

FIG. 8. Sections through center of one side of various types of ball courts. *a*, Chuchun, open-end type. *b*, Chichén, Structures 1 and 2, open-end type. *c*, Chalchitan, Structures 23 and 24, early phase, open-end *a* type. *d*, Huil, open-end *a* type. *e*, Xolchun, Dept. of Huehuetenango, enclosed type. *f*, Chutixtiox, enclosed type. *g*, enclosed *a* type. *h*, a possible section of the "palangana" type. 1, probable portion of stone jaguar head with tenon. 2, remains of stucco figure. 3, mortise. 4, probable position of stone snake head with tenon in enclosed *a* type ball court. 5, probable position of stone head with tenon in "palangana" type ball court.

FIG. 9. Schematic ball court with nomenclature. *a*, playing alley. *b*, bench face. *c*, bench top. *d*, playing wall. *e*, range. *f*, end zone. *g*, mortise. *h*, vertical upper zone or molding of playing wall.

the Department of Jutiapa, and five in the Motagua Valley in the Department of Progreso. Most of these sites are small groups with the ball court either on the edge or near the center. There does not seem to be any particular position. These courts were probably constructed in Late Classic times.

Not much can be said about the masonry used in enclosed *a* ball courts as little was showing. In Ball Court I at Asunción Mita the bench face is built of slate slabs laid in clay mixed with lime,[16] and the sloping bench tops are paved with fist-sized, brown lava cobbles except for the top of the bench face which is paved with slate slabs. At Guaytan, Ball Court I, the benches were faced with thin slabs of schistose rock set vertically. The only trace of surfacing on the bench tops was a layer of hard gray adobe 10 cm. thick.

Stone markers were found with several courts. At San Pedro Pinula a stone head with a tenon was discovered lying in the center of the ball court. The head is of a snake with a human face in its open mouth.[17] The tenon is constructed to fit into the center of the playing wall as shown in figure 8, *g*. A serpent head with a tenon made in the same manner as the one at San Pedro Pinula was found just outside the west wall of Ball Court II at Asunción Mita.[18] No markers were found in Ball Court I at Asunción Mita, but two parrot heads with a human face in the open beak, in the nearby town, are said to have come from the site. These heads are made to stand vertically as do the Copán marker heads.[19] One of the four unnamed Motagua Valley sites has a tenoned stone snake's head with a human face in its open mouth associated with its ball court. Fragments of two human heads sculptured in tuffaceous rock lay on the surface of Ball Court I at Guaytan, but their original position is unknown. They are quite unlike the tenoned heads found in the other courts and probably were not used as markers.[20]

"PALANGANA" TYPE BALL COURTS

Little excavation has been carried on in the "palangana" type ball court. The name "palangana" (wash basin) has been used because it is the name by which this kind of construction is known among the inhabitants of the area in which most of them occur. Only four of these courts have been tested; three at Kaminaljuyu and one at Zacualpa. These excavations consisted of trenching across the center of the courts.

The "palangana" court is a rectangular enclosure, with no indication of end zones, surrounded by walls that normally are of the same height. According to Shook,[21] who located most of them, the ball court at Cotio is typical of 35 other "palanganas" in the Guatemala Valley. Its playing field is about 9.50 m. across and 33 m. long, and the surrounding walls rise 1.50 m. Courts A and B at Kaminaljuyu are larger than the average court, the former having a playing field 10 by 42 m. and the latter 16 by 44 m. The walls of Ball Court A are about 4.50 m. above the court floor.

What may be the largest "palangana" court is not far from Kaminaljuyu Court A. According to Lothrop's plan,[22] its playing field measures 45 by 110 m., about twice the size of the Great Ball Court at Chichén Itzá. If it truly is a ball court, and there is no reason to believe it is not as it has all the features of the typical "palangana," it is the largest of all ball courts so far reported from Mesoamerica. Three huge stone statues found at the southwest end of the court, and part of a large carved stone altar on the southeast side, were probably not in their original position. The former may have been originally on the mound enclosing the southwest end and the latter on top of the southeast range.

Though no exact measurements of the profile of a "palangana" were obtained, we were able, from our excavations, to get a few hints as to what it may have been like. It consisted of a vertical bench face, a wide sloping bench top, and a vertical playing wall (fig. 8, *h*). This profile is very much like the profile of the enclosed *a* type ball court and Acosta's Type B.[23]

There are 52 recorded "palangana" type ball courts, two-thirds of which are in the Guatemala Valley. The rest, with the exception of a few in the Department of Guatemala, are located in the Department of Sacatepéquez, Chimaltenanga, Jalapa, Santa Rosa and in the Zacualpa and San Andres Sajcabaja regions of Quiché. From the ceramic evidence these ball courts were constructed during the late Classic Period.

In all but a very few instances "palangana" courts were made without the use of stone and were probably surfaced with adobe plaster.

In eight cases, including the extra large court at Kaminaljuyu, "palangana" courts have mounds on one side; and in one case, Ball Court A at Kaminaljuyu, a mound rests on the enclosing wall at the end. These mounds are located near the centers of the walls, and probably they were platforms supporting buildings of perishable materials.

As all the "palangana" courts are completely enclosed, they undoubtedly had drains. We found one in Ball Court B of Kaminaljuyu.

Stone markers were found in Ball Courts A, B and C at Kaminaljuyu. These markers were carved in the forms of parrot, snake and human heads. All had tenons constructed to fit in the playing wall as shown in figure 8, *h*. It is likely that excavation of other courts of this type would yield more markers of this kind.

MISCELLANEOUS BALL COURTS

Of the 132 ball courts considered in this report 20 have been placed in a miscellaneous group because they do not fit any of the five types into which the rest have been divided. In most cases it is the plan rather than the profile that is difficult to place in a type. In discussing these courts I suggest the types which they most closely resemble.

The ball court at Zaculeu in the Department of Huehuetenango[24] has a profile similar to the enclosed-type court at Chutixtiox; but, although its end zones are well defined, giving it the shape of a "capital I," it is not completely closed. A wide gap exists at one end between the walls forming the end zones and the two ranges. Ceramic evidence places its construction in Post-Classic time. It resembles the enclosed type more closely than any of the others, and it may be a precursor of that type. Three other sites, also in the Department of Huehuetenango, have ball courts resembling the enclosed type. They are: Piol,[25] where the end zones are marked by low walls; Xetenan,[26] with the end zones defined with low walls but not completely closed at one end; and Uaxac Canal,[27] with possible low walls defining the end zones and a small platform at each end. Two other courts, also with low walls marking end zones and resembling the enclosed-type court, occur at Pantzac and Patzac in the San Andres Sajcabaja region of the Department of Quiché.[28] These courts all date from the Post-Classic and Proto-historic periods.

The ball court at Tzicuay, Department of Quiché in the Nebaj-Cotzal-Chajul region, was probably built in Post-Classic times.[29] Its profile is similar to that of the enclosed-type court, and it has low walls defining end zones. The southern extremity has a gap between the west range and the wall on the west end of the end zone. Benches extend around the extremities of the ranges. Chuitinamit, also in the Department of Quiché but in the Sacapulas region, has a ball court that resembles the enclosed type.[30] It is a defense site with Post-Classic and Protohistoric pottery. The end zones of the court are defined by a combination of high walls and terrace edges.

Another site in the Sacapulas region, Xolchun, is closest to the open-end *a* type.[31] Before it was partly cut away by the river there had been an end zone at the east defined by a wall and the side of another building. The west end opens into a plaza with an altar platform in line with the playing alley. The plaza, however, is not as clearly associated with the court as is the case with the open-end *a* type. Although the ball court at Chijolom, in the Department of Alta Verapaz,[32] has one enclosed end zone, it is more like the open-end court on the east edge of the ruins of Chichén (fig. 4, *b*). The limestone masonry, the most beautifully cut and fitted I have seen in any part of the Guatemala Highlands, was laid without the use of mortar and had no plaster facing. Like Chichén, the benches extend around the ends of the ranges, and the faces of the playing walls are made of huge single stones extending from bench top to the vertical upper molding.

There are two ball courts at Iximche, Department of Chimaltenango, the ancient capital of the Cakchiquels. Being a conquest period site, these were most certainly constructed in Protohistoric times. According to Pollock[33] both courts are the same: small, completely enclosed, and without end zones. In this respect they are like the "palangana" type, but they differ in that the side mounds are considerably higher than the end mounds. No profile is given, but it is stated that the inner surfaces of the side mounds may have been vertical.

The remaining eight miscellaneous ball courts are all in the Motagua

Valley between Progreso and Zacapa. Their profiles, where visible, are of the enclosed *a* type, but the shapes of the courts vary. At Guaytan, Ball Court 2, the end zones are defined by a combination of walls and terrace edges (fig. 5, *b*). At El Terron one end has a well-defined end zone enclosed by walls and the other has only a partly enclosed end zone.[34] At La Vega de Coban one end of the court is open and the other has an enclosed zone.[35] Another court at one of the five unnamed sites in the valley is like that at La Vega de Coban; three others have parallel ranges and unattached mounds at either end; and one is open at both ends. This last was not considered an open-end court, however, because its profile resembles the enclosed *a* style. In fact all eight of these courts are closest to this enclosed *a* type.[36]

Several of the miscellaneous ball courts had construction on one or both of their ranges. At Zaculeu both ranges had long structures formed by low walls with the open sides of the buildings facing the playing alley (fig. 3, *b*). At Tzicuay the east range supported the low walls of a long narrow room with a square platform in the center.[37] At Chijolom both ranges carried long platforms (fig. 5, *c*), and at El Terron there was a square platform on the east range at its south end.[38]

The only markers associated with the miscellaneous courts were in Ball Court 2 at Guaytan. Here five sculptures of tuffaceous rock were found in the court in the positions shown in figure 5, *b*. They represent tenoned snakes' heads, three with human heads in their open jaws.[39] Probably, they were tenoned horizontally into the vertical wall as shown in figure 8, *g*. One would assume that originally there were six heads, three on a side, but we were able to find only five.

SUMMARY

Several features found in ball courts elsewhere are lacking in the ball courts in the Highlands of Guatemala. No stone tenoned rings such as were used in the Mexican Highlands and occasionally in the Maya Lowlands were found. The possibility of portable rings or other type markers that might have been used in the mortises in the enclosed-type courts has already been mentioned. Also lacking are altar-like stones set in the center and at the ends of the playing alley flush with the floor. These markers occur in the Monjas Court at Chichén Itzá, Yucutan; Lubaantun, British Honduras; Tenam Rosario, Chiapas; Yaxchilan, Chiapas; Piedras Negras, Guatemala; and Copán, Honduras. Niches, set generally in the faces of end walls, found at Azompa, Oaxaca, at Tula, and at Monte Alban were absent in all the courts investigated.

Markers occur in ball courts in the Guatemalan Highlands in the form of stone tenoned heads set horizontally in the center of the playing walls near the top in all types except open-end and enclosed. Sometimes elaborate stucco heads were attached to the center of the playing wall where the vertical upper molding begins in open-end *a* type courts. There is also one case of a carved stone laid flat in the lower central part of the playing wall of an open-end court (Chichén).

An interesting feature found, as far as I know, only in two courts in the Highlands of Guatemala, is a hole in the exact center of the playing alley. Tozzer[9] explains it as conceivably being the entrance to the underworld. In discussing it Stern (1948, p. 54) says:

It is striking, therefore, to find Alvarado Tezozomoc, the scion of Aztec royalty, describing the court as having a hole in the center, larger than a bowling ball in diameter, called the *itzampan* (Seler translates this as "place of the skull"). When the court is divided in half he continues, a triangle is drawn about the hole, which is termed the well of water. The details of the play he mentions indicate that both hole and triangle function together in a manner identical with the paired rings described by other writers.

There have been more structural ball courts reported in the Highlands of Guatemala than in any other area of equal size and in this area the Guatemala Valley has the greatest concentration. The most common court is the "palangana" type of which 52 have been found, most of them in the valley of Guatemala. These courts were built in Late Classic times, a period when the ball game must have reached a high point of popularity for it was during this same period the open-end and enclosed *a* type courts were being constructed. With the exception of the two early ball courts at Copán which Stromsvik places in the Early Classic Period (1952), I know of no structural ball courts before the Late Classic Period. In the Late Classic Period, however, they spread all over the Guatemalan Highlands. The open-end court, which in profile is not unlike ball court R-11 at Piedras Negras,[4] was fairly well distributed throughout the area whereas the "palangana" and enclosed *a* types had definite areas where they were concentrated more than others, the former, as mentioned above, in the valley of Guatemala and the latter in the Motagua valley between Progreso and Zacapa. The open-end *a* court first made its appearance in post-Classic times and continued on into the Protohistoric period. It, too, had its area of concentration which was in the Nebaj-Cotzal-Chajul region of the Department of Quiché. Finally, we come to the enclosed-type ball court which was the style court of Protohistoric times and was being built right up to the Spanish Conquest. This type court had a fairly wide distribution throughout the Guatemalan Highlands, although over half of them occur in the Department of Quiché.

It is an interesting fact that during the Late Classic Period ball courts were usually in sites that were in valleys and that by Protohistoric times it was the general rule to build sites, most of which had ball courts, on hill tops and protect them with defense walls. This certainly would indicate a change from a more peaceful existence in Late Classic times to a warlike state in Protohistoric times. It is strange that in both the Highlands of Guatemala and in the Highlands of Mexico the game was so popular in Protohistoric times and that in the Maya Lowlands it seems to have been abandoned. We have plenty of architectural evidence of its popularity in the Guatemalan Highlands and many records and descriptions of ball courts in the Mexican Highlands. Sahagún mentions two courts at Tenochitlan and shows a plan. In the lowlands, such late sites as Tulum and Mayapan have no ball courts. If the game had been an important factor here it seems logical that Landa would have said more about it. He does describe a large house open on all sides where young men came to play various games, among them ball games,[40] but, as Tozzer says, this probably does not refer to a game in a ball court.[41]

SITES WITH BALL COURTS
IN THE
HIGHLANDS OF GUATEMALA

Site	Ceramic Period	Ball Court Type	Reference
DEPARTMENT OF GUATEMALA			
Agua Caliente	Late Classic	"Palangana" (1)	E. M. Shook, 1952
Amatitlan	Late Classic	"Palangana" (2)	E. M. Shook, 1952
Aycinena	Late Classic	"Palangana" (1)	E. M. Shook, 1952
Balsamo	Late Classic	"Palangana" (1)	E. M. Shook, 1952
Castillo	Late Classic	"Palangana" (1)	E. M. Shook, 1952
Cemeterio	Pre- and Late Classic	"Palangana" (1)	E. M. Shook, 1952
Cerritos	Late Classic	"Palangana" (1)	E. M. Shook, 1952
Chinautla	Pre-Classic through Protohistoric	Enclosed (?) (1)	E. M. Shook, 1952
Clara	Late Classic	"Palangana" (1)	E. M. Shook, 1952
Colonia Abril	Late Classic	"Palangana" (1)	E. M. Shook, 1952
Conception	(?)	"Palangana" (1)	E. M. Shook, 1952
Cotio	Late Classic	"Palangana" (1)	E. M. Shook, 1952a
Cristina	Late Classic	"Palangana" (1)	E. M. Shook, 1952
Cruz	Late Classic	"Palangana" (1)	E. M. Shook, 1952

Site	Ceramic Period	Ball Court Type	Reference
Eucaliptus	Late Classic	"Palangana" (1)	E. M. Shook, 1952
Falda	Pre-, Early and Late Classic	"Palangana" (1)	E. M. Shook, 1952
Fuentes	(?)	"Palangana" (1)	E. M. Shook, 1952
Garland	Pre- through Late Classic	"Palangana" (1)	E. M. Shook, 1952
Guacamaya	Late Classic	"Palangana" (1)	E. M. Shook, 1952
Kaminaljuyu	Pre- through Late Classic	"Palangana" (12)	Shook and Smith, 1942
Lavarreda	(?)	"Palangana" (1)	E. M. Shook, 1952
Palmita	Late Classic	"Palangana" (1)	E. M. Shook, 1952
Pelikan	Late Classic	"Palangana" (1)	E. M. Shook, 1952
Ross	Pre- and Late Classic	"Palangana" (1)	E. M. Shook, 1952
Sanja	Pre- through Late Classic	"Palangana" (1)	E. M. Shook, 1952
San Rafael	Late Classic	"Palangana" (1)	E. M. Shook, 1952
Taltic	Late Classic	"Palangana" (?) (1)	E. M. Shook, 1952
Villanueva	Pre- through Late Classic	"Palangana" (1)	E. M. Shook, 1952
Vuelta Grande	(?)	"Palangana" (?) (1)	E. M. Shook, 1952

DEPARTMENT OF HUEHUETENANGO

Site	Ceramic Period	Ball Court Type	Reference
Chacula	(?)	Open-end (1)	E. Seler, 1901
Chalchitan	Pre-(?), Early, Late, and post-Classic	Open-end (1) Open-end a (1)	A. L. Smith, 1955
Chicol	Early and perhaps Late Classic	Open-end (1)	A. L. Smith, 1955
Chilipe	(?)	Open-end (1)	E. M. Shook, 1947
Cuja	(?)	Open-end (1)	La Farge and Byers, 1931
Huitchun	Classic (?) and Protohistoric	Open-end a (1)	A. L. Smith, 1955
Piol	(?)	Miscellaneous (1)	A. L. Smith, 1955
Tu'Kumanchun	Late Classic	Open-end (1)	S. Miles, field notes
Uaxac Canal	(?)	Miscellaneous (1)	E. Seler, 1901
Uaxac Canal Ventana Group	(?)	Open-end (1)	E. Seler, 1901
Xetenan	(?)	Miscellaneous (1)	A. L. Smith, 1955
Xolchun	Protohistoric	Enclosed (1)	A. L. Smith, 1955
Zaculeu	Early Classic through Protohistoric	Miscellaneous (1)	Woodbury and Trik, 1953

DEPARTMENT OF SACATEPÉQUEZ

Site	Ceramic Period	Ball Court Type	Reference
Florencia	Pre- through Late Classic	"Palangana" (1)	E. M. Shook, 1952
Pompeya	Pre- through Late Classic	"Palangana" (?) (1)	S. F. Borhegyi, 1950

Site	Ceramic Period	Ball Court Type	Reference
DEPARTMENT OF QUICHÉ: SANTA CRUZ REGION			
Utatlan	Classic through Protohistoric	Enclosed (2)	C. Sapper, 1897
DEPARTMENT OF QUICHÉ: JOYABA-ZACUALPA REGION			
Kukul	(?)	Enclosed (1)	E. M. Shook, 1944 field notes
Zacualpa	Early Classic through Protohistoric	"Palangana" (?) (1)	R. Wauchope, 1948
DEPARTMENT OF QUICHÉ: SACAPULAS REGION			
Chuchun	Classic	Open-end (1)	A. L. Smith, 1955
Chuitinamit	Post-Classic (?) and Protohistoric	Miscellaneous (1)	A. L. Smith, 1955
Chutixtiox	Protohistoric	Enclosed (1)	A. L. Smith, 1955
Comitancillo	Protohistoric	Enclosed (1)	A. L. Smith, 1955
Pacot	Protohistoric	Enclosed (1)	A. L. Smith, 1955
Rio Blanco	Late pre-, Early Classic, Protohistoric	Open-end (1)	A. L. Smith, 1955
Xecataloj	(?)	Open-end (1)	A. L. Smith, 1955
Xolchun	Classic, post-Classic, Protohistoric	Miscellaneous (1)	A. L. Smith, 1955
Xolpacol	Protohistoric	Enclosed (1)	A. L. Smith, 1955
DEPARTMENT OF QUICHÉ: NEBAJ-COTZAL-CHAJUAL REGION			
Acihtz	Protohistoric	Open-end a (1)	A. L. Smith, 1955
Caquixay	Late Classic and Protohistoric	Open-end a (1)	A. L. Smith, 1955
Chichel	(?)	Open-end a (1)	R. Burkitt, 1930
Chipal	Post-Classic and Protohistoric	Open-end a (1)	A. L. Smith, 1955
El Tigre	(?)	Open-end (1)	A. L. Smith, 1955
Huil	(?)	Open-end a (1)	A. L. Smith, 1955
Kalamte	(?)	Open-end a (1)	C. Sapper, 1895
Mutchil	(?)	Open-end a (1)	A. L. Smith, 1955
Nebaj	Early, Late, and post-Classic	Open-end (1) Open-end a (1)	Smith and Kidder, 1951
Oncap	Protohistoric	Open-end a (1)	A. L. Smith, 1955
Pulai	(?)	Open-end (1)	A. L. Smith, 1955
San Francisco	(?)	Open-end a (1)	R. Burkitt, 1930
San Francisco del Norte	(?)	Open-end a (2)	A. L. Smith, 1955
Tixchun	Post-Classic	Open-end a (1)	A. L. Smith, 1955
Tuchoc	(?)	Open-end a (1)	A. L. Smith, 1955
Tzicuay	Early, Late, and post-Classic	Miscellaneous (1)	A. L. Smith, 1955

Site	Ceramic Period	Ball Court Type	Reference
Vicaveval	Protohistoric	Enclosed (1)	A. L. Smith, 1955
Vitenam	(?)	Open-end (1)	A. L. Smith, 1955

DEPARTMENT OF QUICHÉ: SAN ANDRES SAJCABAJA REGION

Site	Ceramic Period	Ball Court Type	Reference
La Lagunita	Post-Classic	"Palangana" (?) (1) Open-end (1)	A. L. Smith, 1955
Llano Grande	Late Classic	"Palangana" (?) (1)	A. L. Smith, 1955
Pantzac	Post-Classic	Open-end *a* (1) Miscellaneous (1)	A. L. Smith, 1955
Patzac	Late Classic (?) and Protohistoric	Enclosed (1) Miscellaneous (1)	A. L. Smith, 1955

DEPARTMENT OF BAJA VERAPAZ: RABINAL REGION

Site	Ceramic Period	Ball Court Type	Reference
Chuitinamit	(?)	Enclosed (2)	A. L. Smith, 1955

DEPARTMENT OF ALTA VERAPAZ

Site	Ceramic Period	Ball Court Type	Reference
Chichén	Late pre- through post-Classic	Open-end (2)	A. L. Smith, 1955
Chijolom	Late Classic and post-Classic	Miscellaneous (1)	A. L. Smith, 1955
Las Tinajas	Late Classic	Open-end (?) (1)	A. L. Smith, 1955
Tampoma	Late Classic	Open-end *a* (1)	A. L. Smith, 1955

DEPARTMENT OF CHIMALTENANGO

Site	Ceramic Period	Ball Court Type	Reference
Iximche	Protohistoric (?)	Miscellaneous (2)	H. E. D. Pollock, 1937 field notes
La Garrucha	(?)	"Palangana" (1)	E. M. Shook, 1948 field notes
La Merced	(?)	"Palangana" (1)	E. M. Shook, notes
Mixco Viejo	Late Classic and Protohistoric	Enclosed (2)	A. L. Smith, 1955

DEPARTMENT OF PROGRESO

Site	Ceramic Period	Ball Court Type	Reference
Bucaral	(?)	Open-end (?) (1)	E. M. Shook, 1944 field notes
El Teron	Late Classic	Miscellaneous (1)	Smith and Kidder, 1943
Guaytan	Early and Late Classic	Enclosed *a* (1) Miscellaneous (1)	Smith and Kidder, 1943
Four Motagua Valley Sites	(?)	Enclosed *a* (4)	A. L. Smith, 1940 field notes
Five Motagua Valley Sites	(?)	Miscellaneous (5)	A. L. Smith, 1940 field notes

DEPARTMENT OF JALAPA

Site	Ceramic Period	Ball Court Type	Reference
El Sare	(?)	"Palangana" (1)	E. M. Shook, 1943 field notes

Site	Ceramic Period	Ball Court Type	References
San Pedro Pinula	(?)	Enclosed *a* (1) "Palangana" (1)	G. Stromsvik, 1952
Xalapan	(?)	"Palangana" (1)	E. M. Shook, 1943 field notes

DEPARTMENT OF ZACAPA

Site	Ceramic Period	Ball Court Type	References
La Vega de Coban	(?)	Miscellaneous (1)	Smith and Kidder, 1943

DEPARTMENT OF JUTIAPA

Site	Ceramic Period	Ball Court Type	References
Asunción Mita	Late Classic	Enclosed *a* (2)	G. Stromsvik, 1952

DEPARTMENT OF SANTA ROSA

Site	Ceramic Period	Ball Court Type	References
El Prado	(?)	"Palangana" (1)	E. M. Shook, 1942 field notes
Utzumazate	(?)	"Palangana" (1)	E. M. Shook, 1942 field notes

Ceramic Periods

Late pre-Classic	500 B.C.–A.D. 300	Post-Classic	A.D. 900–A.D. 1200
Early Classic	A.D. 300–A.D. 600	Protohistoric	A.D. 1200–A.D. 1525
Late Classic	A.D. 600–A.D. 900		

Ball Court Types

Open-end	No end zones defined by masonry walls.
Open-end *a*	Open-end court with one end leading into an adjoining plaza that normally has an altar platform in its center.
Enclosed	High walls defining end zones, with stairways leading out at either end. Profile has a level bench top and a steeply sloping wall with a vertical molding at the top (fig. 8, *e* and *f*)
Enclosed *a*	Walls defining end zones. Profile has a sloping bench top and a vertical playing wall (fig. 8, *g*).
"Palangana"	Rectangular enclosure with surrounding walls of even height. No end zones.
Miscellaneous	Ball courts that do not fit into any of the above types.

Carbon copies of the field notes of Pollock, Shook and Smith are in the Peabody Museum, Harvard University. The numbers following the ball court type indicate the number of ball courts at the site.

BACKGAMMON AMONG THE AZTECS

Edward B. Tylor

BACKGAMMON AMONG THE AZTECS.

By *backgammon* we usually mean one particular game played with dice and thirty draughts, on a board with twelve points on each side. But this is only one of a family of games, whose general definition is that they consist in moving pieces on a diagram, not at the player's free choice, as in draught-playing, but conformably to the throws of lots or dice. It can hardly be doubted that the set of games thus combining chance and skill are all, whether ancient or modern, the descendants of one original game. By a stretch of imagination, it may be possible to fancy draughts or dice to have been fresh invented more than once. But when it comes to a game which combines the two ideas, it seems to pass the bounds of ordinary probability to suppose, for instance, that a Greek and an Arab and a Birmese were separately seized by the same happy thought, and said, Go to, let us cast lots, and count them to play at draughts by. If indeed any reader should think such a combination might have happened twice over, he may be asked to look closely into the games presently to be described, so as to satisfy himself that their agreement goes even farther, as in the peculiar principle on which the high and low throws are counted, and, so far as one knows, in there generally being in some shape the rule of hitting a blot, that is, taking an enemy's undefended man off the point one's own man moves to. The exact primitive game whence all known games of the class were derived cannot now be pointed out, and indeed is perhaps lost in pre-historic antiquity. So we may as well keep to our own word, and call the whole set the backgammon family. It is in this sense that I use the word here, with the purpose of proving that before

Hernando Cortés landed with his invading Spaniards at Vera Cruz, one variety of backgammon had already found its way over from Asia into Mexico, and had become a fashionable amusement at the barbaric court of Montezuma. But before following the game on its hitherto unnoticed migration into the New World, let us first glance at its Old World history.

Clearly our English *backgammon* and the more complicated French *trictrac* are descended from the Roman game of the "twelve lines" (*duodecim scripta*) which was played throughout the empire. This is the game which Ovid says has lines as many as the gliding year has months, and he means it where he gives the lover insidious counsel, when his mistress casts the ivory numbers from her hand, let him give himself bad throws and play them ill. Among the Christian antiquities in Rome is a marble slab, on which a backgammon-table is cut, with a Greek cross in the middle, and a Greek inscription that Jesus Christ gives victory and help to dicers if they write his name when they throw the dice—Amen. Carelessly scratched as it is, by some stone-cutter whose faith went beyond his trictrac, it shows that the board was like ours even to the division in the middle, which makes the two groups of six points on each side. From ancient Rome, too, we inherit the habit of making the backgammon-board with a draught-board on the reverse side, at any rate the commentators so interpret Martial's epigram on the tabula lusoria:

"Hic mihi bis seno numeratur tessera puncto
Calculus hic gemino discolor hoste perit."

"Here, twice the die is counted to the point of *size*,
Here, 'twixt twin foes of other hue, the draughtsman dies."

The very mode of playing the men in classic backgammon may be made out from a fifth century Greek epigram, commemorating a remarkable hit, in which the Emperor Zeno got his men so blocked, that having the ill-luck to throw 2, 5, 6 (they used three dice, as indeed we continued to do in the Middle Ages), the only moves open obliged him to leave eight blots. This historic problem, and other matters of Greek and Latin backgammon, are worked out by M. Becq de Fouquières, in his *Jeux des Anciens*, with a skill that would have rejoiced the hearts of those eminent amateurs, the old Count de Trictrac and the venerable Abbé du Cornet, to whose teaching history records that Miss Becky Sharp ascribed the proficiency at backgammon which made her society so agreeable to Sir Pitt at Queen's Crawley.

It is not known so exactly what manner of backgammon the Greeks played in earlier ages. But there are various passages to prove that when they talk of dice-playing, they often mean not mere hazard, but some game of the backgammon-sort, where the throws of the dice are turned to account by skilful moving of pieces. Thus Plato says that, as in casting dice, we ought to arrange our affairs according to the throws we get, as reason shall declare best; and Plutarch, further moralizing, remarks that Plato compares life to dicing ($\kappa \nu \beta \epsilon \iota \alpha$), where one must not only get good throws, but know how to use them skilfully when one has got them. So with Plutarch's story of Parysatis, mother of Artaxerxes. She was "awful at dice" ($\delta \epsilon \iota \nu \dot{\eta} \kappa \nu \beta \epsilon \dot{\nu} \epsilon \iota \nu$), and "playing her game carefully," won from the king the eunuch Mesabates, who had cut off the head and hand of Cyrus; having got him, she had him flayed alive and his skin stretched. This episode of old Persian history is noteworthy in the history of the game, because Persian backgammon, which they call *nard*, is much like the Euro-pean form of the game, which, it has been not unreasonably guessed, may itself have come from Persia. This nard is popular in the East, and orthodox Moslems have seen in the fateful throws of the dice a recognition of the decrees of Allah, that fall sometimes for a man and sometimes against him. It is, said one, a nobler game than chess, for the backgammon-player acknowledges predestination and the divine will, but the chess-player denies them like a dissenter. Not to lose ourselves in speculations on the Oriental origin of backgammon, at any rate it was from Rome that it spread over Europe, carrying its Latin name of *tabulæ* with it in French and English *tables*. This word has dropped out of our use since the Elizabethan period, but an instance of it may be cited in a couple of lines, conveying another little sermon on backgammon, which the English author no doubt borrowed from the Latin of Terence, even as he had copied it from the Greek of Menander :

" Man's life's a game of *tables*, and he may
Mend his bad fortune by his wiser play."

There is an idea which readily presents itself as to how backgammon came to be invented, namely, that the draughts were originally mere *counters*, such as little stones, shifted on a calculating-board to reckon up the successive throws, and that it was an afterthought to allow skill in the choice of moves. This guess fits well enough with the classic draught being described as a stone, $\psi \tilde{\eta} \phi o \varsigma$, *calx* or *calculus*, while in Germany, though now made of wood, it still keeps its old name of *stein*. Also the playing-board on which the stones were moved shares the name of the calculating-board, $\ddot{\alpha} \beta \alpha \xi$, *abacus*. But if the classical varieties of backgammon in this way show traces of the game near its original state, they seem in another respect to have passed out of their early simplicity. They are all played with dice, and indeed the French author lately mentioned seems right in guessing that the division of our board into groups of six points each was made on purpose to suit the throws of cubical dice like ours, numbered on all the sides, from 1 to 6. As to the early history of dice, I have elsewhere endeavoured to show (*Primitive Culture*, Chapter III.) that the origin of games of chance may be fairly looked for in instruments of the nature of lots, at first cast seriously by diviners for omens, and afterwards brought down from serious magic into mere sport. Now the simplest of such instruments is the lot which only falls two ways, like the shell, white on one side and blackened on the other, which Greek children spun up into the air to fall, "night or day," as they said; or like our halfpence tossed for "head or tail." Both in divination and in gambling, such two-faced lots probably came earlier than the highly artificial numbered dice. The kinds of backgammon now to be described seem in general to belong to the earlier stage of development, for it is with lots, not dice, that they are played.

The traveller in Egypt or Palestine now and then comes on a lively group sitting round a game, and in their eager shouts, if he knows some Arabic, he may distinguish not only such words as "two" or "four," but also "child," "dog," "Christian," "Moslem." On closer examination he finds that the game is called *táb*, and that it is a sort of backgammon played on an oblong chequer-board, or four rows of little holes in the ground, where bits of stone on one side and bits of red brick on the other do duty as draughts being shifted from place to place in the rows of squares or holes. Not dice, but lots are cast to regulate the moves; these lots are generally four slips of palm-stick, with a green outer side and a white cut side (called black and white) and when they are thrown against a stick set up in the ground, the throw

counts according to how many white sides come up, thus:—

Whites up:	None	One	Two	Three	Four.
Count:	6	1	2	3	4
	(go on)	(táb)	(stop)	(stop)	(go on)

Notice particularly this way of counting throws, for its principles will be found again in lot backgammon elsewhere. There is evidently a crude attempt to reckon probabilities, giving a higher value to the less frequent throws of all four white and all four black, than to two or three white, which come up oftener. Beside the high count, they have the privilege of a second throw. This, if lot backgammon came first, and was succeeded by dice backgammon, would naturally pass into our rule of giving doubles another throw. The throw of one white, which is called "child," or *táb*, *i.e.* "game," has a special power, for only by it may a "dog," that is, a stone or draught, be moved out of its original place in the outer row, and set at liberty to circulate along the lines of squares or "houses," taking an enemy's dog if found alone in its house. While a draught is still in its first inactive useless condition, they call it a "Nazarene," or Christian, but when the throw of *táb* gives it the right to go forth conquering and to conquer, it becomes a "Moslem." It is not needful to go further into the rather complicated rules of moving and taking. Those who are curious may find much about it in Lane's *Modern Egyptians*, and in the quaintly learned little book *De Ludis Orientalibus*, by Thomas Hyde, who was Bodleian librarian in the reign of William and Mary. But one question suggests itself. Seeing how the modern Fellahs delight in *táb*, one naturally asks, Did they inherit it from the ancient Egyptians? From remote antiquity the Egyptians played draughts on earth, and after death their righteous souls still had the oblong chequer-board, and the men like chess-pawns, to amuse their glorified but perhaps rather tiresome life in the world below. But, as Dr. Birch points out, no Egyptian dice have been found earlier than Roman times, nor any plain mention of backgammon. Even if they played like their descendants in the Nile Valley with such things as slips of palm, something about it should be found in the hieroglyphic texts. But at present nothing appears, and there is no reason to add backgammon to the long list of inventions whose earliest traces are found in Egypt. Perhaps the nearest relative of *táb* is Chinese backgammon, but this is played with dice.

Next, as to India. Here, since ancient times, cowrie-shells have been thrown as lots, their "head" and "tail" being according as the shell falls with mouth or back upward. In Sanskrit literature, there is an old mention of a game called *panchiká*, which was played with five cowries, and where it seems that the winning throws were when all the mouths came up or down, as against the commoner throws when some fell each way. That a game of the nature of backgammon was known in India from high antiquity has been plainly made out by Professor Weber. It was called *ayâ-naya*, or "luck and unluck;" or at any rate that was a term used as to the moving of the pieces, which travelled right and left through the squares, and took an undefended man from his place to begin his course anew. So, as a Sanskrit riddle has it, "In a house where there were many, there is left but one, and where there was none and many come, at last there is none. Thus Kâla and Kâlî, casting day and night for their pair of dice, play with human beings for pieces on the board of the world." Putting these particulars together, it is clearly possible to trace from ancient times the game of *pachisi*, played in modern India, into which game it will now be necessary for our argument to go more exactly; in fact to qualify ourselves to sit down and play a game. English backgam-

mon players will hardly take five minutes to learn it.

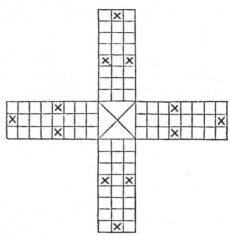

Suppose four players to be seated, each at the end of one arm of the diagram or board, of which a figure is here given. Each player will have four little wooden cones as his pieces or draughts, all of one colour, to distinguish them. If only two play, each will manœuvre two sets of men. Each player's men start one by one down the middle row of his own rectangle, beginning with the square next the central space, and thence they proceed all round the outside rows of the board, travelling from right to left (contrary to the sun) till they get back to their own central row, and up it home to where they started from, he who first gets all his men home winning the game. A solitary man is taken up and sent back to begin again, by one of his adversary's men lighting upon his square, except in the case of the twelve privileged squares, which are marked with a cross, in which case the overtaking piece cannot move. The moving is determined by throwing a number of cowries, which count according to how many fall mouth up; thus, if six cowries are used :—

Mouths up :	None	One	Two	Three	Four	Five	Six
Count :	6	10	2	3	4	25	12
	(go on)	(dás)	(stop)	(stop)	(stop)	(pa-chisi)	(go on)

According to the rules kindly sent me from Dr. Rájendralála Mitra, of

Calcutta, the throws of one-up or five-up (*das* or *pachisi*) alone can start a man on his first square, or get him off if stuck on his last square. These throws, as well as none-up and six-up, give a new throw. Thus the best beginnings are one-up followed by two-up, or five-up followed by four-up, either of which enters a man and carries him on in safety into a "fort." Seven cowries can also be used, but the primitive game was probably more like the ancient game with five cowries just mentioned, for the name pachisi means "five-and-twenty," and was no doubt taken from the throw when five shells come up. The principles of counting the throws and entering the men are plainly like those in the Arab game of táb, and there are Indian forms with only four cowries which come still closer.

Pachisi is a favourite game in India, and an eager player will carry rolled round in his turban the cloth which serves as a board, so as to be ready for a game at any moment. These cloths, when embroidered with the diagram in coloured silk, are quite artistic objects, and one does not often see prettier toys than a set of men in Mr. Franks's collection, little cones (or rather sugar-loaves) of rock crystal, with the colours they are to bear in the game shown by mounting in the top a ruby for red, an emerald for green, &c. There are even stories of yet more sumptuous games, where the board was a courtyard laid out in marble pavement, on which living draught-men clothed in green, red, yellow, and black, walked the circuit and hustled one another off the squares. Our Anglo-Indians sometimes catch the enthusiasm; and there is an often-told tale of that official personage who, when he paid his native servants their wages, would sit down with them to a match at pachisi, and sometimes win his money back. In London toy-shops they sell board and pieces for what they profess to be the game, but these really belong to the modified form of it known in India as *chúpur*, in which, instead of cowries, stick-dice numbered on the four long sides are thrown, these Indian dice being in England replaced by our common cubical ones. This shows the change from lots to dice in games of the backgammon sort, and it is curious to notice how clearly the new rules for counting by the dice are modelled on the old rules for throws of cowries. Having now sufficiently mastered the peculiarities of pachisi, let us pass from Asia to America, and compare them with the details of the Mexican game of *patolli*.

When the Spanish invaders of Mexico gazed half in admiration and half in contempt on the barbaric arts and fashions of Aztec life, they particularly noticed a game, at which the natives played so eagerly, that when they lost all they had, they would even stake their own bodies, and gamble themselves into slavery, just as Tacitus says the old Germans used to do. The earliest particulars of the Mexican game come from Lopez de Gomara, whose *Istoria de las Indias* was printed in 1552, so that it must have been written while the memory of the conquest in 1521 was still fresh. He says, " Sometimes Montezuma looked on as they played at *patoliztli*, which is much like the game of tables, and is played with beans marked with lines like one-faced dice, which they call *patolli*. These they take between both hands, and throw them on a mat or on the ground, where there are certain lines like a chequer-board, on which they mark with stones the point which came up, taking off or putting on a little stone." This may be supplemented from three other old Spanish writers—Torquemada, Sahagun, and Duran. The figure on the mat is spoken of as " a painted cross full of squares like chequers," or as an " aspa," which word means a +, a Greek cross, the sails of a windmill, &c., descriptions which come as close as may be to the pachisi-board. Also, it appears that the stones moved on the board to mark the numbers thrown by the beans were of different colours, one account mentioning twelve stones, six red and six blue, between the two players.

According as the game was played, three to five beans were thrown as lots or dice, and sometimes these beans were marked on one side with a hole and left plain on the other, while sometimes they seem to have had dots or lines indicating various numbers. If both ways were really used, then the game was known in both its stages, that of two-faced lots and that of numbered dice, just as in India it is played as pachisi with cowries, and as chûpur with stick-dice. As to the way of scoring the throws only one of the old writers says anything. This is Diego Duran, an extract from whose MS. history I have obtained by the courtesy of Mr. Oak of the Bancroft Library at San Francisco. He says, as to the holes in the beans which showed how many squares were to be gained, that they were " if one, one, and if two, two, and if three, three, but marking five they were ten, and if ten, twenty." Thus in Mexico we just catch sight of the peculiar trick of scoring, everywhere so characteristic of the game, namely, the advantage given to the extreme throws, which in our own backgammon takes the form of allowing doubles to count twice over. Unluckily the thought had never crossed the minds of these early Spanish historians of the New World that their descriptions of the Aztec game would ever become evidence of use in tracing the lines along which civilization spread over the earth. Had they seen this they would have left us a perfect set of rules, not such careless mentions of a game which plainly they " did not understand." Still they saw enough of Montezuma's patolli to observe that it was in principle like their own game of tables, while clearly they had never heard of the Indian pachisi, or they would have seen how much closer its resemblance came to that. This touches a point in the history of the game. How did the Mexicans get it ? The idea may have already occurred to

some readers of this essay, could not perhaps some stray Portuguese or Spaniard, having lately picked up the game of pachisi in some seaport of the East Indies, have taken his next voyage to the West Indies, and naturalized his newly-learnt game on the mainland of America. But there is no room for a suggestion of this sort when it is remembered that patolli was an established diversion in Mexico at the time of the Spanish entry, which followed within three years of the first landing of Grijalva in the Gulf of Mexico, and indeed within five-and-twenty years of Colon's first sight of Hispaniola. What seems most likely is that the game came direct from Asia to America, reaching Mexico from the Pacific coast.

That the remarkable civilization of Mexico as the Spaniards found it was not entirely of native American growth, but had taken up ideas from Asia, is no new opinion. Alexander von Humboldt argued years ago that the Mexicans did and believed things which were at once so fanciful and so like the fancies of Asiatics that there must have been communication. Would two nations, he asks in effect, have taken independently to forming calendars of days and years by repeating and combining cycles of animals such as tiger, dog, ape, hare? would they have developed independently similar astrological fancies about these signs governing the periods they began, and being influential each over a particular limb or organ of men's bodies ? would they, again, have evolved separately out of their consciousness the myth of the world and its inhabitants having at the end of several successive periods been destroyed by elemental catastrophes ? In spite of Humboldt we often hear Mexican culture talked of as self-produced, with its bronze and gold work, its elaborate architecture and sculpture, its monastic and priestly institutions, its complicated religious rites and formulas. It was my fortune years ago to travel in Mexico and explore its wonderful ruins, and ever since I have held to the view that the higher art and life of the whole Central American district is most rationally accounted for by a carrying across of culture from Asia. Thus it is now a peculiar pleasure to me to supplement Humboldt's group of arguments with a new one which goes on all-fours with them. It may very well have been the same agency which transported to Mexico the art of bronze-making, the computation of time by periods of dogs and apes, the casting of nativities, and the playing of backgammon. What that agency was one can as yet do no more than guess, but too much stress must not be laid on it in speculating on the mass migrations of the American races. Such matters as arts or games are easily carried from country to country; nor can we treat as inaccessible to Asiatic influences the Pacific coast of North America, where disabled junks brought across by the ocean current are from time to time drifted ashore, now and then with their crews alive. The Asiatic communication to be traced in the culture of the Aztec nation may not have been very ancient or extensive; all we can argue is that communication of some sort there was.

Now one thing leads to another, especially in ethnology. Curiously enough, by following up the traces of this trivial little game, we get an unexpected glimpse into the history of the ruder North American tribes. Having learnt about patolli as played in old Mexico, let us take up the account of a Jesuit missionary, Father Joseph Ochs, who was in Spanish America in 1754-68, and who is here writing about the tribes of Sonora and Chihuahua. "Instead of our cards they have slips of reed or bits of wood a thumb wide and near a span long, on which, as on a tally, different strokes are cut and stained black. These they hold fast in the hand, lift them up as high as they can, and let them drop on the ground. Whichever then has most strokes or eyes for him wins the stake. This game is as bad as the

notorious hazard. They call it *patole*. As it is forbidden on pain of blows, they choose for it a place in the bush, but the clatter of these bits of wood has discovered me many a hidden gamester. To play more safely they would spread a cloak or carpet so as not to be betrayed by the noise." Here, then, is found, toward a thousand miles north-west of the city of Mexico, a game which may be described as patolli without the counters, and which still bears the Aztec name, in a district whose language is not Aztec, so that the proof of its having travelled from Mexico seems complete. The people being less intellectual than the old Mexicans, have dropped the skilful part of the game and are content with the mere dicing. Nor, by the way, is this the only place where backgammon has so come down, for in Egypt they will lay aside the board and throw the táb-sticks for fun, those who throw four and six being proclaimed Sultan and Vezir, while the luckless thrower of two gets for his reward two cuts with the palm-stick on the soles of his feet.

Yet another fifteen hundred miles or more up into the continent the game is still to be traced. Among the hunting tribes known under the common name of the North American Indians, there is a favourite sport described by a score of writers under the name of "game of the bowl," or "game of plum-stones." The lots used are a number of plumstones burnt on one side to blacken them, or any similar double-convex pieces of wood, horn, &c. They are either thrown by hand or shaken in a bowl or dish, whence they can be neatly jerked up and let fall on the blanket spread to play on. The counting depends upon how many come up of either colour, white or black, as is seen in the precise rules given by Mr. Morgan in his *League of the Iroquois*. Where six "peach-stones" were thrown, if all six came up, white or black, they counted five, and five up, white or black, counted one, these high throws also giving the player a new turn, but all lower throws counted nothing and passed the lead. It is so curious to find the principle of lot-scoring, which we have tracked all across from Egypt, cropping up so perfectly among the Iroquois, that at the risk of being tedious it is worth while to give in full the mode of counting in the game as played with eight "deer-buttons." The following top line shows how many black or white sides up, with their count below—

Eight	Seven	Six	Five	Four	Three	Two	One	None
20	4	2	0	0	0	2	4	20
go on			stop			go on		

In these games there is no board to play on. The Iroquois use beans as counters, the game being won by one player getting all the beans, but perhaps the white men taught them how to do this. So with the game which will occur to English readers who remember it in *Hiawatha*, where it is described at full length in prose-poetry as "the game of bowl and counters, *pugasaing* with thirteen pieces." This game is real enough, indeed the description of it is taken from Schoolcraft's *Indian Tribes*. But there seem to be no early mentions of this Algonquin game with its ducks and war-clubs and elaborate counting, nor of the Dakota game with tortoises and war-eagles on the plumstones. Thus both may have been lately devised by Indians under European teaching, as improvements on the original *pugasaing* or "play," which was the simple game with black and white-sided plumstones, or the like. This, no doubt, is old, for it is described by the Jesuit Missionaries in 1636 under the name of *jeu de plat*, as a regular sport among the Hurons; and as they clearly did not learn the game from Europe, we are left to argue that it reached them from Asia, very likely through Mexico.

It remains to glance at what may be learnt as to the history of the North American Indians from the fact of their gambling with the bowl and plumstones. It is an interesting question whether "the poor Indian, whose untutor'd mind" has now and then been too easily credited with the invention of all the arts and beliefs he did not get from the white men, may not really before this have largely taken up in his culture ideas of Old World growth. It has long been noticed that looking at the native tribes of what is now the United States and the Dominion of Canada, the tribes on the east side had taken to making pottery and cultivating maize, while the tribes on the west had not, which seems as though there had been a flow or drift of civilization from the Central American district up the eastern half of the continent, which of itself ought to be enough to prevent any ethnologists from looking at the so-called Red-man of New England or the Lakes as the creator of his whole industrial and social life. Nor is it an unknown thing that the myth and religion of the North American tribes contain many fancies well known to Asia, which the men of the prairies were hardly likely to have hit upon independently, but which they certainly did not learn from the white men, who did not even know them. If we are bound, as I think we are, to open a theoretical road for even a well-marked game to migrate by from Asia into America, then there are plenty of other matters waiting for passage along the route. By such conveyance of ideas it may be easiest to explain why the so-called Indians of North America shared with the real Indians of India the quaint belief that the world is a monstrous tortoise floating on the waters, or why the Sioux Indians share with the Tatars the idea that it is sinful to chop or poke with a sharp instrument the burning logs on the fire. But these considerations lead too far into the deepest-lying problems of the connexion and intercourse of nations to be here pursued farther. It is remarkable, too, how vast a geographical range the argument on the migrations of a game may cover. The American farmer now whiles away the winter evening in his farmhouse parlour with a hit at back-gammon, on the spot where not long since the Iroquois played peach-stones in his bark hut. Neither would have recognized the other's sport as akin to his own, though when we trace them through the intermediate stages they are seen to be both birds of one nest. It is by strangely different routes that they have at last come together from their Asiatic home—one perhaps eastward through Asia, across the Pacific, into Mexico, and northward to the St. Lawrence; the other no doubt westward down to the Mediterranean, up northward to England, over the Atlantic, and so out into the American prairie.[1]

EDWARD B. TYLOR.

[1] For special details, copies of original documents, &c., see a paper by the author "On the Game of Patolli in Ancient Mexico, and its probably Asiatic Origin," read before the Anthropological Institute on April 9, 1878.

ON THE GAME OF PATOLLI
IN ANCIENT MEXICO AND
ITS PROBABLY ASIATIC ORIGIN

E[dward] B. Tylor

On the GAME *of* PATOLLI *in* ANCIENT MEXICO, *and its* PROBABLY
ASIATIC ORIGIN.   By E. B. TYLOR, Esq. D.C.L., F.R.S.

THE group of games to which our *backgammon* belongs is ancient
and widely spread over the world.   In it a number of pieces are
moved on a diagram or board, not at the player's free choice as
in draughts or chess, but conformably to the throws of lots or
dice.   One can hardly doubt, from the peculiar combination of
chance and skill here involved, that all the games coming under
this definition must be sprung from one original game, though
this cannot now be clearly identified, and may indeed have disappeared many ages since.   The closeness of correspondence
between the abacus or reckoning-board with its little stones or
calculi moved on its lines or spaces, and the board and pieces
for ancient backgammon, which were even called by the same
names, strongly suggests the idea that the original backgammon
arose out of the sportive use of the calculating-board.   Its
descendants, the backgammon family, fall into two groups of
games : those played with numbered dice, and those played with
two-faced lots which can only fall in two ways, as we say " head
or tail."   These two groups of games may be conveniently called
dice-backgammon and *lot-backgammon*.   Dice-backgammon makes
its appearance plainly in classic history.   The game of the
" twelve lines " (*duodecim scripta*) was played throughout the
Roman Empire, and passed on with little change through
mediæval Europe, carrying its name of *tabulæ, tables*; its modern
representatives being French *trictrac*, English *backgammon*, &c.
Among ancient Greek games, the *kubeia* or " dice-playing " is
shown by various classical passages to have been of the nature
of backgammon.   It appears from Plutarch that in early times

it was played in Persia, where it still flourishes under the name
of *nard*. There are also in Sanskrit literature mentions of
related games in ancient India. For the purpose of the present
paper, however, it will not be needful to go at length into the
history of dice-backgammon. It is with the less familiar lot-
backgammon that we are principally concerned. This, there is
fair reason to believe, was the earlier, as it is the ruder form ;
dice-backgammon being a later improvement. That such is the
case is made likely by the following descriptions of lot-
backgammon, which show how clumsily the throwing of a
whole handful of lots accomplishes what is done easily with one
or two numbered dice.

One variety of lot-backgammon is to this day popular in
Egypt and Palestine, under the name of *tab* or " game." It is
described in Lane's *Modern Egyptians*, and in Hyde's *De Ludis
Orientalibus*, part ii, p. 217. The lots thrown are tab-sticks,
four slips of palm-branch about a span long, cut smooth on one
side so as to be white, while the other side is left green, these
sides being called the white and black respectively. The tab-
sticks are thrown against a wall or stick, and the throw counts
according to how many white sides come uppermost, thus :—

Whites up,   none,   one,   two,   three,   four,
Count   6   1   2   3   4
(go on) (go on,) (stop) (stop) (go on).

Here there is an evident attempt to fix the values of the
throws according to the probability of their occurrence, though
this is very crudely carried out. Not only do the rarer throws
of none-up and four-up score high, but they and one-up (tab)
give the player a new throw, whereas the common throws of
two-up and three-up lose the lead. This principle runs through
all varieties of lot-backgammon. If, as is probable, such lot-
scoring represents the earlier form from which dice-scoring is
derived, then the privilege of a new turn being given to the
extreme throws is the origin of the same privilege being given
to doubles in our backgammon. Next as to the tab-board. This
is divided into four rows of squares, each row having 7, 9, 11,
13, or other odd number of squares or " houses," thus :—

Rows of holes on a flat stone or on the ground will serve, and
the pieces or " dogs " are bits of stone for one side and red brick

for the other, the players starting by putting a piece in each
square on his own side as shown in the figure. Now a "dog"
or draught can only be moved from its original square by a
throw of tab (one-up). While still inert in its original place the
draught is called a Nasara or Christian, but by the throw of tab
it is made a Moslem, and can go out to fight. Suppose a player
at the beginning throws tab, then four, and then two, he uses the
first to bring forward his right-hand draught to the square in
front, then moves it on six squares to the left, and then, his last
throw having lost the lead, the other player takes his turn.
When a throw enables a draught to be moved to a square
occupied by one of the enemy's draughts, this is taken, but a
square occupied by several draughts is safe. That is to say, our
familiar rule of taking a man or hitting a blot belongs to lot-
backgammon. The game is ended by one player losing all his
men. It remains to be pointed out that the lot-throwing part of
the game is sometimes played by itself. The player who throws
four is called Sultan, and he who throws six receives the title of
Wezır, while the unlucky thrower of two or three gets blows on
the soles of his feet.

We now turn to the kind of lot-backgammon played in
India, and now generally known under the name of *pachisi*.
It is a popular mode of gambling in India, and even Europeans
have been known to catch the enthusiasm of the natives, as
witness the well-known story of that English official who,
having paid his servants' wages, would sit down with them to a
match at *pachisi* and sometimes win his money back. At the
time of reading this paper, the best account of the game accessible
to me was that in Herklot's *Qanoon-e-Islam*, but Mr. Arthur Grote
has since kindly procured, through Dr. Rajendralala Mitra, of
the Calcutta University, a more complete and consistent set of
rules, which are here followed. The game may be played by
two, three, or four persons severally, or by two pairs, the partners
sitting opposite one another. A cloth, with coloured patches on
it, to form the pattern or diagram, is generally used as a board,
zealous players often carrying one rolled round in their turbans.
The diagram or board is as shown in the illustration.

Each of the four arms contains 24 squares, of which the
three crossed squares are called forts (*chik*). The pieces played
with (*got*) are usually of turned wood or ivory, of a conoidal shape,
much like our present rifle-bullets, and in sets of four, each of
the four players having a set all of one colour, red, green, yellow,
black. The moves of the pieces on the board are determined by
the throws of cowrie-shells, which count according to how many
fall mouth upward. The scoring is as follows when six cowries
are used :—

Mouths up,	none,	one,	two,	three,	four,	five,	six.
Count,	6	10	2	3	4	25	12

         (go on)   (stop)   (go on).

Suppose now four players to be seated, each at the end of one cross-arm. The object of each player is to move his men

from home down the middle row of his own arm, and then along the outside lines of squares from right to left (against the sun) till having made the circuit of the whole board, they come back to the end of their own arm, move up its middle row where they came down, and get back into the central space or home, the winner being he who gets his four men round first. The pieces move onward as many squares as the score of the throw. But a piece can only be started in the game when its owner throws a 10 (*das*) or a 25 (*pachisi*), which throws give a starting 1 (*puá*) in addition to the ordinary score, by which 1 a-piece is put on the first square and so started on its course. The high throws 6, 10, 12, 25, entitle the player to a new throw as doublets do in our backgammon, but at the lower throws the lead passes to the other player. Thus when the game begins, the throws are useless till one player throws 10 or 25 ; suppose he throws 10, and this giving him a new throw, afterwards 2, he is able to start a piece on the first square, and then move it 10 and 2 squares onward. A single man on a square is taken by an enemy's man moving on to that square, and the taken man being dead (*mará*) is put back in the home to start afresh, but two or more men of one set on a square hold it safely, all which is as in our backgammon. In *pachisi*, however, taking or cutting (*kátá*) a man gives the player a new throw. Also in *pachisi*, the crossed squares or forts are places where a single man is in safety, and even blocks an enemy's man from moving there. The throws just mentioned, 10 followed by 2, are favourable as entering a man and putting him in safety in a fort ; a 25 followed by a 4 is good in the same way. When a piece, after making the circuit of the board, comes back to go up its own middle row, it is called ripe (*pakká*) and is laid on its side to distinguish it from the starting-pieces on their way down. If the ripe piece gets again on the last square before home, it can only be got off the board as it got on, by a throw of *das* or *pachisi.**

The comparison of this Hindu game of *pachisi* shows close connection with the Arab *tab* ; we have even the privileged throws giving a new throw, and a particular throw required to start a man. In India there is also played another game like *pachisi* except that the cowries are superseded by a kind of long dice, numbered on the four long sides but not at the ends ; as thus played the game is called *chúpur*. The *pachisi* board has been introduced into England, with four sets of four small draughts as the pieces, and ordinary dice. In this state the game has made its nearest approach to our backgammon, and any one who tries the set of games will be likely to admit that in the *pachisi* played with cowries as lots, he has before him an early and rude stage of the game as lot-backgammon, out of which it passed into dice-backgammon. He may also be

---

* Further details. If 25, 10, or 12 are thrown thrice running, they are called rotten (*pachá*) and destroy one another, but a new throw of 10 or 25 may restore them, and so with six consecutive throws, restored by a seventh. In going home up the middle row, a player cannot use a throw for which there are not sufficient squares left. When players are in partnership, their pieces can be in the same squares. A partner whose pieces are all home can throw on his partner's behalf, after getting a new starting 1. He may also make a ripe man on its way home into an unripe one, for the purpose of cutting off an enemy's man, or revive and bring out again a piece which has got home. Sometimes a player having two pieces on one square moves them as a couple (*jora*) which can take an enemy's couple. Such couples can move at option to the 12th or 25th square with a throw of 25 or to the 5th or 10th square with a throw of 10, but uneven throws other than 25 disjoin the couple. This system of couples (which is allied to the plan of joining pieces in the Arab *tab*) is said not to be recognized by good *pachisi* players.

disposed to think that our own dice-backgammon, though tolerably ancient, came into existence by a similar course of development. It should be added that both as played with cowries and dice, games like *pachisi* are ancient in India. Having looked into the Sanskrit references and consulted Professor Jolly, of Würzburg, I am inclined to think that a game called *panchikā*, played with five cowries, may represent one of its earliest forms, for the name of *pachisi*, meaning " five-and-twenty," is clearly derived from the scoring of the throw of five cowries. Leaving this for further examination, it will be sufficient to have given an idea of the nature of the Hindu *pachisi*, for it is to this game that a variety of lot-backgammon appearing in Old Mexico will now be seen to present the most striking analogy.

Among the accounts of this Mexican game given by the Spanish chroniclers the earliest is that by Gomara, whose history was printed in 1552, so that his account must have been written while the conquest in 1521 was still fresh in memory. He writes as follows: " Sometimes Montezuma looked on as they played at *patoliztli*, which much resembles the game of tables and is played with beans marked like one-faced dice, which (beans) they call *patolli*, which they take between the hands and throw on a mat, or on the ground, where there are certain lines like a merrel (or draught) board, on which they mark with stones the point which fell up, taking off or putting on a little stone.* Torquemada, partly following this account, gives more details, showing the diagram played on to have been of the shape of a *pachisi* board, and the players to have had men of different colours. He says that "they call it the game of *patolli*, because these dice are called so; they throw them with both hands on a thin mat . . . . on which are made certain lines after the manner of a + cross and others crossing them marking the point falling up (as at dice) taking off or putting on little stones of different colour, as in the game of tables."†

---

* Francisco Lopez de Gomara, " La istoria de las Indias, y conquista de Mexico " [Saragossa] 1552, fol. 42. " Algunas vezes mirauia Moteççuma como jugauan al Patoliztli, que parece mucho al juego de las tablas. Y que se juega con hauas, o frisoles raiados como dados de harinillas que dizen Patolli. Los quales menean entre ambas manos. Y los echan sobre una estera, o en el suelo, donde ay ciertas rains, como alquerque, en que señalan con piedras el punto que cayo arriba, quitando, o poniendo china."

† Juan de Torquemada, Monarquia Indiana, Seville 1615, Book xiv., c. 12. " Auia otro juego que llaman Patolli, que en algo parece al juego de las tablas reales, y juegase con hauas y frisoles, hechos puntos en ellos, a manera de dados de arenillas, y dizenle juego Patolli, porque estos dados se llaman assi ; echanlos con ambas manos sobre una estera delgada que se llama petate, hechas ciertas rayas a manera de aspa y atrauessando otras señalando el punto que cayò hazia arriba (como se haze en los dados) quitando, o poniendo chinas de diferente color, como en el juego de las tablas." The word " aspa " means an equal-armed cross, the

Next come the particulars given by Sahagun, which though not adding much to our knowledge of the game, explain why it ceased to be played some time after the conquest. "The lords for their pastime also played a game called *patolli*, which is as the game of merells (or draughts) or the like or dice-playing, and there are four large beans, each having a hole, and they throw them with the hand, as one plays at knuckle-bones, on a mat where there is a figure drawn. At this game they used to play and win precious things, such as gold beads and precious stones, very fine turquoises. This game and that of ball they have left off, being suspicious on account of some idolatrous superstitions in them." In another place he says: "The second pastime they had was a game like dice; they made on a mat a painted cross, full of squares like the game of draughts, and sitting down on the mat, they took three large beans with certain points made in them, and let them fall on the painted cross, &c.*

At the reading of my paper, I was only able to refer to the work of Diego Duran as cited in Bancroft's *Native States of the Pacific*, vol. ii, p. 300. The part of his work containing the account of *patolli* is still in MS., but there is a transcript in the Bancroft Library at San Francisco, from which Mr. Oak, the librarian, has since kindly furnished me with an extract. The game they played on the mat (says Duran) they called *patolly*, which is the same name we now give to cards. On this mat they had a great cross painted taking the mat from corner to corner. Within the hollow of the cross were certain transverse lines forming houses or squares, which cross and squares were marked and drawn in lines with liquid ulli (indiarubber). For these squares there were twelve small stones, six red and six blue, which they divided between the players, to each so many. If two played, which was the ordinary way, one took six and the other the other six. The dice were certain black beans, five or ten

arms of a windmill, &c.; "arenillas" are dice with points only on one face or side, they are numbered from one to six.

* Fr. Bernardino de Sahagun, "Historia Universal de las Cosas de Nueva España," printed in Lord Kingsborough's "Antiquities of Mexico," vol. vii., book viii., c. 10. "Tambien los Señores por su pasatiempo jugaban un juego que se llama Patolli, que es como el juego del castro ó alquerque ó casi, ó como el juego de los dados; y son quatro frisoles grandes que cada uno tiene un agujero, y arrojanlos con la mano, sobre un petate como quien juega a los carnicoles donde está hecha una figura. A este juego solian jugar y ganarse cosas preciosas, como cuentas de oro y piedras preciosas, turquesas muy finas. Este juego y el de la pelota hanlo dejado, por ser sospechosos de algunas superstitiones idolatricas que en ellos hay," c. 17. "El segundo pasatiempo que tenian era un juego como dados; hacien en un petate una cruz pintada, llena de cuadros semejantes al juego del alquerque o castro, y puestos sobre el petate sentados, tomaban tres frisoles grandes, hechos ciertos puntos en ellos, y dejabanlos caer sobre la cruz pintada, y de alli tenian su juego;" &c.

or as they chose to lose or gain, which had certain white holes in each bean where they marked the number of squares which were gained on each hand; where five were marked they were ten, and ten twenty; and if one, one; and if two, two; and if three, three; and if four, four; but marking five they were ten, and if ten, twenty; and so those little white dots were lots and markers of the lines that were gained, and for shifting the stones from square to square. Duran goes on to describe (as the other authors do) the eagerness with which the Mexicans played at this game; how gamesters went about with the mat and stones in a little basket under their arms; how they spoke to them as though they were things with sense and intelligence; and having talked to them with a thousand loving words and requests, would set up the little baskets with the instruments of the game and the painted mat, and bringing fire would throw into it incense and sacrifice before those instruments, bringing offerings of food. Having finished the offering and ceremonies they went off to play with all the confidence in the world. The author continues, that the name of the god of the dice was Macuilxochitl, which means Five roses (five flowers would have been more correct). Him the players invoked as they threw the beans from the hand, which was in the following manner: That the beans serving as dice are five in honour of that god named Five Roses, and to throw the lot they keep rubbing them a while between their hands, and on throwing them on the mat where there is the figure of the fortune and its counting which is in the manner of two clubs, they called with a loud voice on Macuilxochitl and gave a great clap, and then looked to see the points that had come, and this Macuilxochitl was only for this game of the dice. It seems, however, that they would also sometimes call on the god of gambling, Ometochtli, to give them a good point, &c.*

* Diego Duran, "Hist. Indias," MS., tom. iii., cap. xxii. . . . . . al juego que sobre esta estera jugaban llamaban "patolly," que es el mismo vocablo que ahora llamamos naypes. Sobre esta estera tenian pintada una aspa grande la que tomaba el petate de esquina á esquina. Dentro del hueco de la aspa habia atravesadas unas rayas que servian de casas, la cual aspa y casas estaban señaladas y rayadas con ulli derretido . . . para estas casas habia doce piedras pequeñas las seis coloradas y las seis azules, las cuales pedrezuelas partian entre los que jugaban á tantas á cada cual: si jugaban dos que era lo ordinario tomaba el uno las seis y el otro las otras seis; y aunque jugaban muchos jugaba uno por todos ateniendose á la suerte de aquel, como entre los Españoles se juegan los albures ateniendose á la mejor suerte, así se atenian acá al que mejor meneaba los dados, los cuales eran unos frisoles negros cinco ó diez ó como querian perder ó ganar, los cuales tenian unos ahugerillos (*sic*) blancos en cada frisol por donde pintaban el numero de las casas que se aventajaban en cada mano, donde se pintaban cinco eran diez y diez veinte, y si uno, uno, y si dos, dos, y si tres, tres, y si cuatro, cuatro; pero pintando cinco eran diez, y si diez veinte, y así aquellas pintillas blancas eran suertes y cuenta de las rayas que se ganaban; y darmua para la

K 2

These accounts of *patolli* are the only ones to be trusted, the newer ones being hardly to the point, except where they are following the old authorities. Clavigero repeats what he has read, adding that "he who first got three stones in a row, won." * But this may only be an amplification of his predecessors' comparison of the game to alquerque, which seems to have been like our merells, where counters are moved on a diagram with the object of getting three in a line, whence it is also called in Spanish "tres en raya," or "three in a row." Again, Brasseur says that he who returned first into the squares won the game.† Probably it was so, but this author in stating it may only have gone upon the earlier statement that the game was played like tables.

Putting all this together, it is plain that the Spanish chroniclers were right in comparing *patolli* to their own game of tables or backgammon, but had they been acquainted with *pachisi*, they would doubtless have pointed out the closer connection of *patolli* with this Indian game. The playing backgammon-fashion with coloured stones as counters, on a diagram like a cross, full of squares, on which the moves were made by counting squares according to the throws of marked lots, in scoring which a disproportionate advantage was given to the high throws, all corresponds to *pachisi*. And where the beans

piedras de unas casas en otras . . . Andaban los taures de este juego siempre con la estera debajo del sobaco, y con los dados atados á un pañito como algunos taures de este tiempo, que siempre andan apercibidos con los naypes en las calzas de tablage en tablage; aquellos dados juntam^te con las piedrezuelas del juego traian en una bascrita (*sic*) pequeña á los cuales hacian reverencia como á Dioses fingiendo en ellos haber alguna virtud, y asi les hablaban cuando jugaban como á cosa que tubiese algun sentido ó inteligencia de lo que le pedian . . . . asi estos naturales hablaban á los frisolillos y al petate y decian mil palabras de amor y mil requiebros y mil supersticiones, y despues de haberles hablado ponian las petaquillas en el lugar de adoracion con los instrumentos del juego y la estera pintada junto á ella y traia lumbre y echaba en la lumbre incienso y ofrecia su sacrificio ante aquellos instrumentos ofreciendo comida delante de ellos. Acabada la ofrenda y ceremonias ivan á jugar con toda la confianza del mundo."

" El nombre del Dios de los dados era Macuilxuchitl, que quiere decir cinco rosas: á este invocaban los jugadores cuando arrojaban los frisoles de la mano, lo cual era á la manera que dire; que los frisolillos que sirven como de dados son cinco á honra de aquel Dios que tiene nombre de cinco rosas; y para echar la suerte traenlos un rato refregándolos entre las manos, y al lanzallos sobre la estera donde está la figura de la fortuna y cuenta suya que es á la manera de dos bastos, llamaban á alta voz á Macuilxuchitl, y daban una gran palmada, y luego acudia á ver los puntos que le habian entrado; y este Macuilxuchitl era solamente para este huego de los dados."

" . . . invocaban á este Dios cuando jugaban, diciendo ' el Dios Ometochtly me de buen punto,' " &c.

* Clavigero, "Storia Antica del Messico," Cesena, 1780, vol. ii., p. 185, " e chi prima aveva tre pietruzze in fila, quegli vinceva."

† Brasseur de Bourbourg, "Histoire des Nations Civilisées du Mexique et de l'Amérique Centrale," Paris, 1858, vol. iii., p. 671, " et celui qui retournait le premier dans les cases gagnait la partie."

used as lots at *patolli* seem to have been sometimes only marked on one side to distinguish them from the other in head-and-tail fashion, while sometimes they were numbered; this matches with the two ways of playing the Hindu game, with cowries as two-faced lots, or with the numbered stick-dice. It seems so clear that the Mexican game must have come from Asia, that the question first arises—Could any Spanish or Portuguese sailor have learnt it in the East Indies, and then on a voyage to the West Indies have been, perhaps, wrecked on the Mexican coast, and taught his new acquisition to the natives? But the dates do not allow room for this supposition.

Vasco de Gama's voyage to India was about 1500, and the conquest of Mexico was in 1521. It is by earlier direct communication from Asia that we must explain the presence of *patolli* in Mexico. That such communication took place has been proved by Alexander von Humboldt's well-known argument from the occurrence in Mexico of a chronological calendar in which signs were combined to date days, years, &c., on a complex perverse principle closely resembling that on which the Tibetans, Chinese, &c., still reckon dates. Not only were the signs, tiger, dog, ape, hare, &c., used to date periods of time both by these nations and the ancient Mexicans, but they combine such signs in series, so that as in Japan "younger Fire Hare" denotes the fourth year of the cycle, so in Mexico "two Hare Fire" stands for the 28th day of a year. The correspondence between the myths of successive destructions of the world in Asia and Mexico is hardly less remarkable. The same causes which brought Asiatic calendars and myths into Aztec culture, may have brought over the Indian game of *pachisi*. It is not needful to account for this connection between nations of the two continents by supposing migrations of population on a large scale. The necessary contact might even have been made by the drifting over of boats or junks, with the crews alive, from East Asia to the Pacific coast of North America: an event which happens every now and then, as it probably has done for ages. By whatever communication Asiatic calendars and cosmic myths found their way into America, the Hindu game of *pachisi* or some allied form of it may have passed over from somewhere in Asia, and established itself in Mexico as *patolli*.

The evidence derived from this game, however, by no means ends here. Father Joseph Ochs, a Jesuit missionary who was in Mexico in 1754–68, in the following passage is no doubt speaking of the natives in the Tarahumara and Pima district. "Instead of our cards they have slips of reed or bits of wood, a thumb wide and almost a span long, on which, as on a tally, different strokes are cut in and stained black. These they hold together tight in the hand, raise them as high as they can, and let them fall on the ground. Whoever then has most strokes or eyes for him, wins the stakes. This game is as bad as the notorious hazard. They call it *patole*. As it is forbidden under pain of blows, they choose a place out in the woods, yet the noise of these bits of wood has discovered me many sharpers hidden in the bush. To play the more safely they spread out a cloak or carpet, not to be betrayed by the noise."* Thus toward a thousand miles from the city of Mexico, we find a game going on which still keeps the Aztec name of *patolli*, although the language of the district is not Aztec, and which seems to be the Mexican game so far as the casting lots are concerned, but without the counters. The use of slips of wood as lots is curiously like the Egyptian *táb*, which game also, it was noticed, is sometimes played without the counters, though only for sport, not gambling.

If now we travel another thousand miles and more north-eastward, into the region of the great lakes, we shall find among the so-called North American Indians a game which on examination appears closely connected with the Mexican *patolli*. It is widely spread, and has been mentioned by many authors as the game of plum-stones, game of the bowl, &c. It was clearly not derived from the Europeans, and is noticed as a regular Indian game by the Jesuit missionaries among the Hurons as early as 1636 ;† they call it *jeu de plat*, and say it was played with six plum-stones, white on one side and black on the other, in a dish which was hit hard against the ground so that the stones turned over anyhow, the game being to get them all black or all white. They clearly did not quite understand the game, of which the best account is that given by Mr. L. H. Morgan, as played among the Iroquois.‡ It appears in two forms. As *gus-ga-e-sá-tä*, or deer buttons, it was strictly a fireside game,

---

* Murr, "Nachrichten von verschiedenen Ländern des Spanischen Amerika," Halle, 1809, part i., p. 256. "Anstatt unserer Karten haben sie daumenbreite, fast spannenlange Rohrschnitze, oder auch Hölzergen, in welche, wie auf einem Kerbholze, verschiedene Striche eingeschnitten und schwarz getränkt sind. Diese halten sie in der Hand fest zusammen, heben sie so hoch sie können in die Höhe, und lassen sie auf die Erde fallen. Wer denn mehrere Striche oder Augen über sich hat, gewinnt den Einsatz. Dies Spiel ist so schlimm, als das verruchte Würfelspiel. Sie nennen es Patolo. Weil es bey Strafe der Schläge verboten ist so erschen sie sich hiezu einen Ort im Gebüsche aus ; jedoch hat mir der Klang dieser Hölzerchen manche im Gebüsche versteckte Gauner entdeckt. Sicherer zu spielen breiteten sie einen Mantel oder Teppich aus, um nicht durch den Schall verrathen zu werden," &c.

† "Relations des Jesuites dans la Nouvelle France" (reprinted Quebec, 1858), 1636, p. 113. See also Loskiel "History of Mission of United Brethren among the Indians in North America," translated by Latrobe, London 1794, part i., p. 106.

‡ L. H. Morgan, "League of the Iroquois," Rochester (N.Y.), 1851, p. 302-307.

though sometimes introduced as an amusement at the season of religious councils, the people dividing into tribes as usual and betting upon the result. Eight buttons, about an inch in diameter, shaped like a double-convex lens, were made of elk-horn, rounded and polished, and slightly burned on one side to blacken them. The game was played by two or more, all the players continuing in their seats till it was determined. A certain number of beans, fifty perhaps, were made the capital, and the game continued until one of the players had won them all. Two persons spread a blanket, and seated themselves upon it. One of them shook the deer buttons in his hands, and then threw them down. If 6 turned up of the same colour, it counted 2, if 7, it counted 4, and if all, it counted 20, the winner taking as many beans from the general stock as he made points by the throw. He also continued to throw as long as he continued to win. When less than 6 came up, either black or white, it counted nothing, and the throw passed to the other player. In this manner the game was continued until the beans were taken up between the two players. After that the one paid to the other out of his own winnings, the game ending as soon as either player's beans were all lost. Or four could play, either with a partner or independently. When deer buttons was played as a public game, the arrangement was as in the peach-stone game.

The peach-stone game, *gus-kä-eh*, was a betting game, played by the people divided into tribes, and by custom it was the con-cluding exercise on the last day of the Green Corn and Harvest Festivals, and also of the New Year's Jubilee. Its introduction among them is ascribed to the first *To-do-dä-ho*, who flourished at the formation of the " League," and a popular belief prevailed that it would be enjoyed by them in the future life, in the realm of the Great Spirit. It was played in the public council-house, by a succession of players, two at a time, under the supervision of managers. A number of beans, usually 100, made the bank. When the bets had been made, and the articles staked delivered into the custody of the managers, these seated themselves on a raised platform, the throng arranged themselves in two divisions, and two players sat down to play, one on each side, each pro-vided by the managers on his own side with five beans out of the bank. Six peach-stones were used, ground or cut down to the flattened roundish form required, and burnt on one side to blacken them. They were put in a wooden or earthen bowl and shaken by the player. When they ceased rolling, if all came up of one colour, white or black, it counted 5, entitling the player to receive 5 beans from his adversary; if 5 came up of one colour, it counted 1, giving 1 bean; if less than 5 of either colour came up, it counted nothing, and the lead passed to the opponent. When either player had lost all his stock of beans, he retired, and a new player with a new stock replaced him, till one side had gained all the beans, thus winning the game.

This using of beans as counters may possibly have been learnt by the Indians from the white men, so that we must not found any ethnological argument on it, nor can we with safety treat as properly belonging to the Indian tribes of America the varieties of the game which are described in Schoolcraft's " Indian Tribes," Part II., p. 71, as played by the Dacotas under the name of *kun-ta-soo,* and by the Ojibwas as *puggesaing.* The Dakota game is played with eight plum-stones, but some of them are marked with figures of tortoise, war-eagle, &c., and the counting is elaborate. The Ojibwa name is well known to English readers from Longfellow having embodied in ﹐his " Hiawatha " a long description of it from Schoolcraft, under the title of " the game of bowl and counters, puggesaing with thirteen pieces." It has in it brass discs and pieces of bone cut to represent ducks, war-clubs, &c, and these all have a right and wrong side, the reckoning of the combinations thrown ranging from nothing up to 158 for a single throw, in a most complicated way. Now though modern Indians have played these games, there are no early mentions of them, as there is of the simple game of the bowl and plumstones. It is therefore quite likely that these more complex games may be modern varieties of the old American game of the bowl, made with European help.

To sum up the argument from the presence of these games in America. Lot-backgammon as represented by tab, *pachisi,* &c., ranges in the Old World from Egypt across Southern Asia to Birma. As the *patolli* of the Mexicans is a variety of lot-backgammon most nearly approaching the Hindu *pachisi,* and perhaps like it passing into the stage of dice-backgammon, its presence seems to prove that it had made its way across from Asia. How it came is uncertain, though the drifting across of Asiatic vessels to California offers the readiest solution. At any rate, it may be reckoned among elements of Asiatic culture traceable in the old Mexican civilization, the high development of which in metal work, architecture, astronomy, political and religious institutions, &c., seems to be in large measure due to Asiatic influence. From Mexico, it appears that gambling by means of lots spread among the ruder north-west tribes, bearing the Aztec name of *patolli,* and being in fact the lot-casting part of that game but without the board and stone counters. Moreover, similar gambling by lot-casting was early found among the tribes of the great American lakes. This method of lot-casting, which corresponds to that of lot-backgammon, was certainly not introduced into America by the Europeans, who were not acquainted with it. We are therefore left to consider that the North American Indians got it probably through Mexico, but at any rate in some manner from Asia. Now if any item of culture, even a matter so trifling as a game, can be distinctly made out to have passed over from Asia and established itself among the rude tribes of North America, this opens a way by which various other features of their culture may be fairly accounted for as due to Asiatic influence.

DISCUSSION.

Lieut. Col. GODWIN AUSTEN said : I have listened with very great interest to Mr. Tylor's paper on the striking similarity of the old Mexican game of "*patolli*" with the common Indian game called "*pachisi.*" I became acquainted with this last when employed on the survey of Kashmir some years ago. It was the favourite game of the natives of my establishment, and this led me to learn the game, which I often played with them, and I became then well acquainted with the rules. Knowing that Mr. Tylor was writing on the subject, I have put a few notes and the rules together of the game as played by the Kashmiris, Punjabis, &c.

The game is well known all along the northern part of India to Assam. I do not know whether it extends to Burma, but very probably is known there, from the larger Hindustani element now in the country. I can, I think, clear up the meaning and similarity of one of the statements regarding the Mexican game so described by the old Historian (Clavigero) who very probably did not thoroughly know the game of *patolli*, and described it as a looker-on would do, and as most Europeans in India would now if explaining the game of *pachisi* He says the game ends when three of the coloured pieces are *all in a row.* Now in the game of *pachisi*, played with four sets of three-coloured markers, "Gúti", as they are played out they are placed in a row within the centre square or goal, and opposite to the player's own arm of the cross-board, and this position shows plainly to those engaged how many each individual has played out round the table; the first to place them all in a row being the winner, the others in succession.

Rules of the Game of Pachisi.

The game is played by two, three, or four persons (A B C D) having three markers (Gúti) or counters of different colours each (to shorten the game only two are often agreed on to be played), these are moved over the squares of the board, commencing at A to a′, a″, a‴, &c. Certain squares are marked with diagonal lines ; in these a marker is safe and cannot be taken up ; the term for this is "*Gúché baithna,*"—*Gúché* being probably a corruption of *Gosha*, used in the sense of "*Gosha Nishin*"—a hermit.

2. The moves are regulated by the throw of seven cowries in different combinations.

A cowrie falling with the aperture uppermost is called "*chit*," with the aperture down or flat, "*put*."

The highest throw, "*pachis*," gives the name to the game —is	=	25
Six cowries with aperture up, one down—		
The next highest all seven cowries with aperture upwards	=	12
All seven with aperture down	=	6
All down and one up	=	1
All down and two up	=	2
All down and three up	=	3
and so on up to five.		

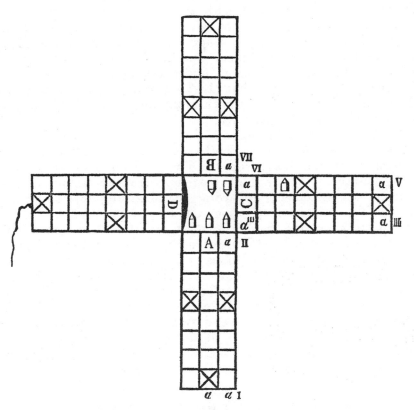

The Board is made of Cloth, with a pocket at D to hold the markers. It then folds up and is tied by a string. The markers are made of wood coloured with lac worked in on a lathe.

3. A throw of twenty-five, twelve, or six must be made to enable a player to come in. Place the first marker on the board and commence play, and so for each marker, this is called *pauwa*—or getting an ace; a throw of the above numbers gives an extra throw

4. On playing out, should the marker get into the last square a throw of twenty-five, twelve, or six must be made to take it off the board.

5. Markers are taken up "*guti marna.*" when by the throw of the cowries a marker can be placed in a square already occupied by an adversary—who then has to commence again from his original side of the board.

It will be seen from the construction of the board that from one corner square to the opposite and inner corner square is 25, or from a′ a i. to a″′ a vii.

Mr. HYDE CLARKE suggested to Mr. Tylor that the Tarahumara language possesses elements independent of its Aztek affinities, and that, too, it is related to remarkable languages of the Old World. He considered the discovery of Mr. Tylor's had another important link in the connection between the Old World and the New, and could not concur with him in attributing the calendar, the creation legend and the attoli, and he would add the measurements of Mr. Petrie, and so many other proofs of connection, to the casual influence of Chinese and Japanese wrecks before the time of Monteruma. He attributed them to specific migration, of which they had now so much evidence.

Mr. WALHOUSE, Capt. DILLON, and the PRESIDENT took part in the above discussion, and Mr. TYLOR replied.

Part II

NORTH AMERICA

IROQUOIS GAMES

W. M. Beauchamp

IROQUOIS GAMES.[1]

SOME Iroquois games have a high antiquity, having survived the test of time. Two forms of the game of white and black still exist, and there are frequent allusions to one of these in the Jesuit Relations, where it is termed that of the plate or dish. It excited the highest interest; for though it was of the simplest nature, nation played against nation, and village against village. From the floor to the ridgepole of the cabin the eager spectators looked at the two players, showing their sympathy by their cries.

Two forms of this simple game of chance remain, and perhaps there were never more than these. Father Bruyas alluded to one of them in his Mohawk lexicon of radical words, speaking of it as the game in which the women scatter fruit stones with the hand. This distinction of throwing remains, although disks of bone or horn are now used instead of the stones of fruit. L. H. Morgan described this as the game of deer buttons, called Gus-ga-e-sá-ta by the Senecas. They used eight circular buttons of deer horn, about an inch in diameter, and blackened on one side. These are about an eighth of an inch in thickness, and bevelled to the edge. He said: "This was strictly a fireside game, although it was sometimes introduced as an amusement at the season of religious councils, the people dividing into tribes as usual, and betting upon the result." In public two played it at a time, with a succession of players. In private two or more played it on a blanket, on which they sat and threw. His counting differs at first sight from that which I received, but amounts to the same thing. Beans were used for the pool, and Morgan said that six white or black drew two, seven drew four, and all white or black drew twenty. Less than six drew nothing, and the other player had his throw until he lost in turn.

Among the Onondagas now eight bones or stones are used, black on one side and white on the other. They term the game Ta-you-nyun-wát-hah, or Finger Shaker, and from one hundred to three hundred beans form the pool, as may be agreed. With them it is also a household game.

In playing this the pieces are raised in the hand and scattered, the desired result being indifferently white or black. Essentially, the counting does not differ from that given by Morgan. Two white or two black will have six of one color, and these count two beans, called O-yú-ah, or the Bird. The player proceeds until he loses, when his opponent takes his turn. Seven white or black gain four beans,

[1] Paper read at the Forty-fifth Meeting of the American Association for the Advancement of Science, Buffalo, N. Y., August 26, 1896.

called O-néo-sah, or Pumpkin. All white or all black gain twenty, called O-hén-tah, or a Field. These are all that draw anything, and we may indifferently say with the Onondagas, two white or black for the first, or six with the Senecas. The game is played singly or by partners, and there is no limit to the number. Usually there are three or four players.

In counting the gains there is a kind of ascending reduction; for as two birds make one pumpkin, only one bird can appear in the result. First come the twenties, then the fours, then the twos, which can occur but once. Thus we may say for twenty, Jo-han-tó-tah, you have one field, or more as the case may be. In the fours we can only say, Ki-yae-ne-you-sáh-ka, You have four pumpkins, for five would make a field. For two beans there is the simple announcement of O-yú-ah, Bird. There is often great excitement over this game.

The game of peach stones, much more commonly used and important, has a more public character, although I have played it in an Indian parlor. In early days the stones of the wild plum were used, but now six peach stones are ground down to an elliptic flattened form, the opposite sides being black or white. This is the great game known as that of the dish nearly three centuries ago. The wooden bowl which I used was eleven inches across the top and three inches deep, handsomely carved out of a hard knot. A beautiful small bowl which I saw elsewhere may have been used by children.

The six stones are placed in Kah-oón-wah, the bowl, and thence the Onondagas term the game Ta-yune-oo-wáh-es, throwing the bowl to each other as they take it in turn. In public playing two players are on their knees at a time, holding the bowl between them. When I played, simply to learn the game, we sat in chairs, the bowl being on another chair between us. Beans are commonly used for counters, but we had plum stones. Many rules are settled according to agreement, but the pumpkin is left out, and the stones usually count five for a bird and six for a field. All white or all black is the highest throw, and five or six are the only winning points. In early days it would seem that all white or all black alone counted. The bowl is simply struck on the floor; and although the game is said to be sometimes intensely exciting, the scientific spirit restrained my enthusiasm. I was not playing for beans, but for information.

This ancient game is used at the New Year's or White Dog Feast among the Onondagas yet. Clan plays against clan, the Long House against the Short House, and, to foretell the harvest, the women play against the men. If the men win, the ears of corn will be long, like them; but if the women gain the game, they will be short, basing the results on the common proportion of the sexes.

As of old, almost all games are yet played for the sick, but they are regarded now more as a diversion of the patient's mind than a means of healing. The game of the dish was once much used in divination, each piece having its own familiar spirit, but it is more commonly a social game now. Gambling at a feast is called Ken-yent-hah.

Brébeuf vividly described this game as he saw it among the Hurons in 1636. He said: " The game of the dish is also in great credit in matters of medicine, especially if the sick man has dreamed it. The game is purely chance; they have for use six plum stones, white on one side, black on the other, within a plate, which they throw violently against the ground, so that the stones jump and turn themselves, sometimes on the one side, sometimes on the other. The match consists in taking all white ones or all black. They usually play village against village. The whole company crowds into one cabin, and arranges itself on the one side and the other, upon poles raised even to the top. They bring in the sick man in a blanket, and that one from the village who is to shake the dish (for there is but one on each side appointed for this purpose) walks after, his face and his head enveloped in his robe. Both sides bet loud and firmly. When the one on the opposite side holds the dish they scream loudly, *Achinc, Achinc, Achinc,* Three, three, three; or else *Io-io, Io-io, Io-io,* wishing that he may throw only three white or three black." As men are said to act much alike under similar circumstances, the cries of the spectators at a baseball game may illustrate the shouts and interest of the ancient Hurons.

Brébeuf adds the methods of some players who were in high repute for their skill. As they often anointed the pieces for good luck, this may have served a further purpose; but he was astonished to see how, in a covered vessel, they could produce all white or all black at their pleasure. Bruyas defined Twa-ten-na-wé-ron, to play with the dish, deriving it from the Mohawk word At-nén-ha, a fruit stone. He gave many words relating to this game and to casting lots, another common thing. From this Loskiel fell into a curious error, saying: " The chief game of the Iroquois and Delawares is *dice*, which, indeed, originated with them. The dice are made of oval and flattish plum stones, painted black on one and yellow on the other side."

In Le Jeune's Relation of 1634 is an interesting but obscure allusion to a game of Iroquois children. The missionary had noticed a resemblance between the Canadian and European children's games of that day. He said: " Among others I have seen the little Parisians casting an arquebuse ball in the air, and catching it with a slightly hollowed stick; the little savage Montagnards do the same, using a small bundle of pine branches, which they catch and pitch in the air with a pointed stick. The little Iroquois have the same pastime, throwing a small perforated bone, which they enlace in the air in another little bone. A young man of that nation told me this, seeing the Montagnard children playing." The meaning seems to be that the perforated bone was caught and pierced by the point of another. Our cup and ball may illustrate these games, though we often attach a rubber string. Bruyas gives the Mohawk word Gan-nák-ti as meaning "a spindle, at the end of which is grafted a little stick that the children cause to run upon the ice." Then, as now, children used pieces of bark for sliding on the ice or snow.

Children, of course, have many games. That of interlocking violets, and pulling them apart, to the certain destruction of one at least, has a spice of savagery, and gives its name to the flower, Ta-keah-noon-wí-tahs, Two heads entangled. Some they have adopted from us, as Mumble-the-peg, which is elaborate and popular. The Onondagas term it Da-yu-sah-yéh-hŭh. Pull-away, and fox and geese in the snow are out-door games; blind man's buff and others are favorites within, as well as that of the bell and shoes, which I recently described. There is also a choosing by clasping hands alternately on a stick until it can be held no longer; but some of these I have mentioned before. Two games of the javelin are yet popular among the Onondagas. In one a group of boys may be seen with their hands full of peeled sumac sticks, often gayly colored. These they throw in the air, and often to a great distance, as they are very light. As a game it is simply a contest of throwing farthest, but a boy will sometimes amuse himself alone. The javelin and hoop requires opposing sides, as one must roll the hoop while the other throws the javelin at or through it. It is little played now. Archery, too, is somewhat out of fashion, though expert archers may still be found. In my boyhood every wandering Indian party was ready to shoot at coppers placed on edge in a crack, and these were rarely missed. The true Onondaga arrow, for ordinary use, is blunt-headed, expanding into a pointed knob, and I suspect, as they believe, that these have always been very largely used. Flint arrow points are rarely abundant on early Iroquois sites, and are usually small and triangular. The Iroquois, too, were not fond of working in stone, and were likely to make an arrow entirely of wood whenever it could be used. For small game it was always available, and they preferred it because it made noise enough in returning to make its recovery easy. This is the reason they now assign for their preference.

Among ball games that of lacrosse may be the oldest remaining and the most widely spread. Almost three centuries ago, at least, the Hurons and others played it, village against village, almost as it is played to-day. This also was played for the sick. The game is too well known to require description in any minute detail, but the leading features are the two bands of contestants trying to carry or throw the ball between the two guarded poles at either end of the ground. The ball must not be touched with the hand, but may be caught up, carried, or thrown with the broad bat. This bat is bent into a broad hook at one end, and is there provided with a network of sinews. It is one of the most picturesque and exciting of ball games, the contestants racing, dodging, throwing, struggling, digging up the ball in the liveliest manner possible. With all its occasional rudeness it is less dangerous than baseball or football, but the Onondagas are not insensible to its boisterous character, and call it Ka-che-kwā-áh, Hitting with their hips. They like baseball, too, and a group of boys may often be seen playing one or two old cat. I have described another native game of ball before, which is little known.

Foot-races hardly hold their own now, though formerly quite popular, but they differ little from our own. In early days, and before the adoption of the pantomimic western war dance, sham fights were a popular amusement. Indeed, as the Iroquois children were to become warriors, many of their sports were of a savage and warlike nature. In December, 1634, Arent Van Curler saw a sham fight among the Mohawks. Twenty men armed themselves with sticks and axes, but wisely wore their Indian armor of strings and reeds. After much skirmishing " the parties closed and dragged each other by the hair, just as they would have done to their enemies after defeating them, and before cutting off their scalps."

The game of the snow snake, called Ka-whén-tah by the Onondagas and Ga-wá-sa by the Senecas, is not mentioned by any early writer, and yet seems purely Iroquois in character. It is a simple test of power and skill in throwing the long and slender rod upon the snow or ice. Often, now, a channel is cut in the snow in which the snow snake glides along. The implement is from five to seven feet long, and has an upturned pointed head loaded with lead. This is run into grooves, and thus the head is blackened by the heat. Originally no metal was used ; in fact, this is a very recent addition. As the long shaft bends in its swift career over the ice or snow, it has a striking resemblance to a gliding snake, and thus receives its common name. The Seneca and Onondaga forms are easily distinguished, though the difference is not essential.

Among the analogies between savage and civilized life may be mentioned a funeral game of the Hurons, some centuries since. Our young collegians once adopted an ancient Indian custom, only terming it a cane rush. It is thus described in the Jesuit Relations : " The captain places in the hand of one of them a stick about a foot long, offering a prize to any one who will take it from him. They throw themselves headlong upon him, and sometimes remain engaged in the contest for an hour." The Jesuits also mentioned the game of the straw as one of importance, but only by name. It may have been a masquerade of the Jugglers at the Dream Feast, who tied bundles of straw before them. If this is correct there were good reasons for withholding a fuller account.

I do not find that climbing a greased pole was ever an Iroquois sport, though the Hurons knew of it. There is an amusing account of this among the Nipissiriniens, at the great funeral feast described in the Relation of 1642, which is not unlike some scenes in modern holidays. "There was a May-pole planted, of a pretty reasonable height. A Nipissirinien, having climbed to the top, fastened two prizes there, namely, a kettle and a deerskin, inviting the youth to show their agility. Although the May-pole was without bark and very smooth, he greased it, in order to make the taking of these more difficult. He had no sooner descended than there was a crowd to mount it ; one lost courage at the beginning, one at a less, one at a greater height, and such a one seeing himself almost arrived at the top, suddenly saw himself at the bottom." A Huron at last got the prizes by an unfair stratagem, but other Hurons made this good.

As in ancient Europe, funeral feasts were commonly accompanied by games of many kinds. Thus in the Huron feast of the dead in 1636, for several days gifts were made. "On one side women were drawing the bow to see who should have the prize, which was sometimes a girdle of porcupine quills or a necklace of beads ; on the other hand, in several parts of the village, the young men were drawing clubs upon any who would try to capture them. The prize of this victory was a hatchet, some knives, or even a beaver robe. Every day the remains were arriving." Mourning and rejoicing mingled, as among the ancient Greeks, and this was not confined to the Huron Iroquois. In fact, even now, as the mourning for an old chief is often accompanied by the installation of the new, we are reminded of the French proclamation : "The king is dead, long live the king."

In connection with funeral rites it seems proper to refer to the game of plum stones used by the Sioux in dividing the property of the dead, for it has a resemblance to the old Iroquois game. It is not one of white and black, and is much more intricate than that of the present Onondagas. A description will be found in Yarrow's "Mortuary Customs of North American Indians," First Annual Report of the Bureau of Ethnology. From the plate it would seem that the mode of throwing the stones was from a bowl upon a hide extended on the ground. Women used seven plum stones, men eight, and those who play are of the sex of the deceased. The game is known as the "ghost gamble," and one Indian represents the ghost of the dead. Cards now take the place of the stones, and each person plays against the ghost for a portion of the property. The stones are not merely black and white, but each has its own mark, and there are six winning throws, as well as five entitling the player to another throw. Buffalo heads, crosses, and dots are among the markings. It will thus be seen that the game is very distinct from the Iroquois game of white and black, while having a marked resemblance. It is more complex, and is used on a very different occasion.

Similar resemblances will be found among western games to that of the snow snake, and yet with the same contrasted features. The deep snows of the eastern forests, we may suppose, developed a form especially adapted to a winter game. The spear or javelin slightly changed one or two features in its new and local use. One barb was cut away, the point slightly turned, and there was no obstruction hindering its flight on the snow.

I have spoken of the game of the bell and the shoe as though it might have been adapted from the whites. A bell is hidden in one of three shoes, by the Onondagas, and the opposing party must guess in which of these it is. In Tanner's Narrative, however, about seventy years ago, he described a similar game somewhat differently played by the Ottawas and Crees. The former used four moccasins, in one of which was hidden some small object. These were touched in due order, with varying results to the guesser and his party. The Crees put the hand successively into all the moccasins, endeavoring to find the hidden object last of all. In this case, therefore, the Onondagas have preserved an old game, substituting the bell for something more primitive.

He also described a game of the dish or bowl, much like that of the Iroquois. Small pieces of wood, bone, or brass were used, not less than nine in number, and blackened on one side. These were placed in a wooden bowl, and the edge was violently struck, throwing the pieces into the air. Each one played until he missed. The principal game of the bowl among the northern tribes, as described by Schoolcraft, has thirteen pieces, and is quite elaborate. The pieces represent men, fishes, ducks, etc. Catlin also described a game of the bowl among the Indian women of Iowa, as well as the moccasin game already mentioned.

Charlevoix's description of the great Iroquois game, as he saw it played in a Huron village in 1721, may well be quoted, as it differs a little from others. "The game of the platter or bones is played between two persons only ; each person has six or eight little bones, which I at first took for apricot stones, these being of the same size and shape; but upon viewing them nearer I found they had six unequal faces, the two largest of which are painted, the one black and the other of a straw-color. They fling them up into the air, striking at the same time against the ground or table with a round hollow dish, in which they are contained, and which must first be made to spin round. When they have no dish they content themselves with throwing the bones up into the air with the hand. If all of them after falling to the ground present the same color, the player wins five points, the party is forty, and the points won are discounted in proportion to the gains on his side; five bones of a color give only one point for the first time, but the second the winner sweeps the board ; any lower number goes for nothing."

The persistence of these Iroquois games is remarkable. As long as known they have had the game of white and black, and have retained it almost unchanged. As long, certainly, they have played lacrosse, in common with most other Indian nations, and other games seem quite as old, although unmentioned by early writers. The moccasin game may have been adopted, but the snow snake seems to have been original. The curious thing is that it attracted so little attention. I think Morgan first described it, but I saw it played many years before any notice of it seems to have appeared in print.

I have spoken merely of things properly called games, wherein there was some kind of a contest. Some would include mere sports under this head, and to the Jesuits the Hononhouaroia, or Dream Feast, with its masquerading and guessing, assumed something of this character. The masking survives only in the annual ceremonies of the False Faces, and these have now lost their religious features, and have become a great frolic. One day last winter I encountered these maskers on their annual round at the Onondaga Reservation. They were approaching a house where they would be welcome, and I stopped to see what would be done. They were dressed in old clothes, some of them well padded, and all had masks, some from the toy-shops and others of paper or wood. One or two wore feathers besides. They danced about the house, and pounded its sides with sticks and turtle-shell rattles. They crawled on their hands and knees on the piazza floor, pounding all the time. The door opened at last, and their leader entered. He danced around the room a while, putting ashes on the heads of the inmates, and crying "Ho! Ho!" The door opened again, and his comrades came in. They danced around, taking up double handfuls of ashes, and puffing these over the heads of their hosts. Then they took up the inmates in chairs, a man on each side, and danced around the room with them. Pounded parched corn was given the visitors to eat in the house, and provisions were taken away for the evening feast, in the basket which one of them carried. I met them on the road an hour or two later, returning from a distant cabin. The change is great indeed in this old custom, but if it has lost its meaning the participants have plenty of fun.

There are minor sports and games which might be mentioned, but those described have the flavor of antiquity. Some reveal a natural failing. Our aborigines had an innate love of gambling, and the idea of gain or loss entered into most of their simple sports. The Iroquois were accustomed, as our western tribes are yet, to stake everything on games of chance or skill. The turn of the plum stone might give them poverty or wealth. It certainly would give them the excitement they craved.

W. M. Beauchamp.

THE PRACTICE OF SPORTS AMONG THE INDIANS OF AMERICA

R. Blasiz

The Practice of Sports Among the Indians of America

R. Blasiz

Translated by Fred E. Foertsch

The author states that he gathered his information from Richard N. Wegner, a noted South American athlete. The account was first published in the "Umschau" 1932.

According to Wegner's observations the physical activities engaged in by South American natives were not designed to train for the use of weapons of war. Sports held an important place in the life of the Indian because of the religious significance attached to them. A victory brought to the members of a particular group the highest glory of the gods and held in abeyance the evil spirits. It was their belief that sickness, sterility, and misfortune do not follow in the wake of the victor and the members of his group. Much more, victory is sufficient to make atonement unnecessary and has the power to free a person from even a death penalty. This accounts for the fact that the Indians entered competition with great emotional feeling.

Certain practices related to the outcomes of the contests as well as certain peculiar customs accompanied the contests. For instance, betting on teams or certain athletes was quite a common practice. Some even risked all their worldly possessions in the gambling adventures. Preparations for the contests were highly important. The contestants held watch all night, they fasted, they adhered to strict dietary rules, and they refrained from contacts with the opposite sex.

The Indian artist Catlin who lived among the wildest tribes about the tenth century describes a game which is very much like Lacrosse. In this game a racket was used. He states that the ball was tossed up in the air in mid-field by a neutral person. The object of the game was to put the ball, by means of the racket, through the opponents' goal which was at the end of the field. Whenever a goal was made there came a rest period of about a minute before resuming the contest. To win a game a team had to score one hundred goals. Before the game was started the goals were erected with much ceremony, including songs and the beating of drums. The racket which was used was similar to our tennis racket but the handle was somewhat longer and the surface area was slightly smaller. Often the racket consisted of a stick with a semi-circular hook at one end to which a net was attached. A racket of this kind was found in an old grave in Nazca. This racket, however, was smaller than the one described by Catlin and was probably the toy of a child.

Certain phenomena in nature determined the time when athletic festivals were to be held. The Indians felt that by following the signs of nature the evil spirits could best be appeased. Thus the Indians of North America with the first snowfall placed a snowshoe on the end of a highly decorated pole, placed it erect in the ground, and proceeded to dance around the pole in a gliding fashion.

In South America the Indians were interested in certain water sports, in feats of skill, and running events. On Lake Titicaca they engaged in boat races. The boats used were very crude and were made of bulrushes. At the head of the Amazon River many races in canoes were held. Races in sailing boats were engaged in with great enthusiasm.

The Uracare Indians were much interested in deflecting an arrow from its path after being shot from a bow. It was common practice to shoot at a human target. The arrow was aimed at shoulder level and slightly to one side of the one representing the target. As the arrow came toward the one representing the target it was his business to strike it down or deflect it from its path with a knife just as it passed by him.

In the mountainous regions of South America and Mexico the Indians were particularly efficient in running. Among the Taharumara tribes in northern Mexico it was not uncommon to see whole villages come together to participate in running contests. The representatives from each village were distinguished by different colored head bands. Competition took place on a circular track which had been staked off. The running course was, however, not prepared as in modern days. It was left as nature had developed it. The length of the course varied for 3 to 15 miles. Endurance races of various lengths were promoted, some of which reached a distance of 145 miles. The Spaniards in their conquest of Peru found that the Indians had well organized across country relay teams which were used for delivering messages and fresh sea food to the capitol at Inka and to other parts of the country. Even today in some parts of Bolivia and Peru the mail is carried by such means.

Antagonistic contests were also enjoyed by the Indians. In many places pushing contests with the use of padded shields were common. Each contestant held the shield in front of himself and in contact with that of his opponent. Each tried to push the other out of a certain area or attempted to make him fall. The Karaja and the Savaje tribes in South America often entertained and feasted visitors, but before the feast could take place a series of wrestling matches were engaged in. Dancing youths came forth and challenged the visitors to matches. In these wrestling matches victory came to the one who succeeded in putting his opponent's back to the ground. After the wrestling bouts were concluded the visitors were feasted and entertained.

Among the Paressi-Kabisi tribes the youths had to pass a strength test before they could be admitted to the field of activities of adult men. The apparatus used for testing the strength was peculiar. It consisted of two heavy uprights which were placed securely in the ground and about a meter apart. In each upright there was a hole. The holes were so placed that a horizontal bar of wood could be drawn through them slightly below the level of the shoulders of the youth. The youth then stepped under this horizontal bar and by means of an upward push from the back and shoulders attempted to break the bar.

Ball games which were similar to our game of soccer were played by a number of tribes in the territory extending from Brazil to Chaco. As far back as 1726 the Jesuit missionairies were astonished by the skill these people displayed. Father Fernandez gives us the first description of this game. The teams all consisted of 4 to 6 members. The ball was made of a sort of crude rubber and had a diameter of about 3 1-2 to 4 1-2 inches. The game was begun by tossing the ball into the air. The players then volleyed it back and forth with their heads. A ball which had fallen to the ground could not be picked up. The players had to use their foreheads to get it into play again. The object of the game was to keep the ball in the air. The side which allowed the ball to fall five times lost the game. The Jesuit Gumilla also observed a similar type of game in another section of the country but here the ball had to be propelled with the right shoulder instead of with the head. Among the ancient tribes of Central America a similar game was played but here they used their hips and buttocks. The field here was divided into 4 parts. At each end of the field a stone ring was erected against a wall and each team tried to put the ball through the opponent's goal. Points were scored each time the ball struck the wall which the opponents were defending. A definite number of points decided the winner. If, however, the ball was put through the ring the game was won regardless of the points previously scored.

Hockey was also a familiar game to the Indians. In Chaco the natives were very fond of this game. The sticks used were very light and were formed from the middle ribs of palm leaves. The field had goals similar to those of today, one at each end. The object was to put the ball through the opponent's goal. Rules were also enforced. Striking the opponent's shins or legs was prohibited. Sometimes guards were made and used as a protection for the thighs. It was not uncommon to see older men participate, frequently with much enthusiasm. Even though they were no longer fit to play in the most active positions, they at least served as goal tenders. —*Leibesuebungen und Koerperliche Erziehung.*

A CHOKTAW BALL GAME

George Catlin

GEORGE CATLIN

A Choktaw Ball Game

Of fifteen thousand, are another tribe, removed from the Northern parts of Alabama, and Mississippi, within the few years past, and now occupying a large and rich tract of country, South of the Arkansas and the Canadian rivers; adjoining to the country of the Creeks and the Cherokees, equally civilized, and living much in the same manner.

In this tribe I painted the portrait of their famous and excellent chief, *Mo-sho-la-tub-bee* (he who puts out and kills), who has since died of the small-pox. In the same plate will also be seen, the portrait of a distinguished and very gentlemanly man, who has been well-educated, and who gave me much curious and valuable information, of the history and traditions of his tribe. The name of this man is *Ha-tchoo-tuck-nee* (the snapping turtle), familiarly called by the whites *"Peter Pinchlin."*

These people seem, even in their troubles, to be happy; and have, like all the other remnants of tribes, preserved with great tenacity their different games, which it would seem they are everlastingly practicing for want of other occupations or amusements in life. Whilst I was staying at the Choctaw agency in the midst of their nation, it seemed to be a sort of season of amusements, a kind of holiday; when the whole tribe almost, were assembled around the establishment, and from day to day we were entertained with some games or feats that were exceedingly amusing: horse-racing, dancing, wrestling, foot-racing, and ball-playing, were amongst the most exciting; and of all the catalogue, the most beautiful, was decidedly that of ball-playing. This wonderful game, which is the favorite one amongst all the tribes, and with these Southern tribes played exactly the same, can never be appreciated by those who are not happy enough to see it.

It is no uncommon occurrence for six or eight hundred or a thousand of these young men, to engage in a game of ball, with five or six times that number of spectators, of men, women and children, surrounding the ground, and looking on. And I pronounce such a scene, with its hundreds of Nature's most beautiful models, denuded, and painted of various colours, running and leaping into the air, in all the most extravagant and varied forms, in the desperate struggles for the ball, a school for the painter or sculptor, equal to any of those which ever inspired the hand of the artist in the Olympian games or the Roman forum.

I have made it an uniform rule, whilst in the Indian country, to attend every ball-play I could hear of, if I could do it by riding a distance of twenty or thirty miles; and my usual custom has been on such occasions, to straddle the back of my horse, and look on to the best advantage. In this way I have sat, and oftentimes reclined, and almost dropped from my horse's back, with irresistible laughter at the succession of droll tricks, and kicks and scuffles which ensue, in the almost superhuman struggles for the ball. These plays generally commence at nine o'clock, or near it, in the morning; and I have more than once balanced myself on my pony, from that time till near sundown, without more than one minute of intermission at a time, before the game has been decided.

It is impossible for pen and ink alone, or brushes, or even with their combined efforts, to give more than a *caricature* of such a scene; but such as I have been able to do, I have put upon the canvas. I will convey as correct an account as I can, and leave the reader to imagine the rest; or look to *other books* for what I may have omitted.

While at the Choctaw agency it was announced, that there was to be a great play on a certain day, within a few miles, on which occasion I attended, and made three sketches, and also the following entry in my note-book, which I literally copy out:

Monday afternoon at three o'clock, I rode out with Lieutenants S. and M., to a very pretty prairie, about six miles distant, to the ball-play-ground of the Choctaws, where we found several thousand Indians encamped. There were two points of timber about half a mile apart, in which the two parties for the play, with their respective families and friends, were encamped; and lying between them, the prairie on which the game was to be played. My companions and myself, although we had been apprised, that to see the whole of a ball-play, we must remain on the ground all the night previous, had brought nothing to sleep upon, resolving to keep our eyes open, and see what transpired through the night. During the afternoon, we loitered about amongst the different tents and shantees of the two encampments, and afterwards, at sundown, witnessed the ceremony of measuring out the ground, and erecting the "byes" or goals which were to guide the play. Each party had their goal made with two upright posts, about 25 feet high and six feet apart, set firm in the ground, with a pole across at the top. These goals were about forty or fifty rods apart; and at a point just half way between, was another small stake, driven down, where the ball was to be thrown up at the firing of a gun, to be struggled for by the players. All this preparation was made by some old men, who were, it seems, selected to be the judges of the play, who drew a line from one bye to the other; to which directly came from the woods, on both sides, a great concourse of women and old men, boys and girls, and dogs and horses, where bets were to be made on the play. The betting was all done across this line, and seemed to be chiefly left to the women, who seemed to have martialled out a little of everything that their houses and their fields possessed. Goods and chattels— knives—dresses—blankets—pots and kettles—dogs and horses, and guns; and all were placed in the possession of *stake-holders,* who sat by them, and watched them on the ground all night, preparatory to the play.

The sticks with which this tribe play, are bent into an oblong hoop at the end, with a sort of slight web of small thongs tied across, to prevent the ball from passing through. The players hold one of these in each hand, and by leaping into the air, they catch the ball between the two nettings and throw it, without being allowed to strike it, or catch it in their hands.

The mode in which these sticks are constructed and used, will be seen in the portrait of *Tullock-ckish-ko* (he who drinks the juice of the stone), the most distinguished ball-player of the Choktaw nation, represented in his ball-play dress, with his ball-sticks in his hands. In every ball-play of these people, it is a rule of the play, that no man shall wear moccasins on his feet, or any other dress than his breech-cloth around his waist, with a beautiful bead belt, and a "tail," made of white horsehair or quills, and a *"mane"* on the neck, of horsehair dyed of various colours.

This game had been arranged and "made up," three or four months before the parties met to play it, and in the following manner:—The two champions who led the two parties, and had the alternate choosing of the players through the whole tribe, sent runners, with the ball-sticks most fantastically ornamented with ribbons and red paint, to be touched by each one of the chosen players; who thereby agreed to be on the spot at the appointed time and ready for the play. The ground having been all prepared and preliminaries of the game all settled, and the bettings all made, and goods all "staked," night came on without the appearance of any players on the ground. But soon after dark, a procession of lighted flambeaux was seen coming from each encampment, to the ground where the players assembled around their respective byes; and at the beat of the drums and chaunts of the women, each party of players commenced the "ball-play dance." Each party danced for a quarter of an hour around their respective byes, in their ball-play dress; rattling their ball-sticks together in the most violent manner, and all singing as loud as they could raise their voices; whilst the women of each party, who had their goods at stake, formed into two rows on the line between the two parties of players, and danced also, in an uniform step, and all their voices joined in chaunts to the Great Spirit; in which they were soliciting his favour in deciding the game to their advantage; and also encouraging the players to exert every power they possessed, in the struggle that was to ensue. In the mean time, four old *medicine-men,* who were to have the starting of the ball, and who were to be judges of the play, were seated at the point where the ball was to be started; and busily smoking to the Great Spirit for their success in judging rightly, and impartially, between the parties in so important an affair.

This dance was one of the most picturesque scenes imaginable, and was repeated at intervals of every half hour during the night, and exactly in the same manner; so that the players were certainly awake all the night, and arranged in their appropriate dress, prepared for the play which was to commence. at nine o'clock the next morning. In the morning, at the hour, the two parties and all their friends, were drawn out and over the ground; when at length the game commenced, by the judges throwing up the ball at the firing of a gun; when an instant struggle ensued between the players, who were some six or seven hundred in numbers, and were mutually endeavouring to catch the ball in their sticks, and throw it home and between their respective stakes; which, whenever successfully done, counts one for the game. In this game every player was dressed alike, that is, *divested* of all dress, except the girdle and the tail, which I have before described; and in these desperate struggles for the ball, when it is *up* (where hundreds are running together and leaping, actually over each other's heads, and darting between their adversaries' legs, tripping and throwing, and foiling each other in every possible manner, and every voice raised to the highest key, in shrill yelps and barks)! there are rapid successions of feats, and of incidents, that astonish and amuse far beyond the conception of any one who has not had the singular good luck to witness them. In these struggles, every mode is used that can be devised, to oppose the progress of the foremost, who is likely to get the ball; and these obstructions often meet desperate individual resistance, which terminates in a violent scuffle, and sometimes in fisticuffs; when their sticks are dropped, and the parties are unmolested, whilst they are settling it between themselves; unless it be by a general *stampedo,* to which they are subject who are down, if the ball happens to pass in their direction. Every weapon, by a rule of all ball-plays, is laid by in their respective encampments, and no man allowed to go for one; so that the sudden broils that take place on the ground, are presumed to be as suddenly settled without any probability of much personal injury; and no one is allowed to interfere in any way with the contentious individuals.

There are times, when the ball gets to the ground, and such a confused mass rushing together around it, and knocking their sticks together, without the possibility of any one getting or seeing it, for the dust that they raise, that the spectator loses his strength, and everything else but his senses; when the condensed mass of ball-sticks, and shins, and bloody noses, is carried around the different parts of the ground, for a quarter of an hour at a time, without any one of the mass being able to see the ball; and which they are often thus scuffling for, several minutes after it has been thrown off, and played over another part of the ground.

For each time that the ball was passed between the stakes of either party, one was counted for their game, and a halt of about one minute; when it was again started by the judges of the play, and a similar struggle ensued; and so on until the successful party arrived to 100, which was the limit of the game, and accomplished at an hour's sun, when they took the stakes; and then, by a previous agreement, produced a number of jugs of whiskey, which gave all a wholesome drink, and sent them all off merry and in good humour, but not drunk.

After this exciting day, the concourse was assembled in the vicinity of the agency house, where we had a great variety of dances and other amusements; the most of which I have described on former occasions. One, however, was new to me, and I must say a few words of it: this was the *Eagle Dance,* a very pretty scene, which is got up by their young men, in honour of that bird, for which they seem to have a religious regard. This picturesque dance was given by twelve or sixteen men, whose bodies were chiefly naked and painted white, with white clay, and each one holding in his hand the tail of the eagle, while his head was also decorated with an eagle's quill. Spears were stuck in the ground, around which the dance was performed by four men at a time, who had simultaneously, at the beat of the drum, jumped up from the ground where they had all sat in rows of four, one row immediately behind the other, and ready to take the place of the first four when they left the ground fatigued, which they did by hopping or jumping around behind the rest, and taking their seats, ready to come up again in their turn, after each of the other sets had been through the same forms.

In this dance, the steps or rather jumps, were different from anything I had ever witnessed before, as the dancers were squat down, with their bodies almost to the ground, in a severe and most difficult posture.

KANSU

A Sioux Game

Z. T. Daniel

KANSU: A SIOUX GAME.—This is a very ancient game of the Sioux Indians, played mostly by elderly women, although young women and men of all ages play it also.

Kansu is an abbreviation of kanta su, which means "plum seed." They drop the *ta* and call the game kansu because it is played with plum seeds. It is used for gambling and amusement, and is more like our dice than any other of our games. When playing, the seeds are thrown up in a basket or bowl, and the markings on the seeds that are up or down decide the throw.

The seeds used are those of the wild plum of the Dakotas and indigenous throughout the northwest region of the United States generally. They are seven in number. On one side of all they are perfectly plain and of the natural color, except some fine marks on four to distinguish them whem the burnt sides are down, but on the reverse side of all there are burnt markings. These markings are made by a piece of hot iron, such as a nail, the blade of a knife, or a piece of hoop iron. Before the natives had iron they used a hot stone. Six of the seeds are in pairs of three different kinds, and one only is of a different marking from all the others. One pair is scorched entirely on one side; another pair has an unburnt line about two millimeters wide traversing their longitudinal convexity (the remainder of their surfaces on that side being scorched); the remaining pair have one-half of one side burnt longitudinally, the other half of the same side unburnt, but traversed by three small burnt lines equidistant, about one millimeter wide, running across their short axes. The remaining and only single seed has an hourglass figure burnt on one side, the contraction in the figure corresponding to the long diameter of the seed. They are all of the same size, about sixteen millimeters long, twelve wide, and seven thick, and are oval, having the outlines and convexity on each side of a diminutive turtle shell. When the Sioux first obtained our ordinary playing cards they gave to them, as well as to the game, the name kansu, because they were used by the whites and themselves for the same purposes as their original kansu.

The men do not use the seeds or the original kansu now, but they substitute our cards. Their women, however, do use the game at the present time. When the ration ticket was issued to them they gave to it the name of kansu, because it was a card; so also to a postal card, business card, or anything of the description of a card or ticket; a railroad, street-car, milk, store, or circus ticket would all be called kansu; so that the evolution of this term as applied to a ticket is a little interesting.

The description of the game kansu, as related by the Sioux, is as follows: Any number of persons may play, and they call the game kansu kute, which literally means "to shoot the seeds." When two persons play, or four that are partners, only six of the seeds are used, the hour-glass or king kansu being eliminated. The king is used when a number over two are playing and each one for himself. The three-line seeds are called "sixes;" the one-line, "fours;" those that are all black, "tens." When two play for a wager they each put 16 small sticks, stones, corn, peas, or what not into a common pile between them, making in all 32. The play begins by putting the seeds into a small bowl or basket and giving it a quick upward motion, which changes the position of the seeds, then letting them fall back into the receptacle, care being taken not to let any one fall out. The markings that are up decide the throw, precisely on the principle of our dice. As they count they take from the pile of 32 what they make, and when the pile is exhausted the one having the greatest number wins the game. If all the white sides are up, the throw counts 16. The 2 "tens" up and 4 whites count 16. Two pairs up count 6, and the player takes another throw. Two "sixes" down count 4. If both "tens" are down, either side, symmetrically, it counts 10. If all burnt sides are up, it is 16. If both "fours" are down, it is 6. If two pairs are up, it counts 2. One pair up does not count unless all the others are down. When more than two play, and each for himself, the "king" is introduced. If the king is up and all the others down, the count is 16. If they are all up, the count is the same. If two pairs are up, the count is 6. If the king is down and the remainder up, the count is 16.

Z. T. DANIEL.

CANUTE

A Game Handed Down From the Indians
to Spanish Settlers in New Mexico
Still Lives in Native Homes

Reginaldo Espinosa

A Game Handed Down from the Indians to Spanish Settlers in New Mexico Still Lives in Native Homes

By Reginaldo Espinosa

IT was Friday evening of a cold winter and at *Don* Juan Martinez's long-porched *adobe* house several women passed to and fro in preparation for the night's *cañute* contest.

Don Juan Martinez, bulky and dark, with a big, black mustache, and dressed in a black serge suit, moved about seeing that all was prepared. He shouted to his oldest son, *"Tomás, parte mucha leña!"* (Chop lots of wood!")

Tomás, a handsome, dark, slender y o u t h, came out accompanied by his younger brother, the former to chop the wood and the latter to carry the chopped wood into the big porch.

A while later arrived *Don* Pedro Sanchez, a small gray-haired man, with a slender face and light complexion; his wife *Doña* Leonor; and family of two daughters, Toña a n d Lola, and son José—a neighboring family t o t h e Martinezes.

The Sanchezes were a l l light complexioned and showed no signs of the Indian m i x t u r e which t h e Martinezes did. All had now come dressed in their best, as i f t o a *baile* (dance). *Doña* Leonor w o r e over her dark hair a black *tapalo* (shawl) of early Spanish make which had been used by her mother and grandmother long before her. It now framed her plump, white face and shaded her big, brown eyes.

Toña and Lola resembled each other very much in their slenderness, black, silky hair, big, dark eyes, rosy complexion, and dashing beauty. José was a quiet lad of fourteen, resembling his father in his frank, kind face.

They were all cordially received and escorted to the Martinez's dining-room for supper—*Señora* Luisa Martinez and daughter Eloisa beaming as elegant hostesses in their beautiful dresses and with their old jewelry. *Doña* Luisa fitted her part becomingly, with her well-shaped

THE FOUR CANUTES, SHOWING THE END MARKINGS

body finely dressed, her dark face lit by welcoming smiles, and her dark eyes shining brightly. Her young daughter, Eloisa, who resembled her very much, also looked her part well in her beautiful attire and with her welcoming airs.

A good supper of hot *chile con carne, tortillas, frijoles* (beans), *buñuelos, enchiladas, tamales,* and a bountiful assortment of other Mexican and Spanish delicacies were now generously served to the guests. The supper was finally finished and all went into another room where t h e flickering fire in an old fire-place in one of the corners gave a w a r m welcome.

Immediately, after a refilling of t h e men's pipes w i t h *p u n c h e Mejicano,* (h o m e - grown tobacco) f o u r cylindrical p i e c e s of wood, the *cañutes,* were brought forth.

"M i r e Compadre," s a i d *Don* Juan Martinez, rubbing his black mustache and addressing *Don* Pedro Sanchez, *"Ise cañutes nuevos."* ("I made a new set of *cañutes".)* He passed them over f o r inspection.

The *c a ñ u t e s* that w e r e passed t o *Don* Pedro were as the name implies, pipes — round, cylindrical wooden pipes—hollow at the center for three-fourths of their length—leaving one end of each *cañute* closed and the other with an open hole.

One of these four *cañutes* was striped all over by narrow lines, running from the center, which was marked by a line all around the middle of the wooden cylinder, to the two ends like the bars on a barber's pole. These lines were burnt into the *cañute's* surface and produced a fascinating brown. At the closed end it had four straight lines burned into it. By name this *cañute* was called *"El Mulato"* (the Mulatto).

Another of the *cañutes* was striped only one-fourth of

its surface—the burned stripes running to the hollow end. At the other end, the closed end, it had one line drawn. This *cañute* was called "*El Uno*" (the One).

Another of this quartet of *cañutes* was striped at the two ends of its surface and with its middle unmarked. From one-fourth of its surface at each end it was striped to its end with the usual burned lines running in curves. At the closed end it had two straight lines drawn on it. This *cañute* was called "*El Dos*" (the Two).

The last of the four was striped at its middle for one-third of its surface with the usual burned stripes. At its closed end it had an X burned into its surface. This one was called "*El Cinchado*" (the Belted One).

All four *cañutes* were the same size and had the one end closed and the other open. They were being brought out so that the game could be started, as that was the reason for the night's social gathering of these two families—to have a *cañute* match.

A large space was cleared in the middle of the room, and one family took one end of the space and the other

and it was the Sanchezes turn to guess in which *cañute* the nail was hidden. If the first *cañute* one of them picked had the nail in it then Tomás would have to pay ten kernels of corn out of the *Troja Mayor* to the Martinezes, who would put them in their *troja*.

If the second *cañute* one of them picked had the nail in it then Tomás would pay the Martinezes six kernels of corn. If the third which one of them chose had the nail Tomás would pay the Martinezes no kernels of corn, and the Sanchezes would takes the *cañutes* and hide the nail in one of them as *Doña* Luisa and Eloisa had done, then let the Martinezes do the guessing.

However, if neither of the first three *cañutes* the Sanchezes picked now had the nail in it Tomás would pay the Martinezes four kernels of corn.

Every time the Martinezes would receive payments of corn they would hide the nail again, until they gave up the *cañutes*. The side that finally held all the one hundred and one kernels of corn in its possession won the game.

After all the kernels in the "*Troja Mayor*" were given

SIDE VIEWS OF THE MARKINGS ON THE CANUTES--WOULD THEY KEEP YOU UP ALL NIGHT?

the other end. Three small Indian earthen pots were then brought into the room. The largest one was given to Tomás, making him the *trojero* of the *Troja Mayor*. (The holder of the main granary). One hundred and one kernels of corn were then put in his pot—his *troja*.

The other pots were given one to each family—both empty. They were to be their *trojas*, (granaries) into which the kernels of corn they won would be put.

Doña Luisa and Eloisa then squatted themselves in the center of the group with the four *cañutes* and a nail in their hands. *Don* Juan covered them up with a red woolen *fresada* (blanket). While the two, covered under the *fresada*, fingered and moved the *cañutes*, the others smiled, the men blowing puffs of smoke from their pipes. Finally the covered ones removed the *fresada* from their heads and moved back about a yard, leaving the four *cañutes* in a row, one next to the other, with the hollow ends facing them and the sealed ends toward the Sanchez family.

Now the game had begun—*Doña* Luisa and Eloisa had hidden in the hollow part of one of the *cañutes* the nail

out, each side had to pay the other for their losses out of their *trojas* until one side held all the corn and won the game.

So the game was started; *Doña* Luisa and Eloisa looked away from the *cañutes* so that they wouldn't show a sign of where the nail was hidden when one of the Sanchezes pointed.

"*Esta en el Mulato*," ("It's in the Mullato,") said Toña, the black-eyed daughter of *Don* Pedro Sanchez, who was going to do the guessing this time.

"*No en el Cinchado, yo creo*," ("No, in the Belted One, I believe,") said her younger sister Lola, her pretty face beaming with smiles.

Toña picked "*El Cinchado*", shook it and found the nail in it.

"*Te dije!*" ("I told you!") exclaimed Lola angrily, drawing up her dark eyebrows.

Tomás gave *Don* Juan ten kernels of corn, and again the Martinez women hid the nail, and set the *cañutes* for the Sanchezes to guess.

Toña now fixed her dark eyes on the *cañutes* and thought for a long while, then she picked *"El Mulato"*, and found it empty. A sigh of relief she gave, and again concentrated. Now she picked *"El Uno"*, and found the nail in it.

Tomás again reached into his *troja* and handed his father six kernels of corn. A third time Toña attempted to pick the right ones and again failed.

Don Pedro said smilingly, *"Estas muy herrada Toña."* ("You are oside Toña.")

Again *Doña* Luisa and Eloisa covered themselves and hid the nail. This time Lola was going to do the guessing.

"Esta en el Uno yo creo," ("It's in the One I believe,") she said.

"No, esta jachado," *Doña* Leonor declared, meaning that the naid had been left in the same *cañute*.

Doña Luisa now began to sing mockingly:

> *"Seguido, Seguido,*
> *Seguido, Seguido,*
> *Se—gui-do, Se—gui-do."*

By this song she meant that they were going to miss again.

Lola picked up *"El Uno"* and found it empty. In haste she picked up a second *cañute* and found the nail.

Again Tomás paid *Don* Juan six kernels of corn out of the *"Troja Mayor"*, stealing covert amorous glances at Lola.

"Anden muchachas," ("Come on girls,") urged *Don* Pedro.

Again *Doña* Luisa and Eloisa hid the nail. This time *Doña* Leonor was going to do the guessing. She picked up the first *cañute* and found it empty; hurriedly she picked a second and found it empty, too.

"Cuidese mama!" ("Look out mama!") advised Toña. *Doña* Leonor smiled.

Now *Doña* Luisa and Eloisa again sang:

> *"Seguido, se-guido,*
> *Seguido, se-guido,*
> *Se-guido, se-gui-do."*

Doña Leonor cautiously picked a third *cañute*, but the nail wasn't in it. She shook her head disgustedly and smiled.

"Estuvo mejor," ("It was better,") declared *Don* Pedro as the four kernels of corn were handed to *Don* Juan.

Again *Doña* Luisa and Eloisa hid the nail in the *cañutes*.

"Dejen al viejo ahora." ("Let the old man now,") portuned *Don* Pedro, and squatted himself in front of the *cañutes*. He fixed his brown eyes on them for a long while, thinking deeply and in great meditation, as if a sage was regarding a difficult problem. Finally he slowly picked a *cañute* and found it empty. A smile beamed on his slender face. He then set his eyes on the *cañutes*, and again began to think deeply. A second he picked and found it empty too. Once more *Don* Pedro's face lighted with a smile.

Again he set his eyes on the remaining *cañutes*, knitted his brows, and began studying them deeply. *Doña* Luisa began to sing out in a high, clear voice the following:

> *"Dicen que viene gente,*
> *Dicen que viene gente,*
> *Y rastros por la cañada,*
> *Y rastros por la cañada,*
> *Dicen que se los llevan,*
> *Dicen que se los llevan,*
> *Pero no se llevan nada,*
> *Pero no se llevan nada.*
>
> *Cañutero, sí cañutero,*
> *No canta bonito que ya la jerro,*
> *No canta bonito que ya la jerro.*
>
> *El Mulato y el Cinchado,*
> *El Mulato y el Cinchado,*
> *Fueron nombrados en un jurado,*
> *Fueron nombrados en un jurado,*
> *El Uno juez de distrito y el Dos un licenciado.*
> *Gallalo, gallalo."*

> *Nunca más contento que hora,*
> *Nunca más contento que hora,*
> *Porque mate venadito,*
> *Porque mate venadito,*
> *Hora comeremos carne del diez que nos de este Indito,*
> *Hora comeremos carne del diez que nos de este Indito.*
> *Gallalo, gallalo."*

By this song *Doña* Luisa boasted that the *cañutes* would remain on her side and that the Sanchezes wouldn't take anything.

Cautiously *Don* Pedro now picked a third *cañute*. It had the nail in it, so the *cañutes* were turned over to the Sanchezes, amidst laughter and clapping of hands.

Now *Doña* Leonor and Toña took the *cañutes* and the nail in their hands, and covered themselves with the red *fresada* as *Doña* Luisa and Eloisa had done. It was the Martinezes turn to guess, and the passing of the kernels of corn was from the Martinez's *troja* to the Sanchez's.

The game proceeded for several hours, until finally the Martinezes had confiscated the one hundred and one kernels of corn from the *"Troja Mayor"* and the Sanchez's *troja*, winning the first game.

It was past midnight and the first game was over. *Doña* Luisa and Eloisa called everyone into the dining-room for a *merienda* (light lunch) of *biscochos* (home-made cookies) and coffee— *vino* (wine) also. They made a jolly bunch around the big table. The conversation drifted naturally to the game. They discussed how it had first been introduced by the Indians to the Spaniards; and how it had flourished all over the state of New Mexico in territorial and pre-territorial days as a gambling game in place of the present card games; of how different old-timers had loved the game and lost all their property playing *cañute*.

"Ya los muchachos no, (Now the boys don't,) *compadre,"* declared *Don* Juan, shaking his big, dark head, and followed saying that when the word *cañute* was heard now, the boys thought of plumbing—not as in the old days, of the game they loved.

Don Pedro agreed, saying that cards and that game called bridge were the popular games now.

The *merienda* was finished, and again they moved to the next room for more *cañute*. Another game was started and the guessing and passing of corn kernels resumed. Finally that game ended, the Sanchezes winning it. The score now stood one to one and both games had been long. A third game was started. Again the guessing and exchanging of corn kernels took place.

A strong wind roared and whined outside, but the frequent replenishing of the fireplace kept the room cozy and warm. The night gradually wore into dawn; a song flitted into the game now and then; and the third game lasted. Eagerly the two sides looked out through the windows to the east for a glimpse of the sunrise when their respective sides held possession of the *cañutes*, as the sunrise was the "rub" and the score now stood one-to-one, so the one having possession of the *cañutes* at the rise of the sun would win the night's contest. The winning side would take the *cañutes* home and hold the next contest at its home.

Slowly, over the far eastern horizon of snow-covered *Sangre de Cristo* Mountains the sun rose, throwing upward and forward bright rays, which changed the color of the fleecy banks of clouds in the light blue skies to a dark pink, and coloring the snow-covered mountain-tops to a bloody red.

The wind outside still whined fiercely and the Sanchezes clapped their hands in glee as they held possession of the *cañutes* at the sunrise, winning the night's play. They prepared to leave for home with the *cañutes*, and invited the Martinezes to their home the next Friday night for another contest.

LEGENDS OF THREE NAVAHO GAMES

Lisbeth Eubank

LEGENDS OF THREE NAVAHO GAMES

LISBETH EUBANK*

THESE LEGENDS of Navaho games are told, with variations, to Navaho Mountain children. Nearly always the same characters are used, and the same ritual remains intact.[1]

The Moccasin Game

Long ago, in the beginning, the gods were busy creating this world. The gods all worked well together, and so this world was made quickly. Sometimes the gods were tired of just "being gods" and changed themselves into animals, birds, rocks or elements. There arose a dispute over light and dark; some of the gods wanted the world always to be dark—some wanted it always to be light. So they changed themselves into two groups, animals and birds. They agreed to play a game, and the winning side would decide whether the world was to be in lightness or darkness. They played the moccasin game as it is played today—a turquoise was hidden in one of a pair of moccasins by one side and the opposing side tried to guess which moccasin held the turquoise. Finally, after playing for a long time, the score was even so it was decreed that half of the day would be light and half of the day would be dark. That is why the rules and ways of playing the moccasin game are always the same for the gods taught the people the *right* way to play.

Thirteen Chips

Long ago, when the gods lived upon this earth, there was a great Kisani (Pueblo) Gambler who lived at Blue House (present site of Pueblo Bonito). Gambler had everything that he wanted, but always, he wanted more and was willing to gamble for it.

Now it so happened that the Rain-god had two beautiful young wives. They lived at "Tse,naa,ahaa,ni" (Rainbow Bridge). These women were highly skilled in the art of embroidery. The

* This work is part of the results of the Indian Education Research Project sponsored jointly by the Committee on Human Development of the University of Chicago and the United States Office of Indian Affairs.

1. For a full account of these games see Washington Matthews *Navaho Legends.*

Rain-god left his wives one day, and while he was gone Gambler visited Rainbow Bridge. He saw these lovely ladies and immediately wanted the embroidery they were doing. So he changed himself into a butterfly and hovered nearby where the women were working. The ladies, ever anxious for a new pattern, seized upon the butterfly thinking to copy the lovely design on its wing spread. When the Gambler was secure in the house of the Rain-god he changed back into his own form and carried these two women to his own domicile where they might make "beautiful designs" for him. Of course, when the Rain-god learned of his loss he sought to recover his wives. The yellow canary offered to help him. So it was arranged that the Rain-god would go to Blue House and challenge the Gambler to play "Thirteen Chips" with him.

This game is played using thirteen chips, each of which has designs in yellow on one side, and is black on the other; each player throws four chips for three turns each, then each player throws one or the remaining chip for the last turn. The chips must all fall between two designated lines, and, in order to count must fall with the design side up. Rain-god was to sprinkle corn-pollen over the bird's wings; then Little Canary was to fly over the Rain-god's chips, as they fell and thus sprinkle yellow corn-pollen on the chips, thereby creating a design on the chip. This Little Canary did, and the Gambler lost. Thus Rain-god and his beautiful wives and "beautiful design" came back to the Navaho.

Forty Stones

"No-hoi-ilth-pi" or Navaho Gambler invented the game of Forty Stones. First, he made a circle using forty stones, quartering the circle with ten stones to each quarter. Three sticks, painted black on one side and white on the other were used. The sticks counted according to color and position—i.e., they must fall *within* the circle of stones. All three white sticks falling in the proper place counted ten points; thus the players could rapidly move clockwise around the circle to the "'home" goal. Navaho Gambler went to visit Pueblo Gambler at Blue House. Here Pueblo Gambler challenged Navaho Gambler to beat him at his own game. Gentle Eastwind, whose ceremonial color is white came to aid Navaho Gambler. She told him she would blow on the sticks when his turn came, thereby causing the sticks to fall in the proper place, white side up. This she did, and Navaho gambler won. So now all Navaho are very good at this game; always they win this game from their Kisani (Pueblo) friends, but prefer to play it among their own tribe, because competition is keener.

SOCIAL MECHANISMS IN GROS VENTRE GAMBLING

Regina Flannery
and
John M. Cooper

SOCIAL MECHANISMS IN GROS VENTRE GAMBLING

REGINA FLANNERY AND JOHN M. COOPER

INTRODUCTION

THE PRESENT PAPER is offered as a modest start toward opening up what looks like a promising field, namely, the social implications of gambling.

Our anthropological sources yield a fairly generous amount of information on the world distribution of gambling,[1] the games and sports gambled on, the valuables wagered, the payment of gambling debts, and the ritual accompaniments of gambling. On the other hand, the same sources yield extremely meager information, and for most gambling peoples none at all, on such social aspects of gambling as: its mode of meshing into the prevalent social organization (who gambles, with whom, and for what); its effectiveness in fulfilling or thwarting the wishes of the individual gambler and in meeting or blocking the needs of integral and fractional social groups; individual differences in participation and the motivations responsible for them; native attitudes toward gambling; the economic and other factors that are favorable or unfavorable to the rise and persistence of gambling in culture as such or in given cultures. Field and library studies of these and most other social aspects of gambling have been almost entirely neglected by anthropologists.[2] And, so far as the present writers have been able to discover from rapid search among the sociological sources and from random inquiries among their sociological friends, such studies have also been almost entirely neglected by the sociologists, even by those specializing in the area of delinquency.

The following pages are an attempt to present the gambling complex, with emphasis on certain of its social aspects, as it existed during the second half of the last century among the Gros Ventre of Montana. Most of the complex is now a thing of the past. New gambling games, particularly playing cards, have superseded the old, and gambling itself, on the reservation and among the Gros Ventre in general, is not the tense and meaningful activity it used to be.

The data on which this paper is based were gathered, incidentally to a gen-

---

1 World distribution is spotty and far from universal. A summarized world distribution, based on several hundred sources, is given in J. M. Cooper, *Temporal Sequence and the Marginal Cultures* (Anthropological Series, Catholic University of America, no. 10, 1941), pp. 67-68.

2 Father Gerald Desmond's *Gambling among the Yakima*, from his field study of 1944, a manuscript now being prepared for publication, is devoted largely to the social aspects.

Vol. 2, 1946

eral study of the social organization and religion of the Gros Ventre, at the Fort Belknap Reservation, Montana, in about equal proportions by Flannery in the summers of 1940 and 1945 and by Cooper in the summers of 1939 and 1940, from Gros Ventre informants, mostly of the older generation. In most cases we used interpreters; in some, we communicated in English. Our chief informants on gambling were: The Boy (b.1872, our most important source, who had gotten a good deal of his information from his father, Lame Bull, b.1825, d.1908), Thick (b. ca. 1870-71), Charles John Buckman (b.1872), Mrs Takes-a-Prisoner Warrior (b. ca. 1850-55) and Mrs Singer Sleeping-Bear (b. ca. 1860). These informants were exceptionally intelligent and dependable, and were not only willing to give us the information they had but anxious to do so. In spite of this, not all the past could, of course, be recaptured, and in certain parts the picture we got is far from complete, particularly regarding individual differences and motivations. However, we have had extremely little reconstruction proper to do, as most of the older gambling complex survived up to near the turn of the century, and had been actively participated in and/or witnessed and was vividly remembered by our informants, while some parts of it, especially many of the social aspects thereof, have persisted down to the present.

WAGERS AND BETTING PROCEDURE

Stakes wagered by the Gros Ventre may be divided into small or trivial ones and big or valuable ones. Small stakes consisted of such things as arrows, bows, bags, beads, pipes, knives, handkerchiefs, dishes, and so forth; big ones, of such things as guns, saddles, lodges, and especially horses (the chief wealth in the old days). Wives were never wagered. Two teams might play mostly for fun, the losers being merely expected or obligated to provide a smoke, or, as more commonly, refreshments or a meal—"to cook," as the current expression goes—for the winners. This last was seemingly the only type of non-dyadic wagering in vogue among the Gros Ventre, if it can be called wagering at all, for such provision of smokes or food for relatives and friends was an everyday custom. Mrs Sleeping-Bear stated that in a gambling game she once played with her husband's brother, she forfeited her eyebrows, which he pulled out, but whether this was an exceptional occurrence or a customary one within the prevalent pattern of rough familiarity between brother-in-law and sister-in-law we could not discover.

Betting was typically dyadic, a given individual matching the wager of another individual, and the stakes going to the winning individual. The dyadic system was kept to even where, as was common, betting was by sides, each side, composed of several or many participants, betting on its favorite player or team. There was no pooling of bets by groups, with equal division of gains among the winners, apart from the "stakes" of food or smokes above mentioned. A given person could put up two or more wagers in a given contest with two or more other persons, but any one wager laid by any one person had to be matched by a single individual. Thus a handkerchief might be matched by another one of equal value, a good horse by another good horse, and so forth. In one case we recorded, a watch was matched against a pair of field glasses, the matching being calculated more by use-value to the respective owners than by money-value or "store-value." Finally there was seemingly no gambling on the promissory principle. Bettors had to have the stakes on hand and to put them up on the spot in full sight of players and onlookers, except of course where a man's lodge or perhaps a given horse at pasture was wagered. Consequently gambling debts proper were not incurred; at most a man lost all he actually possessed at the time. If in the course of a game, he had lost all he had actually at hand and wanted to bet more, he would send for or fetch the articles he wanted to put up.

In gambling activities, certain rather elaborate rules obtained as to who could gamble and could not gamble, with whom, and for what—rules which will be explained later in connection with the wheel game and especially with the hand game.

GAMBLING GAMES AND SPORTS

The Gros Ventre gambled, or gamble, chiefly at the following games and sports: 2-button hand game, wheel (hoop-and-pole) game, horse and foot races, dice, ring-and-pin, bow and arrow contests, and, more recently, playing cards. Of these the more important, as judged by size of wagers, by degree of participation, and by intensity of interest, were the 2-button hand game, the wheel game, and the races. We shall take up, first and briefly, the minor gambling games and sports, and get them out of the way, and after that, in more detail, the above three major ones.

Minor Gambling Games and Sports

The dice game, played with four dice having marks carved or painted on them, was a woman's game.[3] The dice were rubbed in the hands and then thrown down. Ordinarily the wagers were small, but sometimes even horses were lost and won by the women.

---

3 Illustrations of Gros Ventre-dice are given in S. Culin, *Games of the North American Indians* (Twenty-Fourth Annual Report, Bureau of American Ethnology, 1907), figs. 54-55, p. 71, and A. L. Kroeber, *Ethnology of the Gros Ventre* (Anthropological Papers, American Museum of Natural History, vol. 1, pt. 4, 1908), figs. 14-18, pp. 184-186.

Women (and men?) also gambled at ring-and-pin, the "ring" being made of four bones from deer feet.[4] The contest was mostly just for fun; the losers would have to "cook" for the winners.

Several types of bow and arrow contests, serving as archery practice as well as gambling sports, were indulged in by boys, young men, and sometimes older men, not, however, by girls or women. Both distance and accuracy contests occurred. In the latter, the target was a stick or arrow stuck upright in a small mound, or an arrow shot by one contestant a desired distance, say, 100 or 150 yards. In another kind of contest, a bow was set slanting, string upward; the string was vibrated by an arrow and the arrow on release flew toward the target about 35 or 40 feet away. In these bow and arrow contests, the wagers were small, usually arrows, sometimes a bow. Wagers were made by the players, and at times by onlookers too.

The modern 4-button hand game, distinct from the earlier 2-button one, is played more for fun than for winnings. At most the losers may be expected to "cook" for the winners. This modern non-gambling hand game came to the Gros Ventre through an Arapaho, Dances All Night, in 1897, shortly after the time the Ghost Dance was introduced among them (in 1891). The Ghost Dance itself had little popularity among the Gros Ventre and after a couple of years died out among them, but the non-gambling hand game took root and survived. At first, we were informed, it was played with two buttons, but after 1903 with four.

Gambling at playing cards, sometimes for large stakes, occurs today, but usually at the nearby white settlements, between Gros Ventre and white males. Some of the older Gros Ventre are shrewd poker players, and the younger ones play poker among themselves, but we obtained no record of ruinous stakes at cards among the Gros Ventre themselves on the reservation.

Major Gambling Games and Sports

The three more important gambling games and sports of half a century or more ago were races, the wheel game, and the 2-button hand game.

1. Races

On horse races, usually between the two soldier-police societies, the Stars and Wolves (the latter became later the "Grass Dancers"), or between the Gros Ventre and other tribes, such as the Piegan, at intertribal gatherings, were placed large bets—horses, saddles, and so forth—by the men, not however by

---

4 Illustration in Culin, op. cit., fig. 706, p. 537.

women or children. The winners would twit the losers with such remarks as: "Don't use that horse to race with. Use it to pack meat." Horse races for prizes, as distinct from wagers, did not occur.

Bets, often large ones, of horses and so forth, were laid on foot races, particularly on foot races between champions of the two above-mentioned soldier-police societies.

2. The Wheel Game

While large bets were often laid on horse and foot races, the most intense gambling interest of the Gros Ventre appears to have centered on the wheel game and the 2-button hand game.

The wheel game, as the present-day English-speaking Gros Ventre call it, was a variety of the hoop-and-pole game. The implements used in it were: a small buckskin-wrapped hoop about 3-5 inches in diameter, with variously colored large trade beads strung within the rim,[5] a "pole" consisting of an arrow or a stick, and a set of short sticks serving as tallies or counters. The court was about 25-30 feet long with, at each end, a log or other obstruction against which the wheel bumped and then fell. One of the two players would roll the wheel underhand with his right hand, and the two players, each with his pole, would trot on toes, sideways or backwards, stooped over somewhat, alongside the rolling wheel. As the wheel bumped against the obstruction, each would hurriedly but deftly throw down his pole for the wheel to fall upon. If according to the count of beads the roller lost the throw, the other player then rolled. The wheel was rolled back and forth in the court alternately. The roller had a slight advantage over his opponent, but he had to play fairly and roll the wheel vertically, for if he rolled it slanting so that it fell toward him too often he was not considered a good sport.

Before the game started the two players agreed upon the number of counters (say ten for each player) that would constitute a game, upon the value in counters of each bead, and upon one particular bright- or odd-colored bead which would win all the counters and with them the game and the stakes. The counters were not put in one single pile, as they were in the 2-button hand game. They were "bought" with the wagers in equal numbers by the two players from a man widely known for his honesty and integrity who functioned in the game as keeper of these wheel-game counters. This man sat all through the course of the game and "sold" counters to the two players. Each player had a second or representative who looked after his counters, receiving or giving

---

5 Illustration in Kroeber, *op. cit.*, fig. 22, p. 188.

according to the fortunes of play on orders from the principals. Each player also selected a watcher who had to see that the game was played straight.

If the wheel after falling came to rest on neither player's pole, no counters were won by either player, but the player towards whose pole the wheel came to rest closer won the right to roll the wheel next. Whether counters were won by relative closeness of pole to bead or by actual contact only, is a minor point we could not clear up.

Once a player had thrown his pole, touching it was strictly forbidden: "You could not even blow on it," as one informant expressed the matter. At times there were close decisions and arguments would arise over the lay. If the two opponents could not come to an agreement, each would look over the spectators and each would pick out some man of known fairness and probity to act as referee. To be chosen as referee in a big game was looked upon as a high honor. The two referees might have to lie down flat on the ground in order to get as close view as possible, and each might argue his case for his chooser. An agreement reached by the two referees was supposed to be final and without appeal. Sometimes, however, the argument would end in blows.

The wheel game was ordinarily played outside the camp circle, not as the result of any strict prohibition, but merely to be out of people's way. For a big game would attract a large number of spectators and backers, and interest was intense, so intense in fact that in an all-day series of games neither player nor onlookers might go back to their lodges to cook and eat, but might forego eating or else have the food brought to them by the women. Relatives and other partisans of the winning player might provide food for all present, with boasting comments, such as: "Our 'race-horse' here is not just a young fellow. He can feed this whole crowd here too. We will show you how this is done, just as he is showing his opponent how to play."

The onlookers had to keep from getting in the way of players, and could not interfere in any way. Nor was there any rooting by them. In fact, while the game was all-absorbing for players and for spectators, it was played tensely, quietly, and gravely, without the noise and hubbub that characterized the 2-button hand game. And no songs were sung by any one during it; the winner would merely give a yell at the end. Should the winner's pole touch the "joker" bead, he would just walk away, and some one or more of the crowd would walk up to the spot where the wheel lay and would say: "Yes, that's the 'joker' bead." The winner, however, might twit the loser, with some such remark as: "My friend, haven't you any better sense than to gamble with me. You know or ought to know that you don't amount to much."

The wheel game, too, in contrast to the 2-button hand game, was accompanied with no legerdemain and no grace or fancy movements. The players might run or trot in a rather awkward or ridiculous fashion, "awfully funny, like a chicken walking backwards," as one informant put it; but they did not care what the crowd might think of their queer or clumsy gait; they were out to win; they would await some other occasion "to show off handsome."

Likewise, in the wheel game, no prayers to any being were said and there was no resort to supernatural power gotten from prairie chickens or ghosts (see *infra* under hand game). Even if a given wheel-game player had such power, it was of no avail in the wheel game and was not called upon. In the gambling-for-scalps story, to be mentioned presently, the Gros Ventre prayed to the Supreme Being to win, but here there was question not so much of winning material goods as of preserving physical wholeness and life itself, things within the peculiar keeping of the Supreme Being in Gros Ventre theology.

Success in the wheel game depended on two things: skill and what may be called thought-wish power. In the play all effort was concentrated by the players on the utmost exercise of skill and adroitness acquired through long practice and of judgment, in following the rolling wheel and in throwing the pole at just the precise moment and in just the right manner. But, in at least some of the big wheel games, a sort of thought power or thought-wish power was used by the players. In how far such power can be considered "supernatural" is hard to say; it seems to have been more "natural" than "supernatural," as judged by most definitions of "supernatural." At any rate, it was not a power gained, as most other Gros Ventre supernatural powers were gained, from some being by crying, fasting, and dreaming on mountain tops or along timbered water courses.

Its efficacy was derived ultimately from the player's previous war exploits. Its exercise was along the following pattern. There being no set time for wheel games, one might get under way any time, with relatively small stakes, and develop in the course of play into a really big game, or the game could be a big one from the start. In such a big game, between outstanding opponents, for large stakes and for status (see *infra*), before starting to roll the wheel, each player would in turn take the wheel in one hand and with the other touch his pole (arrow or stick) under the wheel on a particular bead. While doing so he would think with intense concentration of one of his past war deeds—e.g., a horse he took from the very door of his enemy's lodge at great risk of life—and would say in his mind, silently and not audibly: "I am not telling a lie [about this deed]. The powers know I am not telling a lie." He would rehearse the event in his mind, and probably (the point was not fully cleared up by us) would think of some object connected with the deed, which was of the same color as the bead he was touching.

This thought-wish was a sort of indirect or implicit oath, not a formal audibly uttered one. If he actually had done no such deed, he could not hope to have good fortune from such intense concentration of thought and wish. But it was not a prayer proper; he was not asking anything directly of any being. The act was called beta´c^{tc}et'ª. It may be added here parenthetically that a highly abstract concept of effective power from deeply sincere wish or intense thought or from both combined plays an important part in many phases of Gros Ventre life even today.

While the player was making this silent wish, the spectators would speculate a lot about which of his great war deeds he was thinking. Later the winner would recite publicly the great deed he had been thinking about. In doing so he had to keep scrupulously to the facts, facts well known to the people, for he was looked upon as a man of character and high standing with a reputation gained by merit, sacrifice, and risk of life.

If a player were losing, one of his kinsmen, friends, or backers might volunteer to take his place playing, and also (apparently: our field evidence is not fully clear) to use his own war deeds power.

The main gambling at the wheel game was for stakes wagered by the two players themselves, a given piece of property against an equivalent piece for each game of any agreed number, say 10, of counters won. But the spectators, too, often bet on the game, although not so generally, it appears, as they did at the 2-button hand game. The wagers by players or spectators could be small or large. Two given players might keep at play many hours in succession, playing game after game. In some instances the betting between the two players would result in the loss by one of the last bit of his property—horses, blankets, clothing, household utensils, even his lodge itself. A comparatively wealthy man could thus become a "pauper" in a day. Often, too, the relatives of the players would win or lose almost as heavily in backing their respective kinsmen.

In some of the big wheel games the "social" stakes-were as important as or more important than the property ones, as illustrated in the case of Lame Bull given below. Two prominent men, enemy friends to each other and at the same time rivals for prestige and status in the tribe, would on a given day play the game à outrance. The winner's status and prestige would be greatly exalted; the loser's proportionately lowered. A man's whole career of advancement to prominence in the tribe—a basic ambition among Gros Ventre men—could be brought to ruin in a single day's gaming at the wheel game. He might lose not only his property and so have to begin accumulating again from scratch, but might at the same time lose as well his standing in the tribe and become a defeated and disgraced nobody, of a low standing from which it was very difficult to rise in the scale.

The wheel game was not played by women or children, nor apparently by the very young men, but only by fully adult or middle-aged men and older ones, and by only two players at a time. The really big games with large stakes were in most cases, it seems—almost all, according to our informants—played by two "enemy friends" or "war friends." Such enemy friends or war friends were very different from ordinary friends or "true" pledged friends. An "enemy friendship" was a war-related compact entered into in the following manner. A member of a returning war party would give some trophy or booty he had taken from the enemy—e.g., a scalp, or horse, or weapon—to one of his own compatriots of the same or opposite sex, who had little choice but to accept. Acceptance made "enemy friends" or "war friends" of the two. War friends, particularly if unrelated and both males, could go the limit in twitting and insulting each other and in playing practical jokes, even rather outrageous ones, on each other, and the victim had to take such behavior in good part, at least externally. However, along with the privilege of taking such liberties ran the accepted obligation to stand by each other in real need or hazard of grave nature.

The two war friends could gamble with each other. In fact, gambling among the Gros Ventre reached at times its climax in contests between two war friends. A wheel game between war friends commonly arose out of a "bragging match" between them; one would challenge the other to play the wheel game. If the one challenged declined to accept the challenge, his war friend who challenged him, and his other war friends, would ever after take occasion to deride him publicly for it at the least provocation. So the challenge could not easily be declined. The game often became one in which each enemy friend would go out to strip the other of practically everything he owned—horses, gun, blankets, lodge—and at which the most eager interest was aroused among the relatives, fellow-clansmen, and friends of the respective players and, for that matter, among the whole camp population. Such enemy-friend contests were commonly protracted sessions, often all-day ones, at the wheel game.

The following three narratives of particular wheel-game gambling contests—the first two of which are matters of well-remembered recent history, the third an older traditional story paralleled elsewhere on the Plains—throw some further light on the social role of the Gros Ventre wheel game.

Narrative 1.   In 1893 two Gros Ventre, enemy friends to each other, Red Whip who died in 1912 and Many Tail Feathers, got into a gambling game with the wheel. Many Tail Feathers was losing and he got angry. He grabbed Red Whip and they had a rought-and-tumble tussle. They fell to the ground, with Red Whip on top, astraddle Many Tail Feathers. Red Whip drew his knife, cut off all of the other's hair, at which loss the latter cried while the people cheered a cheer of contempt. Red Whip acting as if he had scalped an enemy, threw the hair in the air, and said in the hearing of all: "What's the matter with you, my friend? You must have a weak heart. Look at me. This is what I did to my enemy [such and such a time]. You know all about it. I just wanted to show you that I am your superior in matters of this kind. But anyhow you can have that good horse of mine."

Narrative 2.   Lame Bull, father of The Boy, our chief informant on gambling, died in 1908 at the age of 83 or 84 years. Lame Bull, when still a fairly young man, a rising one with prospects of rising higher and higher in the prestige scale, had been chosen as an enemy friend by White Owl, an older man, and Lame Bull had, according to custom, accepted the offer. An offer of enemy friendship was on the one hand almost mandatory, and on the other, where it came from an outstanding man of great experience and ability, as in this case, it was a real honor to the recipient and would rarely be refused.

When Lame Bull and White Owl became enemy friends, they "started to act like two roosters" and were saying to themselves: "I am going to get you when you are off your guard." Both knew that at some time or another, sooner or later, they would have to do something to put their enemy friendship to the greatest test. After much sparring around, the two men engaged in a wheel game as just such a climactic test. At this game White Owl had a big reputation (besides all his other accomplishments), while Lame Bull had no reputation at all at it.

On this occasion Lame Bull wagered everything he owned, and all his wife's property, including their lodge. As it was customary at such events for the kinsmen of the respective players to bet on their kinsman, Lame Bull's father, together with other relatives wagered large stakes on him, although the father was strongly opposed on principle to such betting and had always counseled Lame Bull strenuously against it. More, however, than large amounts of property was at stake; the players' relative and absolute standing in the tribe hung upon the outcome. In the case of Lame Bull and White Owl, the former a younger man of great promise, the latter an older one of recognized prominence, the rivalry was keen and, in a very true sense, ruthless. The older man was jealous of his great reputation and did not want any one to get near him in prestige. He was trying to crush Lame Bull's rising career betimes lest later Lame Bull might outdo him. At the same time, White Owl stood to profit even if he lost, for he would still be attached as enemy friend to Lame Bull and would have reflected prestige from being the enemy friend of this rising man. He would thus profit inevitably by the latter's prestige.

Lame Bull lost everything in the contest, and, of course, his father and relatives lost heavily. White Owl's people tore down Lame Bull's lodge and took it away as winnings and took everything in it, even down to the dishes of Lame Bull's wife. At the end of the playing, Lame Bull was an object of charity and a laughing stock.

About the only thing that earned him a bit of recognition was the fact that in spite of his loss of property and of status—to have recognition at all you had to have some possessions to hold and to give away in presents—and in spite of the strutting and crowing and twitting by the winner and his followers after the playing was over, Lame Bull did not lose his temper.

When the playing ended, Lame Bull had nothing of his own except his wife. So his father and mother invited them to eat. Downcast, embarrassed, ashamed, "feeling like a small potato," he ate. When he had finished, his father gave him such a tongue lashing that Lame Bull, who was very fond of his father, cried, and Lame Bull was a strong man who did not easily cry. He felt so bad that he went out on the hills and cried and cried, and slept out there, and came back a pretty sorry young man. And for a long time after, his wife, who also was one of his enemy friends, would throw this up to him: "Oh, you are nothing. You were always weak. Look what your enemy friend did to you. You will never amount to anything." And she would say such things to him especially when others were present. So she set about training him. At any rate Lame Bull was cured of gambling by his great loss to White Owl.

As time went on, Lame Bull recovered from the defeat which might have wrecked for good the career of another. His people had given him enough property to make a new start in life. He would invite White Owl to his lodge and give him big feasts and would make valuable presents of horses and such things to him. And White Owl would make a mental note of these things and would say to himself: "All right, my friend, you wait and see what I will do for you", awaiting the proper time to reciprocate, as was Gros Ventre custom. So a long time afterwards White Owl made very valuable presents to Lame Bull. And they were very good friends.

Narrative 3. Long ago, the story runs, a young Gros Ventre warrior went off alone on a war raid. He got to a mountain, and after nightfall went into a cave to camp overnight. On feeling around in the darkness he found some one else there, and said to himself: "An enemy." To make sure he asked by touching the skin of the other's forearm. The other by wiggling his finger on the Gros Ventre's chest signified: "I am a Snake Indian." So the Gros Ventre took the Snake's hand and made the sign of "big belly" to signify: "I am a Gros Ventre."

The Gros Ventre then said to the Snake: "Let's not fight tonight. You go to sleep and I'll go to sleep. Tomorrow morning we'll see what we'll do." But being afraid of each other, neither slept at all during the night.

The next morning the Gros Ventre asked the Snake: "Friend, where were you going?" He replied: "On the war path." "Alone?" "Yes, all alone." The Snake then asked the same questions and got the same answers. Then the Gros Ventre said: "We are both alone. Instead of killing each other, let's gamble with the wheel. The loser loses his scalp to the winner."

So they started to play, with such things as bow and arrows and clothing for stakes, and the Snake won everything from the Gros Ventre. Then the Gros Ventre proposed: "Friend, you stake all you have won, in a lump, against my scalp," and this was agreed upon. At this point the Gros Ventre got afraid he would lose, so he prayed to Iˣtcibiniạ't'à, the Supreme Being: "Have pity on me, so I may beat this man. I'll make a Medicine Dance when I get back home." And as he prayed, he took his arrow and the wheel, and put the arrow on the winning bead of the wheel, and prayed to the Supreme Being that when the wheel was rolled it would fall just that way on the arrow. So when the Gros Ventre rolled the wheel, it fell as he had prayed it would, and he won back all that he had lost.

Then the two men started all over again, and this time the Gros Ventre won everything from the Snake. So the Snake in turn proposed: "Friend, you stake all you have won, in a lump, against my scalp." They played again and the Gros Ventre won.

The Snake then said: "Now you have won my scalp. Tie my head around [at the level of the forehead], then take your knife and cut, and pull off my scalp. And after my scalp is off, go to that hill yonder and wave it at me and sing. Then you go back home and I'll go back home." All this the Gros Ventre did. But before leaving, he said to the Snake: "My friend, you came from a long way off. So did I. It is bad enough that you have lost your scalp. So I am going to give you back some of your things that you'll need on your way back home." So the Gros Ventre gave him back his robe, moccasins, bow and arrow, and knife, saying: "You'll need these."

3. The 2-Button Hand Game

The wheel game, as played and gambled on in really big contests by outstanding enemy friends, was in some respects the supreme gambling game of the Gros Ventre. It was supreme at least in the intensity of interest it aroused as a spectacle and supreme in the value of what was won and lost, not merely the great amounts of property wagered, but, still more, such prestige and status or loss thereof as could make or break the contestants' careers. On the other hand, as regards everyday popularity, frequency of use, and range of participation, first rank in the gambling complex was held, it clearly appears, by the old 2-button hand game, the predecessor of the modern non-gambling 4-button hand game. In the following pages we shall use the term "hand game" without qualification to designate this earlier pre-Ghost-Dance hand game proper.

The hand game could be played at nearly any time. There were no set occasions for it, though some were more favorable than others, especially intertribal gatherings. Commonly a game started just with some one proposing: "Let's gamble." So somebody would go to the nearest bush and cut the required twelve sticks, each about a foot in length, for counters. Sometimes the bark would then be peeled off the sticks and the ends thereof squared, but this was not necessary. Then agreement was reached on what would serve to hide as the two required "buttons"—such as a bit of "sun-shell" off an earring for the "short" button, and an end of horn off a bracelet for the "long" button. There had to be two buttons, a "short" and a "long" one.[6] Very commonly the game was played inside a lodge, with the main center of interest opposite the door, but outdoor playing also occurred frequently.

When the game took place inside a lodge the arrangement and line up were about as follows. The twelve counters were in one pile at the rear opposite the door. The two teams, of any number each, were lined up from rear to door facing each other, with a tent pole or sections of one before each team to beat time upon and with the wagers placed in view of all between the teams. Each team had its own tally keeper, guesser, hider, assistant hider, and other team-mates, ranged in the foregoing order from the counter pile toward the door. We shall call these teams A and B with their respective A and B tally keepers, guessers, and so forth.

The game began with a gambling song, sung, to the measure of a small hand drum and/or beats with sticks on the tent poles lying in front of the teams, by all present, team members and spectators. In 1940 we recorded, as part of a series of 116 Gros Ventre songs, two such gambling songs, sung by The Boy. These two songs are wordless, except for a short sentence or phrase in the middle of each. The wording of one is: ą́niti be´tanǫ (general sense: "It's no use you trying to guess me; I'm 'holy'"). The wording of the other, incomplete (as The Boy could not recall the full native text) is: ą́tibdjī nǫ´nǫ'tsǫnen ("dogs" "wet legs": allusion not known to The Boy; the full wording was literally: "dogs wet-legs little-legs"). The tunes are lively ones sung in fast time. Only certain songs could be sung in a gambling game; doctors' songs or Medicine Dance songs were taboo therein. If one of the players had his own gambling song gotten from a prairie chicken or ghost (see *infra*), he would start it and the others (only of his own team or side ?) would sing it with him. In the excite-ment of a game well under way, grunts would often take the place of songs proper.

Each team selected its best player. One held the short button, the other the long one. Player A (of and for team A) hid his button in one of his hands, putting on a show with motions, feints, and so forth. Player B (of and for team B) went through his own show, and finally guessed by pointing. Then B hid and A guessed him. If both guessed correctly or both incorrectly, they each hid and guessed again, and they kept this up until one had guessed correctly and the other incorrectly. So one won the preliminary, and the tally keeper of the winner's side, let us say team A, took four counters from the pile and laid them on his side. The preliminary win also gave the winner's team the right to hide.

---

6 Illustrations of buttons and counters in Culin, *op. cit.*, figs. 345-348, p. 271.

Next, hider A and assistant hider A each took one of the two buttons and put on their show together, while team A and only team A sang, this time a song different from the one sung by everybody together at the very start of the game. The rule was that after the opening song before the preliminary round, only the team whose turn it was to hold the buttons to hide could sing. Guesser B watched the two hiders closely, scrutinizing their motions, eyes, expression of countenance, everything, for clues. If he came to the conclusion that hider A had one button hidden in his left hand and assistant hider A the other button in his right hand, guesser B so indicated by pointing with his thumb to hider A and at the same time with his index finger to assistant hider A. Suppose he guessed incorrectly in both cases Tally keeper A would then take two more counters from the pile and team A would cheer, shout, and get up and dance around. Team B would begin to get scared, as team A would then have won six of the twelve counters.

If in the next play, guesser B indicated one of the two hiders A correctly and the other incorrectly, team A got another counter, thus leaving five counters in the pile. The hider A (hider or assistant hider) who had not been guessed this last time then took both buttons and worked with them; if guesser B pointing with his index finger for the long one and at the same with his thumb for the short one, guessed wrong, team A won one more counter, and then both hiders A would hide. By this time guesser B would be getting more and more worried, and the supporters of team A might be booing and twitting him: "Those [of team A] are winning and winning."

Let us say guesser B lost again on the double guess; then team A won two more counters (it would now have ten of the twelve). Guesser B might here appeal half-seriously to his supernatural helper, if he had one: "What is the matter with you, prairie chicken (or ghost)? You are failing me."

As neither had been guessed in the last play, the two hiders A would both hide again—interchanging the buttons perhaps, signaling between themselves, making quick motions, and so forth. Suppose hider A was then guessed correctly, but assistant hider A incorrectly, then team A would win another counter, and only one would be left in the pile. Excitement would here reach a climax. Assistant hider A, who had not been guessed just before, would then take both buttons. Let us assume that guesser B finally guessed him right and thus saved the day at the last minute. His side B would cheer and cheer. The one last counter would remain in the center between the two tally keepers, but now B got a chance to win counters.

If team B then won two counters on the next play, in which guesser A did the guessing, tally keeper B would take the one counter remaining in the center and also draw one counter from team A's won counters. And so the game went back and forth, one or two hiding at a time according to rule, until one team won all the twelve counters.

A session of hand games might go on for many hours; starting, say, in the morning it might continue throughout the whole day and through the night until the next morning. When any of the players or supporters got hungry, they would go home and eat and then return to the game. After a game in which the twelve counters and stakes were won, and before the next one, there would usually be a little time out for a rest and smoke, and for the placing of bets on the next game.

The atmosphere of the hand game was a holiday one. Raillery was a little rough at times. But for players and spectators, the game was a major source of enjoyment, relaxation, and pleasurable excitement. What with the singing, the drumming, the twitting, the shouting, the often loud and uproarious cheering, the hand game—in rather sharp contrast to the quiet, grave wheel game— was apt to be decidedly noisy, not to say boisterous. Not the least appreciated feature of the hand game was the showmanship, the grace and virtuosity of the players, who played to an appreciative and discriminating house. The victors gloated conspicuously over the losers and bantered them unmercifully, but the losers were expected to keep their tempers, an expectation, however, not always realized.

For success in hand game gambling, most players, it seems clear from our evidence, relied on chance and skill—an occasional one on sleight-of-hand proper—rather than on supernatural power or aid. So far as we could determine, the drumming and singing that accompanied the playing were not of the magico-religious order, at least ordinarily and apart from the exceptional games in which individuals with supernatural power (see *infra*) participated. Certain individuals were, from native keenness or from practice and experience, particularly adept at hiding and guessing, and these were apt to play the role of hiders and guessers for their teammates and backers.

Some few men, however—never women, we were informed—had supernatural gambling power. This power might come unsought, as in the case of Keg to be given presently, or, more commonly, was sought. Not many sought it or possessed it. The young were strongly advised against seeking it by their parents and by the tribal counsellors, for the man who sought and obtained it had to pay a heavy penalty. He would be affected with some serious ailment of the limbs, such as pains in and swelling of the joints, and would die before his time. This latter aspect of the belief accorded with the larger Gros Ventre pattern: any acquisition of special supernatural power sought by quest would be apt to lead to shortening of life.

Nevertheless, against the reiterated advice of parents and elders who would so lecture the growing children and of the chiefs and counsellors who would walk around the camp so warning the people, a good many individuals would seek supernatural power, and a few would go out in quest of supernatural gambling power. In some cases such gambling power was sought by a man who had lost heavily or lost his all at the wheel or hand game, as a desperate measure to recoup his losses and to get a new start in his career.

Gambling power was not sought from the Supreme Being, who apparently did not enter at all into the gambling cycle. The appeal to him in the previously given traditional story of gambling for scalps is more a confirmation of than an exception to the rule. Nor was it sought as other power—to be a great warrior or doctor or to acquire wealth or to live long—was sought, by fasting and dreaming on the hill tops. The seeker for gambling power resorted to the brush and timber along watercourses to obtain it from the prairie chickens, or from a ghost. It was more commonly gotten from prairie chickens; but not infrequently from a ghost, not an ancestor of the candidate, at least not necessarily, but, as The Boy put it laughingly, from "any good-natured ghost." This power was gotten for use only in the hand game, not in any other gambling game or sport.

Usually the seeker looked for a place where wild morning glories formed a sort of bower, "like a little lodge or tipi." It was in there that a ghost was believed to live; the morning glory was called tzek'unθänādzu, "ghost rope" (tzek'ʰ or tsȧ·k'ᵃ, "ghost"). The seeker would cry and cry, and when he got sleepy he would crawl into the bower and sleep. Pretty soon a ghost or prairie chicken might ask him: "Why are you punishing yourself so much?" He might answer: "Because I have lost all my belongings." "Is that all? Well, I will help you out," the being or beings would say, and then would give the seeker a song and tell him what rules he must live by and how he must act in the hand game. The person who got such power would not afterwards reveal the details told him by the giver. From the prairie chicken or ghost the person might also get at the same time the power to do marvelous things, such as making an object disappear, swallowing it and then drawing it out of some part of his body, making it go into his skull and come out of his mouth into his hand or go through his veins and come out somewhere else on his person, and so forth (cf. Red Whip story *infra*.)

Gambling power was of a lower order of dignity and solemnity than power obtained by fasting on the mountains and hill tops. It was taken less seriously, more lightly, and, if we may judge from attitudes today, with an undercurrent of amused jocoseness. It was not, as was power gotten on mountains, transferrable by the original possessor to another, or at least it was not transferred. For one reason others did not usually want it, on account of the ailments and shortened life its possession entailed. A man who was known to have such power was further handicapped: his fellow tribesmen would not ordinarily gamble against him and so his opportunities for participation were few, being limited mostly to games played by the Gros Ventre with other tribes. In such intertribal games, however, he would become a popular champion, and would derive therefrom a certain prestige as well as material gains. The possession then of gambling power, while to a certain limited extent an asset to its owner, was in more respects than one a decided liability.

It may be added here that while those who possessed supernatural gambling power are spoken of today by English-speaking Gros Ventre as "professional gamblers," in reality there were no professional gamblers among the Gros Ventre even in the old days, professional, that is, in the sense of making their living or most of their living at gambling.

The following three narratives, related by The Boy, illustrate various aspects of gambling power.

Narrative 1. Lone Bear, The Boy's wife's father, had gambling power. While he was still in his prime, his legs started hurting him. To escape the penalty he quit gambling. But in vain. His legs went bad, and he died before his time.

Narrative 2. When Lame Bull, The Boy's father, was a young boy about ten years of age he had a friend of about the same age, called Keg, to whom he was much attached. Keg, like other boys of his age, had the daily chore of rising long before daylight and driving out the family horses away from camp to graze. One morning he was awakened very early and was told to drive the horses out. He did so, but when he got out to the grazing ground he decided to steal a few winks lying face down. So he fell asleep, and all at once he started to dream. He dreamed that he saw a big hand game going on with high stakes and one fellow winning everything. Keg looked at this fellow closely and saw it was he, Keg, himself. This man spoke to Keg saying: "Do as you see me doing here. Use my throat as an object [button] to hide."

Then Keg woke up and looked around, and there right near where he lay he saw a covey of prairie chickens doing their mating dance and making a whirring noise with their tails. When he got back he said to Lame Bull: "Let's play and see whether what I dreamed is true. I'll put my helper to the test." Lame Bull tried to guess Keg, but Keg would make a noise like a prairie chicken and thereupon would switch the button to the other hand without Lame Bull perceiving it, and Lame Bull could not guess him.

So as the two grew up, Lame Bull always bet when Keg was playing and won a lot of stuff that way. Keg started gambling from his boyhood and always had luck. After he grew up, however, he did not have many chances to play, because everybody, knowing his power, shied away from gambling against him. But when he did play, he would win. When he was resorting to his power in a game, he would imitate the hissing, swishing noise made by the prairie chickens when they ruffle their tail feathers. The prairie chicken had also given Keg its windpipe to use (apparently as a button) in the hand game, and for it Keg used a little metal spring resembling the windpipe.

Narrative 3. During the lifetime of Red Whip (d. 1912), the Gros Ventre on one occasion, about 1873-75, met the Flathead where Lewistown (Montana) now is and camped close together. The latter asked the former to gamble at the hand game. So when night came, they all assembled in a big lodge. The Flathead had a great gambler, nicknamed Crazy Child, who had gambling power and had never been beaten by anyone on the west side of the Rockies. Outside the lodge the young men of both tribes were visiting in a friendly fashion together, and the Flathead young men told the Gros Ventre young men: "Don't get into that game. Our man cannot be beaten," and some of the latter on that account refrained from betting. But the Gros Ventre had a man of their own, Red Whip, who had gambling power from a ghost, greater gambling power than Crazy Child had.

So the hand game started, with big stakes wagered on both sides. Neither champion showed his prowess right away; they just let themselves run along easily for a while. At last Red Whip decided to cut loose: "This Flathead makes me mad. He has hand game power. So I'll have to use mine. Give me a piece of weasel skin and I'll stop his power." They gave him a piece and he rubbed off a small bit of it and put it on the ground and knelt on it with one knee.

Crazy Child, whose hand-game helper was the owl, used every trick his helper had taught him, to hide the button and battle Red Whip, but to no avail, for Red Whip's ghost helper was more powerful than Crazy Child's owl helper. Then Red Whip, when his turn came to hide, said to the Gros Ventre, "I have this Flathead beaten and I know his helper, the owl, has abandoned him; so sing good and loud and beat time fast and lively," and to the Flathead, "Watch closely, and I will let you hunt for the button after I have hidden it." Red Whip then put on a big show, exhibited the button to the Flathead, threw it into the air, and told him to look for it. Crazy Child hooted like an owl and did all sorts of other things like an owl, but finally gave up: "I can't find the button," at which the Gros Ventre cheered uproariously. Then Red Whip got up, showed the Flathead the button, which was embedded in the lodge pole to the left of the door as you go out, and asked him to pull it out. Crazy Child tried to pull it out but failed, but Red Whip pulled it out easily, and said to Crazy Child: "You are nothing. You are just a little fellow. You don't amount to much. I didn't have to try hard to beat you. But I just wanted to show you this."

This great game lasted one whole night; daylight was breaking when the two men called on their helpers. The Gros Ventres won many things of value: many best horses, guns, and clothes; and no Gros Ventre ever gambled against Red Whip after that.

Men, women, and children could participate in a hand game played by men. All, with an exception or two to be noted, could bet thereon, and men and women could bet on both sides. In a game where the men were players, the women would be present and would join in the singing as well as in the betting, but they could not be guessers, hiders, or tally keepers; only men could be such. Women, however, could so function in hand games among themselves.

Actual participation in hand game gambling was high. One of our women informants, Mrs Warrior, never went in for betting, she emphasized; but she seems to have been rather exceptional in this regard. Our other woman informant on gambling, Mrs Sleeping Bear, was much devoted to gambling, for relatively small stakes. Nearly every one, so far as we could make out from our evidence, seems to have gambled, either frequently and habitually or at least from time to time.

Participation, however, followed a well-defined and established pattern as regards who could or should bet with or against whom and for what kind of stakes. For convenience we are calling this the "bettor-wager pattern."

Some persons or classes of persons could not gamble at all or could not gamble against certain others; others could or would gamble against certain others only for refreshments or a meal; others, for small stakes of little value; others still, for big stakes. The Gros Ventre bettor-wager pattern at first glimpse looks complicated, but actually it conforms to a few very simple principles. We shall look first at the pattern itself; afterwards at the principles.

Blood relatives could not gamble against each other either for large or for small stakes. Such blood relatives included parents and children, grandparents and grandchildren, brothers and sisters, uncles and aunts and nephews and nieces, and also all classificatory relatives of the same categories. At most a group of blood relatives might engage in a hand game with the half-serious half-playful agreement that the losing side would "cook" for the winning side. A given gambling team would commonly be composed chiefly of members who were kin to one another, but non-relatives could also be on the team; the opposing team would likewise be commonly composed chiefly of another kinship group. Where blood relatives gambled in the same game for small or large stakes, they always gambled and bet, not against one another, but on the same side, and in wagering they bet on and backed their own kinsman or kinsmen, wagering dyadically against fellow tribesmen or aliens not related to them.

Gambling between blood relatives for property the loss of which would hurt or would entail even small hardship on the loser was evidently looked upon as conflicting with the common loyalty and mutual helpfulness among all blood relatives that were expected by the Gros Ventre social code. The Gros Ventre felt, furthermore, that such gambling might easily give rise to quarreling and ill-will among relatives, whereas the code expected harmony and good will.

As regards affinal relatives, the rules were more complicated and less uniform. Loyalty, helpfulness, and harmony were desired and expected among close relatives by marriage, but the avoidance, respect, and familiarity conventions differed.

A son-in-law could not gamble at all against his mother-in-law, even on different sides for "cooking" for the winners. On the one hand the rule of respect and avoidance was the most rigid and absolute within the avoidance regulations: they could not look at or speak directly to each other, and could not be in the same lodge together. On the other hand they were expected to be very good and generous to each other. It may be added that these restrictions on the son-in-law applied also to his brothers, presumably too to the mother-in-law's sisters, although we failed to inquire about this last point.

As regards all other relatives by marriage, they, even those prohibited from gambling even for small stakes, were permitted, it seems, to gamble as members of groups against one another where the stakes, if they can really be called such, were merely the above-mentioned "cooking" by the losing side for the winners. Some affinal relatives, however, such as father-in-law and daughter-in-law could not engage in a non-group twosome game, even for fun, just as brother and sister could not do so.

A son-in-law and father-in-law could not gamble against each other even for small wagers; the former could not gamble with the latter's brothers or even his close friends—and presumably vice versa, the father-in-law could not with the son-in-law's. Nor, as mentioned, could daughter-in-law with father-in-law. A son-in-law and father-in-law were under certain restrictions of respect and avoidance but not so absolute as those between son-in-law and mother-in-law; the two men could discuss "business" matters with each other, but could not just sit down and chat together about trivial things and especially about anything concerning sex or the eliminative functions. And about the same rule held for daughter-in-law and father-in-law in their personal relations.

Two brothers-in-law, two sisters-in-law, or a brother-in-law and his sister-in-law (wife's sister or brother's wife) could gamble against each other for small stakes, but not for really large ones. A gambling game between two brothers-in-law, small though the stakes had to be, was a good show for the onlookers—not, however, nearly so good as one between two prominent enemy friends. Two sisters-in-law were also "just right" for gambling against each other.

Through all these three relationships run two currents: one of mutual goodwill and helpfulness, the other of familiarity, "teasing" and twitting. Between two brothers-in-law and two sisters-in-law there is relatively more of the first and less of the second; between brother-in-law and sister-in-law relatively more of the second and less of the first.

Two brothers-in-law could not discuss sex or vulgarity and could not go to the toilet together. They would be helpful to each other in giving presents, in a building project, in business matters, and so forth. But on the other hand they could go quite far in "humiliating" each other, in indulging in practical jokes and horse play at the other's expense, and in rivaling each other in war and in war-deed matching contests—but not to the limit, not so far as enemy friends could go. Two sisters-in-law could likewise "tease" each other, but could not go to the same length that brothers-in-law could go.

To her brother-in-law (sister's husband or husband's brother) a woman could go nearly any length in "teasing" and freedom in the way of crude horse play and of vulgar and obscene talk, and vice versa.

The gambling rule that prevailed, and still prevails largely, between these three types of siblings-in-law, namely, gambling for small stakes permitted and encouraged, but not for large stakes, appears to be genetically related to the two currents we have been discussing: the goodwill one prohibiting stakes whose loss would really hurt, the familiarity one permitting and provoking small-stake gambling.

The Gros Ventre, with a population range of between about 800 and 2,000 in the second half of the last century, were divided into about a dozen bands. These bands were not sibs proper, but each was composed largely of kin related by blood or marriage. Members of a given band, whether related or not, would not gamble against one another. There was a well-marked we-feeling among the members of a band, somewhat distinct from and additional to the kinship feeling proper. Actually this was almost equivalent to "tribal" we-feeling, for each band was for the greater part of the year, particularly in the winter months when the bands scattered to separate quarters within the tribal territory, an almost completely autonomous economico-political unit, and any band was free if it wished to secede from the tribe at any time, temporarily or permanently.

Members of one band could and not infrequently did gamble both for small and for big stakes against members of other bands, just as one kinship group used to gamble against others. Tribal we-feeling certainly existed, but seemingly not as intense as band we-feeling, just as, in turn, the latter was not as intense as kin we-feeling. In inter-band, as in inter-kin, gambling, spectators, if they bet at all, would lay their wagers on the players of their own band, as required by band loyalty, regardless of the relative skill and reputation of the contesting players or teams.

For Gros Ventre men who had reached full adulthood and were still in the prime of life, there were two age-societies, called the Stars and the Wolves (or Wolf-men). These two groups, with soldier-police functions, would join forces when necessary in keeping order, in fighting fires, and in defending the whole tribe against enemies, but for the rest rivalry between them was pretty keen. Stars would gamble against Wolves in big games for large stakes, but ordinarily a Star would not gamble against a Star or a Wolf against a Wolf, except for refreshments or a smoke or similar trifling "stakes." Inasmuch as membership in the two societies cut across the lines of kinship and band membership, inter-society gambling suffered an important restriction: if a Star were gambling in a given game, his relatives among the Wolves would not play or bet against him in that particular game. Kinship ties took precedence over society ties.

Gros Ventre would of course gamble for big stakes against members of other tribes with whom they happened to be at the time on sufficiently good terms, or at least not bitterly and actively hostile, to meet and foregather peacefully, such as the Piegan, Flathead, Nez Percé, and Cree. In such intertribal contests they would often go out to win every possession of their opponents.

The Gros Ventre distinguished three kinds of friends: ordinary friends, true or pledged friends, and enemy or war friends. As a rule ordinary close friends would not take opposite sides in a big gambling game. This was all the more true of pledged friends. Two boys, for instance, who liked each other and who had perhaps grown up together would, though belonging to different bands, enter into a sort of "sworn brotherhood," give each other presents, exchange intimate confidences, and promise, without religious rite of any kind, to stand by each other always, even to death if necessary. Two girls could also enter into a similar pact. Such "true" or pledged friends never gambled against each other either as players or as backers, at least never for stakes of value.

Of enemy or war friends we have previously spoken when describing the wheel game. Two enemy friends would gamble against each other for small stakes or big, the bigger the better. In fact a hand game for big stakes between two enemy friends to strip the loser bare of everything he owned, down to his very lodge, was, like a wheel game of the same order of magnitude, a crowning event in Gros Ventre gambling, one arousing most intense popular interest. One of our informants was, in view of this fact, of the opinion that gambling among the Gros Ventre may have been first invented by enemy friends.

The keepers of the two most sacred pipes, the Flat Pipe and the Feathered Pipe, were not allowed to gamble with any one, nor were their wives, nor (probably: our chief informant was not sure) ex-keepers. Rare exceptions may have occurred in practice. Should an enemy friend of a keeper taunt him into betting and should the challenger lose, he would lose not only his wager but also in a sense his life. For his life would in consequence be shortened, unless the keeper took pity on him and through submitting him to the appropriate ritual procedure averted the penalty. It was believed too that the keeper could not lose if, against the rules, he really did gamble. Gamblers, at least notorious ones, were not selected as pipe keepers.

Keepers and their wives were subject to a great many other restrictions. They had to maintain a high degree of dignity, to practise many kinds of abstention and "asceticism," and to be benefactors to and intercessors for all the people. It seems probably that the taboo on their gambling was related to one or more of these aspects of the keepership.

Ritual "grandfathers" among the Gros Ventre were of two kinds. A retiring sacred-pipe keeper became automatically "grandfather" to the incoming keeper and instructed him in the ritual, prerogatives and duties of the keepership; a candidate for a sacred lodge chose an older man who had been through the rite as a ritual "grandfather" who would instruct him in the ceremonies and observances of the lodge in question. A person would never gamble against his ritual grandfather. The relationship established between grandfather and grandchild in both cases was predominantly a respectful and sacred one. Against his ritual grandfather a man would not even play in the modern non-gambling 4-button hand game.

The foregoing rather intricate "bettor-wager" gambling pattern appears to be the result of the orderly interplay of five chief determinants or conditioning factors.

The most important and most basic determinant was that of in-group altruism, cohesion, and loyalty, decreasing in intensity from closer and smaller circle to more distant and larger circle, from biological family, to kinship group, to band, to lodge and society, to tribe as such, to more or less friendly alien tribe, and stopping short of hostile alien tribe. In general, the less intense the we-group altruism, cohesion, and loyalty, the more gambling and the greater the stakes and vice versa.

Two less important, secondary determinants were the rules of avoidance and respect on the one hand and those of familiarity and license on the other. In general, the greater the degree of avoidance and respect demanded between two persons or classes, the less gambling and the smaller the stakes; the greater the degree of familiarity and license permitted, the more gambling and the bigger the stakes.

A fourth determinant was the element of the sacred (and/or ascetic) associated with certain offices and with the persons occupying them, an element which barred gambling by and/or against these persons, namely, pipe keepers and ritual grandfathers.

A fifth determinant was obviously in operation, although the field evidence therefor is not abundant. We got no record, however, of Gros Ventre gambling with their ancient, hereditary and bitter enemies, the Sioux. Gambling, even to strip opponents completely, presupposes a minimum of friendliness between the players, or at least the absence of deadly and unqualified hostility.

If we diagram along a horizontal belt the full range of human relationships from unqualified friendliness and altruism on the extreme left through the various gradations to unqualified hostility and malevolence on the extreme right, Gros Ventre gambling may be represented on this belt as absent from the extreme left end, gradually increasing in frequency and in size of stakes as we pass along the central section toward the right, and then suddenly dropping and completely disappearing near the extreme right end.

Besides these five determinants or conditioning factors in Gros Ventre gambling, there were perhaps others, but this is as far as our evidence and our analysis thereof have gone. Of course, one cannot have gambling without some kind of close-range or long-range contact between the gamblers, without some kind of property or other valued thing to wager, and so forth, but working out a list of such requisites would be labor lost.

Before leaving this subject, we should emphasize that, while the preceding pages have referred particularly to the bettor-wager pattern as holding for the hand game, the same pattern held as well for all other Gros Ventre gambling games and contests.[7]

---

7 In our world sources on gambling we have noted only two explicit references, and these extremely brief, to the bettor-wager pattern: G. Goodwin, *The Social Organization of the Western Apache* (Chicago, 1942), p. 375, "certain types of gambling" are prevented "between members of the same clan," for it would be "like winning it [property] from yourself"; R.

NATIVE ATTITUDES

The attitude of the Gros Ventre toward their own gambling was a somewhat ambivalent one. Toward gambling practised within the limitations of the bettor-wager pattern, there was, by and large, no strong disapproval. Such gambling was in the main taken for granted. Yet such approval as was given, even as regards much of the gambling that conformed to the bettor-wager pattern, was in certain respects qualified and circumscribed.

Pretty near everyone gambled who had anything to wager. Boys and girls, men and women participated. We recorded only one specific exception, in the person of Mrs Warrior, although there may have been others. There appears to have been no disapproval at all of gambling for "cooking," and very little of gambling for takes of trivial or small value, within of course the bettor-wager pattern. There was a good deal of disapproval of gambling for big or ruinous stakes—how widely shared, how serious, and how "intolerant," it is hard to say.

Parents, however—some at least—commonly counseled their children against

Landes, *The Ojibwa Woman* (Columbia University Contributions to Anthropology, vol. 31, 1938), p. 28, differences between gambling by members of same household and by persons from different households. Under date of September 9, 1939, Father Herbert Prueher wrote to Cooper that among the Wachaga of Tanganyika Territory, East Africa, gambling is [only] by non-relatives, distant friends and strangers; under date of June 30, 1944, Father Berard Haile wrote that among the Navaho no gambling occurred between relatives or between members of same clan.

In short reconnaissance field studies among the Sinkaetku (Southern Okanagon) of Washington, the Kalispel of St Ignatius Mission, Montana, and the Blackfoot of Browning, Montana, in 1938, and the Assiniboine of Ft. Belknap Reservation, Montana, in 1939, Cooper gathered the following fragmentary data on the respective patterns:

Sinkaetku: No gambling against one's brother, sister or cousin: "If my brother wants anything I have, I say to him, 'Take it,' without any question." No gambling between members of same family, nor between members of a group wintering together. Not right to gamble except with "strangers." Intertribal gambling for big stakes customary.

Kalispel: No gambling between brothers. No twosome gambling between cousins, but cousins might gamble as members of opposing teams. Two teams from same village might gamble sometimes, but not often. Gambling is mostly between teams from different villages or tribes.

Blackfoot: Two brothers or two members of same band could gamble against each other only for small stakes; two members of different societies, such as the Brave Dogs and the Doves, could gamble against each other for big stakes, such as horses.

Assiniboine: Blood relatives, such as brothers and other close relatives, would not gamble on opposite sides against one another; they would gamble on same side always. Two brothers-in-law or two sisters-in-law could gamble against each other, but a son-in-law could not gamble against his father-in-law or his mother-in-law on account of current avoidance and respect conventions. Intertribal gambling is customary.

In our own American white culture there are clear indications of a bettor-wager pattern in gambling. No systematic field study thereof has, however, been made, so far as the present writers can discover.

gambling, even for the small stakes, mostly arrows, which children could put up. Further, advice against gambling was commonly given by tribal leaders as well as by relatives and friends, presumably with more particular reference to gambling for high stakes.

Excessive or inveterate high-stake gamblers easily lost the respect of the people and were looked down upon. Such were not likely to be chosen as "chiefs," and could not be chosen as keepers of the sacred pipes. The possession of gambling power from prairie chickens or ghosts netted the possessor a certain prestige, but not nearly the prestige that came from achievements in war or medicine, or even from skill in hunting. Keg, whose story we have given above, had little real prestige, we were told. Red Whip had more, it seems, but this or much of it may well have been the result of his outstanding war record.

The foregoing ambivalent attitude can, we believe, be accounted for, in large part at least, by the data we have, incomplete though these data are. It is pretty clear from the prevalent bettor-wager pattern that the Gros Ventre recognized two more or less conflicting aspects of their gambling: a recreative one and a predatory one. Certain kinds of gambling were indulged in predominantly for friendly recreation, to have a good time together. The minor wagering therein merely added a little spice and zest to play, while the losers suffered no appreciable loss or hurt. Other kinds, the common games for large stakes and the occasional ones for career prestige, were indulged in predominantly for gain and this at the expense of the losers, for acquisition in which the losers suffered losses that were grievously felt and that seriously hurt. As the bettor-wager pattern shows, gambling of the first kinds was recognized as consistent with the accepted canons of in-group altruism and benevolence; that of the second, as inconsistent therewith.

Actually gambling contributed both to social concord and solidarity and to social discord and disunion. It must have contributed in some measure to social concord and solidarity inasmuch as it provided a large measure of pleasurable recreation and excitement shared in common and a relatively innocuous outlet for aggression and dominance. The Gros Ventre were consciously concerned with fomenting solidarity within their ranks: for one thing they were a fighting people beset with powerful enemies. But whether they were aware of the role their gambling played in positively and constructively promoting solidarity is not possible to say on the evidence we have and at this distance of time.

As regards, however, discord resulting from gambling, this was common and they were keenly aware of it. The code demanded that losers should take their losses, together with the associated twitting and strutting by the winners, in good part and as good sports, but actual behavior not infrequently fell short of the code's demands. Bad feeling was at times engendered and could and did end in blows and violence, as was noted earlier in our account of the wheel game. Quarrels among gambling boys must have been fairly common. One of our informants, Thick, recounted three different bow and arrow contests for arrows, in which contests he had engaged as a boy with other boys. All three ended in violence started by the losers. In one of the three set-tos, Thick, the winner, was shot in the hand with an arrow by the other boy who lost his temper, and Thick still, at the age of 75, carries the scar. That the Gros Ventre were perfectly aware, as of course they must have been, of the discord hazard in gambling, is clear from such counsel as, for example, Thick's mother used to give him when he was a boy: "If you join in those gambling games somebody is going to get mad on account of getting beaten and he may pound you up." Further, that gambling often led to bad feeling was given to us by The Boy as the reason why the Gros Ventre disapproved of gambling between relatives.

So far as we could make out, Gros Ventre attitudes on gambling were determined in only minor measure by economic considerations. In the days before the disappearance of the buffalo in 1883-84, the Gros Ventre lived under a normal economy of abundance. Moreover, generosity in parting with their possessions, through gift and sharing, was focal in code and practice. Criers around the camp would counsel the people in words such as: "Men and women, don't love your property. You will always acquire other property. Only life never comes back, but property you can have back any time." In the long run for most individuals winnings would balance losses, just as gifts tended to balance gifts—a system of exchange which incidentally must have served to prevent unhealthy accumulation of wealth in the hands of any individual or small group. The cases of really ruinous loss of property through gambling, of reduction to "pauperism," appear to have been rare, and even in these cases the losers would ordinarily be looked after temporarily and tided over by their kin or friends. At any rate we got no record of individuals or their dependents suffering grave privation of the necessities of life as a result of gambling losses.

How far such facts entered into the Gros Ventre attitude toward gambling cannot be determined confidently from such evidence as we have. In our hours of free discussion with informants, there was almost no intimation of economic considerations leading to disapproval. One of the themes in the tongue-lashing Lame Bull got from his father after the disastrous contest with White Owl may have been the economic, but this was not expressly stated by The Boy. Mrs Warrior kept away from gambling because, she said: "I liked what I had and did not want to lose it," and her grandmother used to advise her against gambling lest she lose valued things. All in all it looks as if economic considerations had little to do with such disapproval of gambling as was current among the Gros Ventre; if anything, economic considerations and concepts of property use and disposal would in the main have reinforced approval.

To sum up, Gros Ventre attitudes on gambling appear to have been influenced very much by concern for altruism and accord, very little by economic values.

PAST AND PRESENT

To round out the picture we have tried to give of Gros Ventre gambling, we are adding a brief sketch of its history.

Gros Ventre myth, folk lore, and tradition have little to say on gambling. According to one folk story, given by Mrs Sleeping Bear, but unknown to Mrs Warrior, the hand game was first gotten from the thunder by a certain Tsē·ganis (Little Short Horns). There is no reference to gambling in the fairly complete cycle of sacred myths we gathered or in the trickster (Nihāt'ⁿ) cycle.[8] This absence, particularly from the trickster cycle, may give some slight ground for suspecting that gambling may not go back very far in Gros Ventre culture history.

Apart, however, from such speculative surmise, what is clear is that gambling was in full vigor among the Gros Ventre in the second half of the last century, and had been since at least around the early part of the century. It was in full swing from at least the early boyhood days of Lame Bull who was born in 1825.

Gros Ventre gambling, especially with the wheel and hand games, suffered a severe shock after the disappearance of the buffalo in 1884, as did the main structure of Gros Ventre culture and society. With the rapid collapse of the broad framework into which gambling had so trimly fitted, gambling itself, especially with the older games, rapidly toppled down. The last big wheel game remembered by five older informants—The Boy, Thick, Charles Buckman, Steven Bradley, Philip Shortman—occurred in 1893; the last big hand game in 1891.[9] Around the turn of the century not much of the older complex was

---

8 Gambling does however occur in the Found-in-the-Grass Gros Ventre folk story, according to The Boy. Gambling at the wheel game between Clotted-Blood and the Bull is recorded in the Clotted-Blood tale, by A. L. Kroeber, *Gros Ventre Myths and Tales* (Anthropological Papers, American Museum of Natural History, vol. 1, pt. 3, 1907), p. 86.

9 When in the field we failed to obtain these exact dates. We are indebted for them to our conscientious, high-minded and exceptionally able interpreter, Thomas Main, who procured them for us from the above five elder informants and forwarded them to us with some other supplementary information by letter of September 25, 1946.

left, although we still have reports of a hand game between the Gros Ventre and the Flathead, staged at Glacier Park, Montana, as late as 1922, in which Joe Assiniboine represented the Gros Ventre. Today neither the wheel game nor the 2-button hand game is played.

Hard times, for a short period near-famine conditions, prevailed for a while after 1884; an economy of abundance gave place to an economy of scarcity. While a world survey of gambling reveals, so far as we can discern, no significant correlation between gambling and abundance or scarcity economies, extreme and sudden economic shock and shift, such as occurred among the Gros Ventre in the years immediately following 1884, may well have slowed up the gambling pace.

Around 1897 the non-gambling hand game was introduced, won favor, and persists down to the present. Today there is little gambling among the Gros Ventre on the reservation. Most of what occurs among them takes place off the reservation, at nearby white villages and towns, in the form of poker or other card games for money, between Gros Ventre and whites.

CATHOLIC UNIVERSITY OF AMERICA
WASHINGTON, D. C.

THE CHIPPEWA OR OJIBWAY
MOCCASIN GAME

George A. Flaskerd

CHIPPEWA MOCCASIN GAME

COMPLETE SET OF ARTICLES FOR THIS GAME

FRONT

DRUM-TWO FACED
CORD INSIDE WITH WOOD PEGS
TWISTED RAWHIDE HANDLE
2½" DIA. SOLID BLACK CENTER

2½"

END

TWO PIECES
RAWHIDE
LACED WITH
DEERSKIN
THONG
1-5" DIAMETER

1-5"

3'-3"

DRUM STICK
½" DIAMETER—OAR
DEERSKIN PAD END

5¾"

8¾"

—FOUR CLOTH PADS—
EDGING ALL AROUND

TWO STRIKIN
TURNING STI
¾ DIAMETER —

12"

BUNDLE OF 20 STICKS
USED FOR COUNTING
IRONWOOD OR OAK—¼" THICK

10 ADDITIONAL STICKS FOR COUN
9 PLAIN AT 20 EACH = 180 STI
1 WITH 13 NOTCHES EACH EDGE
IRONWOOD OR OAK—½" WIDE—¼"

3"

DEERSKIN
STORAGE
POUCH FOR
BALLS

½" DIAM
BALLS FULL

3 STEEL BALLS-PLAIN
1 BRASS BALL SCORED FACE

COLLECTION OF GEORGE FLASKERD

SCALE ⅛ INCH = 1 INCH

THE CHIPPEWA OR OJIBWAY MOCCASIN GAME

by George A. Flaskerd

The Chippewa were originally known as the Ojibway Indians and are of the Algonquian linguistic stock. They resided in Minnesota, Wisconsin, Michigan and Southern Canada for the most part.

The Chippewa name for the moccasin game is "Mukesinnah-Dahdewog". It was being played long before the first white man came to this country. Today entertainment is the prime purpose of the game. The location of a marked ball with as few guesses as possible being the objective. Most games are played solely for pleasure while gambling is of secondary importance. This was not always the case according to early writers.

The game is also referred to as the hidden ball game or the bullet game by some writers. The Indians, however, still call it the moccasin game since moccasins were originally used for hiding the four bullets or balls. The bullets referred to were the round lead balls used in smooth bore muzzle loading flintlock or percussion cap guns not the bullets used in the breech loading arms of today.

The writer is of the opinion this was a man's gambling game since he has never seen any women playing the game alone, with men, or taking any part in it. The game is still being played by the older and middle aged men and to a lesser degree by the younger men. However, in a very few years the game will cease to be played as has been apparent for some time.

Drumming was and still is a very important part of the game. The writer has never seen it played without the drum being used. The drummer, and occasionally others, used to sing the many moccasin game songs while the game was being played. In recent times, however, singing has been discontinued due to the fact the songs have been forgotten.

The game is usually played out of doors since most Indian homes and buildings are small and would not accommodate the players which are usually four to six in number as well as the many onlookers who enjoy the game as much as the players. A blanket, or occasionally a piece of cloth or canvas, is spread upon the ground and fastened down by means of pegs driven into the ground around the outer edges to make a flat surface.

Remarks concerning the songs and type of drumming have been purposely omitted since these phases of the game have been ably covered by Frances Densmore in Bureau of American Ethnology Bulletins 45, 53 and 86.

The game is played in many diverse ways that are basically very similar. The manner of scoring or counting the various plays is quite complex. For the reader who is especially interested in this phase of the game the writer recommends the Bureau of American Ethnology Report No. 24, "The Games of the American Indians" by Stewart Culin as well as most of the references given in the bibliography.

This paper will be confined to a discussion of the equipment known to have been used in playing the game. It is possible that other materials were used in other areas or in the past. The plate accompanying this article shows a complete set of the equipment used in the moccasin game. All of the pieces shown were obtained by the writer from the White Earth Indian Reservation, which is located in northwestern Minnesota, in 1955. A description of each article will be given followed by comment by the writer relating to similar pieces that he has in his collection.

The drum shown is 17 inches in diameter, $2\frac{1}{2}$ inches thick, and has both heads closed. The frame is made of bent wood 3/8 inch in thickness and is lashed with thongs. There are two twisted rawhide strings $3\frac{1}{2}$ inches apart across the drum with six small pegs fastened at inter-

vals in each string. These strings are set in place before the heads
are fastened to the frame. Their purpose is to vibrate against the head
to give a snare drum effect. The drum heads are made of one piece of
wet rawhide tightened by rawhide thongs drawn diagonally through holes
punched in the edge. After the wet rawhide dries the drum heads are
taut. The drum handle is made by extending the twisted thong used to
tighten the heads. Both heads of this drum have $2\frac{1}{2}$ inch solid black
circles in their centers. This type of decoration seems to be typical
for moccasin game drums. Colors other than black are occasionally used.
When in use the drum is held by the handle and beaten with a stick having a pad covered with deerskin at the end.

The writer also has a drum with a single head that measures 3 by
20 inches that has two strings, one with five pegs and the other with
six, stretched across the lower side of the head. The string arrangement is for the purpose of giving a snare drum effect. Many drums, this
one for instance, have old frames with new heads. The rawhide head is
tightened by 8 twisted thongs laced through holes. Red yarn covers the
knots where the thongs are tied together. The hide of which the drum
head is a part is also nailed to the frame with tacks. It is not colored
in any way. A single twisted cord runs across the face of the drum to
give additional vibration. This drum is held by the thongs that are
tied together at its back and beaten by a single drum stick having a
deerskin-covered pad at the end. Densmore mentions small bits of jing-
ling tin set along the rim of this type of drum to give an additional
sound effect. This the writer has never seen nor has he ever seen ornamentation other than the black circle in the center of the head. Densmore also states some drums were painted red with a 6 inch blue circle
in the center of the head. This is not the case today though when

89

Densmore was making her observations it may have been done in some areas, or by persons departing from the ordinary.

The drum stick shown is made of oak wood. It is not colored. In length it measures $14\frac{1}{2}$ inches. It is round and tapers from 3/4 to 1/2 inch and has six diagonal cuts or notches. The striking end is padded and covered with tanned deerskin.

Winchell, page 601, states that two drum sticks were used as a rule. The writer does not recall ever reading any other reference to this effect. He has never seen more than one stick used. The drum is played by only one man who holds it in one hand and beats it with the other. If the drum were flat on the ground when played it could be beaten by two sticks held by one or two men. This the writer has never seen.

The two "striking" or "turning" sticks shown are 3/4 inch in diameter and taper gradually to a blunt point. One is 39 inches long, the other 41 inches. Both are made of plain oak. The handle ends are different. This may be due to the user having the idea that the nature of the handle might affect his luck. These sticks are used to strike or flip over the moccasins or pads under which the four bullets or balls are hidden. The wood from which they are made must be clear straight grain since they take quite a bit of abuse when in use. Ornamentation is usually absent. The writer has never seen painted sticks. Tanner, and Kinietz on page 90, state that the players touched the moccasins or pads with their fingers and also with a stick. Culin, page 342, mentions that striking sticks are painted red.

There are four pads shown under which the four bullets or balls are hidden. They are 5 and 3/4 inches wide and 8 and 3/4 inches high with square tops and rounded bottoms made of two thicknesses of heavy dark brown cloth sewed crosswise many times to give stiffness. The edges are bound with a lighter colored cloth. The writer has another set made of black cloth with light green edging. While the Indians originally used four entire moccasins to hide the bullets or balls, pieces of buckskin, socks, mittens, or pieces of birch bark and cloth are also used.

The four balls shown are hidden under moccasins or cloth pads. Three of them are plain steel balls from bearings while one is made of brass and has its surface scored. The balls are $\frac{1}{2}$ inch in diameter. The writer has some other sets of these game pieces. One is made up of four lead bullets $\frac{1}{4}$ inch in diameter with one of the bullets marked distinctively. Another set is composed of three lead bullets $\frac{1}{4}$ inch in diameter and one scored copper ball $\frac{1}{2}$ inch in diameter. These pieces were valued quite highly for the luck they brought to their owner, and some of the sets could be quite old.

The pouch is made of Indian-tanned deerskin and was used for carrying or storing the round balls. This bag is not colored or beaded. This type of pouch is quite scarce and very seldom seen except at the start or finish of the game.

Various small objects were used in lieu of the lead bullets or balls described. Tanner, and Kinietz on page 90, mention the use of small sticks or pieces of cloth. Winchell, page 601, states that small stones were used. Culin, page 340, says that sets of three copper and one lead ball, one plain ball and three covered with twisted wire, as well as three beads and one bullet have been used. Thayer, page 2, mentions the use of three copper and one lead ball. Hodge, page 485, mentions that hair balls (bezoars) from the stomachs of buffalo were sometimes employed. Fred Blessing, Minnesota Archaeological Society, has a set of four balls with wood centers enclosed in thin shells of brass. These are from Mille Lacs, Minnesota. Densmore, page 211, states that

91

the sets of round bullets were valued at one blanket in the early days.

Frances Densmore, Bureau of American Ethnology Bulletin 53, pages 210-211, states "The following incident indicates the manner in which the game. was formerly regarded. It is said that one of the most successful players of the game at Leech Lake (Minnesota) in the early days obtained the secret of his success from his wife, who returned to him in a dream after death. He had been a gambler for many years before her death and had been fairly successful, but after she died he met with nothing but failure until finally he lost everything. In despair he went into the woods to fast and 'dream'. After a time his wife appeared to him and told him that somewhere in the woods were hidden four bullets, which would bring him success in the Moccasin Game, and that he must let them lie in the water before using them. Then the man began his search for the bullets. He had no further clue to their whereabouts, but he searched constantly, wandering in the woods day after day. At last he found four bullets and, as he had been directed, placed them in the water at the edge of the lake. He then announced that in a certain number of days he would have a moccasin game. By using the bullets which had been in the water he won everything and thereafter was always successful. With this incident, began the custom of soaking the bullets. Many players do so now, believing this procedure will bring them success in the game."

The writer has never observed any Indian soaking his four bullets for the moccasin game. Since this procedure is one of their legends it could be done in secret. The practice should be checked, especially at the Leech Lake Reservation, as many legends have some actual foundation.

The bundle of 20 counting sticks shown is used for counting or tallying. The sticks are $\frac{1}{4}$ inch in diameter and 12 inches long. They

92

are made of native oak. Twenty sticks comprise a set. The sticks are roughly cut and are without embellishment of any kind. Since they are subjected to rough usage they are usually made of oak or ironwood. Culin, page 340, states that occasionally the sticks are stored in a deerskin pouch or bag. While the writer does not possess such a bag, Fred Blessing, Minnesota Archaeological Society, has a bag with its 20 sticks. Culin, page 342, states also that 11 red sticks 18 inches in length were used.

The writer wishes to call especial attention to the 10 rectangular counting sticks that are shown in the plate since they are uncommon today. He knows of only one Chippewa Indian who still makes and uses them. This man said that they were only used to keep count of individual games won, or when play would not be completed until some future time. These sticks are used in addition to the 20 sticks previously described.

The rectangular sticks are $\frac{1}{2}$ inch wide, $4\frac{1}{2}$ inches long, $\frac{1}{4}$ inch thick and are made of oak. Ironwood was formerly used. They are rough cut with bark removed. Nine of the sticks are plain while one has 13 notches in each side. This is a high value stick and is equivalent to 200 of the sticks in the 20 stick set. Each of the other rectangular sticks is worth 20 ordinary counting sticks. While none of the sticks in this set is colored the writer has one/stick that is colored deep purple. He has seen only one other stick of this kind.

The only reference the writer has seen in which additional counting sticks are mentioned is in the Bureau of American Ethnology Bulletin 53, page 213, in an article by Frances Densmore. She states that at the conclusion of each game a 10 inch stick is stuck into the ground at the edge of the blanket. The stakes are settled after playing a number of consecutive games agreed on at the beginning of play.

When the moccasin game was played at Cass Lake last summer, 1961, additional counting sticks were used to keep tally of single games won. The sticks were plain twigs cut from trees growing where the game was played.

The writer wishes to dedicate this paper to the Chippewa Indians, especially his many friends who are members of this tribe and who have been so helpful and kind to him in his study of their arts and crafts.

BIBLIOGRAPHY

Culin, Stewart: 1907. Games of the North American Indians.
    Bureau of American Ethnology Report 24.

Densmore, Frances: Bureau of American Ethnology.
    1910. Chippewa Music. Bulletin 45, Part 1.
    1910. Chippewa Music. Bulletin 53, Part 2.
    1929. Chippewa Customs. Bulletin 86.

Hodge, Frederick Webb: Bureau of American Ethnology.
    1911. Handbook of American Indians Bulletin 30.

Kinietz, W. Vernon: Chippewa Village. Cranbrook Institution
    of Science. 1947. Bulletin 25.

Tanner, John: Captivity of John Tanner.
    1956 reprint by Ross & Haines, Minneapolis, Minn.

Thayer, Burton W.: Some Minnesota Ojibway Games.
    Minnesota Archaeologist Vol. 1, No. 4, Sept. 1935.

Winchell, N. H.: The Aborigines of Minnesota.
    1906-11. Minnesota Historical Society, St. Paul, Minn.

THE GAME OF DOUBLE-BALL
OR
TWIN-BALL

Melvin R. Gilmore

THE GAME OF DOUBLE-BALL, OR TWIN-BALL

THE game of double-ball, or twin-ball, was played by girls in many different Indian tribes. The implements of the game were the twin-ball and playing sticks. The twin-ball consisted of two small, light balls of equal size, each about three inches in diameter, connected by a thong about eight inches long. The balls made by the Indians for playing this game were made of soft deerskin and stuffed with feathers, hair, or some such light and elastic material. The playing stick was about three feet in length and curved at the end. The ball must be played entirely with the stick. To touch the ball with the hand while in play constituted a foul.

The ground on which the game was played was long, like a football ground or a hockey ground. At each end was a goal marked by two posts or two mounds. The ball was put in play in the middle of the field and the game required that it should be played thence to and through between the goal posts at one end or the other. If the ball were played outside the goal posts and beyond, it must be played back into the field and then properly on through between the goal posts before the side could score on it.

The game was played by two contending sides of eight or more girls on each side. The rules and regulations were very adaptable to various conditions. Two parties playing the game might make their regulations and rules by mutual agreement as to the number of players on a side, the length of ground, and so forth.

We may suppose two opposing sides, which we may call the Reds and the Blues, were playing. We may designate the two goals as A and B. The Reds were facing goal A and the Blues were facing goal B. The twin-ball was put in play between them. As it was tossed into the air the Red players advanced and tried to engage the ball as it fell and to send it over the heads of their opponents, the Blues, and on toward goal A. But the Blues at the same time tried to intercept it and send it toward goal B. Thus the two sides were actively contending, surging forward and backward, the ball now moving nearer to one goal and then perhaps being in turn pressed back toward the other. It was a very active game, requiring the highest coördination of eye and all movements. One may well fancy that the two connected balls would present an infinite number of different positions toward the playing stick, and therefore necessitate the greatest celerity and accuracy in engaging the connecting thong with the playing stick.

MELVIN R. GILMORE

A FEW AMERICAN STRING
FIGURES AND TRICKS

Alfred C. Haddon

A FEW AMERICAN STRING FIGURES AND TRICKS

By ALFRED C. HADDON

If an apology be due for offering so small a number of string figures and tricks from America, my excuse must be that the opportunity for learning them was very limited. It is known that string figures abound on the continent, and now a beginning has been made, it is hoped that many more will be published by other observers.

The method of recording these figures has been fully described by Dr W. H. R. Rivers and myself in *Man*,[1] where a dozen Melanesian examples are given. I here repeat the sections of that paper which deal with the terminology and manipulation:

We employ the term "string figures" in those cases in which it is intended to represent certain objects or operations. The "cat's cradle" of our childhood belongs to this category. "Tricks" are generally knots or complicated arrangements of the string which run out freely when pulled. Sometimes it is difficult to decide which name should be applied.

A piece of smooth, pliable string should be selected which is not liable to kink. A length of about 6 ft. 6 in. (2 meters) is usually the most suitable; the ends should be tied in a reef knot, and the ends trimmed. A spliced, knotless string would be best of all.[2]

Terminology. — A string passed over a digit is termed a loop. A loop consists of two strings. Anatomically, anything on the thumb aspect of

---

[1] October, 1902, No. 109, p. 146.

[2] My friend Dr A. Sheridan Lea, F.R.S., has kindly sent me the following description of the method of making a "long splice":

"The ends of a rope, or of a string when the latter is made of distinct strands twisted together, as is the case with all ropes, may be united so that the join is practically no thicker than the rest of the rope or string. This is done by means of what sailors call a 'long splice.' *To make a long splice:* (*First*) Unlay the strands of each end of the rope or string, for a distance rather longer than half the desired length of the splice, taking care not to destroy the corkscrew-like twists of the several strands. Then interlace or 'marry' the strands, as shown in figure 5, I, by putting each strand of one end of the rope symmetrically in between two strands of the other end. (*Second*) Bring the ends of the string closely together so that strands 1 and 2 (and therefore also the other strands) touch each other as shown in figure 5, II. Then, leaving strands 1 and 2 in the position shown, unlay strand 3 backwards toward A and fill up the space thus made by laying strand 4 into the place of strand 3. This is easily done if the twist has not been taken out of the several strands. Next unlay strand 5 toward B, and, as in the hand is termed "radial," and anything on the little-finger side is called "ulnar," thus every loop is composed of a radial string and an ulnar string. By employing the terms thumb, index, middle-finger, ring-finger, little finger, and right and left, it is possible to designate any one of the twenty strings that may extend between the two hands.

A string lying across the front of the hand is a palmar string, and one lying across the back of the hand is a dorsal string.

Sometimes there are two loops on a digit, one of which is nearer the finger-tip than the other. Anatomically, that which is nearer to the point of attachment is "proximal," that which is nearer the free end is "distal." Thus, of two loops on a digit, the one which is nearer the hand is the proximal loop, that which is nearer the tip of the digit is the distal loop; similarly we can speak of a proximal string and a distal string.

In all cases various parts of the string figures are transferred from one digit or set of digits to another or others. This is done by inserting a digit (or digits) into certain loops of the figure and then restoring the digit (or digits) back to the original position, so that they bring with it (or them) one string or both strings of the loop. This operation will be described as follows : " Pass the digit into such and such a loop, take up

the case of strands 3 and 4, lay up strand 6 into the space left by strand 5. The string will now have the appearance shown in figure 5, II. (*Third*) Knot strands 1 and 2 together by a simple overhand knot (the first half of an ordinary reef-knot), as shown in figure 5, III, and pull the knot tight so that it lies flush with the surface of the string. Knot strands 3 and 4, and 5 and 6, together similarly to strands 1 and 2. (*Fourth*) Pass the end of strand 1 over the strand next to it (*a* in figure III), and under the next

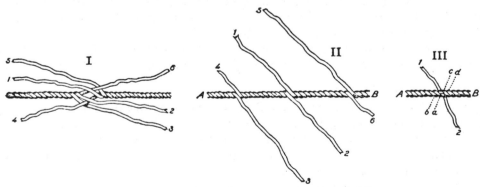

FIG. 5.—Method of making the " long splice."

strand but one (*b* in figure III) and pull tight. Do the same with the end of strand 2 by passing it over *c* and under *d* in figure III and pull tight. Pass the end of strand 1 once or twice again over and under the strands next to *b* toward A, and do the same with strand 2, working it toward B in figure III. Then finish off strands 3, 4, and 5, 6, in a way exactly similar to that given above for strands 1 and 2. (*Fifth*) Roll the splice between two hard flat surfaces. Stretch the splice thoroughly by a prolonged steady pull ; cut off the protruding ends of the strands close to the string, and the splice is finished."

such and such a string, and return.'' In rare cases a string is taken up between thumb and index. A digit may be inserted into a loop from the proximal or distal side, and in passing to a given loop the digit may pass to the distal or proximal side of other loops. We use these expressions as a general rule instead of ''over and under,'' ''above and below,'' because the applicability of the latter terms depends on the way in which the figures are held. If the figures are held horizontally, ''over and above'' will correspond as a general rule to the distal side, while ''under and below'' will correspond to the proximal side. In some cases when there is no possibility of confusion, we have used the shorter terminology.

A given string may be taken up by a digit so that it lies on the front or palmar aspect of the finger, or so that it lies on the back or dorsal aspect. In nearly all cases it will be found that when a string is taken up by inserting the digit into the distal side of a loop, the string will have been taken up by the palmar aspect, and that the insertion into the proximal side of the loop involves taking up the string by the dorsal aspect of the digit.

Other operations involved are those of transferring strings from one digit to another and dropping the strings from a given digit or digits.

The manipulation consists of a series of movements, after each of which the figure should be extended by drawing the hands apart and separating the digits. In some cases in which this would interfere with the formation of the figure, a special instruction will be given that the figure is not to be extended. Usually it is advisable to keep the loops as near the tips of the digits as possible.

There are certain opening positions and movements which are common to many figures. To save trouble these may receive conventional names; the use of these will soon be apparent, but it is better to repeat descriptions than to run any risk of obscurity.

Position I.—This name may be applied to the position in which the string is placed on the hands when beginning the great majority of the figures.

Place the string over the thumbs and little fingers of both hands so that on each hand the string passes from the ulnar side of the hand round the back of the little finger, then between the little and ring fingers and across the palm; then between the index and thumb and round the back of the thumb to the radial side of the hand. When the hands are drawn apart the result is a single radial thumb-string and a single ulnar little-finger string on each hand with a string lying across the palm.

This position differs from the opening position of the English cat's cradle in which the string is wound round the hand so that one string lies across the palm and two across the back of the hand with a single radial index string and a single ulnar little-finger string.

Opening A.—This name may be applied to the manipulation which forms the most frequent starting point of the various figures. Place string on hands in Position I. With the back of the index of the right hand take up from proximal side (or from below) the left palmar string and return. There will now be a loop on the right index, formed by strings passing from the radial side of the little finger and the ulnar side of the thumb of the left hand, *i. e.*, the radial little-finger strings and the ulnar thumb strings respectively.

With the back of the index of left hand take up from proximal side (or from below) the right palmar string and return, keeping the index with the right index loop all the time so that the strings now joining the loop on the left index lie within the right index loop.

The figure now consists of six loops on the thumb, index, and little finger of the two hands. The radial little-finger string of each hand crosses in the center of the figure to form the ulnar index strings of the other hand, and similarly the ulnar thumb string of one hand crosses and becomes the radial index string of the other hand.

The places where the strings cross in the center of the figure may be termed the crosses of Opening A.

TUKTUQDJUNG. CARIBOO OR REINDEER. (*Eskimo.*)

Opening A.— Pass index finger of right hand distal to the little-finger loop, and passing round the ulnar side of that loop, bring it up from the proximal side into the thumb loop, and with the index finger pointing downward, take up with the back of the index finger the radial thumb string and return. There are now two loops on the right index and a twisted loop on the thumb. Let go right thumb. Pass right index finger to the radial side of the right little-finger loop and return, giving it a twist. Pass right thumb into the right double index loop from the proximal side and extend those loops slightly. Remove loop from left index finger and pass it from the distal side through the double loop on the right index finger and thumb, and proximal to the two radial strings, and return the loop to the left index, passing these two strings on their radial side. Drop the double loop on the right index and thumb. Let go left thumb and extend the figure by drawing the hands apart and separating widely the two strings that pass from one hand to the other.

This figure was first described and figured by Dr Franz Boas;[1] indeed, so far as I am aware, it was the first description of a string puzzle published by any anthropologist. Dr Boas demonstrated this figure to me and has kindly given me permission to republish it. The figure apparently is intended to represent the side view of a reindeer's antler.

---

[1] "The Game of Cat's Cradle," *Internat. Archiv für Ethnographie*, I, 1888, pp. 229–230, fig. 1.

DRESSING A SKIN. (*Thompson Indians*, British Columbia.)

Opening A. — Release little fingers and allow the loop thus released to hang down. With a swinging motion throw this loop over the remaining strings so that it falls over their radial side.

Pass each thumb into its own loop distal to the corresponding string of the former little-finger loop and extend the figure.

This and the following figure were learned by Mr Harlan I. Smith, of the American Museum of Natural History, New York, when on the Jesup North Pacific Expedition, and are illustrated by him in the *Memoirs of the American Museum of Natural History*.[1] Mr Smith kindly taught me these two figures and permitted me to publish descriptions of them.

PITCHING A TENT. (*Thompson Indians*.)

Position I. — Take up with the right index the transverse string on the left palm from its proximal side, give it one twist and return. Pass the left index through the right index loop from the distal side and take up the transverse palmar string of the right hand from the proximal side and return through the loop. Drop the thumb and little-finger loops of the right hand and pull the hands apart.

This figure is precisely the same as that known in Torres straits as the " fish-spear." [2]

CROW'S FEET. (*Cherokee.*)

Opening A, but with central loop on the middle fingers instead of on the index fingers. Close together the four fingers of each hand and insert them into the thumb loop from the distal side and transfer the radial thumb string to the ulnar side of the little fingers. Extend the figure. Pass each thumb over the radial index-finger string and into the middle-finger loop from the proximal side. Release middle fingers. By this manipulation the middle-finger loop has been transferred to the thumb. Transfer the loop on the back of each hand to its respective middle finger. Pass each radial little-finger string from the proximal side through middle-finger loop and replace on ulnar side of little finger. A

[1] Vol. II ; Anthropology, vol. I, "The Thompson Indians of British Columbia," by James Teit, edited by Franz Boas ; fig. 270, p. 282.

[2] See *Man*, op. cit., 1902, p. 149.

string passes from the ulnar side of one little finger to the other ; transfer this over the little fingers to their radial side. Release thumbs and draw tight.

This figure was taught to me by a Pullman porter of European, negro, and Cherokee parentage.

THREADING A CLOSED LOOP.   (*Omaha, Pawnee, Kwakiutl.*)

Take a piece of string about eighteen inches in length, and, beginning a few inches from one end, twist the middle portion of the string three or four times round the left thumb in the direction toward the body.   Then make a loop which projects outward between the thumb and index finger of the left hand, and hold it between those digits.   Drop this end of the string and take up the other about half an inch from its extremity with the index finger and thumb of the right hand.   Make movements as if threading the loop with this point of the string.   Suddenly slip the string round the point of the left thumb and it will appear as if the loop had been threaded by the string held in the right hand.

This trick is well known to Europeans and it occurs in Japan. Mr Francis LaFlesche, the talented Omaha collaborator with Miss Alice C. Fletcher, told me that this puzzle was known to the Omaha and Pawnee.

Dr Franz Boas has informed me that he has found this trick among the northwest tribes of America.   There are two shamanistic societies among the Kwakiutl.   This trick is used to identify the members of one of these societies when they hold their secret meetings in the forest.   The members of the other society are recognized by another trick : They employ a little stick, to the middle of which a string is fastened.   The toggle is put in the mouth and when the mouth is opened the stick appears to perforate the tongue.   I understand this is accomplished by means of a second piece of wood secreted in the mouth and placed in a suitable position with the tongue.

AN OMAHA STRING TRICK

Hold the left hand pointing away from the body, thumb uppermost.   Suspend the string loop on the thumb of the left hand so that there is one depending palmar string and one depending string

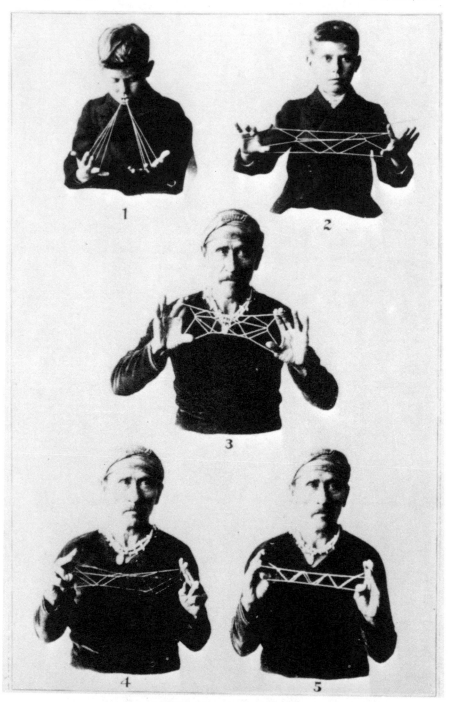

NAVAHO STRING FIGURES
1, Two hogans.   2, Carrying wood.   3, Many stars.   4, Owl.   5, Lightning.

on the back of the hand.   Pass the right index, with its point away
from the body, under the palmar string and between the thumb and
index of the left hand, and take up the dorsal string from the
distal side and bring out a loop on the proximal side of the palmar
string; give this loop a twist, clockwise, and pass it over the index
finger of the left hand and draw tight.   Perform the same manipulation between the index and middle fingers of the left hand and
place the twisted loop on the middle finger, and so on for the
remaining fingers of the left hand.   Release the left thumb and pull
the palmar string; the knots will then run out.

This trick, which is precisely the same as *kebe mokeis* of Murray
island, Torres straits,[1] and which also has been shown to me by
a Japanese, was taught to me by Mr LaFlesche.   The Omaha also
know the trick of taking a ring which is threaded on a loop the
ends of which are fastened.

THE NA-ASH-KLO OR STRING FIGURES OF THE NAVAHO

When visiting Chicago in October, 1901, I was able, through
the good offices of Dr George A. Dorsey, to see something of
two old Navaho men who happened to be passing through that
city.   I very soon found that they were well acquainted with string
figures, but, owing to shortness of time, I was able to learn only
half a dozen of them.   I showed several Papuan string figures and
tricks to the two Navaho, and they were particularly delighted with
the tricks called *lewer* and *monan*, which they learned after considerable difficulty.   I can not tell whether they have remembered these
two tricks; but the fact is here recorded that they have been taught
to two Navaho men.   Dr Dorsey very kindly had the photographs
which illustrate this paper taken for me by the Museum photog-
rapher.   (See plate xv.)

On my return to New York in December, 1901, I had the
pleasure of meeting Mr A. M. Tozzer, who had just returned from
an ethnological expedition to New Mexico.   He too had discovered
the prevalence of these puzzles among the Navaho and had recorded
the names of twenty-six, of which he had made rough sketches.
Following is a list of those for which Mr Tozzer had English names.
" Carrying wood " is the only one he had learned to make.

---

[1] Compare *Man*, op. cit., p. 152.

Man, *dĕnnĕ*.

Sternum with ribs, *ai-yĭt*.

Woman's belt, *sĭs*.

Carrying wood, *chiz-jŏ-yĕt-lĭ*.

Bow, *at^l-ti*.

Arrow, *ka*.

Hogan (or Navaho hut), *hogan*.

Two hogans, *naki-hogan*, or *at^l-sa-hogan*.

Sand-painting figure, *^kos-shis-chi*.

Coyote (prairie wolf), *ma-ĭ*.

Owl, *nas-ja*.

Bird's nest, *a-to*.

Horned toad, *na-a-sho-ĭ-di-chĭzi*.

Butterfly, *ga-hĭ-kĭ*.

Star, *so-a-hinat^lsan-ⁿtĭ-ĭ*.

Large star, *soⁿ-so*.

Two stars, *soⁿ-bĭ-terĕ*.

Many stars, *soⁿ-tlani*.

Lightning, *atsinĭl-klish*.

If the completed figure is carefully released from the hands and placed on the lap, and the two lateral strings are picked up about the center and pulled apart, it will be found that the figure immediately becomes untangled.

The general name for these figures is *na-ash-klo*, according to Mr Tozzer. The term *na* signifies a "continuous movement"; *ash* is "I," and *klo* is the root word of "weaving." Perhaps "continuous weaving" would be a fair translation of the Navaho word.

The Navaho (Navajo of the Spaniards) term themselves *Dĕnnĕ*, which simply means "men" or "the men."

HOGAN

Hold the left hand with the fingers pointing upward. Pass the string over the index and middle fingers of the left hand, allowing a long loop to hang down from its palmar aspect. Place the right hand within the long loop from below, pass the index finger of the right hand between the index and middle fingers of the left hand, and take up from above the dorsal string and pull it out between the fingers as far as it will go toward the right, letting the long loop slip over the back of the right hand. Draw tight. Place the right hand within the long loop from below ; pass the right thumb and index distal to the short transverse string ; take up the two strings immediately between the index and middle fingers of the left hand and draw toward the right so that the loop on the back of the right hand slips over the hand and over the two central strings. Draw tight.

There are now a knot and four strings lying along the palm of the left hand, two central strings which pass between the index and middle fingers, and two lateral strings.   Pass the long ulnar lateral string over the little finger and the corresponding radial lateral string over the thumb.   With the thumb and index of the right hand pick up the transverse string of the knot on the palm of the left hand and draw it gently toward the right.

TWO HOGANS

Opening A. — With the mouth take hold of the two crosses of the figure.   Drop off the hands all the strings except the little finger (or ulnar) string.   Pass both hands from below through the triangle thus formed, and take up with thumbs and indices the loop that has been dropped from the thumb, bringing it over the transverse string and toward the face so as to form an oblong.   Insert the little fingers in the oblong from the distal side, but to the outside of the two strings which form a triangle whose apex is in the mouth, and take up on the backs of the little fingers the sides of this triangle.   Draw the little fingers apart as far as they will go, releasing the mouth strings at the same time.   Hold the middle point of the two central strings with the mouth and place the hands side by side, thumbs outermost.   (See plate xv, figure 1.)

To convert this figure into a single hogan, release the mouth strings and the little finger of one hand and draw tight.

CARRYING WOOD

Opening A. — Pass the thumb and index of each hand distal to the index loop and insert into little-finger loop from the proximal side.   Release little fingers.   Each little-finger loop is now transferred to the thumb and index of their respective hands.

Pass the proximal (that is, the original) loop of each thumb and index over the loop just transferred on to the palmar side of those digits and gently extend the figure.   Insert each thumb from the distal side into the radial of the two loops between the thumb and index and extend the figure.

The two central strings that lie side by side represent the carrying band of the Navaho ; the other strings represent the wood that is being carried.   (See plate xv, figure 2.)

MANY STARS

Opening A. — Pass each thumb distal to the index loop and take up the radial little-finger string from the proximal side and return. Pass each middle finger distal to the index loop and take up the ulnar thumb string from the proximal side and return. Release thumbs. Pass each thumb through the index loop from the distal side and take up from the proximal side the ulnar little-finger string and return through the index loop. Release little fingers. Transfer the middle-finger loop of each hand to the thumb and index by passing these digits to the proximal side of the middle-finger loop, and then round the ulnar middle-finger string to insert them from the distal side into the middle-finger loop. Release middle fingers.[1]

Pass the proximal (or original) loop of each thumb and index over the newly transferred loop on to the palmar side of those digits and gently extend the figure. Insert each thumb from the distal side into the radial of the two loops between the thumb and index ; press the thumb against the palm, and extend the figure by inserting the middle fingers in the index loops. (See plate xv, figure 3.)

OWL

Position 1. — With left index take up palmar string of right hand from the distal side, and return, giving it a twist. With right index take up palmar string of left hand by the side of and not through the left index loop, and return, giving it a twist. Pass each thumb distal to the index loop, and take up the radial little-finger string from the proximal side and return. Continue as in " many stars." (See plate xv, figure 4.)

LIGHTNING

Hold part of the string with the thumbs and forefingers, the hands being about six inches apart ; make a small ring by passing the right hand away from the body and toward the left side, and hold it by the thumb and index of the right hand in such manner that the small ring is away from the body.

---

[1] Another description of this manipulation is : Transfer middle-finger loop of each hand to thumb and index in such a way that the ulnar middle-finger string becomes the radial thumb string and the radial middle-finger string becomes the ulnar index string. In accomplishing this movement the radial middle-finger string passes distal to the

Insert the index fingers, pointing downward, into the small ring, and the thumbs, also pointing downward, into the large loop. Draw tight. With a turn of the wrists make the thumbs point upward. Insert each thumb into its index loop distally and take up the ulnar index string from the proximal side. Pass each middle finger distal to the radial index string and take up ulnar thumb string from the proximal side. Pass each ring finger distal to the ulnar middle finger string and take up the radial index string from the proximal side. Pass each little finger distal to the ulnar ring-finger string and take up ulnar middle-finger string from the proximal side. Extend the thumbs as far as possible; then release them gently and throw the released loops over the other strings. The double element of these loops should be close together. Hold four fingers of each hand firmly together and with the thumbs press down the ulnar ring-finger string. (See plate xv, figure 5.)

INDIAN GAMES

L. F. Hallett

INDIAN GAMES

By L. F. HALLETT

Chairman, Historical Research Committee,
Massachusetts Archaeological Society

Despite the traditional stoicism of the Indians as seen through the eyes of the early colonists, we find occasional references to their various games, many of which were boisterous in nature, and all of which seem to have been blended with sound effects.

One of their dice games, appropriately called "Hubbub," could be heard a quarter of a mile away, according to William Wood.

In any event, gaming occupied a considerable portion of their time, and there were pastimes for all ages and both sexes. Some were reserved for fixed seasons during festivals or religious rites, while others were participated in at will. Some involved a very few individuals, while others pitted tribe against tribe.

Individual games were played in much the same manner among widely separated tribes. The variations were more in the materials employed, due to environment, than in the object or method of play.

Indian games may be divided into two general classes—games of chance, and games of skill or dexterity.

The Indian chance games included dice games and guessing games. In the former, the outcome depended upon the random fall of certain implements employed like dice; in the latter, the guess or choice of the player was the deciding factor. The gaming implements were usually derived from symbolic weapons. Stick dice were often miniature arrows or bows, as were the counting sticks. The engraved and painted tubes used in the guessing game resembled arrow shafts.

The Indians would play at these chance games for long continuous periods of time, often over twenty-four hours, or until all their belongings were lost. If unmarried, they were even known to hazard their own persons, and if chance turned against them, reduce themselves to slavery. Superstitions were nourished with fetishes or lucky stones carried to insure success. During Winslow's visit to Massasoit at Sowams in 1623 sub-chiefs and tribesmen came to visit, and "went to their manner of games for skins and knives."

Dice type games are described as existing among 130 tribes belonging to 30 linguistic stocks, and from no one tribe do they appear to have been absent. From two to four were the usual number of players. This was an ideal game for the long winter nights in the wigwam. Roger Williams describes an "arbour or play house" used in dice games where a village champion would be pitted against a worthy opponent of another village. Each was backed with high stakes by his followers amidst loud shouts of encouragement.

The implements consisted of the dice and the instruments for keeping tally. The small playing discs or dice were made of various materials including split canes, wooden blocks, bone, beaver and woodchuck teeth, walnut shells, peach and plum stones, grains of corn, shell and pottery. Their two faces were of different colors or markings — they could be black and white or other combinations of colors, and were usually eight in number. They could be either thrown by hand or tossed in a bowl or basket.

When thrown by hand they could be tossed in the air against a hide or blanket, struck ends down upon a stone lying on the ground or sometimes held in the hand, or allowed to fall freely upon the ground. If black and white turned up four and four, or five and three, there was no count; six and two counted four; seven and one, ten; and all eight of the same color, twenty. This particular scoring method was used by the Norridgewock tribe of Maine, and varied in other localities. A previously agreed winning number decided the victor. The score was kept with sticks, grains of corn, or other handy material. The Penobscot tribe used counters of cedar wood, and employed six rather than eight dice. William Wood's variation for Massachusetts, the "Hubbub" referred to previously, was played with five small bones in a small tray. One side of the discs was colored black, and the other, white.

Thumping the tray on the ground varied the colors and produced the score. All black or all white gave a double game; three and two a single game; and four and one counted nothing. The player continued while winning, but gave up the tray to the next player after a nothing count.

Card games were mentioned by Roger Williams and William Wood without any detailed account of the play. Williams described the cards as "strong rushes," and Wood used the word "puim" as a card game in which 50 or 60 sticks a foot in length were used. Both probably confused the game of cards as we know it with the Indian stick game, a guessing game having wide distribution.

The guessing games, or stick games, had at least four variations of play. Sometimes a bundle of sticks or arrow shafts was divided in the hands, the object being for the opponent to guess in which hand the odd stick or a particularly marked stick was held; or two or four sticks, one or two marked, were held in the hands, the idea being to guess which hand held the unmarked stick or sticks. Another variation was the use of four sticks, marked in pairs and hidden together, the object being to guess their relative position. Still another, often called the hidden ball or moccasin game, involved some small object—a stone, stick or bullet—which was hidden in one of four wooden tubes, in moccasins, or in the earth. The right guess would locate the object, with the resulting gain or loss of counters. Stick games involved but two persons, and the players continued until all the sticks were won by one or the other.

Games of skill or dexterity included the game of ball in several forms, archery, shooting, racing, swimming, ring and pin, snow-snake, wheel and stick, button hunting, bear baiting, and the harvest game of giveaway.

Among the games in which an implement resembling a ball was employed were the ball stick game or lacrosse, in which the ball was tossed with a racket; shinny, in which the ball was struck with a club; and double ball, a game played mostly by women, whereby two balls or billets were tied together and tossed with a stick. The balls used in these games varied in material. They were commonly covered with buckskin, but some were made of wood, of bladder netted with sinew, of cordage, bone or stone.

By far the most popular, and that having the widest distribution, was the "ball stick game," later called lacrosse. In the North it was played with one racket, and in the South with two. Important intertribal matches were held, and the competing athletes were regularly trained for this game. William Wood observed that the contestants painted their faces as in war. The game was played with a small ball of deerskin, stuffed with hair or moss, or sometimes with a wooden ball of similar size. A ball from Oldtown, Maine, four inches in diameter, covered with buckskin and filled with moose hair is in the Peabody Museum at Cambridge, Mass. The cover, a nearly circular piece of buckskin about nine inches in diameter is drawn up with a buckskin thong around the wad of moose hair; over it is placed a second piece of buckskin, five inches in diameter, which closes the opening. Horizontal goals were set up on a level plain or sandy beach free from stones and other obstacles. The distance between the two goals varied from a few hundred yards to a mile. The participants varied from 8 or 10 on a side to hundreds, and high stakes were wagered. The object of each team was to drive the ball under the opponent's goal by means of the racket, without touching it with the hands. It sometimes required two days to score a single goal, and while the men were playing, the audience sang and shouted encouragement. After the winners had scored the previously agreed number of goals, the entire assembly joined in a feast. Early observers agree that despite the high stakes and the will to win there was no quarreling or bickering, and the rivals parted on amicable terms.

The "ring and pin" game, sometimes called the "lover's game" by the Penobscots, was played throughout New England. A pin or dart of sharp pointed bone or wood about 8 inches long was joined at the middle with a foot long cord, which in turn was fastened to a conical roll of moose hair. The object was to impale the up-swinging cone with the pin. The target could also be a tightly wrapped bunch of cedar twigs, or a hole-punctured strip of moosehide. This game was analogous to the European game of cup and ball.

The lover angle developed when a man called on a maiden and the game was produced. Seated on a robe or skin, the man started the game, and continued until he missed impaling the target. Then it passed to the girl. If his company was agreeable, she continued the game to the end; but if, on her first successful thrust, instead of continuing, she handed the implements back, it meant that his company was not acceptable.

In another form, this was played as a gambling game. In this case the target became six moose phalanx bones strung on a thong, with a little piece of leather on the end to keep them in place. Betting stakes were produced, and each player had ten throws, at the end counting up one for every bone that he caught. When all had played, the man with the highest number won.´ This game was also played as a child's amusement.

The sling game was played between men with slings, the idea being to throw stones as far and accurately as possible. The sling sticks were about a foot and a half in length, with a thong at one end having a loop for the thumb and a groove at the upper end near where the thong was attached. A round stone was placed in the groove, and´was held down by the thong. This in turn was kept taut by the thumb through the loop until release. By this method the stones were hurled a surprising distance.

The snowsnake game, or "skid," was a favorite pastime with the Northern New England tribes within the limit of ice and snow. Highly polished darts or javelins up to ten feet in length were thrown with a motion similar to that used in skipping stones on the water. When used on the snow, a path or track was made by dragging a round log about six inches wide for a considerable distance. Sometimes a boy was seized by the feet and dragged down an incline to accomplish the same purpose. This was probably one of the reasons the boys favored playing on the ice. Sides were chosen and stakes bet upon the result. The greatest distance decided the winner of all the sticks. After choosing those he decided to keep, he threw the remainder in the air and they became the property of those quick enough to seize them. The sticks were carved of hard wood, tapering from an upturned head to a slender tail, and were sometimes oiled to make them more slippery. By spring the custom was to throw away the snowsnakes lest they turn into real snakes.

The wheel and stick game had universal appeal. One player rolled forward a stone disc, or wheel, while his opponent slid after it a stick curved at one end in such a way that the disc, when it fell over, rested within the crook of the stick. This was considerably harder to accomplish than in the telling, and often resulted in prolonged activity to gain the desired result.

A frequent amusement among the younger set was head rubbing. Two contestants clasped their hands behind each other's neck and rubbed foreheads together until one gave up. One refinement involved a sidewise gouging of the foe's temple. This game undoubtedly hardened the head and developed immunity to pain, if not carried to extreme.

A more dangerous pastime was that of bear baiting, observed by William Wood in Eastern Massachusetts. Seeing a bear take to water, an Indian would swim after it, and following a scuffle which could easily end disastrously to the Indian, he would mount the bear's back and ride it through the water until it drowned. Very few achieved this result without being considerably mauled in the process.

Hunt the button games, with other artifacts used rather than buttons in the earlier days, were usually accompanied with songs and movements of the hands intended to confuse those occupied in finding the hidden button.

While dancing generally had a religious or ceremonial significance, there were other occasions when the purpose was purely social. Martin Pring, in 1603, had a talented youth in his company who could play the "gitterne" or zither. With the boy playing tunes in the center of a ring of twenty Indians, they delighted in dancing around in a circle until one broke the ring, whereupon he was punished by the others. Poutrincourt, in the vicinity of Gloucester, Mass., in 1606, observed Indians dancing and playing games to the accompaniment of reed flutes. DeForest, in Connecticut, describes a dancing game in which an Indian stood in the center of a large assembly. Dancing alone, he flourished a valuable article around until it was claimed by one of the bystanders. This continued until the dancer was thoroughly tired or had danced himself out of all his property. Another then took his place and followed the same procedure, and the game of give-away continued; all going away at the end with what they had been able to beg from others. A similar game, called the harvest game because it took place at that period, was described by Roger Williams as an annual ceremony of the Narragansetts of Rhode Island.

Running races were seldom over short distances. The Indian took pride in his power of endurance, and could jog trot for miles with little apparent effort. Couriers between tribes displayed this power, and covered enormous distances in remarkable time.

Morton observed that in the spring, when the fish came up the rivers in large numbers to spawn, the Indians gathered in favorable places and spent considerable of their time in gaming and juggling, each striving to surpass the other in skill and dexterity.

Target practice was universal among the warriors and boys of the various tribes. Spears, knives and hatchets were thrown for accuracy from the hand, and gaming arrows of special design and ornamentation were shot from the bow. As in most other games, betting gave impetus to the contest.

Swimming races undoubtedly took place, although they are not specifically mentioned by the early colonists. According to Josselyn, the Indians took naturally to the water. Their natural stroke was a dog paddle rather than a spreading of the arms. Wood observed them diving and coming up in unexpected places. Roger Williams noted that they could easily swim over a mile, and could float lying as still as a log. Their children were taught to swim when very young.

Games for women included modified forms of shinny, football, and the deer-foot game. In football, the ball was kept in the air as long as possible by kicking it upward. The deer-foot game was played with a number of perforated bones from a deer's foot. They were strung on a beaded cord having a needle at one end. The purpose was to toss the bones in such a way as to catch a particular one upon the end of the needle.

Children had a variety of amusements such as top spinning, target shooting, stilts and slings for the boys; and buckskin dolls, playing-house, forfeit plays and breath-holding contests for the girls. Culin states that the top was one of the most widely diffused of Indian children's playthings. Its antiquity is shown through its use in prehistoric times in Peru. Spinning tops of wood, horn, stone or clay was a winter pastime, commonly played on the ice. In common with all children, the Indian youth took pride in imitating the games of their elders.

The hand wrestling game; so popular today, and reputedly of Indian origin, was not noted by early observers in this area.

Traits which reveal themselves as outstanding in the conduct of the various games played by the Indians include a love of gambling, indifference to losses, enthusiasm expressed through general noisiness, and good sportsmanship on all occasions—a worthy precedent to follow in our present day activities of like nature.

NOTES ON A WEST COAST SURVIVAL
OF THE ANCIENT MEXICAN BALL GAME

Isabel Kelly

NOTES ON MIDDLE AMERICAN ARCHAEOLOGY AND ETHNOLOGY

CARNEGIE INSTITUTION OF WASHINGTON

DIVISION OF HISTORICAL RESEARCH

No. 26

November 10, 1943

Notes on a West Coast Survival of the

Ancient Mexican Ball Game

Isabel Kelly

These notes were obtained in the spring of 1939, during an archaeological survey of the west coast of Mexico. Originally I planned to publish them jointly with Mr. Carlos Linga, who, through his commercial agents in southern Sinaloa, has acquired several accounts of the same ball game from the Mazatlan district, but as this has not been feasible, my Nayarit data are recorded here, without benefit of his somewhat fuller information. The account comes chiefly from Valentin Zamorano, a former player and a manufacturer of balls, with a few supplementary details from his son, Basilio Zamorano. In former times this family was among the rubber workers who supplied balls to the stretch of coast between Acaponeta and Culiacan (Sinaloa), at a price ranging from 25 to 60 pesos.

The game, called _hulama_, was current in the Acaponeta valley, Nayarit, until about 1930. It is said still to be played occasionally in the hills and in small villages, particularly on the feast days of San Juan, San Pedro, and Santiago, and on Sundays and the Saturday of Easter week.

The ball (_hule_, rubber) was round and of solid rubber. The standard circumference was three finger spans plus three fingers;

the weight, 3 kilos, 600 grams. A specimen (3-7565 in the Museum of Anthropology, University of California, Berkeley) purchased from Bernabe Diaz, in the nearby ranch of Camalotita, is undersized and in poor condition from having become flattened during storage. The diameter ranges from 163 to 196 mm., with an average of 180 mm.

Rubber was obtained from the low coastal country immediately south of Acaponeta, and particularly from Pozo de Higuera and Huaritupa. The gatherer climbed the tree and, with a machete, notched the trunk its full length. A leaf of aguama (Bromelia sp.), stripped of the edge spines, was placed against the wound to carry the latex to a corked vessel. A five-gallon tin of rubber latex was sufficient for making one and a half balls.

To coagulate the latex, the root of the machaquana [Operculina rhodocalyx (Gray) Standl.] was diced and added to water. (For this identification I am indebted to Dr. Paul Standley, of the Field Museum of Natural History. Dr. Standley writes that the moonvine, which likewise is a morning glory, frequently is used to coagulate rubber. Prof. Maximino Martinez [Las Plantas Mas Utiles que Existen en la Republica Mexicana, p. 224, Mexico, 1928] notes the use of the juice of Ipomoea bona nox.) The solution was then strained into the latex, three parts solution to one of latex. A small quantity of this mixture was heated to luke-warm, tested with a small pointed stick, and, when of the proper consistency, removed from the fire. The rubber adhering to the stick was shaped into a pellet, which was pressed against the knee and from which the rod was withdrawn. The ball was thus built up, layer by layer, as small quantities of rubber were added to the pellet-like nucleus. After each increment of rubber was squeezed

free of the liquid, the ball was shaped on a flat board held
slanting against the knees to let the liquid run off. From time
to time the growing ball was shaken vigorously beside the ear to
detect any remaining liquid, which was pressed out through the
blister perforated with a small stick. When perfectly round, the
finished ball was smoothed and polished with a stick.

After each game the ball was washed and dried thoroughly,
suspended in a bag so as to hang freely, and turned frequently lest
it become flattened. A well-cared-for ball lasts about six years.
Although the purchased specimen mentioned above is old and neglected, it bounces waist-high when dropped to the ground.

Players were barefoot and ordinarily naked save for a
breechcloth and a special belt or shield, called chimal. The latter
generally was made of the root fiber of the chalate (Ficus sp.),
a fig with aerial roots. A length of root, about 2.5 m. long, was
cut, steeped in water, and beaten with a stick to remove the outer bark. The remaining fiber was opened and spread in the sun to
dry. The belt was not woven; a model made by Basilio Zamorano
consisted merely of a strip of thick bark, 1.5 m. long and 15 cm.
wide. This particular example, however, is not from the chalate
but the haba (Hura sp.). Valentin Zamorano described the belt as
about 10 cm. wide and laced in the front with leather thongs.
The lacing was drawn tight by two men until the player felt "light."
Within the belt was a protective pad of leather or, more recently,
a section of automobile tire, to soften the blow of the ball.
Also in keeping with modern trends is the report that drill or
canvas might be substituted for the bark fiber.

The game was played on a court (<u>taste</u>), long and narrow, "like a street." Valentin Zamorano described it as 1.5 pasos or 3 varas wide by 15 varas long. The informal measure of <u>paso</u>, as used on the west coast, consists of two short paces, totaling a little over 1.5 m. A <u>vara</u> is roughly the equivalent of a yard (actually, 2.78 ft.). It may be assumed, therefore, that the court was roughly between 2.25 and 2.80 m. wide. It was simply a rectangle marked on the ground, with no walls or other permanent construction. Stone or brick marked the four corners, with one marker at the center of either side line to indicate the central, transverse line. Three single markers, indicating respectively the two end lines and the central line, were not used. Stakes might serve as markers but, to avoid injury to players, they were set flush with the surface of the court. The outline of the court and the transverse line across the center (which invariably extended well beyond the side lines) were drawn about 10 cm. wide in the dirt with the foot. The center line was called <u>analco</u>; the zone behind either end line, <u>chiche</u>. According to Cecilio A. Robelo (Nombres geograficos indigenas del Estado de Mexico, p. 43, Cuernavaca, 1900), analco has come to mean "from the other side, on the other shore of a river." Jose Maria Arreola (Nombres indigenas de Lugares del Estado de Jalisco, Boletin de la Junta Auxiliar Jalisciense de la Sociedad Mexicana de Geografia y Estadistica, p. 6, Guadalajara, 1935) gives the same meaning.

The number of players varied. There might be but one on either side, but generally a team consisted of from two to five. If there were five, one of each team was stationed at the center line, with the remaining players of his side strung diagonally be-

hind him, so as to cover their half of the court most effectively.
The rearmost player of each team remained at his station by the back
line; he was called the golpeador 'striker'. Other players seem
not to have had names.

At the beginning of the game an umpire (juez) -- or two,
one for each team -- stood at the center line. He started the
play by rolling the ball into the court. It was recovered (in
the hands) by any player who happened to be near. He then threw
the ball swiftly (again, with the hands) into the court of the
opposing team. One of the latter returned it, either at full
volley or on the bounce; he was required to receive it either on
the hip or on the thigh, to within four fingers' distance of the
knee. Disputes were settled by examining the welt left on the
body. If the ball hit outside the acceptable hip-thigh zone, or
if it were not returned to the other court, a point was scored for
the opposing team. Apparently the ball need not be returned on the
first bounce. A player fell to the ground to receive a low ball
and leapt in the air for a high one. He could receive on either
hip, according to personal preference, but a given player always
used the same hip. In the accompanying photographs a lad of
Camalotita obligingly gives an impromptu demonstration. In figure
1a he awaits the ball; in figure 1b he has just struck it. It
need scarcely be remarked that the game was dangerous. If the
player misjudged by a few centimeters, he received a heavy, moving
body in the solar plexis. Injuries frequently were fatal.

It is said that if the ball were received initially by the
center player and if the latter did not touch the central line
with any part of his body, his team had the right to invade the

territory of the opponents. The advantage of such an invasion
is not understandable <u>unless the end lines functioned as goals</u>.
Basilio Zamorano stated that if the ball hit within the court
and bounced over the back line without being returned, a point
was scored for the attacking team. But this is simply another
way of saying that a ball which hit within the proper court and
was not returned scored a point for the opposing team. Neither
of the Acaponeta informants appeared to regard the end lines of
any particular significance in scoring, although they were questioned specifically concerning this detail. In so far as I could
determine, scoring was exclusively by means of fouls or failures
made by the opposing team: by failure to return the ball by means
of the hip-thigh blow; by having the ball fall in one's own court;
or by knocking the ball out of bounds. A ball which fell outside the court, without first having bounced within, was called
<u>muerta</u> (dead). The earlier accounts which were sent to Mr. Linga
from southern Sinaloa indicated a scoring basically similar to
that just described. He tells me, however, that in a later account
the end lines do function as goals. It may be assumed that my data,
was well as Mr. Linga's earlier information, should stand corrected.

The ball remained in the possession of the team which scored.
Succeeding plays were started according to the number of points
held by the team in possession of the ball. These may be out-
lined thus:

<u>Una</u>: The ball was put into action by the golpeador of the
team which scored on the opening play. He bounced the
ball one to three times, touched it to his hip, and
threw it into the air (with the hand) so that it would

fall into the opposing court. As the ball left his hand,
he called "una."

Dos: If we assume that the same team scored on the play just
described, the same golpeador again opened the play. He
rolled the ball swiftly along the ground into the opponents'
court, calling "dos."

Other plays were started according to the same pattern: una, cuatro,
and cinco (1, 4, 5) being thrown overhead (arriba); dos, tres,
seis, and siete (2, 3, 6, 7) being rolled on the ground (abajo).
At each play the golpeador called the appropriate number as the ball
went into action. J. Eric S. Thompson suggests that actually the
golpeador called the score (raya) of his team rather than any number of play. This seems entirely plausible since, as stated above,
the mode of putting the ball into action was determined by the number of points held by the team in possession of the ball. In any
case, the initial play, followed by the 7 specified above, would
account for a total of eight, which number of points presumably constituted a game. Rolled plays (abajo) were called male; overhead
plays (arriba, en viento) had no special name.

Ordinary progression of score was relatively simple. A team
which won a play gained a point and one which lost a play relinquished a point. In other words, the scoring was double and that
of both teams changed on a single play. After each play the ball
was held by the scoring side. There were, however, some exceptions
and ramifications, a number of which remain entirely obscure.
For example, it was said that if a team had three points and lost
one, it had the privilege of putting the next play into action abajo.
This is not clear, for a team which lost a point presumably would
not have the ball at the start of the succeeding play. Moreover,
it was said that a team holding two points, but which then lost one,
might start the next play by calling for 3. The same difficulty
applies here. However, this would appear to be a means of giving

a team a gambling chance -- that of gaining the score of three or
of losing all. Unfortunately, these complexities of scoring could
not be disentangled because of linguistic handicaps, and it is
hoped that when Mr. Linga publishes his Sinaloan data many of these
obscure points will be clarified. If a team held either three or
seven points it stood to lose all. If a team with three points permitted its opponents to gain two consecutive scores, then instead
of losing two points, it yielded all three. So also, if a team
had seven points and the opponents scored four times successively,
the losing side relinquished all seven points, while the opponents gained four points and retained the ball. The above conditions were called urre de tres and urre de siete. The same situa-
tion may have held for the score of six, as well as for three and
seven, for mention was made of urre de seis, said to obtain when
a team with six points lost four consecutive plays. It may be
noted that the urre applies exclusively to the abajo plays, but
of these, Score 2 is exempt.

A game generally lasted from about 4 o'clock until dark, without rest periods. With good players a game might have to be continued three or four days, being resumed at the score of the previous
afternoon. The implication is that a score of eight constituted
the game, but Basilio Zamorano thought that a game could be played
for any number of points arranged at the start. If, as has been
suggested above, the present data are faulty and the end lines
actually served as goals, presumably the passing of the ball across
the opponents' back line would terminate the game.

The modern version of the ball game at Acaponeta appears to
have been entirely secular, except for the fact that religious

feast days were favored for play. No mention was made of inter-village or inter-group competition, but such rivalry may well have existed. A team was organized by an interested individual who might or might not function as umpire. He was called the "owner of the game" and apparently fed the players and supervised prac-tice. Players were expected to train conscientiously, and an inattentive one might be whipped by the organizer. Training fare was normal, though supervised, until the day of the game, when diet was restricted to liquids, especially milk; but if the game was continued another day, solid food was eaten. Players were expected not to leave the house, to abstain from sexual inter-course, and to bathe immediately following a game. The organizer and financial backer apparently received his compensation in the attendant prestige and in winning bets. Heavy gambling invariably accompanied the ball game, and in this the women participated. A losing team gained nothing but "puros golpes" (just blows).

The above data presented a number of interesting points. Although the account manifestly is incomplete, it is at least definite and, in parts, detailed. Obviously, the modern game of Nayarit and Sinaloa is far from identical with that recorded for the high cultures of central and southern Mexico. But, at the same time, a genetic relationship is implied: both games in-volve corridor-like courts, a ball of solid rubber, the obligation to strike with the hip or thigh, and an accompaniment of lavish betting.

Unfortunately, the early accounts of the game, both in the Mexican and Maya areas, are so vague that little is known of the manner of play. Fundamentally it was probably not unlike that

I have described, although undoubtedly it was much more complex.
Masonry walls against which the ball must have bounced, elaborate
I-shaped courts, wall rings -- these and other traits all indicate
a more elaborate ensemble. Probably this west coast occurrence
should be regarded as a modern, peripheral survival either of
an archaic form or of a simplified version of the classical game.
In any case, it would appear that the chief hope of expanding knowledge concerning this famous Mexican-Maya institution is through
study of the modern survival, the genetically related, albeit simpler, game of the west coast. It is noteworthy that such a survival should be found in a straight mestizo rather than in an indigenous milieu.

The distribution of the Sinaloa-Nayarit game is imperfect-
ly known, but has been established definitely as far north as the
Rio Fuerte (R. L. Beals, The Comparative Ethnology of Northern
Mexico before 1750, p. 188 [quoting Perez de Ribas]). Dr. Gordon
Ekholm was told that the ball game still is played at Bacubirito,
on the Rio Sinaloa, and at Mocorito. Dr. Beals writes me (June 8,
1940) that a similar game is reported for the Cahita; he suspects
that it may not have been general among them, but may have been
confined to the Rio Sinaloa area. He mentions another modern game
which may be an offshoot of the one under consideration. It is
played with a small rubber ball, batted against the right forearm,
on which a protective guard is worn. It is a foul if the ball
touches any other part of the body. This game is specifically reported in Guasave, Nio, Bamoa, Tamazula, and Mocorito. The southern limits of the coastal distribution of hulama are not known
below Acaponeta, in northern Nayarit. There are no data from the

Jalisco littoral, although the game is known in Teocaltiche, in the old Caxcana province, along the modern Jalisco-Zacatecas border (Noticias Varias de Nueva Galicia, p. 357, Guadalajara, 1878).

In view of the informal court herein described for modern Nayarit, it is evident that this, or a similar, ball game may have flourished in an area without having left any perceptible archaeological trace. Perhaps for this reason, there is no mention of prepared ball courts from the west coast of Mexico, from northern Sonora to the Colima-Michoacan frontier. The Sonoran court, said to be of the "Arizona type," was located during an archaeological survey by Dr. Gordon Ekholm, who placed it a few miles south of Santa Cruz, Sonora, on a mesa above the river. The Colima-Michoacan court is at Puente de Cerritos, in the Coahuayana valley, and has been dubiously identified from surface evidence alone. It consists of a long, narrow plaza enclosed by four low mounds, 1-1.5 m. high. The end mounds are broader and slightly lower than the side mounds, which are long, narrow, and their surfaces cobble-strewn. In profile the side mounds are sharply peaked, and their upper surface averages less than 1 m. in width, obviously too narrow to have served as a house foundation. Moreover, the floor of the "court" is flat and at a slightly higher level than the surrounding plain. The whole, from the floor to the mounds, appears from surface indications to be an artificial structure.

The historical and modern occurrences of the ball game in northern Nayarit and virtually throughout Sinaloa suggest a former continuous or nearly continuous distribution into the American Southwest where, in recent years, a number of ball courts have been recognized and excavated. Although the modern version of the game may explain the apparent lack of prepared courts on the west coast, it by no means explains the reappearance of such courts in the Southwest. It is unlikely that the Arizona Hohokam and their neighbors would have gone to the tremendous effort of building courts unless the latter were an integral feature of the game as it was adopted by them. Thus, despite the suggestion of a nearly continuous distribution, it seems probable that the west coast can not be regarded as the potential source of the Southwestern game.

Archaeologically the west coast of Mexico still is little known, and it is possible that ball courts have hitherto escaped notice but will be found in the course of more intensive investigation. In northern Nayarit there are repeated rumors of stone ball courts in the adjacent sierra. These reports were not localized and time did not permit a search. Furthermore, ball courts have been reported in the nearby Sierra Madre of Durango by J. Alden Mason (Late Archaeological Sites in Durango). The Teocaltiche account noted above establishes the game as current in the Caxcana during the late sixteenth century.

As far as present information goes, there is no demonstrable evidence of Hohokam--west coast interplay in any sphere of culture, either ball courts or otherwise. Some inland route of contact, therefore, must be sought. It may be noted that, in addition to ball courts, pseudo-cloisonné painting is common to the Hohokam and the western highlands. Both ball courts and inlay painting are well dated in the Southwest, and occurrences in the western highlands should be examined, for both distribution and chronology. It may well be that the occupation of the western highlands -- like that of the west coast -- will prove to have been far too recent to have bearing on the comparatively early Hohokam occurrences.

INDIAN SPORTS

J. C. McCaskill

INDIAN SPORTS

By J. C. McCaskill – Supervisor of Boys' Activities

Traditionally the North American Indians have been great sportsmen. The vigorous outdoor life to which they were accustomed was conducive to the growth and development of sports. Archaeologists excavating recently in the ruins of Xochicalco, a buried city in Mexico, found evidences that the former inhabitants of this city played the game of basket ball. They unearthed the court with its baskets, and later found the ball. Thus long before Dr. Naismith and Springfield College were ever heard of, the Indians of Mexico were playing basket ball.

When Indian sports are mentioned a great array of famous athletes passes in review. They are headed by the famous Jim Thorpe, Sac and Fox Indian, conceded by many authorities to be the greatest athlete ever produced. At the Carlisle Indian School he became reknowned as a football player under the coaching of Pop Warner. At the 1912 Olympics at Stockholm he completely stole the show. A great runner, a marvelous kicker, a hitter every pitcher feared, Jim Thorpe embodied the Indian ideal of physical prowess.

In addition to Thorpe, the names of Exendine, Hanley, Levi, Chief Bender, Gyon and scores of others occupy prominent places in the sports Hall of Fame.

Indian boys and girls have taken to the sports of the white boys and girls with great enthusiasm. Down in the desert of Arizona miles from any town several years ago I discovered a football game going on. Many of the players were old Carlisle athletes still carrying on in the Pop Warner tradition. In small rural schools throughout the Indian country boys and girls play baseball, football, basket ball and other American games. Stuart Chase tells of finding Indian boys playing basket ball in the sleepy plaza of the town of Tsintsuntsan amid the moldering churches and the ancient graves, a town a million miles from nowhere, once the capital of the Tarascan Indians, in Mexico.

The Indians also have given to the white youth some of their own games. If you have ever seen a lacrosse game you have seen America's oldest and roughest game, played by the American Indians before the coming of the white man. Lacrosse is played by many of the Northern Indians. The Cherokees, Creeks, Choctaws and other Southern Indians play similar games known as rackets. In the north they use a single racket; in the south they use two. In the old days the game was a part of a religious ceremony, and included fasting, bleeding and prayers. Each tribe had its team. The goals were set several hundred yards apart and the ball, made of deerskin stuffed with hair or moss, was advanced by running, passing, or kicking. One's hands were not supposed to touch it.

29

Indian Ball, as it is now called in the south, is played in many places. The Cherokees in western North Carolina still play it, especially at their festivals. A group of young men on the Potawatomi Reservation in Kansas have a team. Several of the Indian schools have teams. Had the Boy Scouts' jamboree in the summer of 1935 not been called off, thousands of Boy Scouts would have had an opportunity to witness this game. The delegation of Creek boys from the Euchee School in Oklahoma were planning to put on a demonstration game.

Many Indians have become famous as long distance runners. This is not surprising. A few years ago I witnessed a stick relay of the Zunis down in the southwest. On the day preceding their Rain Dance they had run the stick relay. Running in bare feet, they throw the sticks with their toes from one runner to another. The course runs for a distance of several miles around the fields and irrigation reservoir.

Archery is another sport followed by many Indians. One of the favorite archery contests of the Cherokee is to place two stacks of cornstalks one hundred yards apart, shooting from one stack to the other with sharp pointed arrows. The first contestant to pierce a given number of stalks is declared winner. The style of shooting of these Indians is quite different from that usually employed by white archers. They give the impression of shooting quickly, with a forward striding motion, as though a deer or rabbit, or other animal had suddenly jumped from the bushes.

Shooting arrows at a moving target is also quite an old game that still survives. The streamlined version of it I saw recently among the Navajos, where an old automobile tire had been made into a target and was rolled down a hill. The object was to see how many arrows the shooter could put into the target before it got to the bottom of the hill.

Many Indian games were developed for the use of two or three persons out on long treks hunting or visiting neighboring tribes. Snow Snakes was quite popular among the Winnebagos and others in the northwest. The snow snake was a nicely whittled and polished stick with a rounded knob on the end. These were thrown in such a way as to skid along the ice for long distances, the object, of course, being to see whose snake could be made to go farthest. They played "for keeps" too.

Stilt walking, found among children of every nook and cranny of this country, is thought by many anthropologists to be indigenous to the Indians. It has been found to have existed among the Hopis, the Shoshones and the Mexican Indians before the coming of the white man. It is quite possible, of course, that other primitive groups, likewise, have developed stilt walking. All Indian games were either games of dexterity, like those described here, or games of chance. Games of pure skill and calculation, such as chess, are unknown among the Indians.

THE SEMINOLES WERE RECOGNIZED AS THE LEADING BALL PLAYERS YEARS AGO

B. McKenzie

The Seminoles Were Recognized As The Leading Ball Players Years Ago

BY B. F. McKENZIE

What has become of the old-time Indian ball game, one of the favorite pastimes of the American Indian?

It is a thing of the past, but still in many Indian homes we find rackets, relics of the days gone by. We cannot go into the Indian camp and see today the interesting ball game as played in the days when our forefathers were young.

If you had the pleasure of being a spectator at one of the ball games you would have seen something which not only held your attention, but, also, your admiration more than the big championship baseball games of the present day.

We seldom see now the ball club used in earlier days which required skill to manipulate so as to hit the goal.

The old Indians consider their ball game a noble and manly exercise. The more modern game of baseball has been substituted for the old time Indian ball game among the younger Indians. While the Indian ball game has nearly passed away, nevertheless, it has helped to advance the modern day baseball game.

The Indian ball game is somewhat different from that of baseball. I will try to give you a short narrative of the game as played by the Seminoles of Oklahoma.

The sides that are to play choose their leaders. They get together and select the most suitable ground. This being done about two weeks before the scheduled game. They talk over matters pertaining to the number of players to be used in the game. They generally selected a stretch of prairie, because it being very smooth, and with grass not more than five inches high.

The ground is about 50 by 150 yards. After selection of the ground has been made, the date of the game is agreed upon. The leaders then notify the members of the whole tribe. Everyone is invited to attend and take part.

Many Indians outside the Five Tribes use one long pole with a feather on top to serve as a goal. The Seminole use two goals, one for each side represented. The goal posts are made of the body of a small tree, four to five inches in diameter, and about 15 feet in length. These goals are made of three poles, two of which are set about three feet in the ground, leaving 12 feet above ground. These posts are set about three feet apart, while a third pole is then placed across the top. These goals are about 100 yards apart.

The Seminole Indians generally play their game in the afternoon, beginning about 1 or 2 o'clock, and lasting until one side makes twenty points. This is the number of goals which constitute the game. It sometimes is very difficult for either side to make points, and often the game lasts until sundown without either side scoring.

They then discontinue the game which is to be finished at some future date. The Seminole Indians are very rough in their games as well as others of the Indian tribes. The players wear very little clothing, usually wear a breech-cloth made of bright red flannel or any color they desire. They also paint their faces and stick eagle feathers in their hair. When they have done these things they are ready to begin playing.

In the forenoon on the day of the game the women sing and dance in order to cheer the men and boys taking part in the ball game. They are very superstitious and the singing and dancing, they believe, will help them win a victory over their opponents.

There are five positions which the players occupy while playing: The first is near one goal; second, between the center and the goal; third, in the center; the fourth and fifth, between the center and the opposite goal. You might consider the positions somewhat similar to those of basket ball as they have a center and what might be called a forward.

The number of players is not limited, and often as many as seventy-five Indians take part in the game. The scoring is done by the men sending the ball between the goal posts, or when the ball hits one of the poles forming the goal.

The Seminoles use short handled sticks. One is used in the left hand to hold the ball, the other is used in the right hand in order to guard the ball. This way it is easy for them to throw the ball through the goals.

The ball is covered with calf or deer skin and is a little larger than a walnut. The inner part of the ball is filled with feathers or cloth, thus making the ball very light in weight.

They use only one ball in playing the game but have three more in readiness to be used only in case one is lost. The cover of the ball is cut like the cover of a baseball. The sewing on of the cover is done very neatly and one unfamiliar with the game might think they were factory made.

When it is nearing the time for the game to be called the men taking part go a short distance away from the camp and get ready for the game. Then as they march toward the ball ground there are two women who go with them. One has a drum made of a small water keg with a piece of hide stretched across one end. The other has a small rattle which is made of a cocoanut shell filled with small gravel. These women lead the players to the ball ground beating the drum and shaking the rattle. Both side go through the same preparations before going into the game. After all the players have reached the ball ground they retire to their respective goals and give their whoops and yells after which they then come to the center of the ball ground where one of the older men gives them some good advice and an encouraging talk on the way to play ball. He also tells them all to go into the game with the determination to win and to always be loyal to their side. That is what makes the game interesting and fierce, because each side is trying its hardest to win the game.

They do not have an umpire as is the custom at the baseball games of the present day. Instead there is a man who tosses the ball into the air at the beginning of each game. They also have two men from each side whose duty it is to stand near each goal to see that no cheating is done. There are many who do not take part in the game and are inclined to cheat for their side. If one of the players is caught cheating the ball is then brought back to the center and the game has to start anew.

As I have said before, there are twenty points in the game and the side making that number of points wins the game and there is always a hard struggle between the opposing sides. It sometimes happens that the two sides playing get into a fight which makes it impossible to finish the game that day. One might consider the game very rough indeed, but that is the Seminole's way of playing ball. After the game the players go to their camps and talk over the results of the game and see how badly they have been bruised up by their opponents.

The long handled sticks are used mostly by the blanketed Indians on the reservations. They take both hands in using this stick and are very skilfull players. The Indians playing with the long handled sticks play a game somewhat similar to that of tennis. The net in the end of the sticks is stretched across very tight, thus forming a racket. The ball is then knocked back and forth over a single goal which is made of a single pole. This game is not so rough as the game played by the Seminoles. These Indians are very skillful players and one of their characteristics is sticktoitiveness. If all of the younger generation of Indians had the courage enthused into them that their ancestors displayed in their ball games, they would make a great success in the world.

NAVAJO GAMBLING SONGS

Washington Matthews

NAVAJO GAMBLING SONGS.

BY DR. WASHINGTON MATTHEWS, U. S. ARMY.

The Navajos have a great number of songs which have been handed down in the tribe for generations and whose forms are well established. Those songs, which pertain to their rites and mythology, are so numerous that I have no hope of ever making a collection that will approximate completeness.

In addition to these transmitted songs, they have countless improvisations, heard at all dances and social gatherings not of a religious character. The difficulties in the way of the Navajo improvisators may not seem to us very important when we learn that meaningless syllables may be added at will to fill out the verses, and that rhyming terminations are not required. Yet they undoubtedly have prosodical laws understood, if not formulated, to conform to which they are often obliged to take liberal poetic licenses and employ terms not used in ordinary conversation.

The songs selected for. presentation here were sung in a game called *Kêsitcè*,* which, in the winter season, is the favorite game for stakes. Only a few can I give. To collect all, even of this particular set of songs, would take more time than I will, probably, ever be able to devote to all branches of Navajo ethnology. One old man, in reply to my question as to the number of songs sung in this game, replied that there were four thousand. Of course, this was an exaggeration and intended to be understood as such ; but the statement was designed to convey some idea of the great number that existed. Another Indian, an inveterate old gambler, who had made *Kesitcè* "the study of his life," said that there was not a thing that walked or flew or crept or crawled in all the world (as

---

* From *Ke*, moccasins, and *sitce*, side by side, parallel to one another in a row.

(1)

known to the Navajos, of course) that had not at least one appropriate song in the game, and that many had more than one song.
He further stated that it took him four years to learn all he knew.

I have not contented myself with hearing these songs from the
mouth of one individual, but have had them sung to me by many
persons from widely distant parts of the Navajo country—persons
who had, perhaps, never exchanged a word with one another in
their lives. The perfect uniformity with which they were repeated
in most cases, and the close approach to uniformity in all other
cases, were wonderful.

These, like all other transmitted songs of this tribe, depend on a
legend for their explanation. Recited by themselves, they seem
almost meaningless; sung in connection with the story they are intended to embellish, their significance is at once apparent. It is,
therefore, necessary that I should tell something of the myth of the
Kesitcè; and, in order that the myth may be fully understood, a
brief description of the game must be given.

THE GAME OF THE KESITCÈ.

This is, to some extent, sacred in its nature, for the playing is
confined to the winter, the only time when their myths may be told
and their most important ceremonies conducted. It is practiced
only during the dark hours. The real reason for this is probably
that the stone used in the game cannot be hidden successfully by
daylight; but if you ask an Indian why the game is played only at
night, he will account for it by referring you to the myth and saying that he on whom the sun shines while he is engaged in the game
will be struck blind. I have heard that on some occasions, when
the stakes are heavy and the day begins to dawn on an undecided
contest, they close all the apertures of the lodge with blankets,
blacken the skin around their eyes, place a watch outside to prevent
intrusion, and for a short time continue their sport.

The implements of the game are eight moccasins; a roundish
stone or pebble about an inch and a half in diameter; a blanket
used as a screen; a stick with which to strike the moccasins; a
chip blackened on one side that they toss up to decide which party
shall begin the game, and one hundred and two counters, each
about nine inches long made of a stiff, slender root-leaf of the
Yucca angustifolia. Two of these counters are notched on the
margins.

The moccasins are buried in the ground so that only about an inch of their tops appear and they are filled to the ground level with powdered earth or sand.   They are placed side by side a few inches apart in two rows, one on each side of the fire.   The players are divided into two parties, each controlling one row of moccasins.   When, by tossing up the chip, they have decided which party shall begin the lucky ones hold up a screen to conceal their operations and hide the ball in one of the moccasins, covering it well with sand.

When all is ready they lower the screen and allow that person to come forward whom their opponents have selected to find the ball. He strikes with a stick the moccasin in which he supposes the ball to lie.   If his guess is correct he takes the stone, his comrades become the hiders and his opponents the seekers; but if he fails to indicate the place wherein the pebble is hid the hiders win some of the counters, the number won depending on the position of the moccasin struck and the position of the one containing the stone. Thus each party is always bound to win while it holds the stone and always bound to lose while its opponent holds it.

The system of counting is rather intricate, and though I perfectly comprehend it I do not consider a full description of it in this connection as necessary to the proper understanding of the myth.   It will suffice to say that the number of counters lost at any one unsuccessful guess can only be either four, six, or ten; these are the only "counts" in the game.

When the game begins the counters are held by some uninterested spectator and handed to either side according as it wins.   When this original holder has given all the counters out, the winners take from the losers.   When one side has won all the counters the game is done.   The original holder parts with the two notched counters, called "grandmothers," last.   One of the party receiving them sticks them up in the rafters of the *hogan* (lodge) and says to them "Go seek your grandchildren" (*i. e.* bring the other counters back to our side).   The possession of the "grandmothers" is supposed to bring good luck.

A good knowledge of the songs is thought to assist the gamblers in their work, probably under the impression that the spirits of the primeval animal gods are there to help such as sing of them.   A song begun during an "inning" (to borrow a term from the field) must be continued while the inning last.   Should this inning be short it is not considered lucky to sing the same song again during the game.

EPITOME OF THE MYTH OF THE KESITCE.

In the ancient days there were, as there are now,. some animals who saw better, could hunt better, and were altogether happier in the darkness than in the light; and there were others who liked not the darkness and were happy only in the light of day. The animals of the night wished it would remain dark forever and the animals of the day wished that the sun would shine forever. At last they met in council in the twilight to talk the matter over and the council resolved that they should play a game by hiding a stone in a moccasin (as in the game now called *Kesitce*) to settle their differences. If the night animals won the sun should never rise again, if the day animals succeeded never more should it set. So when night fell they lit a fire and commenced the game.

In order to determine which side should first hide the stone they took a small weather-stained fragment of wood and rubbed one side with charcoal. They tossed it up; if it fell with the black side up the nocturnal party were to begin, but it fell with the gray side up and those of the diurnal side took the stone. These raised a blanket to conceal their operations and sang a song, which is sung to this day by the Navajos when they raise the screen in this game [No. 1, Screen Song], and the game went on.

They commenced the game with only one hundred counters but a little whitish, old-looking snake called *lic-bitcòi*, *i. e.* maternal grandmother of the snakes, said they ought to have two more counters. Therefore they made two, notched them so that they would look like snakes and called them *bitcòi*, maternal grandmothers, which name the two notched counters used in the game still bear.

The cunning Coyote would not cast his lot permanently with either side. He usually stood between the contending parties, but occasionally went over to one side or the other as the tide of fortune seemed to turn.

Some of the genii of those days joined the animals in this contest. On the side of the night animals was the great destroyer *Yeitso*, the best guesser of all, who soon took the stone away from the day animals. Whenever the latter found it in the moccasins of their moon-loving enemies they could not hold it long for the shrewd-guessing

Yeitso would recover it.   They lost heavily and began to tremble
for their chances, when some one proposed to them to call in the
aid of the gopher, *nasizi.*   He dug a tunnel under the moccasins
leading from one to another and when *Yeitso* would guess the right
moccasin the gopher, unseen by all, would transfer the stone to
another place [See Song No. 7].   Thus was *Yeitso* deceived, the
day party retrieved their losses and sang a taunting song of him
[No. 2, Yeitso Song].

But when they had won back nearly all the counters, luck appeared to again desert them.   The noctivagant beasts came into
possession of the pebble, and kept it so long that it seemed as if
their opponents could never regain it.   Guess as cleverly as they
might, the stone was not to be found in the moccasin indicated by
those who longed for an eternal day.   Then the owl sang a song
expressive of his desires [No. 4, Owl's Song], and when he had
done, one of the wind-gods whispered into the ear of one of the
diurnal party that the owl held the stone in his claws all the time,
and never allowed it to be buried in the moccasin.   So, when next
the screen was withdrawn, the enlightened day animal advanced,
and, instead of striking a moccasin, struck the owl's claws, and the
hidden stone dropped out on the ground.

After this the game proceeded with little advantage to either side,
and the animals turned their attention to composing songs about
the personal peculiarities, habits, and history of their opponents,
just as in social dances to-day the Navajos ridicule one another in
song.   Thus all the songs relating to animals [Nos. 7 *ad fin.*],
which form the great majority of the songs of the *Kesitce,* originated.

Later the players began to grow drowsy and tired and somewhat
indifferent to the game, and again the wind-god whispered—this
time into the ear of the magpie—and said, "Sing a song of the
morning," whereat the magpie sang his song [No. 5].   As he
uttered the last words, "*Qa-yel-ká! Qa-yel-ká!*" |(It dawns! It
dawns!) the players looked forth and beheld the pale streak of
dawn along the eastern horizon.   Then all hastily picked up their
counters and blankets and fled, each to his proper home—one to
the forest, another to the desert, this to the gully, that to the rocks.

The bear had lent his moccasins to be used in the game.   They
were, therefore, partly buried in the ground.   In his haste to be off
he put them on wrong—the right moccasin on the left foot, and

vice versa; and this is why the bear's feet are now misshapen. His coat was then as black as midnight, but he dwelt on top of a high mountain, and was so late in getting back to his lair that the red. beams of the rising sun shone upon him, imparting their ruddy hue to the tips of his hairs, and thus it is that the bear's hair is tipped with red to this day.

The home of the wood-rat, *létso*, was a long way off, and he ran so far and so fast to get there that he raised great blisters on his feet, and this accounts for the callosities we see now on the soles of the rat.

So the day dawned on the undecided game. As the animals never met again to play. for the same stakes, the original alternation of day and night has never,been changed.

TEXT AND TRANSLATION OF SONGS OF THE KESITCE.

NOTE.—In the Navajo words as they appear in this paper the vowels have the continental sounds. There is only one diphthong, *ai;* ‘ denotes an aspirated vowel; *c* has the sound of *sh* in *shine; d* before a vowel has the sound of *th* in *this; j* has the French sound; *l* is always aspirated, as if spelled *hl; n* above the line (ⁿ) is nasal; *q* has the sound of German *ch* in *machen; t* before a vowel has the sound of *th* in *thing;* the other letters have the ordinary English sounds.

No. 1.—SCREEN SONG.

Atcá' dilpá'li taosklè,
Atcá' dilpá'li taosklè.
Kolagà ainà.

TRANSLATION.

The old screen hangs in front
The old screen hangs in front

NOTES.

atcá', in front of; before.

dilpá'li, it hangs.   This is applicable only to something broad and flexible that hangs temporarily.   Of a curtain or *portière* that hangs permanently they say *nipá'li.*

taösklè, something old, frayed, or worn; usually applied only to textile fabrics and clothing; ragged.

kolagà ainà is probably meaningless.

No. 2.—YEITSO SONG.

Yèitso tcinila' nieè,
Tcal azdetsèl tcini "Haèna!"
Yèitso tcinilá' nieè,
Tcal azdetsèl tcini "Haèna! Hanè!"
"Cá'nenánoa'" niyeko.
Tcal azdetsèl tcini "Haèna! Hanè!"

TRANSLATION.

Thus says *Yeitso*,
Weeping while he strikes (at the moccasins,) he says, "Alas!"
Thus says *Yeitso*,
Weeping while he strikes, he says, "Alas! Alas!"
"Put it ye back for me (where it was before)" he says.
Weeping while he strikes, he says, "Alas! Alas!"

NOTES.

Yèitso, an important character in Navajo mythology, a giant who was slain by the children of the Sun.

tcinilá', thus he says, exactly thus he says.

tcal, he cries (while doing something else)—synchronal form.

azdètsèl, he is striking at it.

tcini, he says. This word may be said of one either absent or present. *Vide infra, niyeko.*

haèna! hanè'! exclamations of *Yeitso* expressive of his chagrin and disappointment; herhaps equivalent to Alas!

cá'nenánoa, ca'nánoa, means "replace it all ye for me," and conveys the idea that it must be replaced exactly where it was before. For the extra syllable *ne* I know no meaning. I have been told by the Indians it is "just to make out the song." The luckless *Yeitso* hoped he might find the stone if his opponents were silly enough to do as he requested.

niyeko. Here the singer takes poetic license with the word *nigo*, he says—*i. e.*, some one absent or at a distance says. *Yeitso* is supposed to make his plea while still on the opposite side of the fire, before he approaches to seek the stone. But he says "Alas!" after he comes over.

No. 3.—YEBITCAI SONG.

Yenaqaniya kejòji ke,
Yenaqaniya ooò kejòji ke eè,
Yenaqaniya aà,
Apàna bĭtsĭdi alkìajdolkègo,
Yenaqanĭya kejòji ke, yenaqania kejòji ke,
Yenaqanĭya aà.

TRANSLATION.

He comes to us on toes and feet,
He comes to us on toes and feet,
He comes to us on toes and feet,
With coat upon coat of fine-dressed skin,
He comes to us on toes and feet, he comes to us on toes and feet,
He comes to us.

NOTES.

yenaqaniya, that by means of which one arrives, the "means of transportation." *ye*, a prefix forming with verbs nouns denoting means of motion. *naqaniya*, he arrives at our house, he reaches us, he comes to us.

kejòj, toes.

ke, foot, feet.

apàna, buckskin.

bĭtsĭdi, soft, pliable, devoid of stiffness; said of finely-dressed buckskin, dead grass, etc.

alkìajdolkègo, in layers on the person; refers to layers or coats of flexible material, one on top of another, worn on the body.

Yèbitcai, one of the genii or demigods, came late to the game and those who preceded him sang this song. In the dance of the *Yebitcai* he who enacts this character moves with a noisy, shuffling gait and wears coats of fine buckskin, while the other dancers are nearly naked.

No. 4.—OWL'S SONG.

To-yolkál-nisín-da,
To-yolkál-nisín-da.
Hĭhĭ hihĭ hihĭ.

TRANSLATION.

I wish not the end of all the nights,
or,
I wish not the end of the last night.

NOTES.

tò-da, a negative adverb commonly divided so that the first syllable shall precede, and the last syllable succeed, the verb or sentence which it qualifies. Here we have an example of this arrangement.

yolkal, the end of all the nights, the end of the last night; said of the approach of dawn on the last night of any period as at the end of a festival. The owl here speaks of the last night of all time.

nisin, I wish, I desire. This is usually pronounced *insin*. Transpositions for euphony are common in the Navajo language.

No. 5.—MAGPIE SONG.

A'a'á'i-ne! A'a'á'i-ne!
Ya'a'nì-ainè! Ya'a'nì-ainè! Kòya-ainè
Bitá' alkáigi bikè yiská' ne.
Qayelká'! Qayelká'!

TRANSLATION.

The magpie! The magpie! Here underneath
In the white of his wings are the footsteps of morning.
It dawns! It dawns!

NOTES.

a'a'á'i and *ya'a'ì* are imitations of the magpie's call; *a'a'ì* is the onomatopoetic name of the magpie.

kòya, here beneath, here below, or within; probably refers to a hut or cavern in which the game was supposed to be played.

bitá', his wings.

alkàigi, in the white part; from *kai* or *lakài*, white.

bikè, his feet; hence, also, his footsteps, his trail.

yiská', morning, the morrow.

qayelká', it dawns, it is morning.

ne and *ainè* seem to have no meaning.

2

The black quills of the magpie's wings are margined with white, and thus is the black sky of night bordered at daybreak ; hence, the simile in the song.

In the myth, as related to me, it is stated that the magpie sang this song ; but, in the language of the song, he is referred to in the third person.

No. 6.—CHICKEN HAWK'S SONG.

Yoò qalaenà, yoò qalaenà, yoò qalaenà
Qalaèna enà, qalaèna enò, yoò ayeè, he'ná', he'ná' !
Naestcà qastī[n] cizditìni.
Ta'cijá' ka' nihísye ; ailapà cizáitìni.

TRANSLATION.

The old owl hates me.
When alone I always bring home abundance of rabbits, that is
    why he hates me.

NOTES.

The first two lines have probably no meaning.

naèstcà, the great horned owl, *Bubo Virginianus.*

qastī[n] : *adj.*, old ; *noun*, chief, elder. The two words *naestca qastin* I have rendered "old owl," but they might be translated owl-chief or ancient of the owls.

cizditìni, he hates me ; apparently an obsolete or poetic form ; *cizaìni'* is the ordinary, colloquial form.

ta'cijá', I alone, I by myself.

ka', the little wood rabbit, the "cotton-tail."

nihicye, I bring game home ; said when an animal carries game back to its nest or den or a man carries it home (in quantities and habitually).

ailapà, for that reason, therefore.

This song was sung by the chicken hawk (*Accipiter Cooperi*), called by the Navajos *tsi[n]ya ildjehe*, or he who hunts under the trees. The owl and the hawk were out hunting at the same time. The owl saw a rabbit and flew heavily towards it to catch it. The hawk saw it at the same time, swooped nimbly down, and bore it away before the owl could reach it. When they met at the game the owl, angry with the hawk for his discourtesy, would not look at the latter or speak to him.

No. 7.—GOPHER SONG.

Naasizi tsè'go iⁿ, iⁿ, iⁿ,
Naasizi tsè'go iⁿ, iⁿ, iⁿ,
Yintsel! Yintsel! nieè,
A'ha'èi a'ha'èi a'ha' ìe.

TRANSLATION.

Gopher sees where the stone is,
Gopher sees where the stone is.
Strike on !   Strike on !

NOTES.

nasizi or *nasisi,* one or more species of pouched gopher, probably *Thomomys.*   In the song an extra syllable is added for poetic requirements.

tsè'go, to the stone, in the direction of the stone (*tse'*)—*i. e.,* the stone hidden in the moccasin during the game.

iⁿ, he sees.

yintsel, go on striking it; literally, continue chopping (something lying on the ground).   The motion of striking the moccasin in this game resembles that of chopping a prostrate stick.

As I have intimated, this song was sung by the diurnal party when the gopher was fraudulently changing the position of the stone and *Yeitso* was fruitlessly striking the moccasins.

No. 8.—ELK SONG.

Nisa nagá' i ye-ye-yè.   Nisa nagá'i ye-ye-yè.   Nisa nagá'i ye.
Nàtseli, naapitsilqal; tádi nagá'
Kolacìnìa.   Kolacìnìa.   Kolacìnìa.

TRANSLATION.

He wanders far.   He wanders far.   He wanders far.
The elk, I knocked him down, but still he wanders.
Let him go.   Let him go.   Let him go.

NOTES.

nisa or *niza,* far; this form refers to motion, not to position.
nagá' [*nàga*], he travels, he roams, he wanders.

nàtseli, seems to be an old name for the elk (now called *tse*). The Apaches, a tribe cognate to the Navajos, apply, I am told, this term to a steer.

naapitsilqal, I knocked him down with a club or heavy instrument. *na*, a prefix (seen in *nánigo*, across) denoting that the blow is delivered horizontally; *bi* or *pi*, him; *tsil* implies that the stroke felled him; *qal* notes the action performed in giving one forcible stroke with some heavy implement, as a club.

tádi, still, yet.

kolacĭnìa, said to mean let him go, or I let him go, I allowed him to depart (*not* I released him); but the etymology is somewhat obscure to me; apparently an obsolete or poetic form.

One informant has told me that this was sung by one of the ancient genii named *Tönēnĭli*. One day when hunting he met the elk, knocked him down and thought he was dead, but after awhile elk rose and walked off and *Tonenili*, taking pity on him, let him have his life. When he met elk afterwards at the game he sang this song of the adventure.

No. 9.—CICADA SONG.

Wonĭstcĭd ainà,
Wonistcĭd ainà,
Qàni^{n} qastĭd ainà,
Hiya akè ainà,
Hiyà akè haiyè niiyè.

TRANSLATION.

Cicada!   Cicada!   His nostrils are gone.

NOTES.

wonĭstcĭd, the locust or cicada.

qàni^{n}, nostrils, his nostrils.

qastĭd, an abbreviation of *aqastĭd*, disappeared, obliterated by being filled up. If an arroyo becomes filled by sand washing into it, or if a cellar is filled by natural processes, they say *aqastĭd*.

The other sounds have no meaning.

It is related that when the cicada came to the game some scanned his face closely to see if they were acquainted with him.   They observed that he had eyes and mouth like every one else but no nostrils. They thought he must once have had them, but that they had probably disappeared by a growth of the flesh.

In this song we have a rhyme of the significant words.

NO. 10.—ANTELOPE SONG.

Ainà.   Lapá' owò'!   Lapá' owò'
Ainà.   Tsidì naqotínyagi
Tcádi nagá'ye,
Hi' owò', hi' owò', hi' owò', he.

TRANSLATION.

The dun one, lo!   The dun one, lo!
Truly in distant glade below
Wanders the antelope.

NOTES.

lapá', pale brown, drab, dun.

tsidì [*tsidi, tsída*], surely, certainly, truly. Here it means that, although the antelope may be far away, the singer is sure he recognizes him.

naqotínyagi, in a distant glade below the observer (who is supposed to stand on a hill); *na* here indicates distance; *qoti*^{n} is said of a space seen through an opening, as a room seen through a window; here it is said to refer to a glade; *ya*, below; *gi*, in.

tcádi, the American antelope.

naga'ye [*nàga, nagái*], he travels, he wanders.

The other expressions are exclamatory or have no significance.

NO. 11.—BEAR SONG.

Ti^{n}itì', ti^{n}itè, ti^{n}itì', ti^{n}itè,
Ti^{n}itì' benacá' qàgode nìya?

Ti^{n}itì', ti^{n}itè, ti^{n}itì', ti^{n}itè,
Ti^{n}itì' benacá' qaditlò' qàgode nìya?

TRANSLATION.

(With) these four, these four, these four, these four,
These four things to walk with, whence comes he?

(With) these four, these four, these four, these four,
These four shaggy things to walk with, whence comes he?

NOTES.

*ti**ⁿiti‘*, these four; *tiⁿ* or *tiⁿi*, four; *ti‘*, this, these. The last syllable is changed by poetic license to *tè* alternately.

benaca‘, something to walk with, a figurative or jocose expression for legs.

qaditlò‘, hairy, shaggy, a shaggy coat.

qàgode, from what direction, whence.

nìya, he arrives, he comes here.

This is sung with much emphasis and often in time to motions of head and arms intended to imitate a bear walking.

No. 12.—BADGER SONG.

Ainà,
Nahastcit sitì‘ iii, nahastcit sitì‘ na,
Nahastcit sitì‘ iii, nahastcit sitì‘ na;
" Waurr" — aaa, nìgo, sitì‘ na;
Bità indsokàigo sitì‘ na.

TRANSLATION.

Badger is lying down, badger is lying down,
Badger is lying down, badger is lying down;
"Waurr," he says, lying down;
With a white streak down his forehead, lying down.

NOTES.

nahastcit, the American badger.
sitì‘, he is lying down.
"waurr," an imitation of the badger's growl.
nìgo, thus he says.
bità, his forehead.
indsokài, a white streak running down; said of a "blaze" on a horse's nose; a perpendicular white mark on a wall or a bluff, &c.

No. 13.—SNAKE SONG.

Yùnani atcitèl, yùnani atcitèel, yunani atcitèël-e.
Qàdisislàciⁿ, qàdisislàciⁿ.

TRANSLATION.

He threw him yonder, he threw him yonder, he threw him yonder.
I wonder where he lies, I wonder where he lies.

NOTES.

yùnani, yonder, across, on the other side.

atcitèl, he threw him.   The form of the verb here shows that the object is long and flexible, as a snake or a rope.

qadisislàci[n], I wonder where he lies.   *qadi*, where; *ci* or *si*, I; *silá'*, it lies (*ci* and *silá'* are contracted into *sislà*); *ci*[n] or *cin* denotes doubt and conjecture.

This was sung about a snake.   Its name does not appear, but the forms of the verbs indicate the subject of the song, a snake being, probably, the only animal to which they could well refer.   A Navajo rarely kills a snake.   If one lies in his way, he puts a stick under it and flings it to a distance.   At the game a snake was thus thrown by one party over among the other party, and this act gave origin to the song.

No. 14.—GROUND-SQUIRREL SONG.   I.

Qazài biè_gi kòo sizinèe,
Qazài biè_gi kòo sizinèe,
Altsòzi ko sizìni, notòzi ko sizìni.
Hià àineya, hià àineya.

TRANSLATION.

The squirrel in his shirt stands up there,
The squirrel in his shirt stands up there;
Slender, he stands up there; striped, he stands up there.

NOTES.

qazài, some species of striped ground squirrel, probably a *Spermophilus.*

biè_gi, in his shirt; *bi*, his; *e*, shirt; *gi*, in.

ko, there, in the place pointed to; lengthened by one syllable for poetic reasons.

sizìni, he stands up; the accent is changed for prosodical reasons.

altsòzi, slender, slim; said of wire, etc.

notòzi, striped, marked with long, narrow stripes.

No. 15.—GROUND SQUIRREL SONG.   II.

Qazài nasinéstsin, nasinéstsin.
Tsìdiyaicpìce ca'dadècni;
Kayèl indèilgot, indèilgot.

TRANSLATION.

Squirrel struck me, he struck me.
The titmice are angry on my account;
They put their quivers on.

NOTES.

qazai, ground squirrel.   See Song No. 14.

nasinéstsin, he struck me.   The form of the verb denotes that several blows were delivered horizontally without a weapon.

tsidiyaicpice, the specific name of a very small bird, which I have not identified; I believe it to be a titmouse.   The name refers to their mode of flight in close flocks.   *tsidi*, a bird.

cadadécni, they are angry on my account, for me; *literally*, they close their eyes for me.

kayèl, a quiver; the combination of bow case and quiver in which the Indian carries his weapons.

indèilgot.   I am not certain of the etymology of this word.   It is said to mean that they put their quivers on.   The last line, as a whole, is said to mean "they prepare for war;" as we would say, "they gird their armor on."

This ironic song was sung by one of the big animals in derision of smaller beings who attended the game.

No. 16.—LITTLE OWL SONG.

Ainà
Tánaocliyàgi bitcà yaà o o o,   } Repeat twice
Tánaocliyàgi bitcà yaà ai ai è. }   or oftener.

TRANSLATION.

Do I expect (to find) him down there?   His hat sticks up.

NOTES.

aina, has no meaning; it is an expression used in beginning a song by some people; in most cases it may be omitted at pleasure.

tànaocliyàgi, do I expect him there?   Probably I may hope (to see) him there.   *ta*, a prefix denoting interrogation or doubt. *naocli*, I expect, I look for him.   If I expect a visitor I say *naocli*. *yàgi*, a locative suffix; *ya*, below; *gi*, in.

bitcà, his hat—*i. e.*, his crest.

yaà, it sticks up.

This was sung of the burrowing owl, *glo‘bĭtqá-nastca*, which signifies " owl-among-the-prairie-dogs." This owl was an obscure
little individual at the game and it was difficult to see him, but the
singer sees his little crest sticking up over the surface of the earth
(half hidden, as his crest is when he stands at the mouth of his bur-
row), and thinks he may find him there.

No. 17.—WILD-CAT SONG. I.

Nactùi bikè dinì, yoolni yaàni,
Nactùi bikè dinì, yoolni ya.

TRANSLATION.

Wild-cat's foot is sore,
Wild-cat's foot is sore.

NOTES.

nactùi, the American wild-cat, *Lynx rufus*.
bikè, his foot, his feet.
dinì, it aches, it pains, it is sore.
The rest has no meaning.

This was sung in ridicule of the cautious, delicate tread of the
wild-cat, who walks as if his feet were sore.

No. 18.—WILD-CAT SONG. II.

Ainà, nactùi bitcilyá,
Nactùi bitcilyá;
Qatlè qalkéj.

TRANSLATION.

He looks like a wild-cat,
He looks like a wild-cat ;
The insides of his thighs are striped.

NOTES.

nactùi, the American wild-cat.
bitcilyá, he looks like, his appearance is (that of).
qatlè, the insides of his thighs.
qalkij, spotted, mottled, marked with short stripes or bars; said
of an animate object.
qatlè qalkéj, refers to the peculiar markings on the inside of the
cat's thighs.

3

No. 19.—WILD–CAT SONG. III.

Nactùi ù tcoká'le e,
Nactùi ù tcoká'le e,
Yàgo najdilgòle ;
Qàtce indicgòle ;
"Ráuu" cilnile e.

TRANSLATION.

The wild-cat was walking,
The wild-cat was walking,
He began to run down ;
I ran towards him ;
"*Ráuu,*" said he to me.

NOTES.

nactùi, the American wild-cat.

tcokà'le, he was walking ; said of one who is walking at a distance, not beside the speaker.

yàgo, downwards, down [the hill understood].

najdilgòle, he began to run. The syllables *najdi* indicate the commencement of an action that continues some time.

qàtce, towards (a living object).

indicgòle, I ran at or to him.

ràuu, an imitation of the wild-cat's growl.

cilnile, he said to me.

No. 20.—DOVE SONG. I.

Ainà,
Bide etáge, bide etáge ee,
Bide etáge, bide etáge eee,
Táni-qokàitce etáge ee.
A-ài a-ài-è a-ài a-ài-è.

TRANSLATION.

The dove flies, the dove flies,
The dove flies, the dove flies,
Towards the white alkali flat he flies.

NOTES.

bide, an abbreviation of *qacbide* or *qacpide*, the mourning dove.

etáge, it flies.

táni-qokàitce, toward the white alkali flat; *táni*, that white saline incrustation on the ground known throughout the arid region of the United States as alkali; *qokai* (from the root *kai*), white on the ground; *tce*, towards, in the direction of.

No. 21.—DOVE SONG.   II.

Woc woc naidilàaa,
Woc woc naidilòoo,
Woc woc naidilàaa,
Ke litcìtci naidilàaa,
Tsinolkàji naidilàaa,
Woc woc naidilòoo.

TRANSLATION.

Coo coo picks them up,
Coo coo picks them up,
Coo coo picks them up,
Red-moccasin picks them up,
Glossy-locks picks them up,
Coo coo picks them up.

NOTES.

woc woc, an imitation of the voice of the dove, "coo;" used here as a nickname for the dove, as are also the expressions red-moccasin and glossy-locks.

naidilà [*naidilá'*], he picks them (seeds) up.

ke, feet, foot, moccasin.

litci, red; the duplication of the last syllable is a poetic license. *ke litci* might be translated "red feet," but the given translation is more correct, considering the form the adjective takes.

tsinolkàji, glossy locks; said of a person's hair when neatly combed and well oiled; here said figuratively of the beautiful shining head of the dove.

CHOCTAW SPORTS

Alma Louise Moses

CHOCTAW SPORTS

By Alma Louise Moses

Wheelock Acadamey, Oklahoma – Age 15

The Choctaws love to play. From the earliest time of their history records we read of their games and contests. Our grandmothers and grand-fathers tell us about their merrymakings in Mississippi. Always they played and laughed at trials of strength and fun. Sometimes they commemorated something of a religious nature; sometimes they celebrated an election in the tribe but whatever the event might be, you could depend on the fact that there would be games. Many tribes celebrated their events with tribal dances but the Choctaws had no native dances.

Choctaw ball is still played when members of the tribe meet, but baseball and football have more attraction for the younger Choctaws. I will try to tell you a little about the old game. I have never seen a game but I have read about it and my father used to tell us about games he had seen in Mississippi.

The playing field was about one hundred feet long. At each end of the field was a post, and each team defended its goal post. A man dressed as a medicine man served as a mascot for each team. The players were instructed in the rules of the game and these rules were as strict as those governing any game today. Size, strength and quick action were important.

The players wore little clothing when they played but each went into the game wearing the tail of some animal fastened on the back of his belt. Much of the fun was furnished by the players trying to act like the animals they represented. The spectators shouted and called to encourage the players and the players kept up a continual din of yells that seemed to be a part of the game.

An equal number of players guarded each goal post, and each team had players in the middle of the grounds as is the case with basket ball games of today. Each player used a ball-stick made of a small green hickory limb. One end of this stick was shaved down until it was very thin and then it was turned back and fastened to the shaft by strips of buckskin. These strings were fashioned to form a cup in which to catch the ball.

When the referee throws the ball to start the game, the fight begins. The players seem to be everywhere as they struggle to get the ball and hit the post. Each time that the post is hit by a player that has caught the ball, a score is made for his side. It is not easy to score because the opponents play hard to hinder it.

The Choctaws enjoyed hunting. Sometimes it is said that they liked to hunt better than to work. This is hardly a true statement because wild game was used for the main food and there was a great need for good hunters. The women gladly tended the small patch of corn while their men hunted because they knew that the corn would be very dry food indeed without the wild meat to make "tom-fulla."

Sometimes, when autumn came, a day was set aside for a big hunt. The men went into the forest to hunt wild game. The women and children went to the woods nearer the home to gather nuts and herbs. If the weather was fine this holiday might last for a week or more but when it was over they came back loaded with fruits of the forest and the hunt. There would be much work for all, to salt and dry the meat for winter use. There would be nights of fun around the campfire while the hunters told tales and feasted.

In the spring the streams furnished sport and food for the Choctaws. They fished to provide food for their families and they swam and went boat riding for pleasure. Pony racing has always been a favorite sport among the Choctaws. Even to this day one of the best wishes of a Choctaw girl or boy is to have a pony that is more beautiful and fleeter than all others. Most Choctaws are good riders.

* * * * *

CREEKS, CHOCTAWS AND CHEROKEES LOVE GAMES

Orpha Myounge

<u>CREEKS, CHOCTAWS AND CHEROKEES LOVE GAMES</u>

By Orpha Myounge

Home Extension Agent

An Indian was asked what he considered the most loved Indian sport and his reply was: "Eat". It is true that when planning a meeting Indians always want a barbecue and surely enjoy that part of the meeting!

The Creeks and Choctaws play Indian Ball, a game in which a small hard ball is thrown and caught with sticks some two and one-half feet in length with a cup-like arrangement on one end to catch the ball. This game is considered much rougher than football and is enjoyed by all the tribe, men, women and children.

The Cherokees have what they call a "Corn Stalk Shoot". This is done with bows and arrows. Two piles of corn stalks (with all blades removed) are stacked one hundred yards apart and the contestants shoot from one pile to the other and then walk over to that pile and count the score and shoot back to the other pile; the points are determined by the number of stalks pierced.

Horseshoe pitching is another sport all Indians enjoy. The Cherokees are especially fond of this game. The Cherokees also play a game with a large ball which resembles a hand ball and they toss it around very much in the manner of a basket ball game. Both men and women join in this game.

Fun At A Cornstalk Shoot!

AMERICAN LOVE OF BALL GAME DATES BACK TO INDIANS

John Rinaldo

AMERICAN LOVE OF BALL GAME DATES BACK TO INDIANS

By JOHN RINALDO
ASSISTANT CURATOR OF ARCHAEOLOGY

RECENTLY INSTALLED in the Museum's Hall of Ancient and Modern Indians of the Southwestern United States (Hall 7) is an exhibit that illustrates several important phases in the life and customs of some prehistoric desert farmers of this region

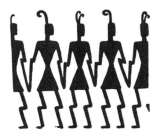

CEREMONIAL DANCERS
As depicted on pottery design

as it existed in the period from about A.D. 700 to 1200. The mode of life shown in graphic form in this exhibit was one of the most highly developed in this area and included such involved techniques as canal irrigation of crops, the fabrication of mosaic plaques, the elaborate carving of stone bowls and paint palettes, and carving and etching (with acid) of shell ornaments and copper working.

What seems most remarkable about this development is that such a complex mode of living was evolved in the face of a harsh desert environment. The climate in southern Arizona, where these people lived, is very hot and dry and the sandy surface of the ground is sparsely covered with salt bush and occasional thickets of mesquite bush—plants that grow where scarcely any other vegetation can survive. Nevertheless these Indians, called Hohokam, managed to grow corn as their staple crop by means of a complex irrigation system extending for miles along the Gila River. Like their modern descendants, the Pima-Papago Indians, they also obtained food by gathering such wild products as mesquite beans and giant cactus fruit and, to a lesser extent, by hunting.

The Hohokam built large villages, consisting of clusters of single-room houses built in shallow excavations. These houses were rectangular or oblong in form. The walls and roofs were supported and framed with timbers and covered with smaller timbers and earth. There was a covered passageway near the middle of one side and a basin-shaped firepit inside near the entrance.

Hohokam pottery was made of clay mixed with finely ground granite and mica. The vessels were made in a number of shapes

POTTERY USED IN CREMATION RITES
The Hohokam Indians cremated their dead

and decorated on the exterior with a great variety of geometric and life-form designs painted in red on a buff background.

However, these people went further than the development of a high culture in the face of an unfavorable environment—they were also devotees of sport. They were among many peoples in this part of the continent and farther south into Mexico and Central and South America who played an unusual and spectacular ball game. This was played with a rubber ball and bears resemblances to tennis, soccer and basketball. The resemblance to court tennis is particularly amazing when the European origin of this game and the American origin of the Indian game are considered. For example, it was played on a court similar to a tennis court divided into halves by markers

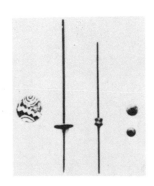

SPINDLE WHORLS
Used in early weaving

and bounded by walls against which the ball was played.

Here our real evidence concerning the Hohokam game stops, although we may infer from these and other details that the remainder of the game was probably much

like that of their southern contemporaries, the Aztecs and Mayas, whose game is pictured on the walls of their ball courts, in the early native codices (manuscripts), and written up in the chronicles of the Spanish explorers. The likeness to soccer is that in most versions of the game the ball could be struck only with the knees, buttocks, thighs or head but never with the hands. In fact in the Indian game, if the

HOHOKAM BALL-COURT
The scene of spectacular athletic games

ball was touched with the hands or with other than the specified parts of the body, it was counted as a fault and the opposing side gained a point. The similarity to basketball is found in one of the Maya versions where an object of the game was to drive the ball through a ring placed high in the wall of the court. Another object was to keep the ball in action while it was on either side of a dividing line and to try to drive it into the field of the opposing party, where, if the ball went dead, a point was scored.

OFTEN 'PLAYED ROUGH'

Among some groups a harder and heavier ball was used than among others, and in these games play frequently involved injury, in which case participation with the heavier ball was often considered a demonstration of manhood. The wagering of high stakes on the outcome was also frequently an element of the game, clothing, featherwork, emblems, and even slaves being wagered.

There is a great deal of evidence in the native codices, the early chronicles, and the decoration and orientation of the ball courts to indicate that the game had a ceremonial significance and symbolism. It has been suggested that the court itself symbolizes the sky and the ball the moon, the morning or evening star, or some other heavenly body. In other associations, it has been suggested that it was symbolic of warfare and quite possibly a substitute for war, in which case the players are the warriors for opposing communities.

The exhibit was planned by Miss Elaine Bluhm, Assistant in Archaeology, and Roger T. Grange, Assistant in Anthropology, and designed by Gustaf Dalstrom, Artist in the Department of Anthropology.

INDIAN "OLYMPICS"

Joe Simon Sando

Indian "Olympics"

By Joe Simon Sando

THROUGHTOUT the world athletes are training for the modern Olympics to be staged at Helsinki, Finland, this summer. Here in New Mexico at Jemez pueblo athletes also are preparing for their Olympics—the ceremonial races of the coming year. The Olympian games date back to the year 776 B. C., the date adopted by the Greeks as the primary date of their chronology, which was reckoned in Olympiads. The origin of the races at Jemez pueblo, like much other Indian history, was unrecorded, therefore, it is unknown. But unlike the modern Olympics which were postponed during World War II, races at Jemez are held annually.

Among the races held during the year are the stick races and the long distance races. These races can be viewed by the general public. The ceremonial relay races are held only occasionally and are restricted to Indians.

Here is how and when the athletes begin their preparation at Jemez.

Early every spring one society group performs its ritual. The ritual, which consists of the usual four days seclusion in singing, fasting and prayer, opens up the new season of growth. The ice along the river has been broken, the hibernating animals have been awakened, and the call for the training of athletes has been echoed. This is the time when the athletes begin to rise at daybreak and go up to the mountains to gather mountain foliage and tree branches which are kept in earthen jars filled with water. The steeped liquid in the jars is then drunk and later regurgitated. This is a practice believed to cleanse the system after a good morning's five or ten-mile exercising run. The distance would depend on the age of the boy and also his condition. The cleansing is done only before breakfast is eaten and preferably after a good workout. The foliage placed in the jars which is brought from the mountains consists of branches from pine, fir, scrub oak, and other brush which is the common food of the deer; whose speed the athlete hopes to acquire. The core of this collection is the heart of a Spanish dagger. The leaves of the dagger plant also are split to tie the collection together. The trips to the mountains generally are made in the early hours and a return to the village by sunrise is a sign of good conditioning, endurance, and much

running. During the time the collection of foliage is in the earthen jar and cleansing of the system is carried on, a traditional vow is made that one will not entertain thoughts of nor flirt and play with the female sex. On the first trip the vow and cleansing period might be twelve days. The second might be for eight, and so on until one reaches the time of four days. All during this time and each morning the runner gets up at dawn and limbers up with a few miles of running.

Why all this sacrifice of sleep and the girl one loves? The reward for all the training is won in the races that take place during the year. There are only two long distance races in which an athlete may win individual glory, but for all the trouble of preparing for the two races, the winner becomes a great hero before the eyes of his fellow competitors and tribe. The first race generally takes place around September 15th. The second race depends on the weather. If the crops should be nipped by frost before the second race, all the running and harvest dancing ceases. Harvest dances begin in September and take place every sixth day, ending with the first frost.

Often a young man journeys to the river immediately upon awakening and before he sets out for the morning jaunt. This is done so that his muscles and reflexes may be hardened to withstand unfavorable weather conditions during training, and keep the trainee from catching cold. It is nothing for a hopeful athlete to literally break the ice to plunge into the water. In the fall a greater number of men of all ages take morning dips in the river. This begins when the herbs in the mountains begin to ripen and spring water flows, carrying the medicinal powers of the herbs.

Before a young boy is ready to go after his own training herbs he is taught the prayers to say when he would be before Mother Nature and all the gods asking for the proper blessings from them while in training and at the races. The prayer went something like this: "Here is some corn pollen for you to eat Mother Nature, and for the god which was posted on this forest to rule and tend the game. If you are satisfied with my offerings, bless me, and through these herbs which I am taking from your domain, give me strength to win any running competitions."

The Indians have a belief that after their departure from this world the Great God will station them to rule a certain area of a mountain, hill, or river. It is therefore that many of the offerings are made to the ruler of the area. For instance, if a young man plans to use a certain territory to train for running, he will ask the god or gods ruling the domain for guidance against anyone who tries to hinder his training. Often one may bury prayer feathers in the ground. These feathers are offerings to the god in return for his expected help in preventing accidents on his domain. Many times an athlete's training may be stopped short by stubbing his toe against an unfriendly rock.

In early spring when irrigation ditch cleaning is in progress, the men entertain with stick races. No men's societies are involved here, but moieties are concerned. In every Indian village among the Southwest pueblos there are two moieties. They are either winter or summer moieties, north or south side moieties, or the Turquoise or Pumpkin moieties. To mention a few villages and their moieties, in Taos and San Ildefonso pueblos it is the North and South side, in Santa Clara and San Juan pueblos it is the winter and summer people; all these are called Northern Rio Grande pueblos. In the Southern Rio Grande pueblos there are Cochiti, Santo Domingo, San Felipe, Sandia, Isleta, Santa Ana, Zia, and Jemez. All these have the Turquoise and the Pumpkin moieties. The colors which they use in dances are turquoise and white for the Turquoise moiety and orange and white for the Pumpkin moiety.

To get back to our stick race. For the race branches from a salt bush are whittled down to pieces three inches long by about five inches circumference and weighing at least a pound. These sticks are painted with the respective colors of turquoise and white or orange and white. The race is started by the two war captains, each of whom is a member of either side. They stand together in the starting position with the sticks on their toes. At a given moment each kicks his stick. Other members waiting and running along the way pick up the sticks and kick them on, each side identifying its stick by the colors. The races generally are held for the traditional four days. The first morning the race is toward the East, the second toward the North, the third morning toward the West and the last day toward the South. The average distance of the round trip is about twelve miles. Generally these races are held at sunrise. Even though this race is a teamwork affair, the well-conditioned participants easily stand out.

Once every few years ceremonial relay races are held in the early spring. The only one in which the writer took part was before the Second World War. A certain group of one of the two men's societies were in the kiva for four days. While in there they had challenged the second men's society to relay races to be held in the confines of the village on the fourth day. On that day the village war cap-

tain announced the race and invited all non-members to side with the second society group. We were competing against a team which supposedly possessed mana or orenda (a kind of force or power).

It may seem a strange way to win a race when our American youth are accustomed to judging as the winner whoever crosses the line first with a baton, but in this race the winner is determined by color. The men's society team coming from the kiva was colored either all black or all red. The object of the colored racers was to beat the laymen and then apply some of their paint onto the losers.

The starter was a person of the clown society, since in any social function concerning ordinary laymen and religious dancers possessing orenda, the clown is the liaison, or intermediary. The starter had a bundled up deer hide on which he banged with a small club. The first bang corresponded to "on your mark"; second, "get set"; and third, "go." The distance was between 150 and 200 yards. The race began shortly after noon and lasted until the painted runners were tired out. Ordinarily the race would have lasted until we laymen were beaten at least once. But during this particular day there were at least five young boys who were never beaten and therefore no paint was applied on us. This was a good sign that some boys had sacrificed their early morning sleep.

The first long distance race is staged around September 15th. The uniform for the biggest event of all races is a loin cloth and bare feet. Before sunrise all the participants go to the starting line, a point five or six miles from the village. Here a representative from the society sponsoring the event recites a prayer to the gods in the clouds and mountains inviting them to watch the mortals in a great game. He invites them to come along to the village and deliver their blessings in the form of abundant crops and plenty of game in the hunting seasons.

In this race a young man is selected who stands 50 yards in front of the starting line with a trophy. The trophy is a corn stalk with appropriate prayer feathers tied to it, giving the trophy mana. After the prayer is said, all the participants and the one in front yell simultaneously, "woooo-who", the front man pointing the trophy toward the sunrise. This is repeated toward the four cardinal directions. After the last one, which is to the South, everyone darts forward as this is the starting sign. It is at this starting time the swiftest runner reaches the front man first, who also is tearing away toward the village. The man who is in a condition to outrun the others takes the trophy and leads the dash until another may overtake him and all those who are able may take the lead. Usually from about the two-mile point the longer distance runners may take over the exchange of leads. And from about the four or five-mile point the potential winners will be coming closer to the lead man waiting for their second breath. Usually near the village, where women and elder folks are watching, the greater runners give with all their strength to outdo each other and bring home the trophy with all the glory. Besides the mana on the trophy, the fact that a young man reaches the village first bearing the trophy makes the winner the great hero of the year.

SIX GAME PIECES FROM OTOWI

Marjorie Ferguson Tichy

SIX GAME PIECES FROM OTOWI

By MARJORIE FERGUSON TICHY

A RARE GROUP of clay specimens came to light recently in the process of cataloging the archaeological material from the ruins of Otowi, New Mexico, acquired by the Museum of New Mexico from the Philadelphia Commercial Museum, which conducted excavations there in 1916 and 1917, under an arrangement with the New Mexico institution. Among the several hundred clay vessels, consisting largely of Abiquiu, Bandelier black on grey and Tsankawi black on cream, dark culinary vessels, Potsuwi-i incised and a few Rio Grande glaze decorated pieces, hundreds of interesting artifacts and ceremonial pieces of stone, bone, and wood, were six actual Biscuit ware "biscuits." These interesting little objects were undoubtedly gaming pieces, the writer believes. Their size and shape must, first of all, exclude them from any practical every day usage, such as our so called "pot lids." While possessing the same general superficial characteristics each one is unique in detail.

Unfortunately, nothing is known regarding their actual excavation history other than the fact that they were recovered at Otowi by Dr. (Mrs.) L. L. W. Wilson during one of her seasons of activities there. The only possible reference to anything akin to these specimens discovered in any of her written works is found in EL PALACIO, Vol. 3, p. 34, which reads as follows: "We found also specimens of clay balls, both white and red." The six pieces under discussion here, while of clay, are neither white nor red, but are

[1]

more nearly a dirty, greyish-buff; also they are more like buns, or biscuits, than balls. If classified according to pottery standards they would stand in the Bandelier black on grey[1] group, although only one actually contains any black decoration.

As already indicated, it is not known whether these gaming pieces were found in a cache or not. Neither can one be sure they were used in a game requiring six "men."

It is a well known fact that Indians of the Rio Grande area, Tewas, Tiguas, and Keres alike, played games in pre-historic times. One of the most popular, and one that dates back to ancient times, it is now believed, is the hidden ball, or stick game, commonly called Canute. The Zunis also played this game and used a disc of stone approximately the size of these clay Otowi pieces to throw into the air in order to determine which group would start the game. Canute, then, is mentioned as one possibility. If the Otowi specimens were used as the pieces to be hidden under the hollow tubes or cups, then the tubes would have had to be large to the bunglesome point in order to contain them. Thus they seem impractical for this phase of the game. It should be noted that Indians of some of the Northern Rio Grande pueblos still play Canute.

Sets of six dice are found in use today in some of the pueblos. These are usually of bone, however, and are not as large as the ones described here.[2] The shape, however, is somewhat the same, and it is barely possible that these could have been dice. That dice were employed in games of chance in pre-historic times is borne out by the finding of an occassional bone dice in pre-Spanish strata in many southwestern ruins. Bo 14/11 (with the nail [3] marks on the under side) rather suggests a marked or "loaded" dice. Bo 14/8 is also uniquely marked. If the six pieces were originally used together in one set, they are all different

---

1. See Table of Specifications.
2. See Table of Specifications
.3 See Table of Specifications.

enough to be easily recognized in a game of chance.

The writer feels that the most logical explanation of these objects is that they were used in a game similar to quoits, shuffleboard, or shinny, the first named being the most likely solution. Any such game as quoits played with these clay objects would have to be played on a fairly soft surface or dirt floor; otherwise it would not be long before they would break.

In spite of the lack of experience in playing quoits, the writer discovered that these specimens made excellent discs in aiming at a target. Their size, rounded tops, and weight aided greatly in making them sail through the air easily. In Culin's *Games of the North American Indians; B.A.E., 1907*, vol. 24, there are several accounts of how the Zunis played quoits. On pages 726-727 the following is given:

"Zuni, New Mexico. Mr. John G. Owens describes this game as follows: *Than-ka-la-wa.*—This game is usually played in the spring, and resembles somewhat our game of quoits. In place of the ordinary quoit they use flat stones. Any number may take part. A small stone, or even a corn-cob, is set up, and on this each places his stake. To determine which shall play first they all throw for some distant point. He who comes nearest the mark chosen pitches first, and each one follows according to his throw; then the game begins. The distance pitched is nearly 100 feet. The object is to knock over the stake or pool. If the pool is knocked over, and the stone pitched goes beyond it, it counts nothing; if just even with it, the one who pitched has another chance; if it remains behind, he takes everything and all put up again. They count it great sport, and some become very skilful in pitching. Frank H. Cushing in 1893 described the game as 'the standing cob game.'

"The specimens in Figs. 951 and 952, page 727, were collected by the writer (Culin) in 1903. [Figure 952, particularly, resembles the Otowi pieces. Its diameter was four inches. The two specimens in figure 951 were four and one-half inches and five inches, respectively, in diameter. They are described as quoits by Culin.] The stones are called *tankalania*. It is a winter game for men and boys. Each one has a quoit. They set a corncob up on the ground and put the stakes—turquoise, silver beads or buttons, or money—on top of the cob and throw at it in turn. The first player throws his stone from the cob at some distant point, about as far as he can. The players then stand at this point and throw at the cob until one of them knocks it down. Then the one whose quoit fell nearest the stakes (not the cob) wins all. After a player throws he draws a ring around his stone to mark where it fell when he takes it up to throw again. A stone, a chip, or any convenient object is put on the cob to lay the stakes on.

"Figure 953, page 727, has a cross incised on one face and on the other the face of the sun. [Its diameter was three and one-half inches, and was called a sun quoit by Culin.] It was presented to the writer by Zuni Dick in 1903. He gave the name as *tankalana yettokia,* and said it was anciently used on Corn Mountain by the Sun Priest."

Bo 14/9 is the only one of the group showing great wear and battering. It apparently had been used a great deal, and such marks as it bore would more likely have been made by a cue or shinny stick than by aiming at a target.

There are examples of stone discs (possible gaming pieces) from ruins throughout the Rio Grande and elsewhere in the Southwest, but data regarding such clay discs as those described from the Otowi ruins are practically non-existent.[4] If their distribution had been common it would seem logical that they should come to light with some regularity in excavated ruins. Likewise, stone discs are also somewhat rare in comparison with the thousands of oddly shaped and rounded, worked sherds occurring in every pottery producing community of the Southwest.

---

4. Dr. Frank Hibben, U. N. M., informs the writer that he knows of one specimen from the Mimbres similar to those of the Otowi group.

TABULATED SPECIFICATIONS OF THE OTOWI GAME PIECES

Cat. No.	Length	Width	Thickness	Description
Bo 14/6	$2\frac{3}{8}''$	$2\frac{3}{16}''$	$\frac{7}{8}''$	Typical biscuit ware paste. Somewhat crackled due to poor mixing. No decoration. Slight concavity on bottom containing smoother slip than rest of body. Bottom shows slight wear.
Bo 14/7	$3\frac{1}{8}''$	$3''$	$1\frac{1}{8}''$	Typical bis. w. paste. Slipped, no design. Rounded top. Chipped and worn from usage. Small punched hole on upper side near rim.
Bo 14/8	$3''$	$3''$	$\frac{7}{8}''$	Typical bis. w. paste. Well smoothed. Black linear design on upper side. Flat top and uneven slightly convex bottom. Surface scuffed and scratched.
Bo 14/9	$2\frac{13}{16}''$	$2\frac{5}{8}''$	$\frac{7}{8}''$	Typical bis. w. paste. Slightly rounded top. Entire surface on both sides so badly worn and chipped that nothing can be said of its original surface treatment.
Bo 14/10	$2\frac{1}{2}''$	$2\frac{7}{16}''$	$1\frac{3}{8}''$	Typical bis. w. paste. Slipped, scraped, and smoothed. High rounded top. Good condition—shows little wear except on bottom.
Bo 14/11	$2\frac{11}{16}''$	$2\frac{3}{16}''$	$\frac{3}{4}''$	Typical bis. w. paste. No slip on under side which contains a series of some 27 finger nail indentations at one end. Top well smoothed with sloping ends and high rounded middle.

However, among these many worked sherds there are quite a good number of a size and shape to make good gaming pieces, and it is possible that these were used instead of stone quoits; although it seems somewhat more difficult to aim with them because of their lightness. The group of pottery discs from Otowi, however, would appear to be unique archaeological specimens.

SIOUX GAMES

[Parts]
I and II

J. R. Walker

SIOUX GAMES. I.

ACCORDING to the information given by the older men among the Lakota, the games described in the following pages have been played among them as far back as the memory of man goes. They all believe them to be very ancient. These games are played but little now, as they have been replaced by others, most of which have been introduced by the white people. Owing to the paucity of their language it is difficult for these Indians to give a differential description, and to secure full and accurate information from them in regard to any matter that is complex is a tedious process. It was necessary, in order to get the correct rules of these games, to see them played, and to question the players in regard to every step relative to them, for no Indian was able to give the rules completely. But after they were secured and written, all who were questioned about them, or to whom they were read, agreed that they were correct.

The writer has used the word "Lakota" instead of "Dakota," because it represents the Teton dialect, while "Dakota" represents the Santee and Yankton dialect, and because the information relative to these games was gathered among the Tetons. The spelling of the Lakota words herein given is that adopted in the "Dakota-English Dictionary, North American Ethnology, U. S. Geographical and Geological Survey," vol. vii.

Apparently the original Sioux language was composed entirely of words of a single syllable, and the vocabulary was very limited. Things, conditions, and actions, not named in the original language, were described by phrases composed of the original words. These phrases became agglutinated, and formed compound words, and the language as spoken at the present time is largely composed of these compound or phrase words. Because of the primitive ideas expressed by the elements of these compound words it is difficult to make an exact translation of them into English, and for this reason the translations herein given are liberal.

The following is a list of the games, in Lakota and English.

LAKOTA WOSKATE EHANA.	SIOUX GAMES, ANCIENT.
A. Wayekiyapi Woskate Wicasa.	Gambling Games for Men.
Painyankapi.	Wands and Hoop.
Takapsice.	Shinney.
Canwiyusna.	Odd Sticks.
Hehaka.	Elk.
B. Wayekiyapi Woskate Winyan.	Gambling Games for Women.
Tawinkapsice.	Woman's Shinney.
Tasiha.	Foot Bones.

| Tanpan | Dice. |
| Icaslohe. | Bowls. |

C. Woimagaga Woskata Wicasa.	Amusement Games for Men.
Tahuka Cangleska.	Webbed Hoops.
Hutanacute.	Winged Bones.
Pteheste.	Young Cow.
Canpaslohanpi.	Throwing Sticks.
Ogle Cekutepi.	Coat Shooting.

D. Woimagaga Woskate Hoksila.	Amusement Game for Boys.
Paslohanpi.	Javelins.
Canwacikiyapi.	Tops.
Titazipi Hoksila.	Boy's Bow.
Hohu Yourmonpi.	Bone Whirler.
Tate Yourmonpi.	Wind Whirler.
Ipahotonpi.	Popgun.

E. Woimagaga Woskate Wicincala.	Amusement Games for Girls.
Hepaslohanpi.	Horned Javelins.
Hosingagapi.	Dolls.
Tipi Cikala.	Little Tipi.

Some of the Sioux dances could be included in a list of their games, but as they are all accompanied with more or less of ceremony, they more properly belong in a list of their entertainments and ceremonies. In describing the various implements used in the games the measurements given are vague, because these Indians had no fixed standard, and could give approximate measures only.

The only previous account of Sioux games is by Louis L. Meeker, published in the "Bulletin of the Free Museum of Science and Arts," University of Pennsylvania, vol. iii. No. 1. In this publication the author gives most of his attention to the objects used in playing the games, without giving very full information as to the rules for playing. As the games played by the Sioux are known to all of the Indians of the Plains, it seems advisable to have a complete account of the rules governing them, for comparative purposes. As the illustrations in the paper by Mr. Meeker are quite satisfactory, the writer will dispense with illustrations in his own.[1]

I. WOSKATE PAINYANKAPI.

(Game of Wands and Hoop.)

Painyankapi is an ancient gambling game played by men. The Indians took great interest in this game, and some became very skilful at it. Sometimes a band of Indians would go a long distance, taking with them their families and all their possessions, to gamble on a game between expert players. Such games were watched by

[1] The author made a collection of the objects described in this paper for the American Museum of Natural History, New York city.

interested crowds, and, as they offer many opportunities for trickery, fierce contests arose over disputed points, which sometimes ended in bloodshed and feuds.

The implements used in the game are: *cangleska,* the hoop; *cansakala,* the wands.

The *cangleska* is made from one piece, as long as the tallest man, taken from an ash sapling in the spring, while the sap is flowing. This is held in the fire, with the bark on, until it becomes pliable, when it is bent into the form of a hoop. It is then trimmed to a uniform diameter of about one inch, the ends lapped about three inches, and fastened together with thongs of rawhide.

Beginning near the lap, on each side of the hoop, four shallow spaces are cut so as to divide the hoop into quadrants. These spaces are about two inches long and half an inch wide, and those on one side are exactly opposite those on the other. Three transverse grooves are cut in each of the spaces nearest the lap, and these are called *canhuta,* or the stump. Two oblique grooves crossing each other at right angles are cut on each of the two spaces next the lap, and these are called *okajaya,* or the fork. Six transverse grooves are cut on each of the two spaces opposite the stump, and these are called *wagopi,* or the stripes. The two remaining spaces are blackened, and are called *sapa,* or black.

The *cansakala* are made of ash or choke-cherry wood, about four feet in length and three fourths of an inch in diameter. One end is flattened, or squared, for about ten inches. From the flattened portion to within about eight inches of the other end they are wrapped with a rawhide or buckskin thong, applied in a spiral manner. They are held together in pairs by a buckskin thong about eight inches long, fastened to each about one third of the length from their rounded ends.

Any one may make these wands, but it is believed by these Indians that certain men can make them of superior excellence, and give to them magic powers which may be exercised in favor of the one who plays with them. It is also believed that certain medicine-men can make medicine over the wands which, if carried when playing with the wands, will give the player supernatural powers in playing the game. But if an opposing player has the same medicine, they counteract each other, or if an opposing player has a more powerful medicine, this will prevail in the game. It is also believed by these Indians that if a player in any game has a talisman, properly prepared by ceremony and incantation, it will protect him against the evil effects of any kind of medicine or form of magic.

The rules governing the game are : —

Before beginning the game the players must choose an umpire, a hoop, and the wands, and agree upon the number of points in the count.

The umpire must watch the game, decide all contested points, and call aloud all counts when made.

One hoop must be used during the entire game.

Each player must use his own pair of wands during the entire game.

If the hoop or a wand becomes unfit for use during a game, the game is declared off, and a new game must be played.

If a player persistently breaks the rules of the game, the game is declared off.

The players roll the hoop alternately.

To roll the hoop, the players stand side by side. One of them grasps the hoop between the thumb and the second, third, and fourth fingers, with his first finger extended along the circumference, with the hoop directed forward, and by swinging his hand below his hips he rolls the hoop on the ground in front of the players.

If a player rolls the hoop improperly, or fails to roll it when he should, his opponent counts one, and rolls the hoop.

After the hoop leaves the hand of the player it must not be touched or interfered with in any manner until after the umpire has called the count.

After the hoop is rolled the players follow it and attempt to throw their wands upon the ground so that the hoop will lie upon them when it falls.

After the hoop has fallen the umpire must examine it and call the count aloud.

The count is as follows : —

To count at all one of the marked spaces on the hoop must lie directly over a wand.

One marked space lying over one wand counts one.

One space lying over two wands counts two.

Two spaces lying over one wand count two.

Two spaces lying over two wands count two.

Three spaces lying over two wands count three.

Four spaces lying over two wands count the game.

The first who counts the number agreed upon wins the game.

If at the end of a play both players count the number agreed upon, the game is a draw, and a new game must be played.

Since this game seems to have important ceremonial associations, the following narrative is added :[1] —

[1] Contributed by Clark Wissler.

HOOP GAME.

A band of Sioux Indians were travelling in the lake country of Minnesota. Game was very scarce, and they had little to eat for a long time. When they were nearly exhausted their chief decided to camp. One of his young men requested that he be allowed to fast for four days. Permission being given, he went to the top of a high hill in full view of the camp. After two days and two nights the watchers from the camp saw a buffalo approach the man on the hill. The buffalo circled around him, and then disappeared on the opposite side. At midday the young man returned to the camp. He stopped and sat down on the top of a small hill, and his younger brother went out to him. The young man told his brother to stand back and not approach him. He said, " I have a message for you to deliver to my father. Tell my father to place a tent in the middle of the camp circle. Tell him to scatter sage grass around the inside, and that he must select four good men to enter the tent and await me." Then the young brother returned to the camp and delivered this message to his father. Every one knew that the young man had something important to tell the people.

The father did as requested. He believed the young man because the people of the camp had seen the buffalo on the hill with him. When the tent was ready, and the four good men had entered, the younger brother was sent to notify the young man. The young man approached, walking slowly. He stopped near the entrance of the tent, and after a few moments he moved still nearer and paused. He then approached the door, walked entirely around the tent, and entered. He produced a large pipe wrapped in sage grass. He sat down at the back of the lodge and asked the four good men to send for a good young man to act as his assistant. When the assistant came, the young man said to him, " Go out and cut a stick for me." When the assistant returned with the stick the young man ordered him to peel it. When this was done, the young man asked the four good men to make a sweat house.

When this was ready, the young man and the four good men entered the sweat house, while the assistant waited outside. When the ceremony in the sweat house ended, the party returned to the tent. Then the young man told them that a buffalo had come to him on the hill, had given him a pipe, instructions, and a message to deliver to his people. He ordered his assistant to bring a coal of fire. With this he made incense with sage grass, held his hands in the smoke four times, took up the bundle containing the pipe, unwrapped it, and took out the pipe. The stem of the pipe was red, and the bowl was of black stone. "This pipe," said the young man, "was given me by the buffalo that you saw upon the hill, and he also instructed me as to its use."

The young man ordered his assistant to go out and cut an ash sapling and four cherry sticks. When these were brought, he gave a cherry stick to each of the four good men for them to peel. He, himself, took the ash stick and began to remove the bark. This done he bent it into a hoop and tied the ends with sinew threads and buckskin strings. He held the hoop in the smoke from the sage grass, then took red paint in his hands, held his hands over the smoke as before, and painted the hoop. Then he placed his assistant at the door of the lodge, himself at the rear, and two of the good men on each side. He instructed the four good men to paint their cherry sticks red in the same way that he painted the hoop. The assistant then smoothed the floor of the tent, while the young man sang four songs. The words of the songs were as follows : —

1. I have passed by the holy floor (earth, smooth and level like the floor of a tipi).
2. I have passed by the holy robe.
3. I have passed by the holy shell.
4. I have passed by an eagle feather, it is good.

Then the young man said, " Now I shall roll the hoop. It will circle the tent. You are to watch the tracks made by it. You will see that it leaves buffalo tracks, returns to me, and lies down." So the young man sang the four songs again and rolled the hoop. The hoop circled the tent and returned to the young man as he had said. The four good men saw in the trail left by the hoop the tracks of buffalo. The young man said that, on the fourth day from this time, there would be many buffalo. Then he took strips of raw hide and wrapped them around the cherry sticks. He tied red cloth around one and blue around the other. Then he put on a buffalo robe and asked the men to follow him. The young man passed out of the door, and the four good men took the hoop and the sticks and played the hoop game, as they walked behind the young man. The people of the camp watched them, and wherever the hoop rolled, buffalo tracks appeared.

The young man requested his assistant to call a good old man. The people of the camp were in a state of famine. When the assistant brought the old man to the tent, the young man requested him to harangue the camp, as follows : " Ho, Ho, Ho, this young man wishes the people to make arrows, to sharpen them, and to sharpen their knives. He says that four buffalo will be here to-morrow morning. Let no one bother them, let no dogs chase them, let them go through the camp in peace. The four buffalo will come from the west."

Early the next morning the four buffalo came as predicted. They passed slowly through the north side of the camp and disappeared in the east. Then the chief of the camp sent a sentinel to stand upon the hill where the four buffalo were first seen. The sentinel looked down into the valley on the other side of the hill, where he saw vast herds.of buffalo moving toward the camp. The chief had instructed the sentinel to run back and forth when buffalo were visible. The people of the camp who were watching saw him run back and forth upon the hill, and began to prepare for the hunt. The young man, who was still in his tent, sent out his assistant to call the people to his door. He requested that they stand around and keep quiet. The sentinel who had returned now addressed the people, telling them of the buffalo he had seen, the direction in which they were moving, etc. The young man then addressed the people, giving them permission to chase the buffalo.

They had a great hunt. Buffalo were everywhere. They even ran through the camp, and were shot down at the doors of the tents. The people had meat in great abundance.

When the hunt was over the young man requested the four good men to keep and care for the hoop and the sticks with which they had played. A tent was always kept in the middle of the camp circle, and the four good men spent most of their time in it. Whenever the people wished to hunt buffalo, the four men played the hoop game, and the buffalo appeared as before. In the course of time all these men died, except one. This last man made the four marks we now see upon the hoop. After his death, the game was played by all the people, and became a great gambling game.

From this narrative it appears that the origin of the game was ceremonial and that the hoop used here is the same as the sacred hoop or ring so often used by the Sioux.

2. WOSKATE TAKAPSICE.

(Game of Shinney.)

Takapsice is an ancient gambling game played by men, and is their roughest and most athletic game. They often received serious wounds, or had their bones broken while playing it, but serious quarrels seldom resulted.

It may be played by a few or by hundreds, and formerly was played for a wager. The wager on important games was often very large; men, women, and children betting, sometimes all they possessed, or a band of Indians contributing to a bet to make it equal to that offered by another band.

In former times one band of Indians would challenge another to play this game. If the challenge was accepted they would camp together, and play for days at a time, making a gala time of it, giving feasts, dancing, and having a good time generally.

The implements used in the game are : *cantakapsice*, the club; *tapatakapsice*, the ball.

The club was made of an ash or choke-cherry sapling, taken in the spring when the sap was running, and heated in the fire until it was pliable, when the lower end was bent until it stood a right angles to the rest of the stick, or into a semicircular crook, about six inches across.

The shape of this crook varied to suit the fancy of the maker.

After the crook was made the stick was trimmed down to a uniform diameter of about one and a half inches, and cut of such a length that the player could strike on the ground with it while standing erect.

Any one might make a club, but certain persons were supposed to make clubs of superior excellence, and some persons were supposed to be able to confer magical powers on clubs, causing the possessor to exercise unusual skill in playing. These magic clubs were supposed to be potent, not only in games, but to work enchantment in all kinds of affairs, for or against a person, as the possessor chose. The medicine-men sometimes included such clubs among their paraphernalia, and invoked their magic powers in their incantations over the sick.

Certain medicine-men were supposed to have the power to make medicine over clubs, so that any one in whose favor this medicine was made, by carrying it and the club during the game for which the medicine was made, would be on the winning side.

One possessing a magic club boasted of it, and the matter was generally known, but one who had medicine made over a club must keep the matter secret, for a general knowledge of the existence of the medicine would either destroy its potency, or others knowing of the medicine might have a more powerful medicine made against it, or the magic of a talisman could be exercised especially against it, and defeat its power.

A player who possessed a magic club was feared by those who did not, and the latter tried to avoid coming in contact with such a club while playing the game. This gave the possessors of such clubs decided advantages over others, and they were eagerly sought as players, and heavy wagers laid on their playing.

The clubs were generally without ornament, but they were sometimes ornamented by pyrographic figures on the handle or body. Certain clubs were highly prized by their owners, who took great care of them, frequently oiling and polishing them.

When a club was held for its magic power alone, as by the medicine-men, it was often highly ornamented with feathers, bead work, porcupine quills, or tufts of hair.

The ball was made by winding some material into a ball, and covering it with buckskin or rawhide, or of wood. It was from two and a half to three inches in diameter.

The game is played where two goals can be set up with a level track of land between them.

The rules of the game are :—

Any number of men may play, but there must be an equal number on the opposing sides.

In a series of games the same persons must play in each game of the series.

After the game begins, if any player stops playing, a player from the opposing party must stop playing also.

The players of a game must fix the goals before beginning to play.

Each of the two goals must consist of two stakes set about fifty to one hundred feet apart, and a line drawn from one stake to the other, which must be nearly parallel to the line drawn at the other goal.

The goals must be from three hundred yards to one mile apart, as may be agreed upon between the players, for each game.

After the goals are fixed the players choose their goal, either by agreement or by lot.

After the goals are chosen the players arrange themselves in two lines, about half way between the goals, all the players on one side standing in one line, and each side facing the goal it has chosen, the lines being about thirty feet apart.

After the players are in line the ball is placed as nearly as can be half way between them.

After the ball is placed on the ground it must not be touched by the hand or foot of any one until the game is ended.

If at any time during the play the ball becomes so damaged that it is unfit for use, the game is called off, and another game must be played to decide the contest.

The club may be used in any manner to make a play, or to prevent an opponent from making a play

After the ball is placed on the ground, at a given signal, each side attempts to put the ball across its goal in a direction opposite from the other goal.

The side that first puts the ball across its goal in the proper direction wins the game.

3. WOSKATE CANWIYUSNA.

(Guessing the Odd Stick.)

Canwiyusna is an ancient gambling game played by the Sioux men.

It may be played at any time, but was generally played during the winter, and at night.

The wagers on the game were generally small.

The implements used in the game were *canwiyawa*, counting-sticks.

These are a large number of rods of wood, about the size of an ordinary lead pencil. They are of an odd number, and generally ninety-nine. They may be plain, but they are generally colored, and when so the color on all is the same, but applied differently, as some may be colored all over, others half colored, or striped, streaked, or spotted.

The rules of the game are: —

The game may be played by two or more men.

Before beginning the game the players must agree upon the number of counts that will constitute the game.

One player must manipulate the sticks during the entire game.

The one who manipulates the sticks must keep his count with each of the other players separate from that of all the others.

To play, the player who manipulates the sticks hides them from the other players, and divides them into two portions, and then exposes them to the view of the other players.

After the portions are exposed to the view of the players they must not be touched by any one until each has made his guess.

Each player may make one guess as to which portion contains the odd number of sticks.

If a player guesses the portion that has the odd number of sticks in it he counts one point, but if he does not the manipulator counts one.

The one who counts the number of points agreed upon wins the wager.

4. WOSKATE HEHAKA.

(Game of Elk.)

Hehaka is an ancient gambling game played by the Sioux men.

It was usually played while hunting for elk, and was supposed to give success in the quest for game.

The wagers were usually small, and but little interest was taken in the game by others than the players.

The implements used in the game are: *hehaka*, the elk; *cangleska*, the hoop.

The *hehaka* is made of a round rod of wood about four feet long and three quarters of an inch in diameter, one end of which is squared or flattened for about ten inches. A small rod of wood about eighteen inches long and one half an inch in diameter at the middle, and tapering towards both ends, is fastened to the round end, and bent and held in a semicircle by a string of twisted sinew or leather, curving towards the other end of the longer rod. This string is fastened at or near the ends of the curved rod and to the longer rod on about the level of the tips of the curved rod.

About eighteen inches from this two other rods are fastened crosswise on the longer rod, on a plane parallel with the plane of the curved rod at the end. One of these rods is similar to, but smaller than, the curved rod at the end, but it curves at a right angle to the longer rod.

The other is square or flattened, and about a half an inch wide at its middle, tapering towards both ends.

About eighteen inches from these, towards the flattened end of the longer rod, two other rods like those above described are fastened in the same manner.

The longer rod is then wrapped with a buckskin or rawhide thong applied in a spiral manner from the curved rod at the round end to beyond where the cross rods are fastened to it, and all the curved and cross rods are wrapped in the same manner.

A banner about two by four inches in size, made of buckskin or cloth, and colored, is attached to the end where the curved rod is fastened.

The ring is about six inches in diameter, made of rawhide or sinews, and wrapped with a thong of rawhide.

The rules of the game are : —

Two persons play the game.

Before beginning the game they must agree upon the number of points that shall constitute the game.

Each player must have one *hehaka*.

One hoop must be used in a game.

The players must toss the hoop alternately.

The hoop must be tossed up in the air.

After the hoop is tossed and begins to descend the players may attempt to catch it on the *hehaka*.

The hoop must be caught on the *hehaka* before it touches the ground. If so caught after it touches the ground no count is made.

After it is caught on the *hehaka*, the *hehaka* must be laid on the ground with the hoop on the point where caught, before a count can be made.

An opposing player may, with his *hehaka*, take the hoop from a *hehaka* at any time before the *hehaka* is laid on the ground.

After a *hehaka* is laid on the ground no one must touch the hoop, either to remove or replace it.

If the hoop is caught on a *hehaka*, and the *hehaka* is placed on the ground, the count is as follows : —

If the hoop is on the flattened end of the longer rod, nothing is counted.

If the hoop is on one of the cross rods, one is counted.

If the hoop is on two of the cross rods, two are counted.

If the hoop is on the curved rod at the end of the *hehaka*, three are counted.

If the hoop falls off the *hehaka* and strikes the ground it cannot be replaced, and nothing is counted.

The count is made for the player whose *hehaka* holds the hoop.

The player who first counts the number of points agreed upon wins the game.

5. WOSKATE TAWINKAPSICE.

(Game of Woman's Shinney.)

Tawinkapsice is an ancient gambling game played by the Sioux women. The implements used and the rules of the game are precisely the same as those for *takapsice,* except that women only play at this game.

The women play the game with as much vigor as the men, and in former times at the meetings for playing *takapsice* the *tawinkapsice* was interspersed with the other games.

6. WOSKATE TASIHE.

(Game with Foot Bones.)

Tasihe is an ancient gambling game played by the Sioux women.

Men, boys, and girls practised at manipulating the implement of the game so that many of them became expert, but it was considered beneath the dignity of men or boys to play the game in a contest for a given number of points, or for stakes.

The game was played by two or more women who sat, after the fashion of the Sioux women, on the ground.

Some women became very expert at the game, and others, men and women, would bet heavily on their play.

The implements used in this game are : *tasiha,* foot bones ; *tahinspa,* bodkin.

The *tasiha* are made from the short bones from the foot of a deer or antelope. There are from four to six in a set, which are worked into the form of a hollow cone, so that one will fit over the top of the other. The convex articulating surface is not removed from the top bone. From four to six small holes are drilled through the projecting points at the wider ends of the cones.

A hole is drilled through the articulating surface of the top bone, and all are strung on a pliable thong, which should be two and one half times the length of the bones when they are fitted together. The bones are strung on this thong with the top bone at one end, and each with the apex of its cone towards the base of the cone next to it.

The apex of each cone should fit loosely into the hollow of the cone next above it so that they will not jam, but will fall apart easily.

Four loops about one half an inch in diameter, made of some pliable material, are fastened to the end of the thong next to the top bone.

The *tahinspa* was formerly made of bone, and should be of the same length as the *tasiha* when they are fitted together. At one end a hole is drilled, or a notch cut, for the purpose of fastening it to the thong.

The opposite end is shaped into a slender point, so that it will pass readily into the holes drilled about the lower borders of the *tasiha*.

Latterly the *tahinspa* is made of wire of the same length as that made of bone, and with one end looped and the other pointed.

The *tahinspa* is fastened to the thong at the end opposite the loops.

Formerly the implement was without ornament, but latterly the loops are made of thread strung with beads.

The rules of the game are : —

Only women may play at the game.

Any number may play in a game.

Before beginning to play the players must agree upon the number that shall constitute a game.

No player shall make more than one play at a time.

A player must hold the *tahinspa* in one hand and toss the *tasiha* with the other.

The *tasiha* must be caught on the point of the *tahinspa* after they have been tossed into the air.

If one *tasiha* is caught on the *tahinspa* this counts one.

If one or more *tasiha* remain on the one that is caught, this counts as many as there are *tasiha* so remaining.

If all the *tasiha* remain on top of the one that is caught, this counts the game.

If a *tasiha* is caught so that the *tahinspa* is through one of the holes at its lower border, this counts two.

If, when a play is made, the *tahinspa* passes through a loop, this counts one. If through two loops, this counts two. If through three loops, this counts three. If through four loops, this counts four.

7. WOSKATE TANPAN.

(Game of Dice.)

Tanpan is an ancient gambling game played by the older Sioux women.

This is an absorbing game, on which some women became inveterate gamblers, sometimes playing all day and all night at a single sitting.

The implements used in the game are : *tanpan*, basket ; *kansu*, dice ; *canwiyawa*, counting-sticks.

The *tanpan* is made of willow twigs, or some similar material, woven into a basket about three inches in diameter at the bottom and flaring to the top, like a pannikin, and about two and a half inches deep.

The *kansu* are made of plumstones, one side of which is left plain, and the other carved with some figure, or with straight marks.

The figures usually represent some animal or part of an animal, though they may represent anything that the maker pleases to put on them.

There are six stones in each set, and usually some of these have only plain marks, and others figures on them.

The *canwiyawa* are rods of wood about the size of a lead pencil, and may be of any number, but there were generally one hundred in a set.

The rules of the game are : —

The game may be played by two, four, or six old women, who must be divided into two opposing sides, with an equal number on each side.

Before beginning the game the players must agree upon how much each figure on the plumstones shall count, how many counting-sticks shall be played for, and place the counting-sticks in a pile between them.

After the game begins, no one must touch the counting-sticks, except to take the number won at a play. No one shall play more than once at a time. To play, the player must put all the *kansu* in the *tanpan*, and cover it with the hand, shake it about, and then pour or throw out the *kansu*.

After the *kansu* are thrown out of the *tanpan*, no one may touch them until after the count is made and agreed upon.

If the plain side of a *kansu* lies uppermost, this counts nothing.

If the carved side of a *kansu* lies uppermost, this counts what has been agreed upon.

When a player has played, and her count is made and agreed upon, she takes from the pile of counting-sticks as many as her count amounts to.

When the counting-sticks are all taken, the side which has the greater number of sticks wins the game.

J. R. Walker.

SIOUX GAMES. II.

8. WOSKATE ICASLOHE.

(Game of Bowls.)

Icaslohe is an ancient gambling game played by the Sioux women.

The implements used in the game are: *tapainyan,* stone ball; *canmibi,* wooden cylinder.

The *tapainyan* are balls made of any kind of stone, from one to two and a half inches in diameter.

The *canmibi* are cylinders made of any kind of wood, from an inch and a half to two and a half inches in diameter, and from an inch and a half to three inches long.

The rules of the game are: —

The game is generally played on the ice, but may be played on the ground.

Two women play at the game.

Each player must have a *tapainyan* and a *canmibi.*

Before beginning the game the players must agree upon the number they are to play for, and they must draw two parallel lines on the ice from ten to thirty feet apart.

The players must take their positions opposite each other outside the parallel lines, and must not be between the lines when they play.

Each player must place her *canmibi* on the line nearest her.

The players must bowl the *tapainyan* alternately, at the *canmibi* on the line farthest from them.

When the *tapainyan* is bowled it must strike the surface before it crosses the line nearest the one who bowled it; if it does not the play counts nothing.

If the *canmibi* bowled at is knocked away from the line it counts one for the player, otherwise nothing.

9. WOSKATE TAHUKA CANGLESKA.

(Game of the Webbed Hoop.)

Tahuka cangleska is an ancient game played for amusement by the Sioux men.

This is an exciting game in which the Indians took great interest, gathering in large numbers to witness the play.

The implements used in the game are: *tahuka cangleska,* webbed hoop; *wahukeza,* spear.

The *tahuka cangleska* is made of a rod of wood from one half to one inch in diameter, which is bent so as to form a hoop from one to three feet in diameter. A web of rawhide is woven across the entire hoop, with interstices of from one half to three quarters of an inch, that in the centre being somewhat larger and called the heart.

The *wahukeza* is made of the sprout of a tree, or a young willow, and is from four to five and a half feet long, and about one half an inch in diameter at the larger end, which is bluntly pointed. The smaller end may be either straight or forked, and sometimes is ornamented with feathers, bead-work, or in any other manner according to the fancy.

The rules of the game are : —

Any number of persons may play in a game, but they should be equally divided into two opposing sides.

Each player may have as many spears as he wishes.

Before beginning the game the players must agree upon how many innings will constitute the game.

Two parallel lines, about fifty yards long, and about fifty yards apart, are drawn.

The players take their positions opposite each other, outside these lines, choosing them either by agreement or by lot.

Any number of hoops may be used in a game, but there should never be less than four, and they should be of various sizes.

One player on each side must throw all the hoops.

The hoops must be thrown alternately, from one side to the other.

The thrower must not have either foot between the lines when he throws the hoops.

The hoop when thrown must cross both lines, and it may do so, either in the air or rolling on the ground ; it may cross one line in the air, and roll across the other, or it may be thrown across one line, and strike between the lines and bound across the other.

After the hoop had crossed both lines, the players towards whom it was thrown, throw their spears at it.

If, while the hoop is in the air, it is speared through the heart, the count is five ; if through any other interstice, the count is two.

If, while the hoop is rolling on the ground, it is speared through the heart, the count is three ; if through any other interstice, the count is one.

If speared while the spear is held in the hand the count is nothing.

If speared after the hoop has stopped, nothing.

When the number of innings that have been agreed upon have been played, the side that has the most counts wins the game.

Another method of playing with these implements is : —

The sides line up as in the former game, and the hoops are all thrown from one side towards the other, which keeps all the hoops they have speared, and returns all they have not, which are again thrown to them.

When all the hoops have been speared, the side that spears them chases the opposite side, and throws the hoops at them, and, if any one of the side that is chased spears a hoop while it is in the air, the chase stops.

Then the opposite side throws the hoops, and the game is repeated.

10. WOSKATE HUTANACUTE.

(Game with Winged Bones.)

Hutanacute is an ancient game played for amusement by the Sioux men during the winter, on the snow or ice.

The implement used is *hutanacute*, winged bone.

The *hutanacute* is made from the rib of one of the larger ruminating animals. A piece about four to eight inches long is taken from the rib where it begins to narrow and thicken, and the wider end is cut square across, and the narrower end rounded up from the convex side.

Two holes are drilled in the wider end, lengthwise to the rib, and at such an angle that when the rods are in them their free ends will be about ten to twelve inches apart.

Two rods are made of plum sprouts, about one fourth of an inch in diameter, and about fourteen inches long. The smaller end of each of these is feathered like an arrow, and the other end is inserted into the hole in the bone.

The rules of the game are : —

Any number may play.

Each player may have from two to four winged bones, but each player should have the same number.

A mark is made from which the bones are thrown.

The bones are thrown so that they may strike and slide on the ice or snow.

The players throw alternately until all the bones are thrown.

When all the bones are thrown, the player whose bone lies the farthest from the mark wins the game.

11. WOSKATE PTEHESTE.

(Game of the Young Cow.)

Pteheste is an ancient game played for amusement by the Sioux men during the winter, on the ice or snow.

The implement used in this game is *pteheste*, young cow.

The *pteheste* is made of the tip of a cow or buffalo horn, from three to four inches long. This is trimmed so as to make it as nearly straight as possible, and a feather-tipped arrow securely fastened into its base, so that it has the appearance of a horn-pointed arrow.

Any number of persons may play.

Each player may have any number of arrows, but all players should have the same number.

Two parallel lines are drawn from twenty to thirty feet apart.

The players take their position on one side of these lines.

A player must throw his horned arrow so that it may strike between the two lines and slide beyond them.

The players throw alternately until all the arrows are thrown.

At the end the player whose arrow lies the farthest from the lines wins the game.

12. WOSKATE CANPASLOHANPI.
(Game with Throwing Sticks.)

Canpaslohanpi is an ancient game played for amusement by the Sioux men in the winter on the snow or ice.

The implement used in this game is *canpaslohanpi*, throwing stick.

The *canpaslohanpi* is made of ash, and is about four feet long.

It is cylindrical on one side, and flat on the other. About five inches from one end it is about two inches wide, and an inch and a half thick. From this place it is rounded up to a blunt point on the flat side and tapers to the farthest end, which is about an inch wide and half an inch thick.

Each player has but one throwing stick.

Any number of persons may play.

The game is played by grasping the stick at the smaller end, between the thumb and second, third, and fourth fingers, with the first finger across the smaller end, the flat side of the stick held uppermost.

Then by swinging the hand below the hips the javelin is shot forward so that it will slide on the snow or ice.

The game is to see who can slide the stick the farthest.

13. WOSKATE OGLE CEKUTEPI.
(Game of Coat Shooting.)

Ogle cekutepi is an ancient game played for amusement by the Sioux men.

The implements used in the game are : *Ogle*, coat ; *itazipe*, bow ; *wanhinkpe*, arrows.

The *ogle* is an arrow that is either painted black or wrapped with a black strip of buckskin, or has a tag attached to it (sometimes it is a plain arrow).

The *itazipe* and *wanhinpe* are the ordinary bow and arrows.

The game is played by shooting the *ogle* high in the air so that it will fall from fifty to seventy-five yards away. Then the players stand where it was shot from, and shoot at it with the bow and arrows.

This is merely a game of skill, and not for points.

14. WOSKATE PASLOHANPI.

(Game of Javelins.)

Paslohanpi is an ancient game played for amusement by the Sioux boys in the springtime.

The implement used is *wahukezala*, javelin.

The *wahukezala* is made of willow. It is from three to six feet long, and from three eighths to three quarters of an inch in diameter at the larger end, and tapers to the smaller end.

The bark is peeled from it and wrapped about it in a spiral manner, leaving an exposed space about a half an inch wide. It is then held in smoke until the exposed part is blackened, when the bark is removed.

This marks the javelin with spiral stripes of black and white.

Each one who plays may have as many javelins as he chooses.

There are two ways of throwing the javelin. One is to lay it across something, as the arm, or the foot, or another javelin, or a stump of log, or a small mound of earth, or anything that is convenient, and grasping it at the smaller end, shoot it forward.

The other way is to grasp the javelin near the middle and throw it from the hand.

In throwing, the contest may be for distance, or to throw at a mark.

The game is merely a contest of skill in throwing the javelin.

15. WOSKATE CANWACIKIYAPI.

(Game of Tops.)

Canwacikiyapi is an ancient game played for amusement by the Sioux boys.

The implements used in this game are: *canwacikiyapi*, tops; *icapsintepi*, whips.

The *canwacikiyapi* is a wooden cylinder with a conical point. The cylinders are from an inch to two inches in thickness, and from a half to an inch and a half in length, and the conical point is from an inch to two inches in length.

The *icapsinte* has a handle and from one to four lashes. The handle is made of wood, and is from fifteen inches to two feet long, and about half an inch thick at its thicker end, and tapers to the other end.

The lashes are made of pliable thongs or strings, about twelve to fifteen inches long, and are fastened to the smaller end of the handle.

The tops are spun in the same manner as whip tops are spun by white boys. A game is played by marking a square about five feet across. On three sides of this square barriers are placed, and the fourth side left open.

The players spin their tops outside of the square, and while they are spinning they drive them into the open side of the square.

After the tops cross the open side of the square they must not be touched.

After the top stops spinning, the one that lies nearest the side of the square opposite the opening wins the game.

Another game is played by marking a circle about six feet in diameter and near its centre making four holes a little larger than the tops and about six inches apart.

The players spin their tops outside the circle, and while they are spinning drive them into it.

After a top enters the circle it must not be touched.

The player whose top lies in one of the holes when it has stopped spinning wins the game.

If two or more tops lie in the holes when they stop spinning, those who spun them must spin them again until one player's top lies in the holes more often than any other.

16. WOSKATE TITAZIPI HOKSILA.

(Game with Boys' Bows.)

The Sioux boys have, from ancient times, indulged in amusement with the bow and arrow.

They play at various games, mimicking battles, hunting, and similar things.

They also shoot at a target, and for distance, but there appears to be no formal game or rules governing their play.

The boys' bow is like the bows for the men, except that it is smaller.

The boys' arrows are like those for the men, except that they are made with heads large and blunt.

17. HOHU YOURMONPI.

(Bone Whirler.)

The *hohu yourmonpi* is a toy that has been played with by the Sioux boys from ancient times.

It is made from the short bone of the foot of one of the larger ruminating animals, and is fastened to the middle of a string of sinews about twelve to eighteen inches long. At each end of the sinew string a short stick is fastened to serve as a hand hold.

These sticks are taken, one in each hand, and the bone whirled about so as to twist the string. The string is then drawn taut, which rapidly untwists it, and rapidly whirls the bone so that its motion will twist the string in the opposite direction. This process is repeated indefinitely, the motion of the bone making a buzzing noise.

The object of playing with the toy is to make the buzzing noise.

A game called "buffaloes fighting" is played with this toy, as follows : —

A number of boys, each with a bone whirler, set them to buzzing, and imitate the actions of bulls fighting ; the buzzing of the bones is supposed to represent the bellowing of the bulls. They approach each other and strike the bones together, and if the bone of a player is stopped from buzzing, he is defeated.

18. TATE YOURMONPI.

(Wind Whirler.)

The *tate yourmonpi* is a toy that has been played with by the Sioux boys from ancient times.

It consists of a blade of wood, usually red cedar, about one eighth of an inch thick, two inches wide, and twelve inches long. One end of this is fastened to a wooden handle by a pliable thong about twelve to eighteen inches long.

The handle is from two to three feet long, and about one half to one inch in diameter.

By holding the handle above the head and swinging it rapidly with a circular motion, the blade is whirled rapidly and makes a buzzing noise.

The object of playing with the toy is to make the buzzing noise, and sometimes a number of boys contest to see who can keep it continually buzzing for the longest time.

19. IPAHOTONPI.

(Pop-gun.)

The *ipahotonpi* is a toy that has been played with by the Sioux boys from ancient times.

It consists of : *tancan*, the body ; *wibopan*, the ramrod ; *iyopuhdi*, the wadding.

The *tancan* was formerly made from a piece of ash sprout, about six to ten inches long, from which the pith was removed, but since the Indians have obtained wire, they burn a hole through a piece of ash from eight to fifteen inches long, and from one and a half to two inches in diameter.

It is generally ornamented by pyrographic figures or markings.

The *wibopan* is made of some tough wood, a little longer than the *tancan*, and of such size as to pass readily through the bore.

The *iyopuhdi* is made by chewing the inner bark of the elm, and using it while wet.

A wad is packed tightly into one end of the bore, and a closely fitting wad is forced from the other end, rapidly through the bore by means of the ramrod, when the first wad flies out with an explosive noise.

The object of playing with the toy is to make the report.

Sometimes the boys play at mimic battle with the pop-guns, or they mimic hunting, when one or more boys imitate the game, and the others try to hit them with the wads from the pop-guns.

20. WOSKATE HEPASLOHANPI.

(Game of Horned Javelins.)

Hepaslohanpi is an ancient game played for amusement by the Sioux girls in the winter on the ice or snow.

The implement used in the game is *hewahukezala*, horned javelin.

The *hewahukezala* is made of a wooden javelin, about four to five feet long and from three quarters to an inch thick at the thicker end, tapering to a diameter of three eighths to one half an inch at the smaller end.

A tip of elk horn, about four to eight inches long, is fastened on the larger end.

The game is played by throwing the javelin so that it will strike and slide on the snow or ice, and the one whose javelin slides the farthest wins the game.

As many girls may play at the game as wish to do so.

21. HOKSINKAGAPI.

(Dolls.)

From ancient times the Sioux girls have played with dolls.

The dolls were rude effigies, sometimes carved from wood, but generally made of buckskin, and stuffed with hair, with their features made by marking or painting.

The dolls were dressed with both male and female attire, which was adorned with all the ornaments worn by the Indians.

The girls would often have doll baby carriers, like those used for the Indian babies, and would carry the dolls on their backs, as their mothers carried their babies.

22. TIPI CIKALA.

(Toy Tipis.)

From ancient times the Sioux girls have played with toy tipis varying in size from a miniature tipi of a foot or so in height to one large enough for a child to enter.

They played with these toy tipis in much the same way as white children play with toy houses.

J. R. Walker.

A CHEROKEE INDIAN BALL GAME

K. E. Wolfe

A Cherokee Indian Ball Game.

KATHARINE E. WOLFE, *Cherokee*.

JUST as the white man, the Indian too has various forms of amusements. The ball game, as played by the Cherokees, is as important to them as football or any other popular game is to other people. The Eastern Band of Cherokees live on the Qualla Reservation in western North Carolina.

The neighborhood in which I live is divided into four main sections, namely: Yellow Hill, Soco, Big Cove and Birdtown.

The Indians living in one of these sections will challenge those living in another to a game of ball. Say for instance the Indian men of Big Cove will challenge those living in Birdtown. They choose their players and agree upon the time and place for playing the game. It is generally played in an open field, far different from the well-graded field upon which the game of football is played.

The evening before the game the Indians, the women included, hold a dance in their respective sections of the country. These dances are held in the open air, usually near some small stream. The women do the singing while the men dance. In their songs they make all kinds of remarks about those of the opposing side. These dances continue all night long. From the time of the dances until after the game, the players are not allowed to eat any food.

The following day, the people from the different sections gather at the appointed place to witness the game. They either sit or stand around the edge of the field.

The ball players each have two sticks similar to those used in the game of lacrosse, only smaller. The ball is tossed up in the center of the field and the game begins. The object is to get it around two poles, placed at each end of the field, a certain number of times. They cannot pick up the ball in their hands. The players who succeed in getting the ball around the poles at their end of the field the greatest number of times, win the game.

INDIAN TRACK MEET

Clee Woods

Lining up alongside the race track

Indian Track Meet

By Clee Woods

B Y THE TIME we were within a mile of Jemez Pueblo we began to meet the runners as they jogged down to the starting point. It was dawn, and the race at the Pueblo was to start just at sunrise. We offered some of our friends a ride, but they smiled and trotted on. They're not allowed to ride to the starting line.

They were young men mostly. But nearer the pueblo, boys of all ages down to little fellows of seven or eight were on

A group of Indian runners

the road. All stripped down to G-strings, or at most a pair of shorts. Clan leaders and race officials gave each boy his station beside the road, at a distance from the pueblo commensurate with his size and age. Older boys were taken on down much nearer to the starting point.

Twenty - five young men lined up across the road at the starting point some two miles below the pueblo. Many of the young fellows were trained athletes who'd been to Indian schools at Albuquerque and Santa Fé. More than half the runners wore their long black hair down their backs.

My wife and I were the only spectators, but the whole pueblo would be waiting eagerly for the finish up there. This was the fall harvest race, October 3rd.

The runners toed the mark. Some fifty yards away four elders took their station in the middle of the road. One of them carried four stalks of corn cut off below the ear and

Two Jicarilla clans meet on the race course

bundled together tightly at the base. Calmly they waited, runners and officials, for the sun.

Just as the sun rounded up over a wide *mesa* the runners tensed. The four starters watched. Then one of them let out a sudden sharp cry and all four of them broke up the road. Behind them the twenty-five runners leaped to the race like flushed quail.

In a moment a seventeen-year-old lad was in the lead. Rapidly he closed the distance between him and the starter who still carried the bundle of cornstalks. Soon he was passing the starter and this man handed him the bundle.

A second runner forged up behind the leader with the cornstalk bundle. They fought it out there for nearly a quarter of a mile, this seventeen-year-old and his older challenger. The challenger had the best of it and the seventeen-year-old passed the bundle to him. That is the inviolate rule.

The second man tucked the bundle back into the crook of his left arm and sped on, as if overanxious to prove his right to the bundle he'd taken from the boy. As the runners sped up the road the boys stationed along in waiting joined in the race. The

little fellows of course played out fast. But it was good training for them, building up in them the spirit of the race and its traditions for the day when they'd be young men and real contenders in the pack.

It was the young fellows who'd been to Indian schools who were the foxy ones. Six or eight of them were lying back just behind the leader. They were content to let him set the pace— and be handicapped with that bundle! Let him wear himself out.

Now the foxy half dozen began to edge up. They were more than halfway to the pueblo. They were challenging each other and driving on that runner up ahead with the cornstalks.

The race grows hotter. The untrained and the unfit drop behind, but they keep on running in spite of the certainty that they can't win. Now a thin, leggy fellow begins to turn on the power. He widens the distance between himself and the foxy bunch, closes the interval between him and the man with the cornstalk bundle. Another runner accepts the challenge, forges up from the foxy group. He comes abreast of the leggy one; they battle for a hundred yards. Mr. Legs beats off the challenge. Now he has just one man to take, the guy with the cornstalks. That man, though, is unwilling to surrender his bundle, the baton of this race. He glances back, makes a valiant spurt.

But that lean Mr. Legs knows how to run. There's still half a mile to go. He encourages the leader to kill himself off. Makes sure no new challenger is coming up dangerously close from the rear. Then he begins to ease up

Jicarillas ride to their Ceremonial grounds for the races

faster, his stride long and smooth and determined. He begins to pass the leader. Reaches out eager hands. Takes the cornstalks!

Now his honor is at stake. He's said that he's man enough to retain that bundle until he reaches home, and let no man pass him to claim it. That's the way it's done. The winner must keep the bundle until he races through his own door in the pueblo. Any time up to then a challenger may overtake him and reach for the bundle as he passes.

Mr. Legs really is running now. The taste of victory has him. The other foxy ones from behind turn on all they have, each man making his last desperate bid. But Mr. Legs still has what it takes. He keeps right on picking them up and putting them down too fast. The pueblo greets him, cheers him, runs to points of advantage to see what the final challengers can do about it. Then Mr. Legs bounds through his own door, and he's the man of the day.

THE ISLETA PUEBLO stages its big race the Sunday before Easter, as a climax to three weeks of ceremonial festivities while the irrigation ditches are being cleaned for summer use. Here the race is between two teams of about a dozen runners each, a team for each of the pueblo's two clans.

It begins with ceremonial reverence. Chanting Medicine Men lead the runners from the big circular *kiva* at the west end of the street. The race course is the center of the main street which runs east and west between the Rio Grande and the tracks of the Santa Fe Railroad.

One half of each team takes its station at the west end of the course; the others come to the east end. Two middle-age runners toe the mark. These two old boys have no intention of winning their laps. It's just part of the tradition that two elders open the event.

Together this pair trot down the course, grinning at each other. Jibes fly at them from all sides. Undisturbed, they go on to the finish side by side. Then the real race begins. A young, eager man touches off his elderly team mate and darts down the street. Right beside him speeds his opponent. They battle for the lead all the way. They're fresh, anxious.

There isn't eighteen inches difference between them when they reach the east end of the lap and new members of the team touch them off and break back the other way. In the many races I've watched among numerous Indian tribes, I've never yet seen a man try to cheat or take the least unfair advantage.

Down the street this second pair of young fellows fight for momentary supremacy. Each knows that if he can give his next man a little lead his teammate will fight all the harder to retain and widen that lead. But into the finish they go about neck and neck. Each puts on a powerful spurt the last ten yards. Back come two more, the race still as hot as ever.

In order to win, a team must gain a complete lap, over and back. This is accomplished when the winning runner overtakes the losing team's man and slaps him on the back. In older times the practice was for the winner to seize the losing man by the hair or *chongo*, hence the name *Chongo* Race.

Today our two clans seesaw back and forth. Now one's in the lead, now the other. Looks as though it's going to be a long race. It's been known to take four and five hours to conclude one of the *Chongo* races.

But not this time. One man on the Pumpkin Clan team is weakening. When it comes his turn to run the third time he just doesn't have enough stuff left. Sensing this, the Turquoise man summons greater effort into his legs. He pulls ahead. Hands his team a good ten-yard lead.

Wider and wider the Turquoise runners spread that lead. Frantically, the Pumpkin Clan rooters appeal to their team to run. Equally frantic Turquoise people implore their team to win.

Now the Turquoise man is reaching the west end just as the Pumpkin man makes it to the eastern starting line. That's half a lap lost. Now the Turquoise men in reality change from the pursued to the pursuer. All they have to do is to gain that other length of the course—about 200 yards. Eagerness spurs them into faster starts. The Pumpkin boys are getting disheartened. Several weak spots develop in their team. Fight doggedly as their best men may, those failing runners keep on yielding distance.

The Turquoise man is only a hundred yards behind the tiring opponent. He still feels pretty good. He had a good emetic before the race. He cuts down the loser's lead by half. His next teammate is not so fresh. He barely holds what was given him.

But now a fast, sturdy Turquoise man comes up. What's fifty yards to him against a disheartened rival? He throws all he has into it, eats up the distance. Just before the Pumpkin man reaches the goal the Turquoise man rushes up from behind, slaps him on the back and it's all over.

IF YOU WANT to see really pretty team work, go watch the Zuñi boys sometime in their long-distance race. They occasionally stage this race at the Gallup Indian Ceremonial.

Three men constitute a team. They not only must run the required distance, two, three, five miles. They must run it barefooted and flip a rock ahead of them all the way, with their feet.

The start is remotely akin to the kickoff in football. Each kickoff man has his rock, most often round but sometimes elongated, ready on his toes for the start. At the signal, he sends the rock as far out over the race course as he can. This is not done with a kick, but with a flinging motion of the foot.

His two teammates rush down the course

like tackles going down under the ball. One endeavors to reach the rock, get his toes beneath it and arch it off down the course again. The third man is racing on at full speed, to be on the rock when it lands from the second man's fling. While this third man is getting toes under the rock and sending it off on its third flight, Number One races hard down the course, so he can take his turn at it again. Number Two also dashes on, for his turn at the rock.

In this way the rock is carried all the way over the course. The race is won by the team whose rock first sails across the finish line.

This race is popular among several pueblo tribes. The Pima and Papago tribes run it in southern Arizona. It comes down from prehistoric times. In pre-Columbian ruins sometimes are found the little round stones used for the football. The usual size is about that of a small apple. In my collection I have one of these stones with a covering of dried pitch over it. An old Pima man once told me that within his time his people used exactly the same type of pitch-covered stone ball for the races.

For sheer fun and keen rivalry, I'll take the Jicarilla Apache race. The Apaches always give you a run for your money, no matter what it is—war, fun, raising sheep, riding a bronc, anything.

The Jicarilla race comes as the culminating event of their three-day fall festival or Thanksgiving *Fiesta* at Stone Lake, on their reservation 12 miles south of Dulce, New Mexico. It is like the *Chongo* race, in that it is a relay event and is run between the tribe's two clans. But there the resemblance ends. The Apaches, both spectators and runners, get a far greater kick out of their race. The whole tribe of about 800 gathers at Stone Lake by September 13th of each year. This *fiesta,* like the others described, dates back to prehistoric times. It originally was held as a celebration for the reuniting of the tribe's two clans each fall, after one clan had gone to the plains of New Mexico for the summer, while the other clan stayed in the mountains to hunt and perhaps to raid the pueblo peoples occasionally, especially when the crops were gathered.

On the second day of the *fiesta* the men of the Ollero or Mountain Clan stage a parade through their half of the encampment. They are all mounted and led by John Ballazar, last tribal chief before adoption of the rule by council and still their number one man. The clan banner, a white strip of cloth with three big dots painted on it, flutters high on a pole at the head of the parade. The parade terminates at their race course on one side of the encampment. The Plains Clan or Llaneros put on a similar parade in their half of the camp and then retire to their own race course.

Each clan holds a trial heat, on its own course. The winner of the heat will lead off as honor man for his team in the big race the next day. The boys put on a real race in the trial heats, on a dead straightaway. These trial dashes are nearly always won nowadays by trained trackmen.

The main race between the two clans comes off on the afternoon of September 15th annually. It's *the* event of *fiesta.* Rivalry between the two clans is keen.

At the north end of the track the Llaneros have a brush circle or *kiva.* At the south end the Olleros have a similar brush shelter. For hours before the race, the Medicine Men and elders of each clan chant and dance inside the *kivas.* The runners come in to get themselves painted and feathered—a job of another hour or more. Medicine Men make sand paintings on the dirt floor.

Just before the race is to start, everyone within the *kiva,* including runners, dances and marches around in the *kiva,* always going clockwise. As each man leaves the *kiva* he steps very carefully onto the sun and the moon sand paintings on the right side just within the door.

Now each clan, men, women and some youngsters, moves away from its *kiva.* Chanting and dancing, they meet about midway the track. Each tribe's banner is held high over it. All other participants wave green branches in their hands as they dance and sing. When the two clans meet, they surge back and forth, bantering and taunting each other—all in high good humor. On the side lines the rivalry breaks out in verbal bantering, jibing. Once I saw an old lady lose her temper and cross the track after some woman who'd got a little too aggravating with her tongue.

Up and down, back and forth they surge. Finally, the dancing ends; they square off for the race.

The race opens much like the *Chongo,* with two elders trotting the first stretch. Then it's snatched away by those two fast lads who yesterday proved themselves worthy of the honor of running the first lap for their respective clans. Down the level, scraped track they dash. A pretty race. Picturesque runners, their nearly naked bodies painted from toes to scalp, eagle feathers and eagle down in their hair.

Awaiting them at the end of the course are the two next fastest. As the turn of each man comes to run, a team captain, who is not a runner, gives last-second coaching. They brush the boy's legs with eagle feathers to put speed and stamina into them.

These boys have both. The Jicarillas do not confine their selection of a team to their own tribe. Each clan strives to import "ringers" from other tribes, and this is considered correct procedure. They'll even run in a white man sometimes if they think he can outrun anything they've got.

This time my Olleros were loaded for bear. They took a lead, began to widen it. Every time a certain runner took his turn, the lead grew still wider. That runner was the very same long-haired young man whom we'd seen win the Jemez race the preceding October. The Olleros had sent word to him and his brother to come run for them, and here they were doing the same good job of it.

The Olleros shouted their delight. Hurled defiant jibes at their Llanero rivals. The Llaneros took it like good sportsmen. They'd won the three previous years. It was about time the Olleros were showing something, even if they did have to get outside Indians to help do it.

The Olleros did show plenty. A speeding Apache, with victory in sight, spurted all the way down the course. He slapped a lagging Llanero on the back—and we'd had two hours of great sport and a lot of fun.

STUDIES IN PLAY AND GAMES

An Arno Press Collection

Appleton, Lilla Estelle. **A Comparative Study of the Play Activities of Adult Savages and Civilized Children.** 1910

Barker, Roger, Tamara Dembo and Kurt Lewin. **Frustration and Regression: An Experiment With Young Children.** 1941

Brewster, Paul G., editor. **Children's Games and Rhymes.** 1952

Buytendijk, F[rederick] J[acobus] J[ohannes]. **Wesen und Sinn des Spiels.** 1933

Culin, Stewart. **Chess and Playing-Cards.** 1898

Daiken, Leslie. **Children's Games Throughout the Year.** 1949

[Froebel, Friedrich]. **Mother's Songs, Games and Stories.** 1914

Glassford, Robert Gerald. **Application of a Theory of Games to the Transitional Eskimo Culture.** 1976

Gomme, Alice B. and Cecil J. Sharp, editors. **Children's Singing Games.** 1909/1912

Groos, Karl. **The Play of Animals.** 1898

Groos, Karl. **The Play of Man.** 1901

Lehman, Harvey C. and Paul A. Witty. **The Psychology of Play Activities.** 1927

MacLagan, Robert Craig, compiler. **The Games and Diversions of Argyleshire.** 1901

Markey, Frances V. **Imaginative Behavior of Preschool Children.** 1935

Roth, Walter E[dmund]. **Games, Sports and Amusements.** 1902

Sutton-Smith, Brian, editor. **A Children's Games Anthology.** 1976

Sutton-Smith, Brian, editor. **The Games of the Americas, Parts I and II.** 1976

Sutton-Smith, Brian, editor. **The Psychology of Play.** 1976

Van Alstyne, Dorothy. **Play Behavior and Choice of Play Materials of Pre-School Children.** 1932

Wells, H[erbert] G[eorge]. **Floor Games.** 1912

Wolford, Leah Jackson. **The Play-Party in Indiana.** 1959